Smalltalk

THE OBJECT-ORIENTED SERIES

D. Coleman, P. Arnold, S. Bodoff, C. Dollin, H. Gilchrist, F. Hayes and P. Jeremaes
Object-Oriented Development: The Fusion Method

S. Cook and J. Daniels
Designing Object Systems

B. Henderson-Sellers
A Book of Object-Oriented Knowledge

B. Henderson-Sellers and J. Edwards
Book Two Object-Oriented Knowledge: The Working Object

H. Kilov and J. Ross
Information Modelling: An Object-Oriented Approach

P. Krief
Prototyping with Objects

K. Lano and H. Haughton
Object-Oriented Specification Case Studies

J. Lindskov Knudsen, M. Löfgren, O. Lehrmann Madsen and B. Magnusson
Object-Oriented Environments: The Mjølner Approach

M. Lorenz
Object-Oriented Software Development: A Practical Guide

M. Lorenz and J. Kidd
Object-Oriented Software Metrics

B. Meyer
An Object-Oriented Environment: Principles and Applications

B. Meyer
Eiffel: The Language

B. Meyer
Reusable Software: The Base Object-Oriented Component Libraries

B. Meyer
Object Success: A Manager's Guide to Object Orientation, its Impact on the Corporation, and its Use for Reengineering the Software Process

B. Meyer and J.-M. Nerson (eds)
Object-Oriented Applications

D. Mandrioli and B. Meyer (eds)
Advances in Object-Oriented Software Engineering

O. Nierstrasz and D. Tsichritzis
Object-Oriented Software Composition

G. Pomberger and P. Blaschek
An Object-Oriented Approach to Software Engineering

R. Rist and R. Terwilliger
Object-Oriented Programming in Eiffel

P.J. Robinson
Hierarchical Object-Oriented Design

R. Switzer
Eiffel: An Introduction

K. Waldén and J.-M. Nerson
Seamless Object-Oriented Software Architecture: Analysis and Design of Reliable Systems

R. Wiener
Software Development Using Eiffel: There Can Be Life Other Than C++

T. Hopkins and B. Horan
Smalltalk: An Introduction to Application Development Using VisualWorks

(Various editors)
Proceedings of TOOLS Conferences, 4 to 16: Technology of Object-Oriented Languages and Systems

Smalltalk

an introduction to application development using VisualWorks

Trevor Hopkins
Bernard Horan

PRENTICE HALL
London New York Toronto Sydney Tokyo Singapore
Madrid Mexico City Munich

First published 1995 by
Prentice Hall Europe
Campus 400, Maylands Avenue
Hemel Hempstead
Hertfordshire, HP2 7EZ
A division of
Simon & Schuster International Group

Typeset in 10/12pt Times
by Photoprint, Torquay, S. Devon

Printed and bound in Great Britain by
T.J. Press (Padstow) Ltd

Library of Congress Cataloging-in-Publication Data

Hopkins, T. (Trevor). 1957–
Smalltalk : an introduction to application development using VisualWorks / Trevor Hopkins, Bernard Horan.
p. cm. -- (Prentice-Hall object-oriented series)
Includes bibliographical references and index.
ISBN 0–13–318387–4
1. Smalltalk (Computer program language) I. Horan, Bernard. II. Title. III. Series.
QA76.73.S59H67 1995
005.13′3--dc20 95–7583
CIP

British Library Cataloguing in Publication Data

A catalogue record for this book is available from the British Library

ISBN 0–13–318387–4

3 4 5 99 98 97 96

Contents

Preface

This book is a complete, stand-alone introduction to application development using Smalltalk-80. It provides a comprehensive description of the VisualWorks 2.0 development environment, the language and major aspects of the class library, including coverage of the Model–View–Controller (MVC) paradigm.

The book is aimed at students attending university/college and software professionals in industry. It can be used by both the specialist and the general reader: the specialist will find a detailed guide to the development of applications using VisualWorks; for the general reader, the book provides an introduction to Smalltalk-80 and the VisualWorks development environment.

Note, however, that this book is not intended as a general programming primer – readers are expected to have a firm understanding of general computer systems and the algorithms used in such systems. They are also expected to be familiar with at least one programming language (such as Pascal, C or Lisp). However, no previous exposure to VisualWorks, Smalltalk-80 or object-oriented programming is assumed.

The structure of the book stresses the relationship between the language syntax, the class hierarchy and the development environment. This reflects the tutorial nature of our approach, with a large number of (relatively) short chapters, each covering specific points. An exhaustive index combined with extensive cross-references ensures that the reader can find what he or she is looking for.

There are a large number of worked examples, each of which illustrates a particular aspect of the Smalltalk-80 language, the VisualWorks development environment or its class library. The examples are frequently accompanied by screen-shots of VisualWorks in operation. Additionally, almost all chapters contain exercises (of various degrees of complexity) which the reader is encouraged to answer using VisualWorks.

Typographical conventions

In this book the standard typeface is a serif font. Other fonts are used to distinguish special terms, as follows:

- Menu items are in bold sans serif, e.g. **Workspace**.
- Smalltalk expressions or variables, as they appear in the system, appear in sans serif, such as Transcript show: 'Hello'.
- Place holders and variables used in examples are in italic sans serif typeface, for example *a Collection*.
- Keys that appear on the keyboard are indicated by angle brackets. For example, the 'carriage return' key: <CR>, or a function key: <F1>.

Trademarks

Acknowledgements

There are many people whom we should acknowledge for their help and support during the production of this book. Firstly we'd like to thank Laura Hill, who reviewed the first draft of the manuscript and provided the original material for Chapter 34. Mario Wolczko deserves special thanks, not only for providing the basis for Chapter 26, but also for his in-depth knowledge and comprehension which has been a constant inspiration. In addition there are a number of (ex-)colleagues who have all helped with ideas, examples and exercises – their contribution was much appreciated; they are Gary Birch, Dave Cleal, Adrian Kunzle, John Nolan, Anthony Nowlan, and Ian Piumarta. We would also like to thank the anonymous reviewers for their often irritating, but nonetheless constructive criticisms; Adele Goldberg for her review, including comments on the technical accuracy of the book; and Helen Martin of Prentice Hall for having the patience to wait for us! Finally, I'd like to express my personal gratitude to my partner, Sandra Ellesley – this book could not have been completed without her advice, support and encouragement.

Bernard Horan, May 1995

1 What is object-oriented programming?

This chapter contains a brief introduction to the ideas of object-oriented programming. It presents basic concepts such as *objects* and *messages*, explains the notions of *class* and *instance*, and the advantages of a *class hierarchy*. The way in which the correct methods are identified after a message-send is also described.

In addition, we discuss the various implementations of object-oriented languages, and identify the Smalltalk approach at an abstract level. The advantages of object-oriented programming to all sorts of environments are emphasized.

1.1 Objects

The fundamental concept that underpins object-oriented programming is that of the *Object*. An object is a combination of two parts:

1. 'Data' – the *state* of the object is maintained within that object.
2. 'Operations' – all the mechanisms to *access* and *manipulate* that state.

The internal representation of an object consists of variables which either hold data directly or act as pointers to other objects (Figure 1.1). The internal variables within the object are not directly accessible from outside that object – the barrier that this provides is called *information hiding*. In an object-oriented language, the 'natural' view of objects is from the *outside*; the *inside* of the object is only of interest to itself. Therefore, no object can read or modify the state of any other object, i.e. unlike a data structure (for example, a Pascal record or a C struct), an external entity cannot force a change of state in an object. Access to any part of the state of an object is only possible if the object itself permits it.

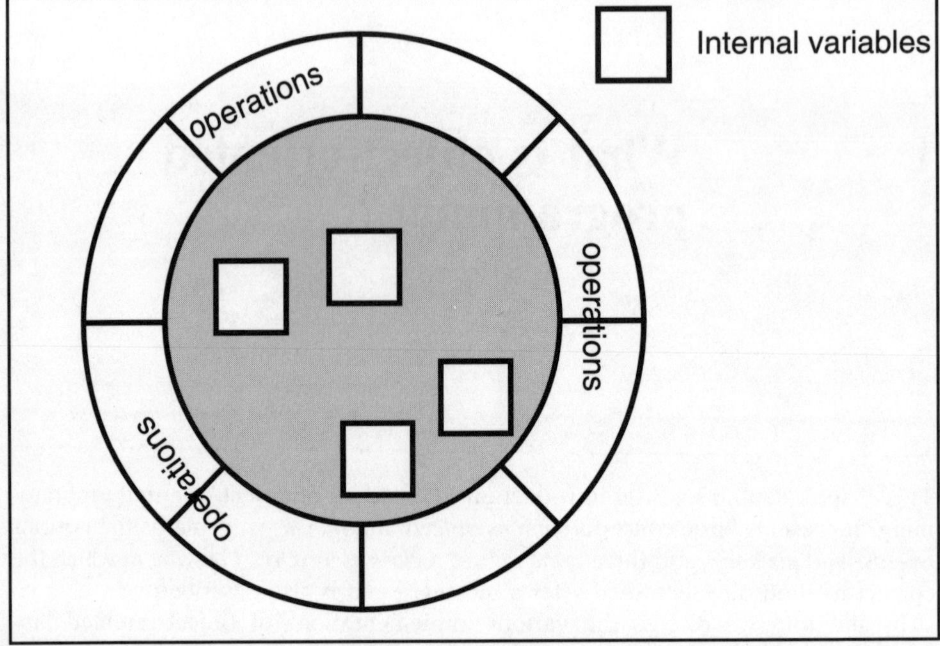

Figure 1.1 An Object.

1.2 Messages

Object-oriented programming languages use *message-sending* as their only means of performing operations. If the receiving object *understands* the message it has been sent, then one of its internal operations (or *methods*) will be performed. This, in turn, may cause some computation to take place (by acting on one or more of the object's internal variables). A result is always returned (i.e. an object).

Since an object's internal state is private and cannot be directly accessed from the outside, the only way of accessing that state is by sending a message to the object. The set of messages to which an object responds is called its *message interface*. However, it is important to note that a message specifies only *which* operation is requested, not *how* that operation is to be fulfilled. The object receiving the message (the *receiver*) determines from its methods (described in some object-oriented language) how to carry out that operation. Similarly, a method that is being performed in response to the receipt of a message may only manipulate other objects (including the receiver's internal variables) by sending them messages. Program flow may therefore be illustrated in terms of communication between many objects (see Figure 1.2).

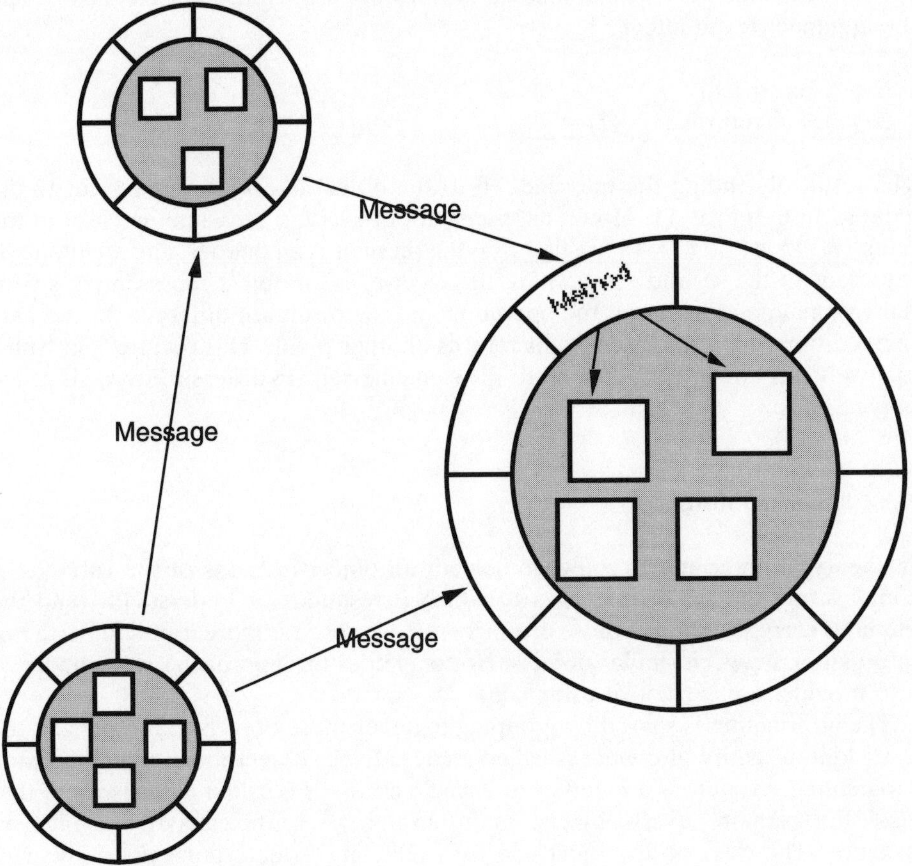

Figure 1.2 Objects send *messages* to each other; the receiver's corresponding *method* determines the operations to be performed.

For example, we could request an object to carry out some activity by sending it a message. One or more arguments may be sent to an object along with the name of the message (called the *selector*). The object receiving the message may be able to perform the action entirely on its own; alternatively, it may ask other objects for information, pass information to other objects, or to carry out computation, all by sending messages.

The same message sent to different objects can produce different results, since it is the receiver of the message, not the sender, that decides what will happen as a result of a message-send. In this respect sending a message is fundamentally different from calling a procedure in a conventional programming language such as C.

Let us examine the result of sending the message +5. Here the selector is +, and the argument is the integer 5.

6 + 5 returns 11
(7@2) + 5 returns (12@7).

The result of sending the message +5 to the object integer 6 (equivalent to the expression 6 + 5) is 11. However, the result of sending the same message to the point (7@2) is (12@7). In the first case the receiver is an Integer, and an Integer is returned. In the second case, where the receiver is an object representing a two-dimensional point in space, the operation and the result are different. In this case the addition of a scalar to a point returns another point. This feature – in which many objects are able to respond to the same message in different ways – is called *polymorphism*.

1.3 Classes and instances

In theory, a programmer could implement an object in terms of the variables it contains and the set of messages to which it responds or understands (and the methods corresponding to those messages). However, it is more useful to share this information between similar objects. Not only does this approach save memory, it also provides a means of re-using code.

The information is shared by grouping together those objects that represent the same kind of entity into what is called a *class*. Every object in an object-oriented programming system is a member of a single class – it is called an *instance* of that class. Furthermore, every object contains a reference to the class of which it is an instance. The class of an object acts as a template to determine the number of internal variables an instance will have, and holds a list of methods which corresponds to the messages to which all instances of the class will respond.

If objects did not obtain their behavior from classes, each object would have to 'carry around' with it a copy of all the code it could evaluate. By using classes we avoid the potential efficiency problems in a fine-grain object-oriented system. Consequently, the behavior of an object, expressed in terms of messages to which it responds, depends on its class. All objects of the same class have common methods, and therefore uniform behavior, but they may have different state.

1.4 Class hierarchy

Classes are arranged in a class hierarchy. Every class has a parent class – or *superclass* – and may also have *subclasses*. A subclass *inherits* both the behavior of its superclass (in terms of its method dictionary) and the structure of its internal variables. At the top of the hierarchy is the only class without a superclass, called class Object in Smalltalk. Class Object defines the basic structure of all objects, and the methods corresponding to the messages to which every object will respond.

For example, referring to Figure 1.3, we can see a class hierarchy where thomas is an instance of class Persian, which itself is a subclass of class Cat, which is a subclass of class Mammal, which may be a subclass of class Vertebrate, and so on.

A superclass of which no instances should be created is known as an *abstract superclass*. Such classes are intended to support partial implementations of features that are completed (differently) in subclasses.

Inheritance supports *differential programming* (or programming by modification), i.e. a new class of object may be defined which is similar to an existing one (its superclass) except for a few minor differences. Subclasses therefore allow the programmer to *refine*, or *specialize*, the behavior of the parent class. This can take a number of forms:

- Additional or modified behavior provided by extra methods
- The re-implementation of the internal representation of the object's state
- The addition of extra internal variables
- Any combination of the above.

We may therefore exploit inheritance as another technique for re-using code. For example, if the message odd is sent to the Integer 12, the result false will be returned even though the class Integer does not have a method specifying how to make this test. This is because the method corresponding to the message odd is defined in class Number, which is a superclass of class Integer. This means that all subclasses of class Number, including integers, are able to respond to the message odd, since they inherit this method.

Within Smalltalk, the class structure is implemented as a *single inheritance* hierarchy. This means that a subclass can only inherit from one parent superclass. Other object-oriented programming languages support *multiple inheritance*, in which case a subclass may inherit from multiple parent superclasses.

1.5 Methods

A message is sent to an object which is an instance of some class. A search is made in the class's method dictionary for the method corresponding to the message selector. If the method is found there, then it is *bound* to the message and evaluated, and the appropriate response returned. If the appropriate method is not found, then a search is made in the instance's class's immediate superclass. This process repeats up the class hierarchy until either the method is located or there are no further superclasses. In the latter case, the system notifies the programmer that a run-time error has occurred.

The object-oriented message-passing mechanism can be compared to a function call in a conventional programming language such as C. It is similar in that the point

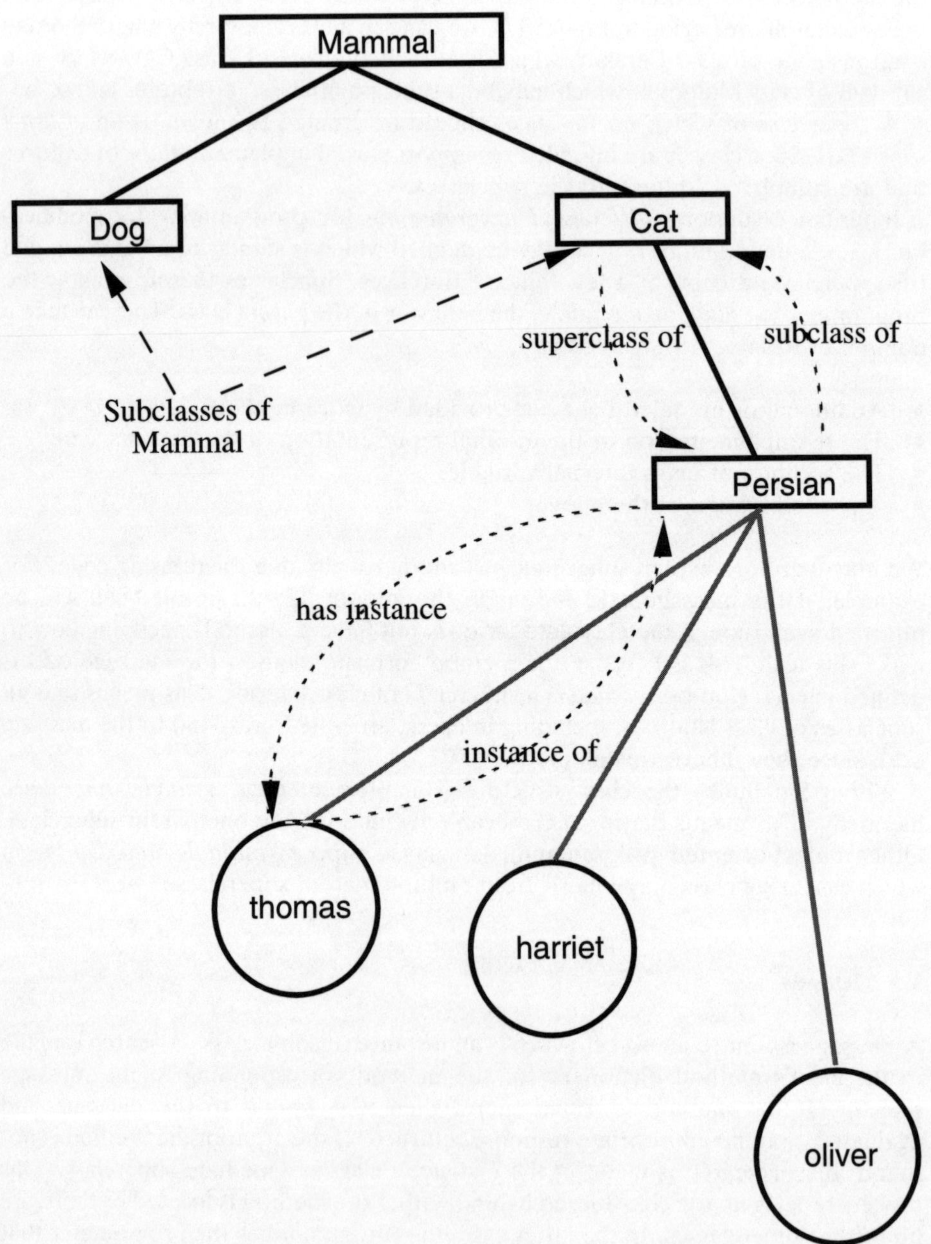

Figure 1. An example of a class hierarchy and its instances.

of control is moved to the receiver; the object sending the message is suspended until a response is received. It is different in that the receiver of a message is not determined when the code is created ('compile time') but is determined when the message is actually sent ('run time'). This *dynamic* (or late) binding mechanism is the feature which gives Smalltalk its polymorphic capabilities.

1.6 Alternative object-oriented programming languages

At present there are many languages that claim to be 'object-oriented'. Of these, many are *pure* in the sense that they consistently adhere to the object-oriented paradigm described in the previous sections. Others take a conventional language and add extensions suitable for object-oriented programming.

However, in these *hybrid* languages, objects are only used to represent higher-level entities; the data types specific to each language are retained. In addition, hybrid languages relax the requirement for information hiding – external procedures or functions may be used to access the internal variables of an object. However, hybrid languages offer the advantage of familiarity, and programmers have the freedom to decide whether or not to make use of the extra object-oriented features. Unfortunately, therefore, these languages lack the rigorous consistency and conceptual clarity that make pure object-oriented languages, for example Smalltalk, such a powerful programming language.

In the following sections we briefly describe several of the most well-known object-oriented programming languages.

Simula

Based on Algol 60, Simula was the first object-oriented language. It introduced the concepts of *class*, *inheritance* and *polymorphism*.

Smalltalk

The Smalltalk language and programming environment was developed at the Xerox Palo Alto Research Center in the 1970s and early 1980s. The graphical programming environment greatly influenced the development of the Apple Macintosh and later windowing systems such as X11 and Microsoft Windows. When first developed, Smalltalk broke new ground as the first uniformly object-oriented language (every data item is an object). Today, over 20 years later, there are still few languages or environments that match the sophistication of its incremental compiler and the extensibility of both its language and environment.

At the time of writing, there are several implementations of Smalltalk available. The ParcPlace Systems implementation is a direct descendant of earlier Xerox versions, whereas others have arrived on the scene more recently. (Chapter 2 discusses the various Smalltalk implementations.)

Eiffel

Eiffel builds on the concepts of Simula by adding multiple inheritance and semi-formal class specifications in an attempt to produce a *pure* object-oriented language compatible with current approaches to software engineering. Class invariants and operation pre- and post-conditions may be expressed algebraically in a class specification. Consequently this allows a large degree of compile-time and run-time correctness checking.

The Eiffel library contains numerous classes for common data structures, parsing and scanning libraries, and an interface with the X11 window system.

C++

This is an extension to C designed by Bjarne Stroustrup of AT&T Bell Laboratories – the home of the C language. The AT&T product is a translator that converts C++ into C, which you then compile with a compiler of your choice, other vendors provide products that compile C++ directly. Its main influence was Simula, rather than Smalltalk, and so it remains a strongly typed language. There is no 'standard' library of classes to compare with that of Smalltalk-80, although there are libraries for different application areas.

Objective-C

Objective-C extends the C language by the introduction of classes and a new data type, *id*, which is a reference to any object. Objective-C is modelled on Smalltalk-80 and has the same typeless nature, although simple data items, such as integers and reals, remain in C.

It is a pre-processor that translates the object-oriented extensions into conventional C code, which is then fed to a standard C compiler. Objective-C comes with a class library in source form which is a useful aid to learning the basics. It initially achieved popularity through its use on the NeXT machine, bundled with Interface Builder (also written in Objective-C).

C+@

C+@ (pronounced 'cat') is another language based on C by AT&T Bell Labs, derived from their Calico language. It is closer to Smalltalk than C++ since it is a true object-based language in which all data items are objects, although it retains the language syntax of C. Again, like Smalltalk, it provides a graphical programming environment and a large class library, written in C+@ and available in source.

Object Pascal

This is an extension to Pascal developed as a systems programming tool at Apple. Object Pascal is a simple object-oriented language, but lacks some of the more complex ideas present in Smalltalk-80.

It has been used to produce a large variety of Macintosh applications. The language is in the Simula mould, and (like C++) it uses an extension of the existing record structure to implement classes. Microsoft's *Quick Pascal* is based closely on Object Pascal, with nearly identical syntax.

CLOS

The Common Lisp Object System is an extension to Common Lisp, itself a standardized version of Lisp. An object in CLOS is an instance of a class and a class may inherit from many other classes (multiple inheritance). However, CLOS does not have any notion of message-sending.

Self

Self is an object-based language whose syntax is similar to Smalltalk. One difference is that Self doesn't have the notion of a class. An object is derived from another (its prototype) by copying and refinement. Another difference is that no distinction is made between instance variables and methods – they are both called *slots*. On the face of it, Self is an immensely powerful language. However, its disadvantages shouldn't be overlooked: it's still a research project and requires a large amount of memory and a big machine to run (Sparc-10 and 64MB, preferably).

Dylan

Dylan (which stands for 'DYnamic LANguage') is a new object-oriented language originally developed by the Eastern Research and Technology Labs of Apple Computer. It most closely resembles CLOS and Scheme, but has been influenced by Smalltalk and Self. At present its design is still fluid, and there are no commercial implementations.

1.7 The advantages of object-oriented programming

To summarize this chapter, it is worth reiterating the main points concerning object-oriented programming:

- An object is a combination of some local state (represented as internal variables) and the operations by which that state may be accessed and manipulated – this is called *encapsulation*.
- The state of an object is not directly accessible from outside that object – this is called *information hiding*.
- Message-sending is the only means of performing operations.
- A message specifies which operation is requested, the corresponding method contains the expressions to be evaluated.
- Every object is an instance of a class.
- Classes are arranged in a hierarchy.
- Every class has a superclass (except class Object in Smalltalk-80).
- A subclass inherits the behavior of its superclass.
- Message-sending is a polymorphic operation.

These properties provide the programmer with the following useful features:

- An object encapsulates state and methods, and consequently the use of objects provides data protection without excessive specification.
- By separating the user of an object from the implementer, the user is no longer aware of how an object is implemented. Users, then, can only manipulate an object by using those messages provided by the implementer. This has the benefit that the programmer can change the internal implementation of an object and, keeping the message interface constant, have no detrimental effect on the applications using that object. This in turn promotes a modular programming style.
- Similarly, separating *what* happens from *how* it happens promotes the re-use of code.
- The use of inheritance and polymorphism promotes differential programming, or programming by modification.
- The description of a system in terms of objects, and of objects in terms of possible behavior (as defined by messages), permits modular design. Object-oriented programming minimizes the number of assumptions that different parts of a program make about each other, therefore re-using some components of a program written for one application in another application is easy.

1.8 Summary

In this chapter we have given a brief overview of object-oriented programming, emphasizing the basic concepts such as encapsulation and polymorphism. We hope that it has provided you with the incentive to go on to explore the use of Smalltalk-80 in more detail. The next chapter describes some of the history of the Smalltalk language, and acts as a precursor to later chapters on the use of VisualWorks.

2 Introduction to Smalltalk

In this chapter we briefly describe Smalltalk, its origins and the way in which it is used. In particular, we outline the elements that combine to make Smalltalk – the language, the programming environment, the class library, and the implementation.

There is a short discussion of the differences between various Smalltalk implementations from the users' point of view, followed by a list of other publications cited within the book.

2.1 What is Smalltalk?

Smalltalk can be seen as just another programming language, with its own rules of syntax for describing classes, objects, methods and messages; and its own rules of grammar for parsing expressions. However, most implementations of Smalltalk provide more than just a language – they supply a programming environment, a library of classes and a persistent object store. Each of these combines to produce a unified framework for the development of object-oriented applications and each is described in detail below.

A language

Compared to conventional programming languages such as C or Pascal, Smalltalk has an unusual syntax. In addition, Smalltalk has no notion of 'type'. Objects are employed to represent everything in Smalltalk, including all the conventional data types that may be found in any programming language: such as integers, booleans, floating-point numbers, characters, strings, arrays. In addition, objects are used to represent display items such as menus, windows, and even the compiler itself. Smalltalk is therefore described as a *uniformly* object-oriented language.

However, the rules of Smalltalk syntax (see Chapter 3) are simple and consistent. When you have mastered these rules and have gained a certain familiarity, it is a straightforward language both to read and write. The problems are no greater than mastering the syntax of Lisp, APL and Forth and, like the adherents of those languages, most Smalltalk programmers argue that the syntax is one of the strengths of the language.

A programming environment

Smalltalk was one of the first systems to pioneer the so-called 'WIMP' interface (Windows, Icons, Menus and Pointer). It is not surprising, then, to discover that current environments provide numerous tools to enable programmers to browse existing classes and copy and modify pre-written code (Chapter 6). Additional editing tools enable programmers to amend and correct newly created code effortlessly. Other tools allow the programmer access to the underlying filing system (Chapter 6), from which existing source code may be 'filed-in'. Additionally, Smalltalk provides change-management tools. These are in the form of *Projects* that may be used to contain code specific to particular software Projects and also Browsers to view recent changes (Chapter 24). Since Smalltalk is extensible, programmers can tailor these existing tools or create new ones for their own use.

Smalltalk also pioneered the use of an incremental compiler. This means that programmers can avoid lengthy sessions of compiling and linking, and get 'instant gratification' from the speed of compilation, thus enabling them to adopt a more exploratory approach to software development. This approach enables the programmer to develop software in a piecemeal fashion, exploring ideas as the application takes shape.

The combination of an incremental compiler and a symbolic debugger (giving interactive access to source code) allows the programmer to inspect and modify currently active objects, carry out in-line testing and modify and recompile existing code, and then restart the evaluation of the expressions. By inserting break points at suitable points, the programmer is able to step through the evaluation of the code (see Chapter 23).

Thus, the Smalltalk programming environment promotes a programming process that employs an iterative development style for creating an application. The programmer is able to develop a partial solution, test it, add new functionality, test it, and so on, until the complete solution is reached.

A class library

Despite its name, Smalltalk is not necessarily small – for example, Smalltalk-80 contains hundreds of classes and thousands of methods, all available on-line in source code form (Smalltalk is written almost entirely in Smalltalk – a small kernel is written in machine code). The classes can be further refined using the inheritance mechanism, or they can be used as internal variables by other objects. Consequently, the effort required to construct new applications is minimized.

The library of classes includes:

- Various subclasses of Number. This includes Integer, Float and Fraction.
- Various data structures. This includes Set, Bag, Array, OrderedCollection, SortedCollection, and Dictionary.
- Classes to represent text, font, color, etc.
- Geometric representations, e.g. Point, Rectangle, Circle, Polygon, etc.
- Classes to assist in the control of concurrency. For example, Process and Semaphore.

A persistent object store

A Smalltalk system consists of two parts:

- The *virtual image* (or 'Image'), containing all the objects in the system.
- The *virtual machine* (or 'VM'), consisting of hardware and software (microcode) to give dynamics to objects in the image. (Each hardware platform requires its own VM.)

This implementation technique was used for several reasons:

- To ensure portability of the virtual image. Any Smalltalk image should be executable on any virtual machine. The image is (mostly) isolated from the VM implementation (hardware and software).
- The Smalltalk system is very large, but most of the functionality is in the image. This eases the problems of implementation, as only a relatively simple VM has to be constructed.

Because the complete working environment is saved (the *image*), Smalltalk also acts as a persistent object store. This allows the programmer to create new classes, and even new instances, and keep them from one working session to another.

2.2 Smalltalk implementations

At present there are four commercial implementations of Smalltalk, with others under development. In addition, there are a small number of implementations in the public domain. The differences between them are generally outweighed by their similarities, and any differences that do exist are likely to be found in the content of the class library and the sophistication of the tools. In the following sections we describe the most popular Smalltalk implementations:

Smalltalk-80

Smalltalk-80 is the latest in a line of Smalltalk development originally started at Xerox Palo Alto Research Center (PARC) in the early 1970s, and can be viewed as the ancestor of all other Smalltalk implementations. (Earlier versions, including Smalltalk-72 and Smalltalk-76, were for research purposes only.)

It became a commercial product in the late 1980s when its current distributor ParcPlace Systems was created out of the Smalltalk researchers at PARC headed by Adele Goldberg. At that time, the release of Smalltalk-80 was numbered 2.2. Release 2.4 introduced a major modification to the VM with the effect that previous virtual images would no longer run on the new VM. However, the most significant recent release was 4.0 (ParcPlace named the product 'Objectworks\Smalltalk') which integrated the windowing system with that of the host platform. (To our knowledge there has never been a 3.*x* release!) Meanwhile, there has been a minor upgrade (with the addition of extra classes) in the form of release 4.1. More recently, ParcPlace has released an extended version of Smalltalk-80, called 'VisualWorks' (now at release 2.0), which provides window-building facilities and database connectivity.

There are three important features that distinguish VisualWorks from its competitors:

1. Its class library – considered to be the most complete and re-usable. (All source is available.)
2. Its portability – VisualWorks is available for several platforms, including Apple Macintosh, SUN, HP, DEC and MS-Windows. A virtual image created on any one of these machines will run on any other *without* recompilation.
3. Its tools – VisualWorks has the richest set of tools available (some of which we have referred to above; others are described in later chapters).

Smalltalk/V

Produced by Digitalk. Current versions are available for PCs (running under MS-Windows, and Presentation Manager) and for the Macintosh. Most of the differences between VisualWorks and Smalltalk/V relate to the size and content of the library of classes provided (which is smaller than VisualWorks), the sophistication of programming tools and the ease of portability across platforms. (Source code is typically not portable between Smalltalk/V and VisualWorks. Some source code – especially that which provides the user interface – is not portable between different versions of Smalltalk/V.)

SmalltalkAgents

Released by Quasar Knowledge Systems in late 1993, SmalltalkAgents is a relative newcomer to the Smalltalk scene. It is currently (Spring 1995) only available for the Apple Macintosh, with versions for MS-Windows and SUN scheduled for late 1995.

The implementation appears closer to Smalltalk/V than Smalltalk-80, and some of the extensions it introduces contravene other Smalltalk conventions. It is packaged with an extensive set of modular class libraries including data structures and support for graphical user interfaces.

VisualAge

IBM advertises VisualAge as its 'object-oriented application-builder technology'. Essentially a 4GL, it combines a visual programming toolkit; a library of 'parts' (to provide database queries, transactions and a graphical user interface); multi-media capabilities (in the form of support for audio and video); team programming tools and configuration management. The reason for its inclusion here is that it also provides Smalltalk as a 'scripting language' for advanced application logic (the language is interpreted). At the moment it is only available for OS/2 and MS-Windows.

Smalltalk/X

Currently a beta product, Smalltalk/X is an almost full implementation of Smalltalk that compiles to machine code using 'C' as an intermediate. Smalltalk/X may be used as a language or a full programming environment. As its name suggests, this implementation is aimed at platforms that use the X11 windowing system, although we understand that versions are being developed for MS-Windows. Smalltalk/X comes with a library of classes to represent data structures, user interface components, etc.

Apple Smalltalk

Developed by Apple, but unsupported by them, this is available from the 'Apple Programmers and Developers Alliance' for a minimum cost.

Little Smalltalk

Little Smalltalk, by Timothy Budd, is designed to run under UNIX on an alphanumeric display (and therefore does not possess the sophisticated programming tools available in other versions of Smalltalk). It is available as a book and sources in the public domain for UNIX, MS-DOS, and the Acorn Archimedes.

2.3 The books

Throughout the chapters of this book you will see occasional reference to the 'Orange Book' or the 'Blue Book'. Here we refer to one of the four books to be written by authors who were (and some who still are) involved with the development of Smalltalk-80. The 'color' of the book indicates the color of the background of the illustration on the front cover (as well as for the Addison-Wesley logo on the spine). The full references of the books are as follows:

Blue Book	Goldberg, Adele, and David Robson, *Smalltalk-80: The Language and its Implementation*, Addison-Wesley, 1983.
Orange Book	Goldberg, Adele, *Smalltalk-80: The Interactive Programming Environment*, Addison-Wesley, 1984.
Green Book	Krasner, Glenn (ed.), *Smalltalk-80: Bits of History, Words of Advice*, Addison-Wesley, 1983.
Purple Book	Goldberg, Adele, and David Robson, *Smalltalk-80: The Language*, Addison-Wesley, 1989. (The Purple Book is an update/revision of the Blue Book.)

2.4 Typographical conventions

In this book the standard typeface is a serif font. Other fonts are used to distinguish special terms, as follows:

- Menu items are in bold sans serif, e.g. **Workspace**.
- Smalltalk expressions or variables, as they appear in the system, appear in sans serif, such as Transcript show: 'Hello'.
- Place holders and variables used in examples are in italic sans serif typeface, for example *a Collection*.
- Keys that appear on the keyboard are indicated by angle brackets. For example, the 'carriage return' key: <CR>, or a function key: <F1>.

2.5 Summary

The overview of Smalltalk provided in this chapter is an introduction to the later chapters of the book. We hope to have given you a glimpse of the way in which Smalltalk is different from other programming languages. In the following chapters this difference will be made more apparent as we consider Smalltalk's language syntax. From now on, when we mention Smalltalk, we shall be referring to the Smalltalk-80 language, unless stated otherwise.

3 Language basics

The Smalltalk language syntax is straightforward, but is rather unusual compared with more conventional languages. Topics in this chapter include the expression syntax, literals and variables, the parsing rules, a brief introduction to blocks and an introduction to variables.

3.1 Smalltalk expression syntax

Clearly, an expression syntax is required to express how objects interact with one another. An expression is a sequence of characters which describe an object, called the *value* of the expression. Four types of expression are permitted:

- *Literals* describe constant objects (numbers, characters, strings, symbols and arrays).
- *Variable names* describe accessible variables. The value of the variable name is the current value of the variable with that name.
- *Message expressions* describe messages sent to receivers. The value of the expression is determined by the method it invokes.
- *Block expressions* describe deferred activities. Blocks are often used for control structures.

3.2 Literals

One of the simplest forms of Smalltalk expression is the 'literal expression'. Here we describe the syntax of these constant objects.

Numbers

A Number is represented as a sequence of digits, with an optional leading unary minus sign and optional decimal point. There is no unary plus sign. Examples include:

```
8   12.7   −0.0007
```

Numbers can also be represented in other bases, by *preceding* the base with a radix and the letter 'r':

```
8r177     16r5E     2r100011
```

Numbers can also be expressed in 'scientific notation', using the suffix letter 'e'. For example:

```
2.23e5     3e-2
```

Finally, numbers can also be represented as 'fixed-point' (used, for example, to represent currency values) using the suffix letter 'f'. For example:

```
2.23f     177f6     3f-2
```

Characters

A Character is an individual letter of an alphabet. It is represented by a single alphanumeric letter preceded by a '$' sign. Examples include:

```
$D     $+     $$     $9     $x
```

Strings

A String is a sequence of Characters surrounded by quote marks. Examples include:

```
'test string'   'string with '' embedded single quote'
```

Symbols

A Symbol is an object that represents a string used for a name in Smalltalk. A Symbol is represented using the '#' sign, and is optionally surrounded by quote marks. Symbols are always unique. Examples include:

```
#initialize     #W80     #temp     #'3x'
```

Literal Arrays

The literals are surrounded by parentheses and preceded by the '#' sign. One array 'embedded' in another may avoid the use of the '#' sign. Examples are:

```
#(40 41 42)     #((1 '2') ('first' #second))     #(1 'one' ($5 'five'))
```

Byte Arrays

A Byte Array is a sequence of bytes (integers between 0 and 255) surrounded by square brackets and preceded by a '#' sign. For example:

```
#[1 2 3 0]     #[16rFF 0 2r111 2e2]
```

3.3 Variables

A variable points to an object and the variable's name is an expression referring to that object. Variable names are identifiers made up of letters and digits with an initial letter:

```
someObject     Integer     Smalltalk     temp3
```

When made up from more than one word, the first letter of each subsequent word in the identifier is capitalized. You are strongly encouraged to conform to this convention – it is used consistently throughout the standard image.

3.4 Pseudo-variables

A pseudo-variable name refers to an object which cannot be changed; these include:

nil – A value used when no other is appropriate, such as uninitialized variables. nil is the sole instance of class UndefinedObject.

true – Represents truth. It is the sole instance of class True.

false – Represents falsehood. It is the sole instance of class False.

Classes True and False are subclasses of Boolean.

3.5 Messages

A *message expression* comprises a *receiver*, a *selector* and possibly some *arguments*. The basic specification for sending a message in Smalltalk is

```
<receiver> <message>
```

where <receiver> is the name of some known object, and <message> is a *unary*, *binary*, or *keyword* message including arguments.

Unary messages

Unary messages are the simplest type of message in Smalltalk. An object is followed by a single word (the message selector) and no arguments. The selector must contain no colons. Examples include:

```
3 negated
100 factorial
Window new
anArray size
theta sin
4 even
```

Binary messages

Binary messages are more complex, since they also have one argument specified with them. The selector is one or two non-alphabetic characters, the second of which must not be a minus sign. Existing binary messages in the current Smalltalk image include:

```
+                              -                      /          *
=                              <                      >          ~=
<=                             >=
& (logical 'and')              | (logical 'or')       //
, (string concatenation)
```

These binary messages will be described in more detail in later chapters. Examples include:

```
2 + 3

true & false

3 * 4

100 // 17

index - 1
```

Keyword messages

Keyword messages are the most complex type of message. The structure of a keyword message comprises one or more keywords each with its own argument. For instance, in the message

```
anArray copyFrom: 1 to: 3
```

copyFrom: and to: are the keywords, and the numbers 1 and 3 are arguments. Note that each keyword must end with a colon. A message can have no more than 255 keywords. An argument can be an expression representing any object. Other examples include:

```
index max: limit
anArray at: first put: 'aardvark'
```

3.6 Parsing rules

The order of evaluation in a Smalltalk statement is:

1. Unary messages left to right
2. Binary messages left to right
3. Keyword messages left to right.

Multiple expressions are separated by full stops. (For North American readers, a 'full stop' is a 'period'.)

These rules are quite unlike those in many other languages, where precedence depends on the function. There is no algebraic hierarchy. However, as with many other languages, parentheses can be used to alter the order of precedence. It is worth considering some examples:

In the example:

```
1.5 tan rounded
```

the unary message tan is sent to 1.5, and the unary message rounded is sent to the resulting object. Similarly, for binary messages:

```
a + b * 2
```

returns the result 'twice (a+b)'. To get '(twice b)+a', the expression should be written:

```
a + (b * 2)
```

Parentheses also have precedence over unary messages. In the example:

```
(anArray at: 14) even
```

the message even is sent to the 14th element of anArray, while:

```
anArray at: 14 even
```

the message even is sent to 14, and an attempt is made to use the resulting object (true) as an index to anArray. This is probably an error.

When multiple keywords appear in an expression, they are parsed as a single keyword message. For example:

```
frame scale: factor max: 5
```

contains a keyword message selector (scale:max:) with two arguments, factor and 5. Conversely:

```
frame scale: (factor max: 5)
```

sends the keyword message max: 5 to factor, and uses the resulting object as the argument to the keyword message selector scale: sent to frame.

It is important therefore to exercise care when putting keyword messages together:

```
2 raisedTo: 3 raisedTo: 7
```

As there is no raisedTo:raisedTo: message selector, the above expression will result in an error. Similarly, it is important to note that:

(2 raisedTo: 3) raisedTo: 7 *is not equal to* 2 raisedTo: (3 raisedTo: 7)

Omitting the parentheses in these sorts of cases is a common source of errors.

Parentheses can always be used to clarify the intention of an expression. Nevertheless, use with care, otherwise your expressions will become very cluttered.

Exercise 3.1

What is the result for each of the following Smalltalk expressions?

```
2 + 3 negated
2 raisedTo: 3 + 7
(2 raisedTo: 3) + 7
2 raisedTo: 3 + 7 negated
(2 raisedTo: 3) + 7 negated
(2 raisedTo: 3 + 7) negated
```

3.7 Assignments

A variable name can refer to different objects at different times. The assignment expression can be used to assign an object to a variable. It looks like:

```
<variable> := <message send>
```

Examples include:

```
newIndex := 1
this := that
someString := 'Part Two'
anArray := #(1 2 3 4 5)
```

Assignment expressions return values (like other expressions) so several assignments can be made together:

```
this := that := theOther
stop := end := 0
```

Exercise 3.2

What is the result of the following assignment expressions?

```
a := 5 - 4.
a := 5 raisedTo: 3.
a := (b := 5) * 66.
a := 3 * (2 raisedTo: (b := 36 // 42)).
```

3.8 Returning

When it has finished evaluating, every Smalltalk method returns an object to the sender of the message. If no object is specified, the receiver itself is returned. If some other object should be returned, the '^' symbol is used to return the object and terminate the evaluation of the current method (though it need not necessarily be at the end of the message sequence). Any object can be returned this way.

3.9 Blocks

A block represents a *deferred sequence of messages*. A block is represented by a sequence of expressions (separated by full stops), enclosed by square brackets. For example:

```
aBlock := [index - 2]
aBlock := [anArray at: newIndex put: 42]
```

The expressions in a block are evaluated when the block receives the message value. For example:

```
aBlock := [a := 0].
aBlock value
```

when aBlock receives the message value, its message expressions are evaluated, here causing the variable a to refer to the integer 0.

Blocks are used to implement control structures (see Chapter 10). Examples include:

```
aNumber even
        ifTrue: [aString := 'even']
        ifFalse: [aString := 'odd']

[index > 0]
        whileTrue: [index := index + 1]
```

3.10 Variables (again)

The permanent 'private' memory of an object has already been introduced. The term used to describe the variables that represent an object's private memory is *instance variables*, since they are used to represent the private memory of an instance of a class.

Instance variables are only available to the specific object in which they are contained. They are simply names for pointers to other objects and always begin life as nil. Each instance of a class keeps its own internal copy of each instance variable.

Other types of variables are also provided and they are as follows:

- **Temporary variables** exist only for the duration of some activity (e.g. the evaluation of a method).
- **Class variables** are shared by all instances of a single class.
- **Global variables** are shared by all instances of all classes (i.e. all objects). Try not to use global variables except for experimentation.
- **Pool variables** are shared by all instances of some classes, and are thus a way of creating common storage between object classes. Pool variables are very rarely used.

By convention, private variables (instance variables, temporary variables) start with an initial lower-case letter, whereas shared variables (class variables, global variables, pool variables) start with an initial upper-case letter.

3.11 Comments

Text that is only for documentation purposes is indicated by its enclosure in double quotes (").

3.12 Summary

This chapter provides an introduction to the syntax of the Smalltalk language, covering all of the most important features. However, later chapters expand on the use of the syntax, in particular we shall return to different kinds of variables later in the book: Chapter 7 gives examples of global variables, and Chapter 12 describes class and pool variables. Also, blocks are examined in more detail in Chapters 10 and 17. Meanwhile, the next few chapters introduce the VisualWorks user interface, so that you can get underway with using the syntax.

4 Getting going with the user interface

In this chapter we present a brief introduction to the items seen on the screen, and their relationship to things within the environment. These include Browsers and Workspaces, Prompters and Menus. The mouse/cursor combination, the screen and the keyboard are also mentioned.

This introduction is followed by an indication of how to start (and stop!) VisualWorks; naturally, this aspect is somewhat dependent on the user's local machine and operating system. A discussion of the importance of snapshots and the 'sources' and 'changes' files is provided.

4.1 Windows

The VisualWorks user interface consists of one or more (potentially) overlapping windows, each of which may contain text or graphics. The windows are managed by the host platform's standard window manager, and not part of VisualWorks. On UNIX systems, this will be X-windows, together with a window manager such as twm, olwm (OpenLook) or mwm (Motif). On PC machines it will be MS-Windows, and on the Macintosh it will be Apple's own distinctive user interface. Each window is manipulated using the mechanisms of the native window manager, but can also be manipulated through VisualWorks.

Several types of windows are available as standard. These include windows with the following labels:

- **VisualWorks** – a window with menu options and buttons for launching other windows (hereinafter known as the 'Launcher'). It may also contain an area known as the 'System Transcript' (see below). We recommend that you keep this window open so that you can see the messages as they are displayed.
- **Workspace** – a general work/edit area.

- **System Browser** – for managing (parts of) the class hierarchy.
- **Class Browser** – for managing a single class.
- **System Transcript** – displaying 'system' messages.
- **File Browser** – access to underlying file system.
- **Inspector** – discover/change state of any object.
- **Debugger** – following/modifying evaluation paths.
- **Change List Browser** – for managing changes made to the image.

The VisualWorks image contains much code and a uniform mechanism for creating new windows.

4.2 Menus, prompters, etc.

A number of other 'things' can appear on the screen. These include:

- **Menus** – These are widely used in conjunction with windows. They allow the user to select one of several items using the mouse.
- **Confirmers** – These request the user to confirm or deny a request.
- **Prompters** – A mechanism for prompting the user for some typed response.
- **Informers** – These typically inform the user that some user request has failed.
- **Notifiers** – The means by which VisualWorks indicates that some event has occurred. This may be an error condition, a user interrupt or some other exception condition.

The use of many of these items will be demonstrated later in the book.

4.3 The mouse

VisualWorks requires the use of some form of pointing device – it is used for much of the user's interaction with the environment. A cursor on the display screen follows the movement of the pointing device. Typically, the device will be a mouse with three buttons. (If you are using a Macintosh or a PC, now would be a good time to consult your manual to discover how to simulate a three-button mouse on your single-button (Macintosh) or double-button (PC) mouse.)

Because VisualWorks also runs on machines with one- and two-button mice, use of the terms 'left', 'middle' and 'right' is discouraged. The names for the mouse buttons are:

<Select> is the left button (for historical reasons, also called the 'red' button in VisualWorks source code).

<Operate> is the middle button (also called the 'yellow' button in VisualWorks).

<Window> is the right button (also called the 'blue' button in VisualWorks).

Despite the recommendations, much Smalltalk code still uses the color names! The following terminology for the use of the mouse buttons is normally used:

Press	– press and hold the button down.
Release	– release the button.
Click	– press and release the button without moving the mouse.
Double-click	– click the button twice without moving the mouse between clicks.

When over a VisualWorks window, the general operations associated with mouse buttons are as follows:

<Select> button	– Selecting and positioning within the 'application' displayed in the window.
<Operate> button	– 'Application' (window) specific menu items.
<Window> button	– Window control function menu items, common to all standard VisualWorks windows.

4.4 Cursors

Eight standard cursors are used to give feedback about VisualWorks' activities and the current mouse position. (Use of these and other cursors is described in Chapter 31.) The eight cursors are described in Table 4.1.

The wait and/or execute cursors are used when evaluating messages that require several seconds to complete. The read and write cursors are used when file I/O is being performed.

4.5 Using VisualWorks

At least the following files should be present in your directory (Macintosh users should substitute the word 'folder' for the word 'directory'):

visual.im – this is the image file, representing the current (suspended) state of your Smalltalk evaluation.

visual.sou – this file contains the source code for all the classes and methods in the image. (On distributed file systems, you may find that this file is elsewhere.)

visual.cha – this file contains the changes made to the image file since the sources file was created. Every new or modified method, and all evaluations performed, are recorded here.

Table 4.1

Shape	Name	Description
	normal	The cursor looks like this for most of the time. The point of selection (or *hot-spot*) is the tip of the arrow.
	execute	The system is compiling a method, evaluating an expression, etc. During this time, mouse button movements are ignored and keyboard inputs are deferred.
	wait	The system is carrying out some operation that prevents it from responding to your input.
	read	Data is being read from an external file. User input is ignored/deferred.
	write	Data is being written to an external file. User input is ignored/deferred.
GC	garbage collector	Non-compacting garbage-collection is taking place. This occurs only during 'low-space conditions'. User input is ignored/deferred.
	memory compactor	Memory is being compacted. This occurs when free memory is heavily fragmented. User input is ignored/deferred.
	compacting garbage collector	A full compacting garbage-collection is taking place. This only occurs during 'low-space conditions'. User input is ignored/deferred.

If any of these files is missing, you will not be able to run VisualWorks. It is very important that the visual.im and visual.cha files remain consistent, so we recommend that you do not directly modify either file.

The actions required to start your VisualWorks session depend on the platform you are using. Here we will consider three possibilities: UNIX, MS-Windows and Macintosh. You should consult your manual or system administrator if you feel you may need help accessing or installing the software.

UNIX

To start the VisualWorks system, type `oe20 visual.im`. This starts the Smalltalk Virtual Machine (known as the 'Object Engine') and loads the image file. A number of messages will be printed in the console window as the image is loaded.

MS-Windows

Double-click on the icon named 'Visual' in the appropriate Program Manager window. This starts the Smalltalk Virtual Machine (known as the 'Object Engine') and loads the image file.

Macintosh

Double-click on the icon named 'visual.im' in the appropriate folder (usually contained in a folder also called 'Visual'). This starts the Smalltalk Virtual Machine (known as the 'Object Engine') and loads the image file. Once the image is loaded, two windows will appear on the screen: the Launcher (labelled 'VisualWorks') and a Workspace.

To leave the VisualWorks environment, select the **Exit VisualWorks . . .** option from the **File** menu of the Launcher. A Confirmer will appear (Figure 4.1); select **Exit** from this. Any changes you have made are not saved. If you want to save the changes you have made to the image, then you should select the **Save then Exit** option. A Prompter will appear, asking for a filename to be used for the image (Figure 4.2).

Figure 4.1 Confirm that you wish to quit the VisualWorks image.

Figure 4.2 Specifying the filename to be used.

Exercise 4.1

Exit and save the VisualWorks image (when asked to specify the filename, simply press <CR>). Then restart the image – you should note that the VisualWorks windows are in exactly the same state as when you quit the image.

The image can also be saved without stopping the VisualWorks system by using the **Save as ...** option from the **File** menu of the Launcher.

Exercise 4.2

Select the **Save as ...** option from the **File** menu of the Launcher. Use the default image filename (visual); type <CR> in the Prompter. Move the existing windows around the screen and then quit without saving. Restart VisualWorks; note that the window positions are those of the saved image.

4.6 The Launcher

The Launcher is a window that is always available (see Figure 4.3). It allows a wide variety of VisualWorks windows to be opened, and may incorporate an area called the 'System Transcript' (see later).

The Launcher consists of a menu bar containing seven menus, and seven buttons (each button acts as a shortcut to a menu option):

File – Various special options, including saving the image to a file, forcing a full garbage-collection cycle, and setting the user's preferences.
Browse – Allows a variety of browsers to be opened, including System and Class browsers (Chapters 6 and 9), and access to VisualWorks' 'resources' (Chapter 34).
Tools – Allows file handling (Chapter 6) and Workspace windows to be opened. Additionally provides access to VisualWorks' window-building tools and other

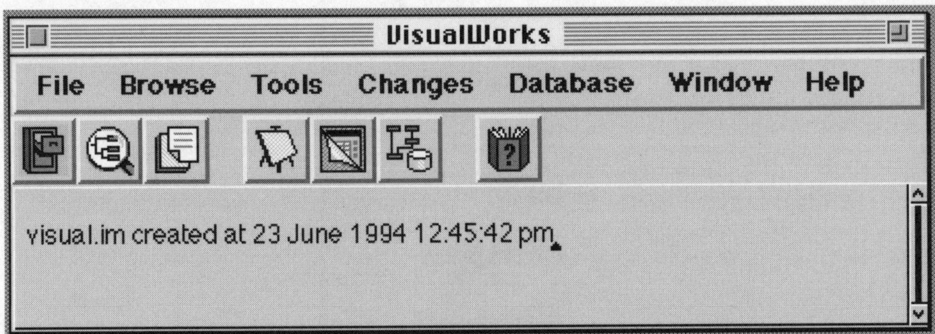

Figure 4.3 The VisualWorks Launcher.

advanced utilities (if available). The menu also includes an option to specify if the System Transcript should be included in the Launcher.
Changes – Allows several different kinds of windows to be opened, which support change management. We will be describing techniques for change management later in the book (Chapter 24).
Database – Allows access to database connectivity tools. (These will not be described further in this book.)
Window – Provides window management features (see later).
Help – Allows access to on-line documentation and examples.

4.7 <Window> button menu operations

Every window has a standard <window> button menu (Figure 4.4), which provides operations to control the window. The options provided by the menu will usually be identical for each window.

relabel as . . . – Allows the user to change the label that identifies the window.
refresh – Redisplays the entire window contents.
move – This permits a window to be moved without changing its size. The window is temporarily removed and its frame may be repositioned using the mouse. Click the <select> button to establish the top-left corner of the window's new position.
resize – This permits a window to be resized. You are prompted for the new top-left and bottom-right positions of the window.
front – Forces the window to the top of any stack of overlapping windows.

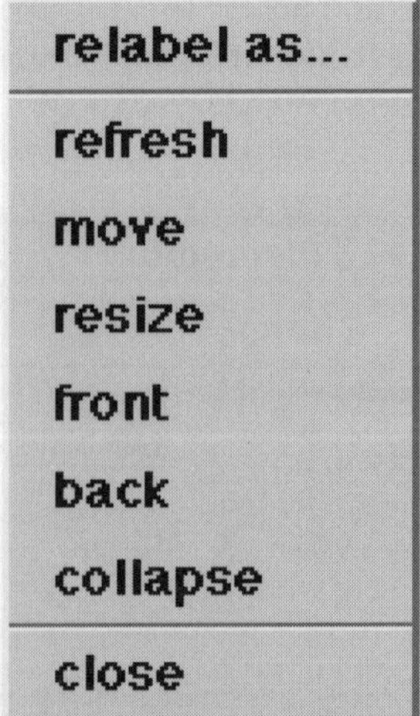

Figure 4.4 The <window> button menu.

back – Forces the window to the bottom of any stack.
collapse – Collapses the window to an icon. (It is not possible to reduce a window to an icon on the Macintosh. Instead the window is collapsed to the size of the window's title bar.)
close – The window is permanently removed. If there is anything in the window that has been changed but not 'saved' (see later), then a Confirmer is used to ensure that this is what you want to do. (Beware of different names: e.g. OpenLook's 'close' is the same as **collapse**, 'quit' means **close**.)

Exercise 4.3

Create a new Workspace by selecting the **Workspace** item from the **Tools** menu of the Launcher. Then experiment with the operations on the <window> button menu. Also, try the window manager operations provided by the host platform.

4.8 The Window Menu

The **Window** menu available from the Launcher (Figure 4.5) contains more options to control window management. The menu options are as follows:

Refresh All – redraws all the open windows.
Collapse All – collapses all the open windows, with the exception of the Launcher.
Restore All – expands all collapsed windows.
Windows – provides a sub-menu containing a list of window labels. Selecting an item from this menu will bring the corresponding window to the front. (The Macintosh version also includes a 'window' menu on its screen menu bar.)

4.9 Help

The **Help** menu (Figure 4.6) on the Launcher provides access to the help system. The menu contains four items; the first two both open the on-line documentation

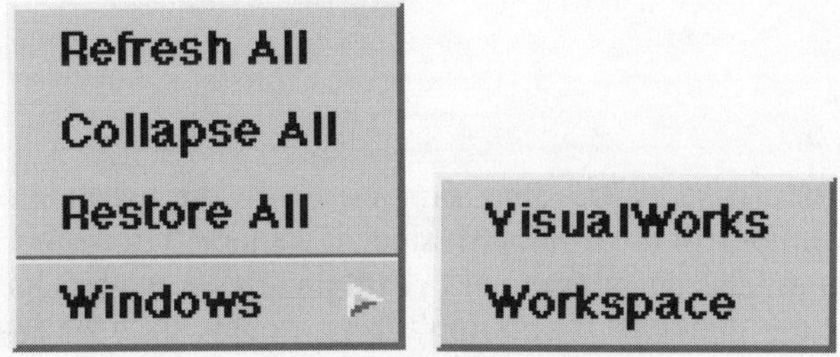

Figure 4.5 The **Window** menu.

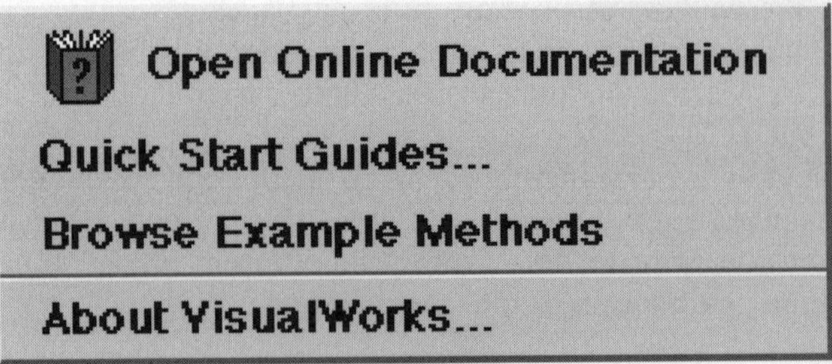

Figure 4.6 The **Help** menu.

(the latter goes directly to the chapter entitled 'Database Quick Start Guides'). The third option opens a Browser containing all the methods in the VisualWorks image that give the user an opportunity to experiment with an example. The last menu option opens a window describing your release of VisualWorks.

Exercise 4.4

Experiment with the example methods.

The on-line documentation is divided into three 'books', containing 'chapters' and pages. The titles of the books are: 'Database Cookbook' (containing one chapter), 'Database Quick Start Guides' (containing six chapters – only one of which is complete), and 'VisualWorks Cookbook' (containing 31 chapters). It's worth taking some time to examine the on-line documentation, using it as a complement to this book. For example, Chapter 1 of the 'VisualWorks Cookbook' describes similar material to Chapter 3 (Figure 4.7). The window containing the on-line documentation also provides buttons to gain access to examples, and to search the chapters.

Exercise 4.5

Browse the examples in Chapter 1 of the VisualWorks Cookbook on-line documentation.

4.10 Summary

It's important that readers become familiar with the user interface to the VisualWorks development environment, since it's almost impossible to write code by any other means. This and subsequent chapters rely on readers having a copy of VisualWorks at their disposal. If you don't have a copy, then we suggest that you buy (or beg!) a copy before reading Chapter 5.

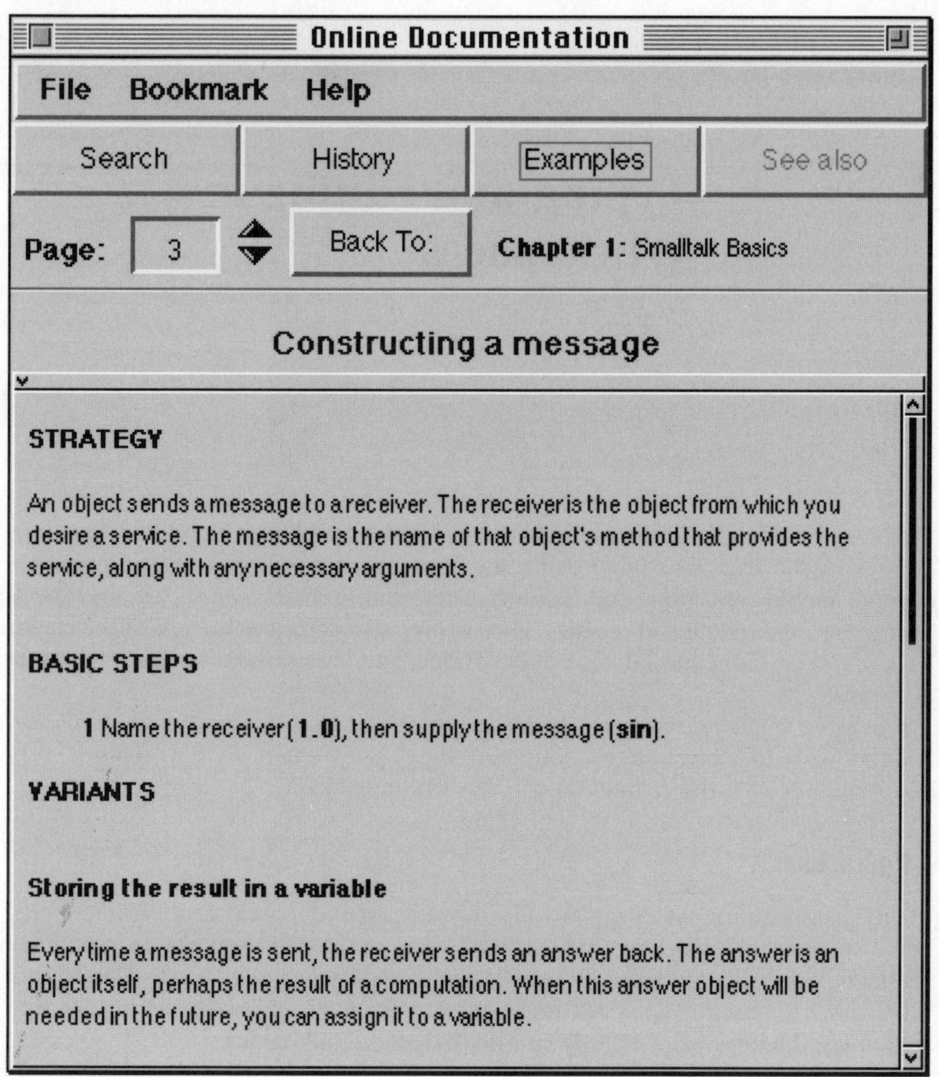

Figure 4.7 The on-line documentation.

5 Typing and editing in Workspaces

This chapter provides a complete introduction to the typing and editing functions built-in to the user interface, using the Workspace as an example. Operations include simple selection and editing using the mouse, *copy*, *cut* and *paste* operations, and *search* and *replace*. The chapter also describes the use of the cursor keys, scroll bars and special key combinations, and discusses the simple evaluation of expressions.

Extensive small exercises are included, to ensure that the reader is completely familiar with this level of operation of the VisualWorks system. This is very important, as all further chapters will rely on these skills.

5.1 Introduction

In any programming system, you will, of course, spend a great deal of time typing at the keyboard. Unless you are a perfect typist, and also never make programming mistakes, you will undoubtedly want to edit what you have typed. The VisualWorks environment recognizes these facts, and much effort has been put into facilitating the process of editing (particularly Smalltalk code).

In this chapter, we will describe how text is manipulated within the VisualWorks system. We will concentrate on using Workspaces, which are a simple kind of edit/compile interface. However, you should remember that the same editing mechanisms are available in all places where you can type, This is because all the editors behind the Workspaces and other text areas are instances of the same class, or at least instances of related classes.

5.2 Typing and selecting

This section considers simple text editing within the VisualWorks system. First, you will need to open a Workspace (unless, of course, you already have one open

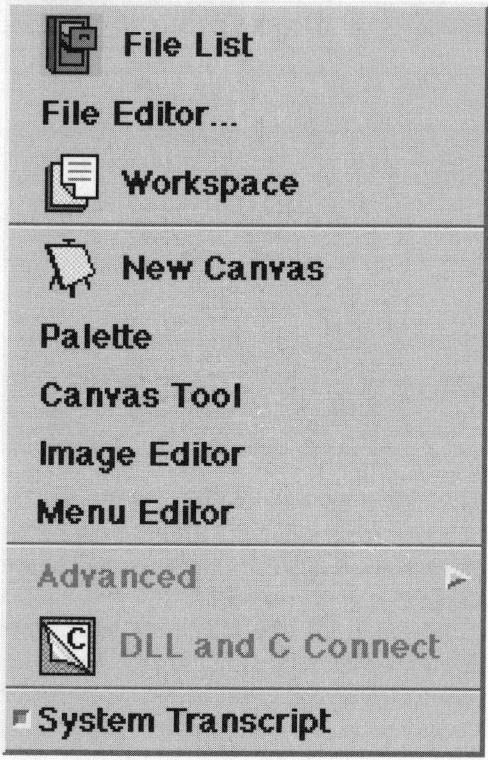

Figure 5.1 The **Tools** menu of the Launcher.

somewhere on the screen). To do this, you need to select the **Workspace** item from the **Tools** menu on the Launcher (see Figure 5.1). (Note that the item is preceded by an icon which matches one found on the Launcher itself.) The Workspace should now be the *active* window (the one in which your typing will appear). If necessary, move the cursor over it and click the <select> (left) button.

Now type some text into the Workspace. You will see that new characters are placed at a location just after the caret, the symbol which looks like '^'. The caret should move along as you type. You can position the caret anywhere within the text by clicking the <select> button at the desired position or by using the cursor keys. In this way, you can add new characters within existing text. The Workspace will now appear something like Figure 5.2. (The description that follows is specific to the 'default look' of VisualWorks, and your window manager may provide an alternative style.)

You should note that the caret always appears between adjacent characters, since you cannot add a new character in the middle of an existing one. Also, the characters are presented using a proportionally spaced font (like the characters in

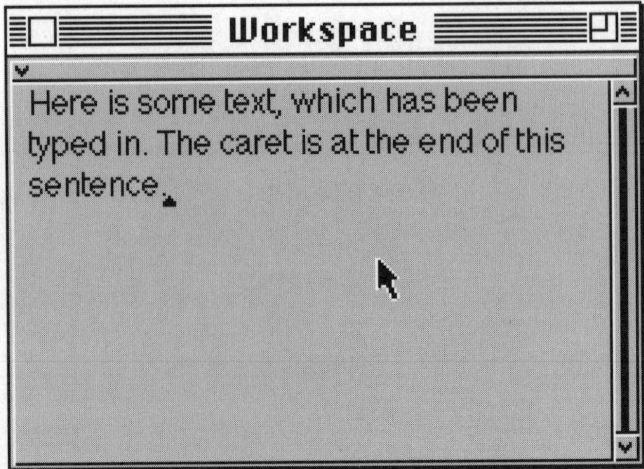

Figure 5.2 Entering text into a Workspace.

this book), rather than the fixed-spaced fonts (like typewritten characters) often used for computer output.

Characters can be deleted using the <delete> or <backspace> key on the keyboard. This key deletes the character immediately to the left of the caret, in the usual way. Also the entire *word* to the left of the caret can be deleted in one go, using the <control-w> key combination (<control> key held down while <w> is typed).

Most of the remaining editing commands rely on the notion of a *text selection* (or just *selection*). Because this notion is so widely used, VisualWorks provides a number of ways in which to make a selection.

One or more characters can be *selected* (i.e. identified as the selection) by positioning the cursor at the desired start position using the mouse, pressing down the <select> mouse button and, while holding the <select> button down, *drawing through* the text. The selected characters will be highlighted (see Figure 5.3). The selection is completed by releasing the <select> mouse button.

The selection can be deleted using the <delete> or <backspace> key. This is a convenient way of quickly deleting a 'chunk' of text. Alternatively, the selection can be replaced simply by typing new characters at the keyboard. The characters are inserted in the place of the current selection.

Note that the caret disappears when a text selection has been made. You can think of the caret as indicating the position of a 'zero-length' selection, and characters you type always replace the current selection. To extend the text selection, hold down a <shift> key and then click at the new end point. To deselect the text selection, simply click once anywhere in the active window.

There are several other 'shorthand' ways of making selections more quickly. One which is particularly useful is to use the <escape-tab> key combination (<escape>

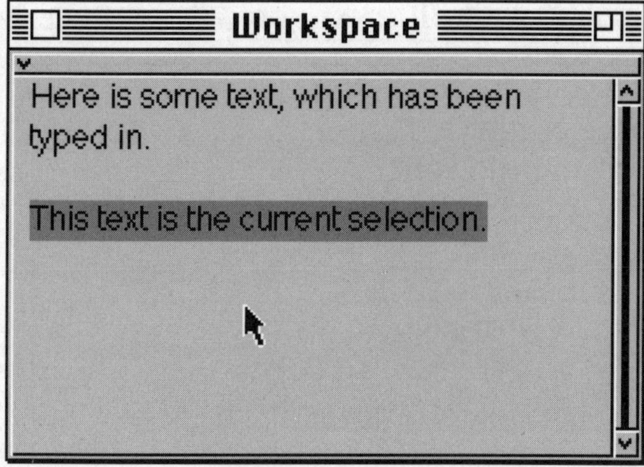

Figure 5.3 Making a text selection.

key *followed* by the <tab> key) to select all the text just typed (i.e. since the caret was last moved, or since an editing operation was performed). This is particularly useful should you wish to perform some operation on everything you have just entered. You may find that this selection method is faster than using the mouse, since you do not have to move your hands from the keyboard.

Another useful selection mechanism is ‘double-clicking’ the <select> mouse button; i.e. pressing and releasing the button twice in quick succession without moving the mouse between clicks. Double-clicking within a ‘word’ selects the entire word; this is handy should you wish to replace an entire word. Double-clicking at the beginning or end of a line of text (up to the next carriage return) selects the entire line. All the text in that Workspace may be selected by double-clicking at its beginning or its end. You should note that the double-click selection is not determined by the speed of clicking, but by location. The first click positions the caret, and a subsequent click in the same location as the caret selects the word, line or complete text appropriately.

A final mechanism by which double-clicking can be used to make selections quickly is where there is a section of text surrounded by *delimiters*. These include parentheses ‘( )’, square brackets ‘[ ]’, curly brackets ‘{} ’, angle brackets ‘< >’, single quote marks ‘ ' ' ’ and double quotes ‘ " " ’. The text within any of these delimiters can be selected by double-clicking between the delimiter and the first (or last) character of the enclosed text. Almost all of these delimiters have some meaning in the syntax of the Smalltalk language.

A great many of the keys on the keyboard have different functions when used in combination with the <control> key or the <escape> key. We have already seen the <control-w> and <escape-tab> combinations in operation. Several other

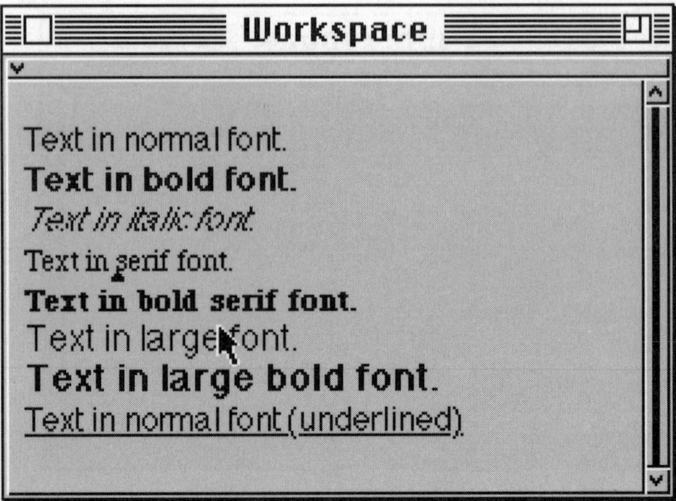

Figure 5.4 Changing text fonts, using <escape> key combinations.

<escape> key combinations affect the selection in interesting and useful ways (see Figure 5.4):

<Escape-b> makes the selected text bold (heavy) font. <Escape-B> makes it normal weight font.

<Escape-i> makes the selected text italic. <Escape-I> reverses the effect.

<Escape-u> makes the selected text underlined. <Escape-U> reverses the effect.

<Escape-+> increases the font size of the selected text. <Escape--> decreases the font size of the selected text.

<Escape-x> 'normalizes' the text to its default size and font.

<Escape-f> removes embedded <CR>'s and <tab>'s from the selected text (effectively rewraps the text into a single paragraph).

The <escape> key with an opening delimiter character key (such as '[' or ' " ') inserts a pair of the appropriate delimiters around the selection, provided they do not already have a pair of these delimiters surrounding them, in which case they are removed. The feature, together with the ability to make a selection by double-clicking within a pair of delimiters, makes it very easy to add and remove various brackets, and so on.

There are also some <control> key combinations that you may find of use later:

<Control-t> inserts ifTrue:
<Control-f> inserts ifFalse:
<Control-g> inserts :=
<Control-d> inserts the current date.

Exercise 5.1

Try opening a Workspace, and then typing some text into it. Add characters at different places within the Workspace, moving the caret by using the <select> mouse button and cursor keys.

Exercise 5.2

Experiment with removing characters from the Workspace using the <backspace>, <delete> and <control-w> keys. Try determining what Smalltalk considers to be a 'word', when using the <control-W key>. *Hint*: consider the syntax of the Smalltalk language (see Chapter 3).

Exercise 5.3

Try making text selections by 'drawing through' using the <select> mouse button. Try deleting the text (using the <delete> or <backspace> key) and replacing the text by typing in new characters.

Exercise 5.4

Experiment with different ways of making selections, including using the <escape-tab> key combination, double-clicking within words and at the beginning of lines and so on. Also, try selecting the text within various kinds of delimiters by double-clicking.

Exercise 5.5

Experiment with changing the font of the text selection using the <escape> key combinations. Also, experiment with inserting and deleting pairs of delimiters around the selection.

Exercise 5.6

Experiment with the <control> key combinations (but be careful trying <control-c>).

5.3 Editing

In this section we will consider further editing operations. These invariably operate on the text selection (introduced in the previous section). Editing operations are selected from the pop-up menu attached to the <operate> mouse button.

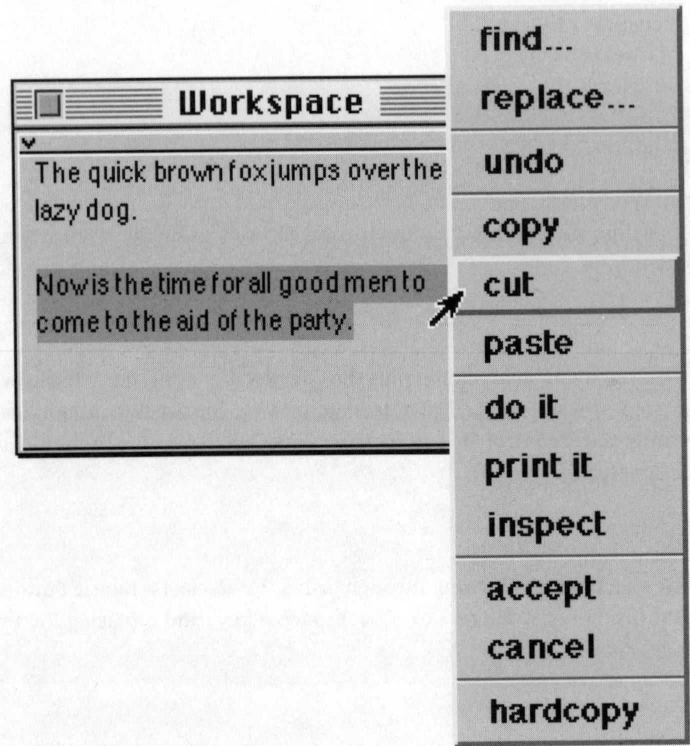

Figure 5.5 Using the **cut**, **copy** and **paste** options (1).

Each <operate> menu can also be invoked by being *pulled-down* (especially useful for single-button mice). This is done by pressing either the <select> or <operate> mouse button while the cursor is over the stripe above each pane (containing a small inverted caret at the left end). Note that the cursor also changes shape. If you don't like the appearance of the stripe, it may be removed (see Chapter 12).

The **copy**, **cut** and **paste** options on the <operate> button menu provide fairly conventional cut-and-paste style editing functions. The **cut** option removes the current selection, and puts it in a (hidden) paste buffer (Figure 5.5). This can be pasted back using the **paste** option; the text is inserted at the caret, or is used to replace the current selection, just as if the text had been typed in at the keyboard (Figure 5.6). The resulting Workspace is shown in Figure 5.7. The **copy** option operates just like the **cut** option, except that the selection is not removed from the Workspace.

You should note that the paste buffer is global, and is therefore shared by all text-editing operations. This means that it is possible to cut or copy text from one

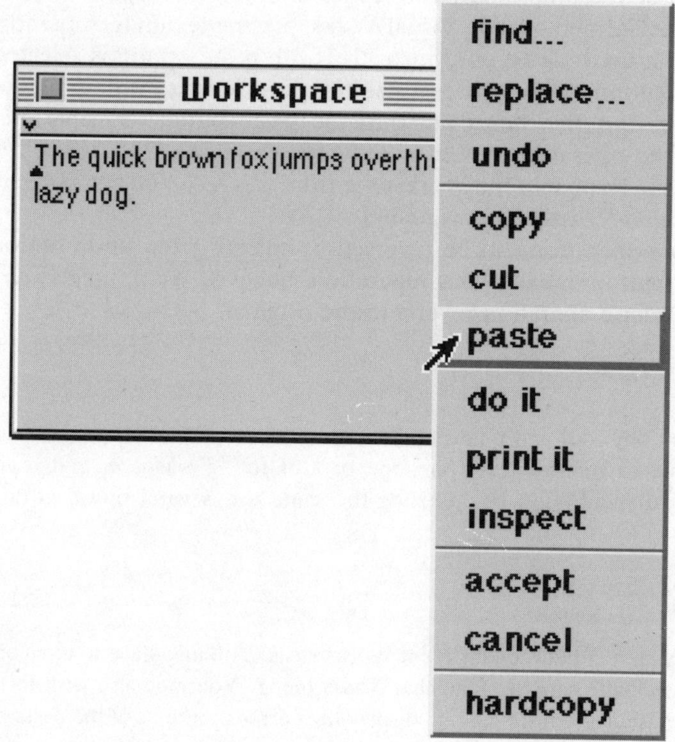

Figure 5.6 Using the **cut**, **copy** and **paste** options (2).

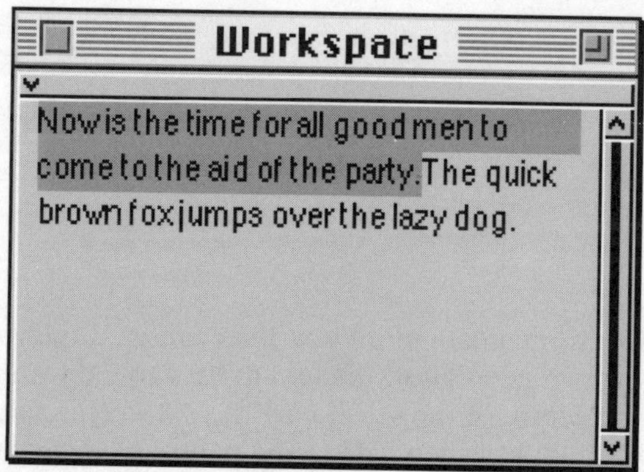

Figure 5.7 Using the **cut**, **copy** and **paste** options (3).

Workspace, for example, and paste it into another Workspace. If a copy or cut operation is performed outside VisualWorks, placing text in the operating system's clipboard, that text will be used instead. If the paste option is selected from the <operate> button menu with a <shift> key held down, a list will appear containing the last five items put into the paste buffer, possibly including the contents of the operating system's clipboard. You can then select the text you actually want to paste into the Workspace from this list. You can also cut and paste to and from non-VisualWorks windows.

Any editing operation can be reversed by selecting the **undo** option from the <operate> button menu. This operation behaves as a toggle; undoing the previously undone operation reverts to the original.

Exercise 5.7

Try using the **copy**, **cut** and **paste** options from the <operate> button menu. You should be able to remove text from one part of the Workspace, and replace it elsewhere. You should also try inserting the same text several times, in different places.

Exercise 5.8

Also, try copying text between different Workspaces. You may have to open another Workspace window, using the Launcher **Tools** menu. You may also wish to try the **paste** option, using a <shift> key, to display the current contents of the paste buffer.

Exercise 5.9

Try repeatedly replacing a piece of text using the **replace ...** option from the <operate> button menu. Also, try the effect of the **undo** <operate> button menu option.

Exercise 5.10

Try searching for text in a Workspace, using the **find ...** options.

5.4 Scrolling

Frequently, a window will contain more text than can be displayed with its visible area; *scroll bars* are provided to allow the text to be scrolled within a window. The thick black line in the centre of the scroll bar (the *marker*) indicates the extent of the visible text. For example, when half of the pane's contents are displayed, the marker is half the length of the scroll bar. The marker also indicates the position of the contents in the pane – when you are viewing the bottom-most portion, for example, the marker occupies the bottom-most portion of the scroll bar. By default, a vertical scroll bar appears to the right of each pane. This may be amended by modifying the class LookPreferences – we will examine this later (Chapter 12).

When the cursor is moved into a scroll bar, the cursor shape changes to an arrow to indicate the scrolling operation. The scroll bar area itself is divided into three parts (horizontal scroll bars are available, and work in a similar fashion):

- When the cursor is above the marker, clicking the <select> mouse button moves the marker up and the text down. The cursor changes to ↑ (see Figure 5.8).
- When the cursor is below the marker, clicking the <select> mouse button moves the marker down and the text up. The cursor changes to ↓ (see Figure 5.9).
- When the cursor is over the marker, the marker and text can be dragged while the <select> button is held down. The cursor changes to ↕ (see Figure 5.10).
- When the cursor is anywhere in the scroll bar the marker and text can be dragged while the <operate> button is held down.

There are also two small 'buttons' (*elevator buttons*) associated with the scroll bar. These scroll the text up and down appropriately, a line at a time (or continuously, if held down), while the <select> button is pressed. The cursor changes to ↑ or ↓ respectively.

Exercise 5.11

Type lots of text into a Workspace. Experiment with the scrolling operations, including the scrolling buttons, and the different parts of the scroll bar. You will be using the scrolling mechanism extensively, so it is worth getting used to it.

Figure 5.8 Scrolling text down in a Workspace.

Figure 5.9 Scrolling text up in a Workspace.

Figure 5.10 Absolute scrolling of text in a Workspace.

Exercise 5.12

How far does the text move when the up or down scrolling actions are performed? *Hint*: try clicking a mouse button in the top and bottom parts of the scroll bar.

Exercise 5.13

What happens when you type in a line of text which is much longer than the width of the Workspace? Try it and see. Also, try resizing the Workspace containing several very long lines of text.

5.5 Evaluating Smalltalk code

Unlike most systems, the primary 'command' interface to Smalltalk is a compiler; in fact, the Smalltalk language compiler. 'Commands' are therefore written in the

Smalltalk language itself. There is no notion of a separate 'command interpreter', as in MS-DOS or UNIX, for example.

Workspaces and other text areas allow textual expressions to be entered by the user and sent to the compiler. Once again, it is the text selection which is important. The **do it** option on the Workspace <operate> button menu evaluates the selection. This means that simple expressions in the Smalltalk language (see Chapter 3) can be typed in and evaluated immediately.

More precisely, the text in the selection is fed to the Smalltalk compiler (an instance of class Compiler, of course). This parses the text and, if there are no syntax errors, generates code that can be evaluated by the underlying virtual machine. This code is then evaluated. In practice, it takes less time to compile and evaluate simple expressions than it takes to explain the process (see Figure 5.11).

Frequently, we will wish to see the result of evaluating an expression. We can do this by using the **print it** option from the <operate> button menu. This compiles and evaluates the selected expression(s) just like the **do it** option but, in addition, the object resulting from evaluating the code is sent the message printString. Every object understands this message, and answers with a String which represents its

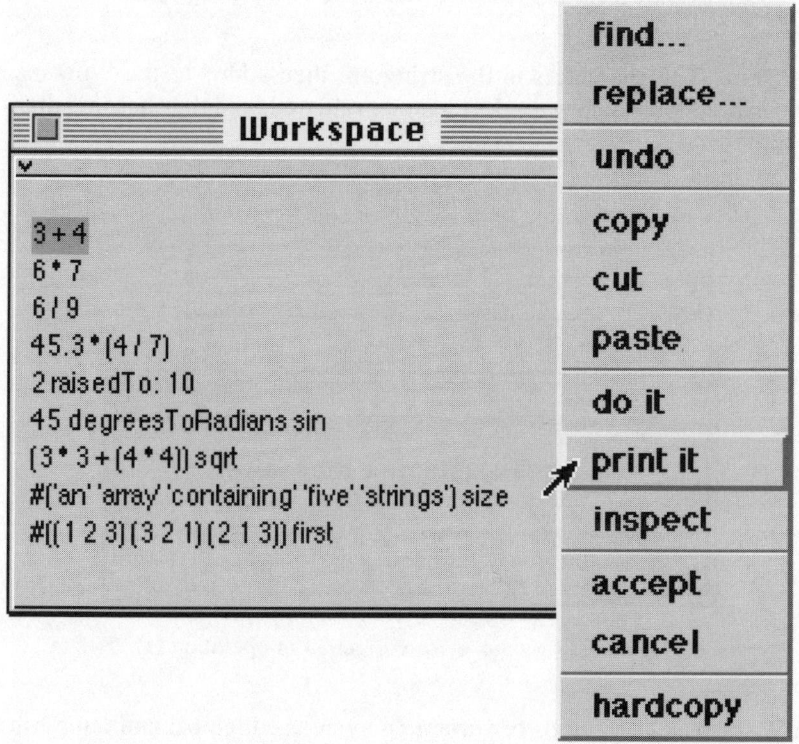

Figure 5.11 Selecting and evaluating a simple expression.

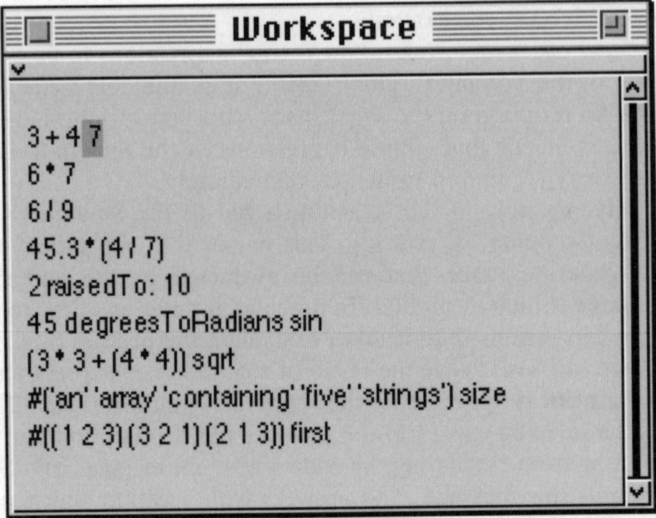

Figure 5.12 The result of evaluating a simple expression.

internal state. The characters in the string are then added to the Workspace just after the expression which was selected and evaluated, and they become the current selection.

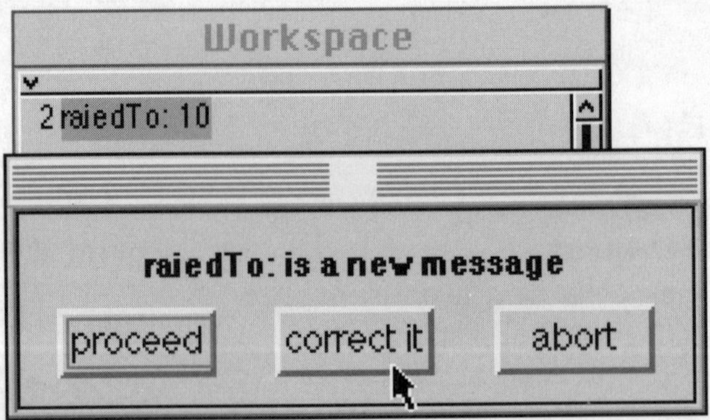

Figure 5.13 Syntax error correction in operation (1).

In a Workspace, two kinds of variable may be used: global and temporary. The code is not being evaluated as a method in some specified class, therefore instance variables, class variables, and pool variables are not accessible.

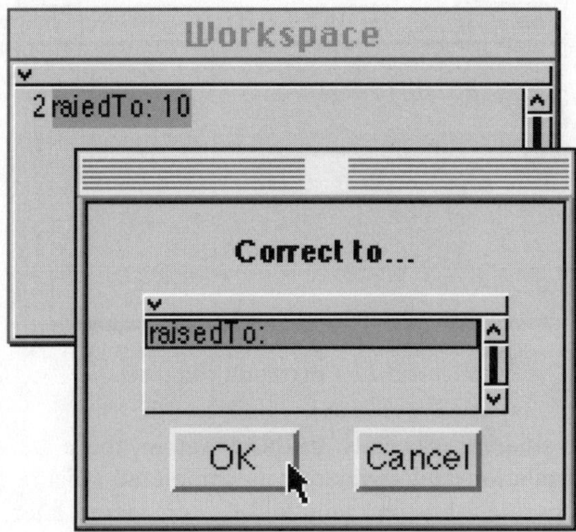

Figure 5.14 Syntax error correction in operation (2).

Look at the example shown in Figure 5.12. When compiled and evaluated, the selected expression 3+4 causes the message +4 to be sent to the object 3 (an instance of class SmallInteger). The message comprises a binary message selector, +, and the argument 4. The resulting object 7 (also an instance of SmallInteger) then receives the message printString. The resulting String, '7', which just contains a single character $7 is then placed in the Workspace and made the current text selection (see Figure 5.12).

But what happens if the expression contains syntax errors? The answer is that the error is detected and indicated. There is also an error correction mechanism available, which attempts to correct simple typing mistakes and other silly errors. Consider selecting and evaluating (using the **print it** option) the following expression:

```
2 raiedTo: 10 "Note the spelling error!"
```

The correct message selector is raisedTo:. On evaluating this expression, a Confirmer appears (see Figure 5.13). The heading of the Confirmer tells us that the message selector is new; there is no corresponding method in any class, anywhere in the image. The Confirmer offers three options: you can give up immediately and edit the text yourself, using **abort**; you can carry on regardless, using the **proceed** option, or you can invoke the correction mechanism, using the **correct it** option. If **correct it** is selected, then one or more message selectors which are the nearest match to the error are found and presented to the user (see Figure 5.14). If you select a suggested correction, the error is corrected in the source text, and the

Figure 5.15 Correction complete.

compilation and evaluation proceeds. In this example, there are no further syntax errors, so the compilation and evaluation is completed (Figure 5.15). The other options on the <operate> button menu will be considered later.

Exercise 5.14

Use the following expressions in a Workspace to discover (a) the current number of unused object pointers; and (b) the current amount of free memory:

```
ObjectMemory current oopsLeft
ObjectMemory current availableFreeBytes
```

Exercise 5.15

Try selecting and evaluating other simple expressions using the **print it** <operate> button menu option. For example, you might like to try some of the other expressions in Figure 5.11.

Exercise 5.16

Try inserting deliberate syntax errors and provoke the correction mechanism into assisting you. You should note that Smalltalk is unable to correct all syntax errors. In some cases, the correction mechanism will give up.

5.6 The Settings Tool

The 'Settings Tool' may be opened by selecting the **Settings** option from the **File** menu of the Launcher. The items available from the Settings Tool (Figure 5.16) provide information useful to install your VisualWorks image. These include initializing the source file manager, selecting the appropriate time zone, default text style and look-and-feel preferences.

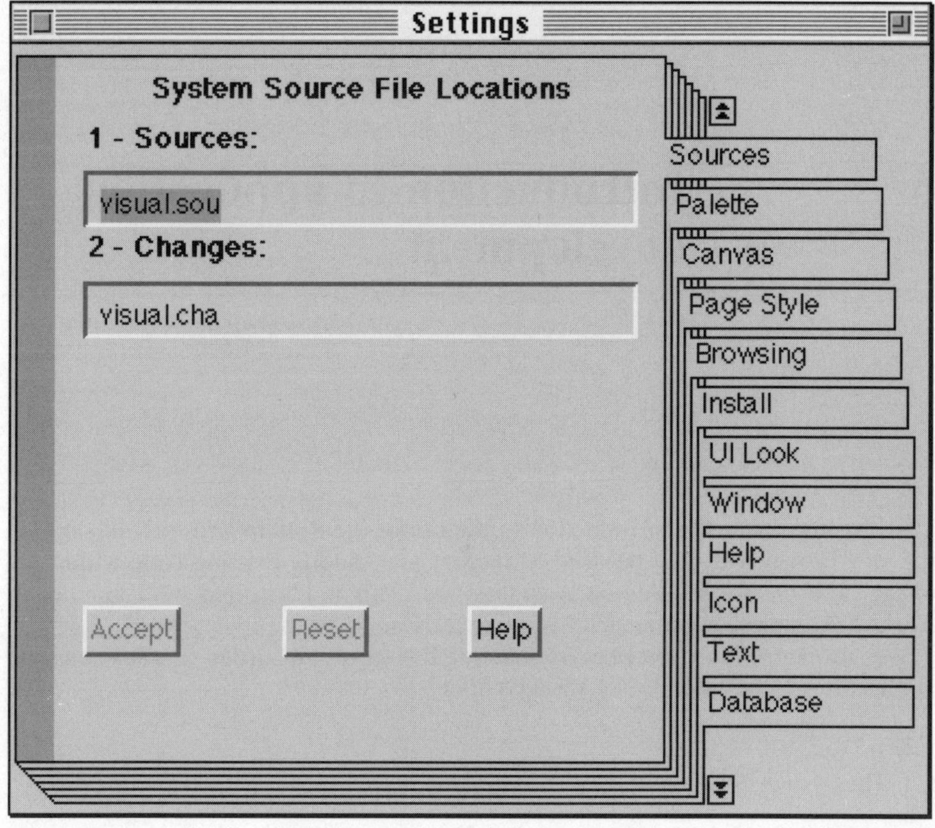

Figure 5.16 The Settings tool.

Exercise 5.17

Change the time zone so that it is appropriate for your machine and geographical location. (You may need to scroll to the tab labelled 'Time Zones'.) Ensure that your setting is correct by printing out the result of the following expression in a Workspace:

```
Time now
```

(i.e. type and select the expression, then evaluate it using the **print it** option from the <operate> menu).

5.7 Summary

By now, we assume that you are familiar enough with the VisualWorks environment to start writing methods and implementing classes. If not, then we suggest you revisit the exercises until you feel confident enough to go on; alternatively, experiment on your own, using a Workspace.

6 Introduction to application development

This chapter forms the introduction to the use of the System Browser, illustrating the way in which it may be used to inspect and modify existing code within the image, and create new methods and classes. This is illustrated by a number of worked examples, together with some exercises.

We also introduce the File Browser at this point, in order to allow existing applications to be 'filed-in' to VisualWorks.

6.1 The System Browser

The System Browser is the primary user interface for entering code in VisualWorks. It allows the user to:

- Create and edit source code
- Perform in-line testing
- Format (pretty print) method source code
- Explain code
- Save ('file-out') source code
- Organize classes and methods
- Find the senders of, implementors of, and messages sent by a method
- Create/alter/remove classes
- Display class hierarchy
- Spawn special-purpose Browsers.

Many of these will be described in later chapters.

The System Browser allows the user to inspect the message interface to any object in the image, and to modify it if required. To open a System Browser, select the **All Classes** item from the **Browse** menu on the Launcher. (Note that the

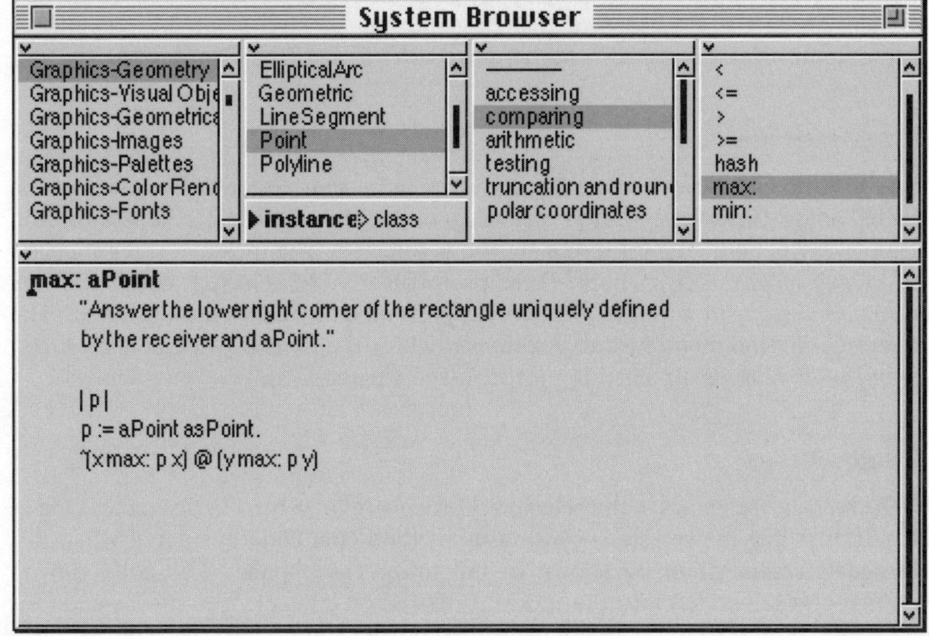

Figure 6.1 The System Browser.

menu item is preceded by an icon, a copy of which is present as one of the buttons below the menu bar.) More than one System Browser can be open simultaneously.

The System Browser (Figure 6.1) is made up of five panes and two buttons, marked **instance** and **class**. From left to right, the top four panes are as follows.

Class categories

These are groups of classes that are categorized for the convenience of the user. The order of the categories and the classes they contain is arbitrary and bears little relationship to the VisualWorks class hierarchy. One of these categories may be selected (by clicking the <select> mouse button). New categories may be added using the **add . . .** item from the <operate> button menu. Categories may also be *removed* or *renamed* (see Chapter 16). The classes in the selected category are presented in the next pane.

Class names

Classes in the selected category are presented in this pane. One class may be selected, causing categories of messages to be presented in the next pane. Selecting a class causes the *class definition* to be displayed in the lower (text) pane.

Alternatively, a display of the part of the class *hierarchy* containing this class or a *comment* about the functions of this class can be selected from the <operate> button menu. Classes may also be *removed* or *renamed* (see Chapter 16).

Message categories

These are the categories of messages which can be sent either to instances of the selected class (**instance** button pressed) or to the class itself (**class** button pressed). By default, the **instance** button is selected. The message categories are also known as *protocols*. One of these protocols may be selected, causing all the message selectors in this protocol to be presented in the rightmost pane. The <operate> button menu includes options to allow the user to *add* a new protocol, or *remove* or *rename* an existing protocol (see Chapter 16).

Message selectors

All the message selectors in the selected protocol are presented in this pane. One of the selectors may be selected, causing its method (the code evaluated when this message is received) to be shown in the lower (text) pane. The code can be modified and reinserted into the image if desired (see later). The source code for the method displayed in the text pane is held on an external file (the 'sources' file – see Chapter 4).

6.2 Example: browsing the implementation of an existing method

Try the following. Select the class category Magnitude-Numbers in the leftmost top pane, using the <select> mouse button. Select Number in the Class Names pane. Select testing in the Protocol pane. Select the selector even in the Message Selector pane.

The code displayed in the lower pane is evaluated when an instance of a Number (or one of its subclasses) receives a message with the selector even. This code returns true if the receiver is even, otherwise false. Note that it sends a message to itself (self), using the selector \\ (modulo) with 2 as the argument.

Exercise 6.1

Verify that the even method evaluates correctly by typing, selecting and evaluating (using **print it**) the following expression in a Workspace:

```
42 even
```

Repeat the above test with other numbers.

Exercise 6.2

Try the effect of the following options from the <operate> button menu in the Class Names pane. First select Magnitude-Numbers (leftmost pane). Select Number in the Class Names pane. Select **hierarchy** from the Class Names pane <operate> button menu. This will display a textual representation of the part of the hierarchical structure of the classes in the image which includes Number in the lower (text) pane.

You can see, for example, that classes Float, Fraction and Integer are all subclasses of Number. Thus, the message even should be understood by instances of all of these classes. Try:

```
4 even
17.91 even
(3/7) even
```

Also examine the definition and comment menu items from the <operate> button menu.

6.3 Defining methods

A new method can be defined from the Browser whenever a protocol has been selected. If there are no protocols to select, one must be created by using the add ... command in the Message Categories pane <operate> menu. The following *template* is provided by the Browser:

```
message selector and argument names
    "comment stating purpose of message"

    | temporary variable names |
    statements
```

This template is relatively straightforward to complete. Any number of statements can be placed in the statements section. There can be no more than 255 temporary variables and arguments.

6.4 Example: creating a new method

A function not currently implemented by instances of class Number is the 'absolute difference' function. Here, we will add this functionality to Number. Select Magnitude-Numbers, Number and arithmetic in the leftmost three panes in the System Browser. Do not select anything from the top rightmost pane. The lower (text) pane should display a 'template' for new methods. Edit (using the normal text editing conventions) the template, so that it appears as below:

```
diff: aNumber
   "return the absolute difference between me and aNumber"
   | temp |
   temp := self - aNumber.
   temp < 0
      ifTrue: [^temp negated]
      ifFalse: [^temp]
```

This method first calculates temp, which is the difference between the parameter aNumber and the receiver (self). It then answers with either temp or a negated version of temp, depending whether temp is negative. The new method can now be compiled and added to the VisualWorks environment by selecting **accept** from the <operate> button menu in the lower pane. Do this. Correct any errors that have inadvertently crept in! (The **cancel** option discards all the text just added to the text pane and restores it to its earlier state.)

Exercise 6.3

Test the functioning of the new method by typing and evaluating (**print it**) suitable expressions in a Workspace. For example, try:

```
42 diff: 17.
17 diff: 42.
- 17 diff: - 19.
10.15 diff: (3/7).
237846527938465 diff: 3456
```

Note that the addition you have made to your VisualWorks image will be there permanently, until you choose to remove it. (This assumes that you save the image eventually, of course!)

Exercise 6.4

In fact, the implementation of diff: used above is not very good (although it works). A better version is shown below.

```
diff: aNumber
   "return the absolute difference between me and aNumber"
   ^(self - aNumber) abs
```

This version eliminates the temporary variable, and uses the abs method, which is already implemented for Number. This minimizes the amount of code added to the image to support this new functionality.

Exercise 6.5

Modify your implementation of diff: by editing and accepting the text in the System Browser. Verify that this has not changed the functionality of the method by repeating the tests above. Note that there is no way in which the implementation can be determined by the sender of the diff: message. You may like to look at the implementation of the abs method in class ArithmeticValue.

6.5 Defining classes

In much the same fashion as methods, class definitions can be added using the Browser when a class category is selected. As with methods, if no appropriate category exists then the **add . . .** option from the Class Categories pane <operate> menu can be used to create one. The Browser provides the following template:

```
NameOfSuperclass subclass: #NameOfClass
   instanceVariableNames: 'instVarName1 instVarName2'
   classVariableNames: 'ClassVarName1 ClassVarName2'
   poolDictionaries: ' '
   category: 'Category-Name'
```

Once again, this is easy to fill out. Remember to keep the '#' symbol in front of the class name, and also that class names should always begin with an upper-case character. For example:

```
Number subclass: #Fraction
   instanceVariableNames: 'numerator denominator'
   classVariableNames: ' '
   poolDictionaries: ' '
   category: 'Magnitude-Numbers'
```

6.6 Example: adding a new 'application'

This example is an exercise in adding a (small) new 'application', based on classes already available within the image. The example itself is adapted from the 'Orange Book', Chapter 17.

Here, we will construct a class corresponding to an individual's 'spending history'. We will not be too concerned about the design or the other classes used. This is an exercise in effectively using the System Browser and compiler. We will describe a new class SpendingHistory with several methods and instance variables. We will also try out this class in a simple manner.

Exercise 6.6

Use the **add . . .** item from the <operate> button menu in the Class Categories pane (top-left) of the System Browser. When prompted, choose a suitable name for the category, such as 'Spending'. This new class category will have no classes in it, as yet. A template for the creation of a new class will be displayed in the lower pane of the System Browser.

Exercise 6.7

Edit the template (using the normal text editor conventions) so that it appears as below.

```
Object subclass: #SpendingHistory
  instanceVariableNames: 'cashOnHand expenditures'
  classVariableNames: ''
  poolDictionaries: ''
  category: 'Spending'
```

This declares the new class SpendingHistory to be a subclass of Object. The new class has two instance variables called cashOnHand and expenditures, and no class variables. Select **accept** from the <operate> button menu. This creates the new class SpendingHistory and permanently installs it in the image.

We now need to add some additional functionality to SpendingHistory, since at the moment all instances of SpendingHistory will have exactly the same functionality as instances of Object. First, we will add a method to the class protocol to create new initialized instances of SpendingHistory.

Exercise 6.8

Select the **class** button in the System Browser and select the **add . . .** item from the <operate> button menu in the Message Categories pane. You will be prompted for the name of a protocol; respond with 'instance creation'. The method template will appear in the lower window. Use the editing functions to create the initialBalance: method as shown:

```
initialBalance: anAmount
  ^self new setInitialBalance: anAmount
```

Note that this uses a method defined further up the class hierarchy (new). Add the method to the image using the **accept** item from the <operate> button menu. This method causes the message selector setInitialBalance: to be sent to the new instance of SpendingHistory. The method corresponding to this message is not yet defined, so you should select **proceed** when prompted with a Confirmer.

We will now add instance protocol to class SpendingHistory.

Exercise 6.9

Select the **instance** button in the System Browser. Create a new protocol (as before) called 'private'. Edit the template to add the setInitialBalance: method. Accept this using the <operate> button menu item.

```
setInitialBalance: anAmount
  "Initialize the instance variables;
  cashOnHand is set to amount"

  cashOnHand := anAmount.
  expenditures := Dictionary new.
```

Exercise 6.10

Repeat the above for method totalSpentOn: in protocol 'inquiries', for method spend:on: in protocol 'transactions', and for method printOn: in protocol 'printing' (see below).

```
totalSpentOn: reason
  "return the amount spent on reason. Answer
  0 if reason is not used for expenditures"

  (expenditures includesKey: reason)
    ifTrue: [^expenditures at: reason]
    ifFalse: [^0]

spend: anAmount on: reason
  "Spend anAmount on reason, reducing the variable cashOnHand"

  expenditures
    at: reason
    put: (self totalSpentOn: reason) + anAmount.
  cashOnHand := cashOnHand - anAmount.

printOn: aStream
  "print a suitable representation of the receiver on aStream"

  super printOn: aStream.
  aStream space.
  aStream nextPutAll: 'balance: '.
  cashOnHand printOn: aStream.
  expenditures keysAndValuesDo: [:reason :amount |
    aStream cr.
    reason printOn: aStream.
    aStream tab.
    amount printOn: aStream]
```

You can now create initialized instances of class SpendingHistory by evaluating the expression:

```
SpendingHistory initialBalance: 600
```

Exercise 6.11

To test the new class, type the expressions shown below in a Workspace. Select and evaluate the code using **print it**.

```
| spendingHistory |
spendingHistory := SpendingHistory initialBalance: 800.
spendingHistory spend: 220 on: 'rent'.
spendingHistory spend: 30 on: 'food'.
spendingHistory spend: 45 on: 'drink'.
spendingHistory spend: 20 on: 'petrol'
```

Before continuing, ensure that you take a "snapshot" of your image, by selecting the **Save As . . .** option from the **File** menu of the Launcher. We will return to this example later in the book.

6.7 Saving your code

Each of the upper panes in the System Browser has a **file out as . . .** option on the <operate> button menu. This option allows the user to produce a file containing the source code for the selected category, class, protocol or method.

Exercise 6.12

Select the category Spending in the Class Categories pane, and choose the **file out as . . .** option from the <operate> button menu in that pane. You will be prompted to complete a filename specification (see Figure 6.2) ending in '.st' (if necessary the filename will be truncated to the constraints of your platform's filing system). Simply press the <CR> key. The cursor will indicate that a file is being written to the disk.

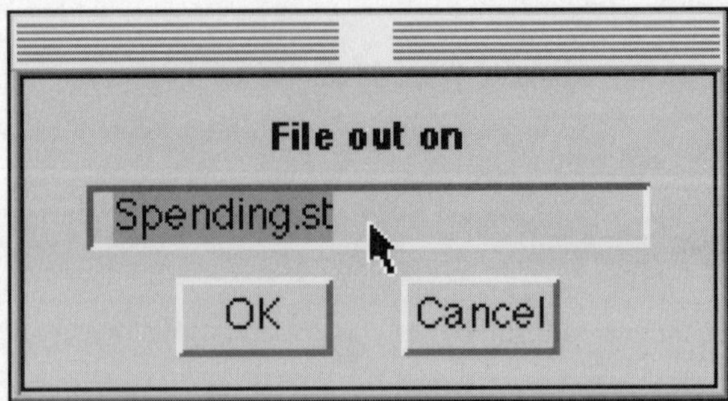

Figure 6.2 Completing a filename specification.

Exercise 6.13

File out the diff: method you created earlier.

6.8 The File Browser

The File Browser provides browsing access to the operating system's file management facilities. It allows the user to:

- Produce a list of files that meet a specified pattern
- Access information about files (e.g. creation date)
- Access the contents of files
- 'File-in' existing source code to create new methods and/or classes
- Create, remove or rename files and directories
- Edit files.

The File Browser consists of three panes and one button (Figure 6.3).

The upper pane

The upper pane permits a file or directory name to be specified. Parts of the directory structure are separated by appropriate characters (e.g. '/' for UNIX, '\' for PC machines, and ':' for the Macintosh). (On the Macintosh the directory structure is replaced by folders. Broadly speaking, each folder on the Macintosh is equivalent to a directory on the other platforms.) This pane is used as the initial access point into the file system. Wildcards may be used in the specification of the file or directory. An asterisk ('*') may be used to substitute for any number of characters, and a hash ('#') for an individual character. Note that the label of the window reflects the currently selected file/directory.

The <operate> menu in the pane (Figure 6.4) is similar to the standard text-editing menu, with the additional option **volumes . . .** which displays a menu of subdirectories in the root directory (UNIX); or currently available disk drives or volumes (Macintosh and MS-Windows).

The middle pane

The middle pane normally contains an alphabetically sorted list of one or more files or directories (e.g. the contents of a directory). One of the items from the list may be selected using the <select> mouse button. Note that the contents of the <operate> menu in this pane depends on whether a file, a directory, or no item is selected. If a file or directory *is* selected then the <operate> menu appears as in Figures 6.5 and 6.6 respectively.

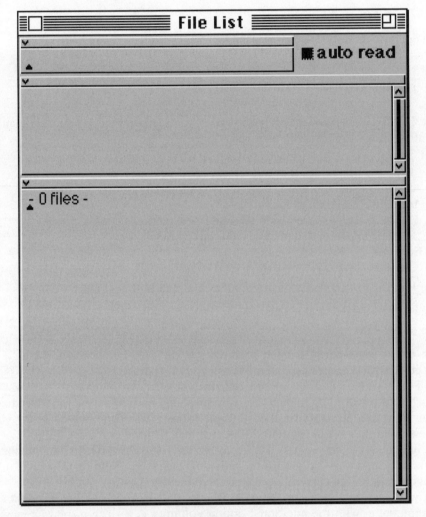

Figure 6.3 The File Browser.

There are a number of options common to both menus that apply to the selected file/directory:

copy name – Copies the path name of the selected file or directory so that it may later be pasted.
rename as . . . – Changes the name of the selected file/directory. (On some platforms this may produce an error if you do not have permission to change the name of the file.) This may cause the position of the file to change in the list of files. A Prompter will appear requesting the new name, with the old name as default.

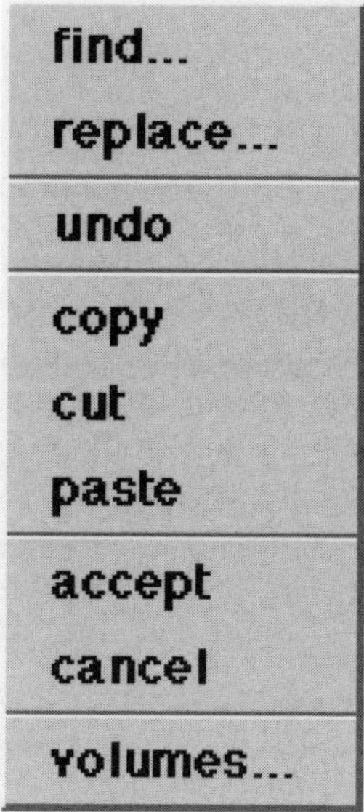

Figure 6.4 The <operate> menu available in the upper pane of the File Browser.

Figures 6.5 and 6.6 The <operate> menu options available in the middle pane of the File Browser when a file or directory is selected (respectively).

remove ... – Deletes the selected file/directory, after prompting for user confirmation.
spawn – Opens a new File Browser in the selected directory, or opens a File Editor (see later) on the selected file.

Those options only applicable to a selected *file* are as follows:

get info – Displays information about the selected file in the lower pane (e.g. creation date, modification date). You should note that this option is replaced by **get contents**, when the lower pane contains file information.
get contents – Displays the contents of the selected file in the lower pane.
file in – Assumes that the file contains Smalltalk code (e.g. that has previously been filed out), retrieves the file contents, reading and evaluating the text.
copy file to ... – Creates a new file after prompting the user for its name. The original file remains selected. If the destination file already exists then the user is prompted to try again (with a different filename) or abort.

The options available when a *directory* is selected are as follows:

new pattern – Copies and accepts the currently selected directory into the upper pane and displays its contents in the middle pane.
add directory ... – Prompts the user for the name of a new directory, and creates a new directory with that name as a subdirectory of the selected directory.
add file ... – Prompts the user for the name of a new file, and creates a new empty file with that name *within* the selected directory.

The lower pane

The lower pane is where the contents of the selected file (or information about it) may be displayed using the **get contents (get info)** option from the <operate> button menu in the middle pane. The contents of a file may be edited using the normal VisualWorks editing conventions.

The options available on the <operate> menu in this pane are dependent on the selection in the middle pane. If a directory is selected then the pane will display the contents of the directory (if any) and the menu will be similar to the usual text editing menu.

If a file is selected in the middle pane and its contents are displayed in the lower pane, then the <operate> menu (Figure 6.7) contains the following extra options:

file it in – Evaluates the text selection as if it were reading it from the selected file.
save – Writes the contents of the file to disk (e.g. after editing the file).
save as ... – Prompts the user for the name of a new file and then writes the contents of the existing file to a file with that name.
cancel – Ignores any edits made to the file since it was last saved, and resets its contents.
spawn – Opens a File Editor on the selected file with any changes that have been made to it. Cancels any edits that have been made in the original File List Browser.

Figure 6.7 The <operate> menu available from the lower pane of the File Browser when a file is selected.

The auto read button

The button is used in combination with the lower two panes, and indicates whether or not the contents of the selected file should be automatically displayed (without recourse to the **get contents** option), rather than information about the file.

Exercise 6.14

Open a File Browser by selecting the **File List** option from the **Tools** menu of the Launcher. (Note that the menu item is preceded by an icon, a copy of which is present as one of the buttons below the menu bar.) View all files in the current directory by typing a '*' in the top pane and using the **accept** option from the <operate> button menu. As a shortcut to using the menu, you may just press the <CR> key here.

Select the file visual.cha in the middle pane, and (if necessary) use the **get contents** option from the <operate> button menu. The contents of the file will be displayed in the lower window.

Note that all changes you have made to the image, as well as all code evaluated in a Workspace, have been recorded in this file.

6.9 Summary

The System Browser provides a user interface metaphor for using VisualWorks – especially by its use of the <select> and <operate> mouse buttons which provide a means of 'selecting' some piece of a window or pane (such as a text selection or an item in a list) and then 'operating' on that selection by choosing an option from a menu. The File Browser continues this metaphor, acting as a means of browsing the underlying file system.

Don't be surprised if it takes you some time to get to grips with this metaphor – very few user interfaces follow the lead set by Smalltalk. It's worth investing some time using the System Browser, as it will pay off in later chapters. In the next chapter we return to using the Smalltalk language: an extension to the syntax and the use of global variables.

7 The System Transcript

This chapter starts by introducing the *System Transcript*, illustrating how it can be used with a number of examples. The Transcript is also used to introduce *Global Variables*, and the TextCollector class is briefly mentioned. The Transcript is also used as a vehicle to introduce *cascaded* expressions, again with examples.

7.1 Introduction

The System Transcript (or just *Transcript*) is primarily used to display warnings or useful information. For example, when you run an explicit garbage-collection operation (by selecting the **Collect Garbage** item from the **File** menu on the Launcher), a message is printed in the Transcript indicating how much memory space was reclaimed, as well as other (possibly) useful information (Figure 7.1).

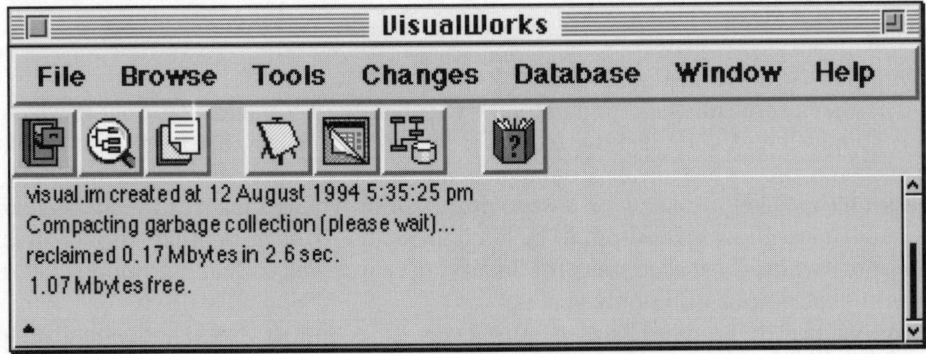

Figure 7.1 The System Transcript.

Similarly, when you save the VisualWorks image into a file (see Chapter 4), some comments are printed in the Transcript.

The Transcript can also be used as a general-purpose text output area, which is very useful for displaying the results of computations which do not require sophisticated presentation. This chapter starts by describing how to use the Transcript in this way. Using the Transcript as an example, we go on to discuss global variables, and a further piece of Smalltalk language syntax called *cascading*.

7.2 Using the System Transcript

The System Transcript is like an ordinary Workspace (see Chapter 5), except that it has the additional property of being able to display messages generated from anywhere within VisualWorks. Therefore the Transcript has the usual Workspace <operate> button menu, and you can type, edit and evaluate expressions just as if it was a Workspace.

You will already have seen a Transcript open on the screen as part of the Launcher when you started VisualWorks. You are advised to have the Transcript open at all times, so that you do not miss any important messages which might be displayed. The inclusion of the Transcript is controlled by the **System Transcript** check-box on the **Tools** menu of the Launcher.

The Transcript is referenced by a global variable Transcript. Global variables can be accessed from any part of the image. The global variable Transcript actually refers to an instance of class TextCollector. The most useful message understood by Transcript (and other instances of TextCollector) is show: ; the argument to this keyword message should be a String. When the object referenced by the global variable Transcript receives the message show: , the argument string is added to the contents of the Transcript.

For example, select and evaluate the following expression in a Workspace, using the **do it** option from the <operate> button menu:

```
Transcript show: 'Hello, world!'.
```

The result is shown in Figure 7.2.

Another useful message understood by instances of TextCollector is cr, which starts a new line. Other useful messages include space, which inserts a single blank space, and tab, which inserts enough blank space to move to the next tabbing position (just like 'tab stops' on a word processor or typewriter). The tab message is very useful to allow text output to be lined up neatly – remember that VisualWorks uses proportionally spaced fonts for displaying characters, so that it is impossible to line up text output using only spaces.

We've already seen in Chapter 5 that every object in the image understands the message printString. The response to the message is a string containing a suitable printable representation of the receiving object. Since everything in the Visual-

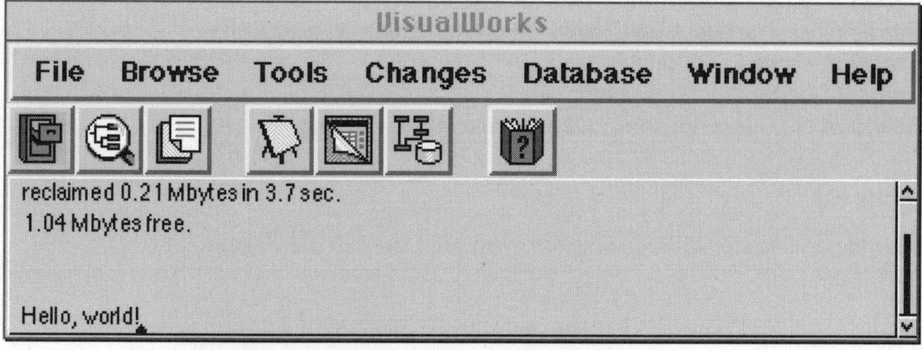

Figure 7.2 Displaying messages using the System Transcript.

Works image is an object, this means that we can print out some representation of anything within the image. The printString method is defined in class Object; the default printing method used to implement this (printOn:) is frequently redefined in subclasses of Object.

Using Transcript and the printString message together provides a very useful way of printing out the results of computations. For example, if the following expression is selected and evaluated using **do it**, the number 1024 will be printed in the Transcript.

```
Transcript show: (2 raisedTo: 10) printString
```

Omitting the printString message is a very common source of programming errors.

Finally, you should note that the System Transcript retains only the last 10 000 characters inserted into it.

Exercise 7.1

Try some further example messages sent to Transcript. You might like to try some of the expressions below:

```
Transcript show: 'Good-bye, World!'
Transcript cr. Transcript tab. Transcript show: 'String on a new line'.
Transcript show: (3+4) printString
Transcript show: (22/7) printString
Transcript cr. Transcript show: (42 raisedTo: 42) printString
```

Exercise 7.2

Try getting an instance of SpendingHistory to print itself in the Transcript.

Exercise 7.3

Try using the System Browser (Chapter 6) to browse class TextCollector. Find out what other messages Transcript can respond to. Try out some of these messages. (This class can be found in category Interface-Transcript.)

7.3 Global variables

The System Transcript illustrates the use of a global variable: a variable name that can be used from anywhere within the image. This is in contrast to the other kinds of variables introduced in Chapter 3: instance variables, which are only accessible from within a particular object, and temporary variables, which are only accessible within a particular method or block. Another important kind of variable, the class variable, is introduced in Chapter 12.

All global variables start with an initial capital letter, unlike instance and temporary variables. Global variables are usually used to refer to objects which we wish to have a long lifetime. For example, the names of classes (names like Object, Number and so on) are global variables. Several other important objects are referred to by global variables within the image, including the object that controls all the windows on the screen (ScheduledControllers – see Chapter 31).

In fact, all global variables within the image are stored in a single table called the *system dictionary*. This is an instance of class SystemDictionary which itself is a subclass of Dictionary (described in Chapter 14). The system dictionary is referenced by the global variable Smalltalk; this means that the global variable Smalltalk appears in the system dictionary referred to by that variable (i.e. is a circularity).

You can look at the contents of the VisualWorks system dictionary by printing its contents in a Workspace (remember that every object in the image can be printed out). Selecting and evaluating (using **print it**) the following expression is one convenient way of doing this. (The expression produces a sorted list of the names of global variables.)

```
Smalltalk keys asSortedCollection
```

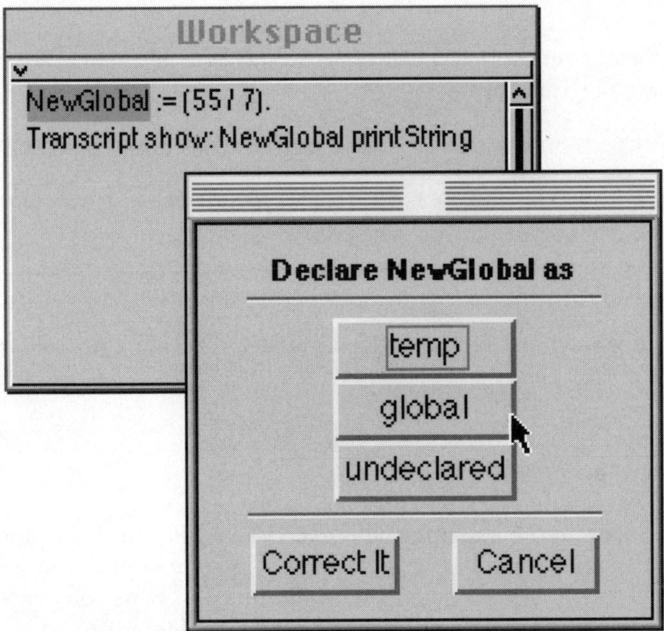

Figure 7.3 Declaring a global variable.

This will display the names of every global variable in the image, including the names of all the classes. You can also more conveniently inspect the contents of the VisualWorks system dictionary using an Inspector (Chapter 8).

Global variables are usually declared simply by typing and 'accepting' the name of the new variable (with an initial capital letter, of course). If the variable does not already exist, a Confirmer will appear, asking what kind of variable is required. You should select the **global** option (see Figure 7.3). You could also select the **Correct It** option, if you had mistyped the variable name.

Alternatively, the new global variable name, together with the object to which it refers, can be inserted directly into the system dictionary, using an expression like:

```
Smalltalk at: #NewGlobal put: (55/7).
```

Global variables can be removed using the following expression:

```
Smalltalk removeKey: #NewGlobal.
```

It's important to note that new global variables are relatively rare in VisualWorks applications, and extensive use of globals suggests that the structure of the application has not been well thought out. A global variable should only be used when you are quite sure that there should never be more than one object with these particular properties.

Exercise 7.4

Look at the contents of the system dictionary Smalltalk, by printing it out in a Workspace (or in the Transcript).

Exercise 7.5

Try creating new global variables, in both of the ways described in this section. Also, try removing the global variables you have created.

Exercise 7.6

What happens if you try and declare a global variable which does not start with an upper-case letter? Try it and find out.

7.4 Cascading expressions

You will have seen in the examples and exercises earlier in this chapter how it is frequently necessary to send several messages in sequence to the System Transcript. In general, repeated message sends to the same object occur quite frequently. To aid this, a syntactic form called 'cascading' is provided. This uses a different separator character ';' (semi-colon). For example, the following sequence of expressions might be used:

```
Transcript cr.
Transcript show: 'The result of 6 times 7 is'.
Transcript tab.
Transcript show: (6*7) printString.
Transcript cr.
```

A series of messages (cr, show:, tab and so on) is sent to the same object (Transcript). Clearly, the repeated use of the global variable name Transcript involves tedious repeated typing.

These expressions could be rewritten using a cascade, to avoid using the 3Transcript identifier quite so often:

```
Transcript cr ;
  show: 'The result of 6 times 7 is' ;
  tab ;
  show: (6*7) printString ;
  cr.
```

You should be able to see that exactly the same sequence of messages has been sent. In both cases, five messages are sent to the Transcript. (Here the message expressions have been spread over several lines for clarity – it is not necessary to do this in practice.)

The use of cascade expressions frequently results in fewer, shorter expressions, with fewer temporary variables being used. However, any cascaded expression can be rewritten as a sequence of message-sends without cascades, possibly with the addition of temporary variables. In some cases, the expressions may be much easier to understand in a form without cascades.

It is important to stress the difference between *cascaded* and ordinary *concatenated* message sends. Consider the following two expressions:

```
receiverObject message1 message2.
receiverObject message1; message2. "Note the cascade."
```

In the first expression, receiverObject receives message1, and evaluates the appropriate method. This method answers with another object; it is this *new* object that receives message2. In the second case, receiverObject receives message1 as before and evaluates the corresponding method. However, this new object is *discarded*, and it is receiverObject again which then receives message2. The two expressions are equivalent only if message1 answers with self; i.e. receiverObject itself.

Exercise 7.7

Try rewriting some of the Transcript examples from Exercise 7.1 using cascades.

Exercise 7.8

The following expressions create an Array containing three elements and put a different string at each element using a sequence of at:put: messages. Rewrite these as three expressions using cascades, keeping the temporary variable array.

```
| array |
array := Array new: 3. "Create a new Array, length 3."
array at: 1 put: 'first'. "Put a string in the first location."
array at: 2 put: 'second'. "Put a string in the second location."
array at: 3 put: 'third'. "Put a string in the third location."
Transcript cr. "New line in the Transcript."
Transcript show: array printString. "Print the array in the Transcript."
```

Exercise 7.9

(Much harder.) Try rewriting the above as a single expression, but with all the same message-sends, removing the temporary variable array. *Hint*: you may need to use the message yourself, implemented in class Object.

7.5 Summary

The System Transcript is most often used as a means of tracing the flow of a sequence of message-sends. It's unlikely that the Transcript would be open when an application is deployed to users, it's far more of a developer's aid. The Transcript is an excellent example of the use of a global variable – only one instance of it is required, and it needs to be accessed from everywhere in the image. We are now going to look at one of the Smalltalk classes – Point – as an example of the way in which objects provide encapsulation.

8 Inspecting an example class – Point

This chapter introduces, as an example, the class Point. This illustrates aspects of the use of *class* and *instance* protocol, the use of instance variables, and the 'information hiding' and 'encapsulation' aspects of the object-oriented approach. Class Point is also used to illustrate the use of *Inspectors*, with many examples.

8.1 Class Point

Class Point represents the abstract notion of locations in a *two-dimensional plane*. This is a particularly useful idea, especially when we are interested in manipulating objects on a (two-dimensional) display screen. Points are very widely used within VisualWorks, particularly in conjunction with rectangles (see Chapter 13), windows and panes (see Chapter 30).

Internally, a Point is represented in cartesian (rectangular) coordinates, although other representations are possible (see later). Two instance variables are defined, x and y, giving the displacement from the origin in the horizontal and vertical directions respectively. Unusually, the coordinate scheme is left-handed (see Figure 8.1), so that, while the *x*-axis runs left to right, the *y*-axis runs top to bottom. (Conventionally, the *y*-axis runs bottom to top.) This is because VisualWorks is frequently concerned with the display of text – usually displayed left to right and top to bottom.

Creating a new Point

Sending the message new to a class will usually result in a new instance of that class. When the class Point receives the message new, the corresponding method returns a new instance of Point with both x and y instance variables uninitialized – i.e. each with a reference to the undefined object nil (see Chapter 21). In other words, a

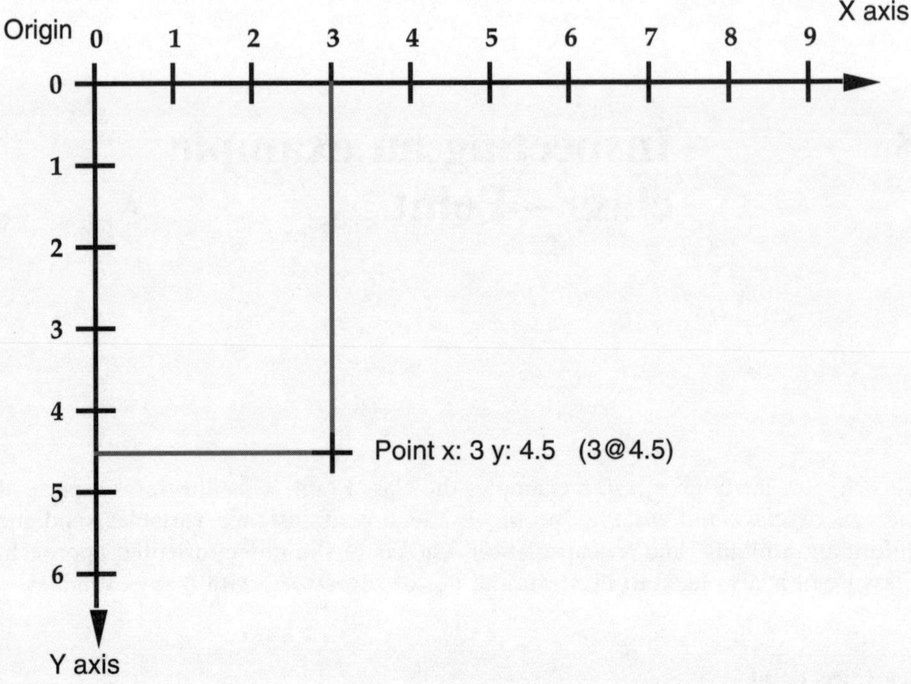

Figure 8.1 The VisualWorks coordinate scheme.

Point is created which represents nowhere in particular. We will then have to define the instance variables by sending further messages to the newly created instance. What we really want is a way of creating initialized instances of class Point – i.e. with their instance variables suitably defined.

An instance creation class method is already available by which initialized instances of Point may be created. This method is called x: y:, and allows new instances to be created with the x and y instance variables initialized by the argument numbers, for example:

```
Point x: 3 y: 4.5.
```

or

```
Point x: 2 y: 3.
```

This is a slight improvement; it is now easier to create initialized instances. However, since points are so widely used, a shorthand way of creating points is provided. The message @ (a binary message selector) is understood by instances of subclasses of Number (see Chapter 13). This answers with a new instance of Point, created from the receiver (for the *x*-coordinate) and the argument (for the *y*-coordinate). This means that points can be expressed simply as 2@3. This mechanism for creating new points using @ is so widely used that the same format is adopted when points are printed.

Class Point has a large number of methods available. You are advised to spend some time browsing this class. The instance protocols provided include the following.

Accessing

The current values of the x and y instance variables can be accessed, using the messages x and y respectively. The corresponding methods (also called x and y) simply return the current value of the appropriate instance variable. Similarly, the instance variables can be set using the x: and y: messages. You should note that the relationship between the instance variable names x and y, and the method names x and y, is simply one of convenience; there is no *a priori* reason why they should have the same names. However, giving the same names to instance variables, and to methods that access those instance variables (often called simply *access methods*) is conventional, and frequently used.

Comparing

Methods are provided to compare Points for equality (=), and various kinds of inequality (<, >, <=, >=, ~=, and so on). For example, a Point is 'less than' another Point if it is both above and to the left of the first Point; i.e. closer to the origin in both coordinates.

Arithmetic

All the usual arithmetic operations (+ and so on) are defined on Points. For example:

```
(3 @ 4.5) + (12.7 @ - 3)
((22 / 5) @ 14) - (2 @ 13)
(3 @ 4) * (2 @ 2)
(99 @ 100) / (4 @ 4)
(- 14 @ 13.95) abs
```

These methods also work if the argument is a scalar (any kind of number), rather than a Point. Examples include:

```
(3 @ 4.5) + 12
(3 @ 4) / (22 / 7)
```

Truncation and rounding

The rounded method answers with a new Point with x and y values converted to the nearest integer values. The truncate: method answers with a new Point with x and y values truncated so that they lie on a grid specified by the argument (another Point).

Polar coordinates

The r method answers with the distance of the Point from the origin. The theta method answers with the angle (in radians) from the *x*-axis. These methods allow locations to be converted to polar coordinate form.

Point functions

Several useful methods are provided in this protocol. These include: dist:, giving the absolute distance between the receiver and argument Points, and transpose, which answers with a new Point with x and y swapped over. There are several other instance protocols provided, which are not considered here.

Exercise 8.1

Try creating various instances of class Point, using each of the instance creation methods mentioned above. Use the show: and printString messages to display the values in the Transcript.

Exercise 8.2

Browse class Point; this class can be found in category Graphics-Geometry. Using the System Browser, find out the effect of dividing a Point by an integer. Type in and evaluate (using **print it**) an expression to find out if your answer is correct.

Exercise 8.3

Try out some of the methods defined in the point functions and polar coordinates protocols. For example, find out the result of each of the following expressions:

```
101.7@77.1 grid: 4@4.
43@17 dist: 45@103.
(4@3) r.
(4@3) theta.
```

Exercise 8.4

(Harder.) The dist: method in the point functions instance protocol answers with the absolute (positive) distance between the argument and receiver Points. This is the length of a straight line joining these two Points. In manhattan geometry, motion is not permitted in arbitrary directions, but must follow horizontal and vertical lines only. (This is just like travelling in a modern city, laid out as a series of 'blocks' – hence the name!) Write a new method called manhattan:, in the point functions instance protocol of class Point, which answers with the absolute distance between the receiver and argument Points, when travelling only in horizontal and vertical directions.

8.2 Alternative representations for class Point

It is worth observing at this point that the internal representation of class Point (in cartesian coordinates) is not the only possible way in which locations in two-dimensional space can be specified. For example, in a polar coordinate representation, a location is specified as a distance ('r') from a defined origin, together with an angle ('theta') from a defined axis through that origin (see Figure 8.2).

It would be perfectly feasible to implement class Point so that each instance had instance variables r and theta. When the message x was sent, for example, the corresponding method would have to compute the appropriate value from r and

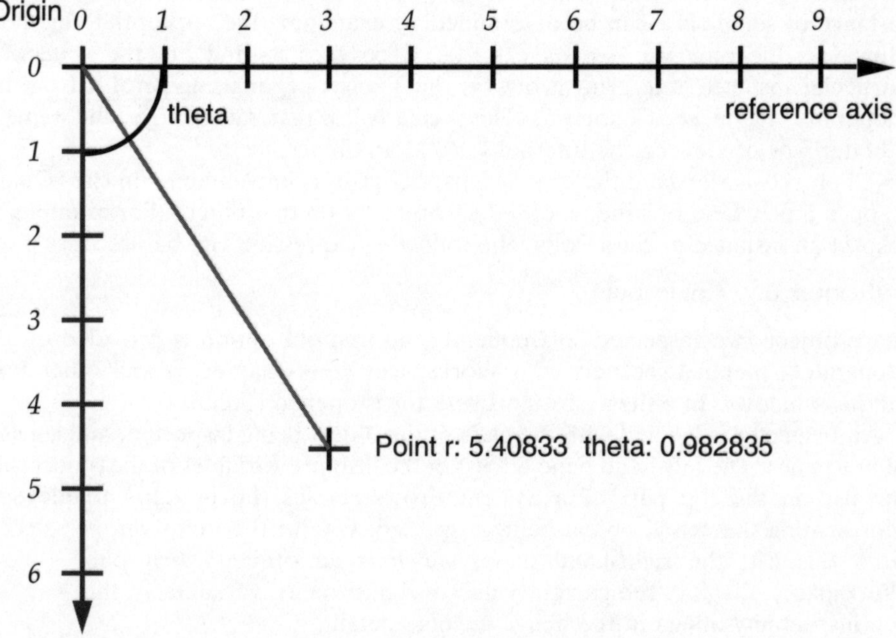

Figure 8.2 Alternative representation for class **Point**.

theta. However, methods such as r could be implemented simply to answer with the value of the corresponding instance variable. All the other methods currently implemented by class Point could be re-implemented using the new instance variables.

Thus, it is possible to implement class Point in a completely different way but, provided that the same methods were implemented to give the same result, there would be *no change* as far as any other object in the image is concerned. This illustrates the information-hiding features provided by an object-oriented system.

Class Point is actually implemented using x and y instance variables for performance reasons. As points are most frequently used to describe rectangular areas (such as panes on the screen), the cartesian operations are the ones most frequently used.

Exercise 8.5

Implement a new class NewPoint that behaves just like Point, but using a different internal representation as suggested above.

8.3 Inspecting instances of classes

We have already investigated the use of Browsers to view the source code of the methods associated with various classes. The effect that a message sent to an instance of some class can be determined by examining the appropriate method. However, the only way we have so far discovered to find out the state of a particular instance is to print it out (in the Transcript, or using **print it** from the <operate> menu, see Chapter 5). This is clearly less than satisfactory, and we need a better way of viewing the internal state of an object.

All objects understand the message inspect. This is implemented in class Object to open a new kind of window called an *Inspector* on that object. For example, to inspect an instance of class Point, the following expression can be used:

```
(Point x: 3 y: 4.5) inspect
```

Since objects are inspected so frequently, an **inspect** option is provided on the <operate> menu associated with Workspaces (see Chapter 5) and other text-editing windows. In either case, an Inspector is opened (Figure 8.3).

An Inspector is labeled with the class of the object being inspected, and consists of two panes. The left-hand pane is a list of the instance variables of the object (like the lists in the top part of a System Browser) plus the pseudo-variable self, representing the actual object being inspected. One of the items can be selected from this list; the right-hand pane, which is an ordinary text pane (like a Workspace), displays the current value of that instance variable. In this way, we can inspect any object in the image in some detail.

The left-hand pane has an <operate> menu; this has one item (**inspect**), which allows the selected instance variable to be inspected; another Inspector is spawned

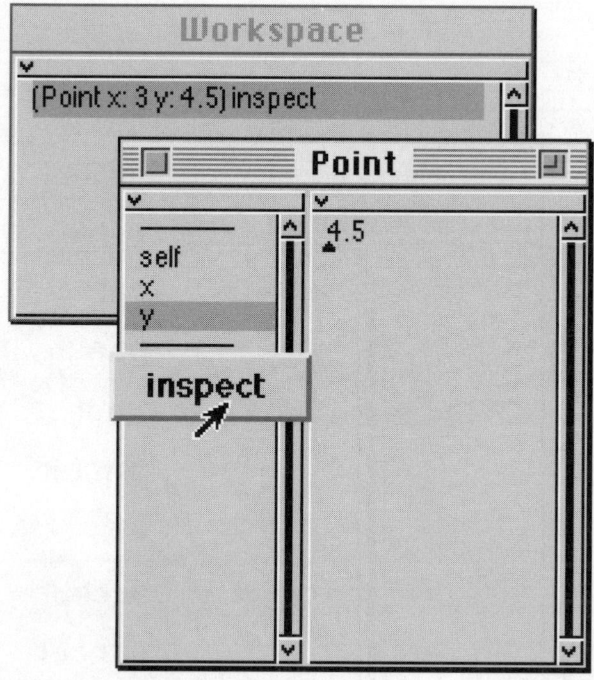

Figure 8.3 Inspecting an instance of class **Point**.

on that object. This allows complex structures of interrelated objects to be explored.

Since the right-hand pane of the Inspector is a Workspace, we can select and evaluate expressions in the usual way. However, we can also write expressions which use the named instance variables and the pseudo-variable self (see Figure 8.4). We say that the expressions we select and evaluate are evaluated 'in the context of the object being inspected'.

As well as being able to view the values of instance variables of any object, Inspectors also allow us to modify these values. Any expression can be typed into the right-hand pane of an Inspector; if the **accept** option is selected from the <operate> menu (Figure 8.5), then the resulting object is used as the new value of the instance variable (Figure 8.6). You should note that you cannot change self in this way.

Exercise 8.6

Create and inspect various instances of class Point, in the ways suggested above. Look at the values of the instance variables. You might also like to try inspecting other

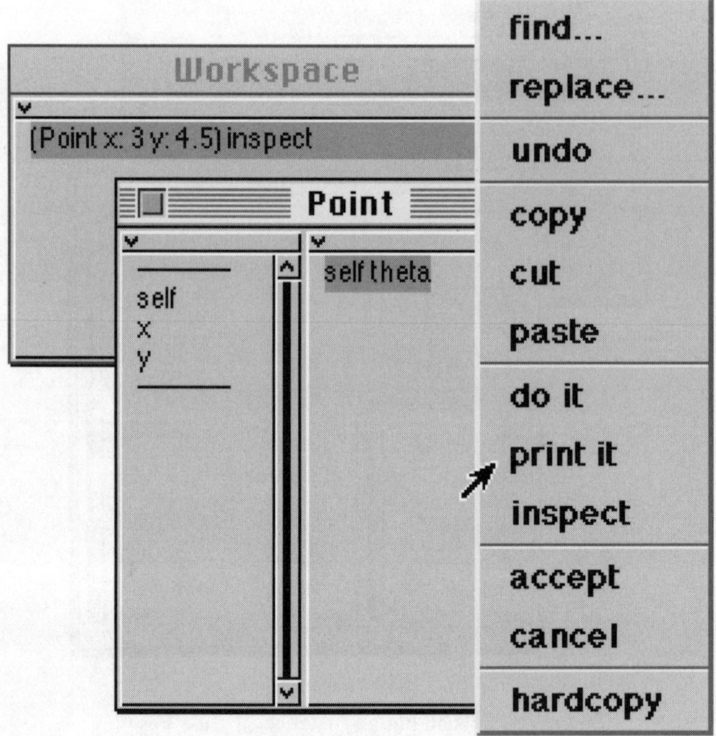

Figure 8.4 Evaluating an expression using **self**, in the context of the inspected object.

objects you already know about. Experiment with the **inspect** option from the <operate> menu in both the left- and right-hand panes of the Inspector.

Exercise 8.7

Try evaluating some expressions using the values of instance variables, or self (as in Figure 8.5, for example). Also, try modifying the value of an instance variable, by typing an expression and using the **accept** menu item.

8.4 Other Inspectors

A small number of special Inspectors are provided for instances of certain classes. In particular, Inspectors are implemented for instances of class OrderedCollection

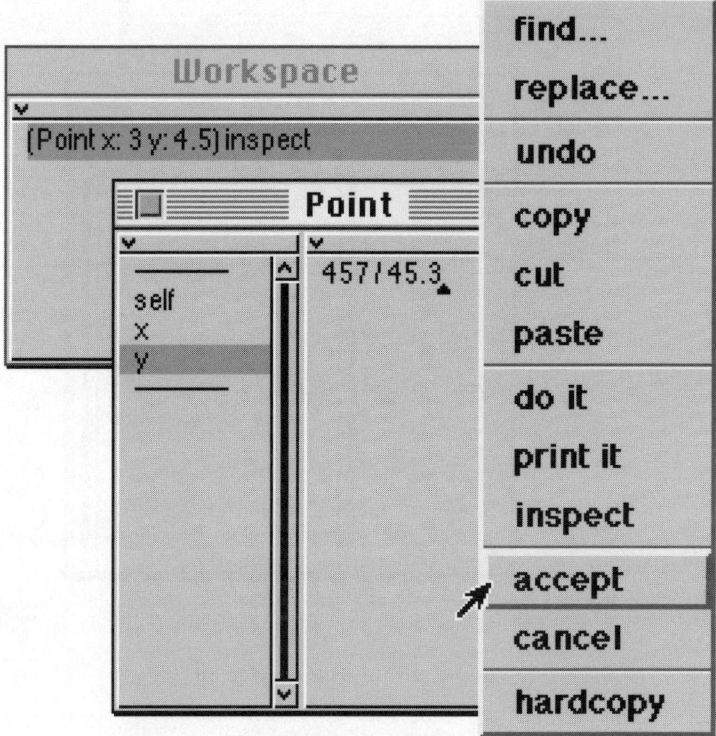

Figure 8.5 Changing the value of a **Point**'s instance variable, using an Inspector.

(see Chapter 15) and its subclasses (Figure 8.7), as well as instances of class Dictionary (Chapter 14) and its subclasses (Figure 8.8). Both these Inspectors have extra items on their <operate> menus to provide a means of modifying the collection (by adding or removing an element), or finding references to an element in a Dictionary.

Exercise 8.8

Try inspecting the system dictionary Smalltalk, which contains all the global variables in the image. *Warning*: be very careful not to remove anything from this dictionary!

Exercise 8.9

You might like to try inspecting a class, to find out its internal structure. Classes are considered further in Chapter 26.

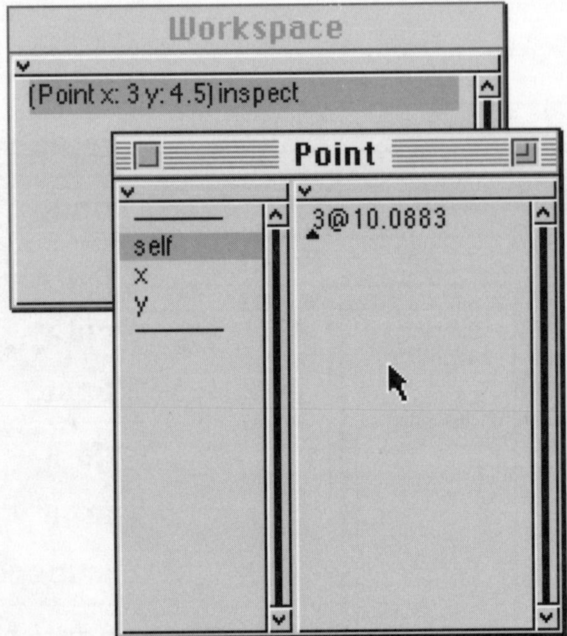

Figure 8.6 The result of changing an instance variable using an Inspector.

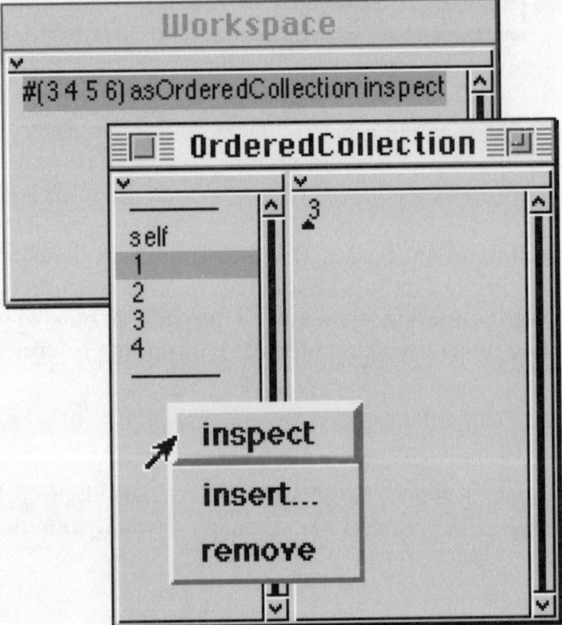

Figure 8.7 Inspecting an **OrderedCollection**.

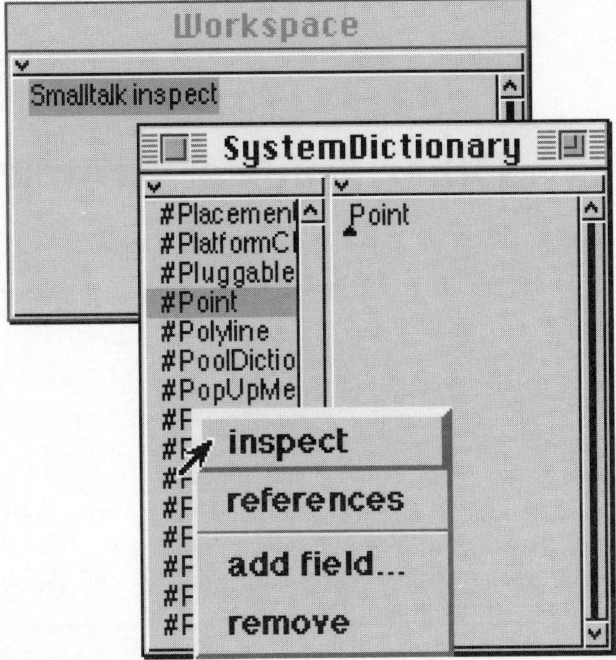

Figure 8.8 Inspecting the system dictionary.

8.5 Summary

Class Point is a simple class, yet it is a good example of the way in which objects both *hide* their state from the outside world and *encapsulate* operations on that state. The suggested alternative representation for Point shows how the internal implementation of a class may be changed without any change in its behavior or message interface. Class Point also demonstrates how a class can have *class* messages as well as *instance* messages.

Inspectors are frequently used when developing, testing and debugging, but it should be emphasized that Inspectors allow direct access to the instance variables of the object being inspected, and therefore deliberately break the information-hiding notion which is central to object-oriented programming. In the following chapter we temporarily revisit the System Browser, before going on (in Chapter 10) to look at the use of blocks.

9 Other kinds of Browsers

This chapter returns to the System Browser, and explains the way in which further Browsers can be 'spawned' to view the image in different ways. It also illustrates some of the other types of Browsers that are available and explores some of the functions available from the pop-up menus.

9.1 Introduction

As we have already seen in Chapter 6, the System Browser permits access to all classes and methods in the image. Using the System Browser, we can view and modify any method in the image, add and remove methods, as well as adding and removing classes. The System Browser is the most generally useful way of exploring the functionality associated with classes within the VisualWorks image.

During application development, however, it is frequently necessary to view methods in several different (and possibly unrelated) classes, and it is often convenient to be able to browse only a part of a class hierarchy. It is always possible to open two (or more) System Browsers on the screen simultaneously for this purpose. However, the System Browsers take up a lot of screen space and the screen can rapidly become very cluttered and crowded.

To alleviate this problem, VisualWorks provides several other kinds of Browsers, each of which permit access to only a limited amount of the image, such as just one class, or even just one method. Although these kinds of Browsers are limited in their access, they occupy less screen space, and are sometimes useful for this purpose. Other kinds of Browser permit classes to be explored in a completely different way from that supported by the System Browser. For example, the *Hierarchy Browser* allows a part of the class hierarchy to be viewed. Both these kinds of Browser are explored in this chapter.

Yet other kinds of Browser permit, for example, methods with the same name to be viewed regardless of the class with which they are associated. These kinds of Browser are discussed in Chapter 16.

9.2 Spawning other Browsers

Each of the panes in the System Browser has a **spawn** option on the <operate> menu. The <operate> menu available in the Class Names pane also has a **spawn hierarchy** option. Each of these options causes a different kind of Browser to be created, on a limited part of the class hierarchy.

Working from left to right across the System Browser, the **spawn** option on the leftmost pane (Class Categories) <operate> menu opens a Browser on only those classes in the selected category – a *Category Browser*. Other classes are not accessible (see Figure 9.1).

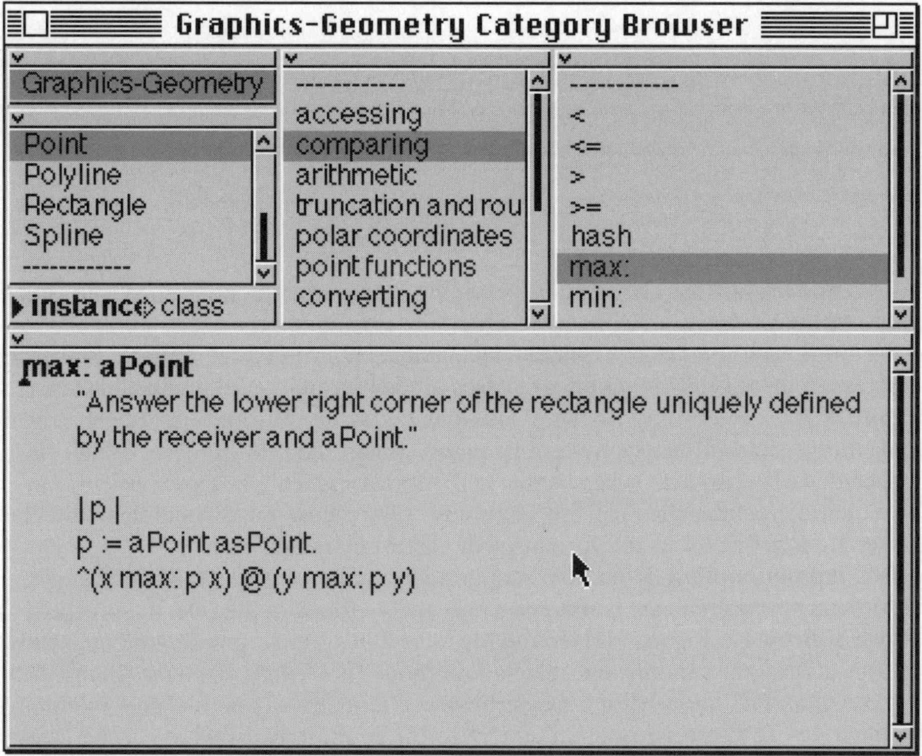

Figure 9.1 A Class Category Browser.

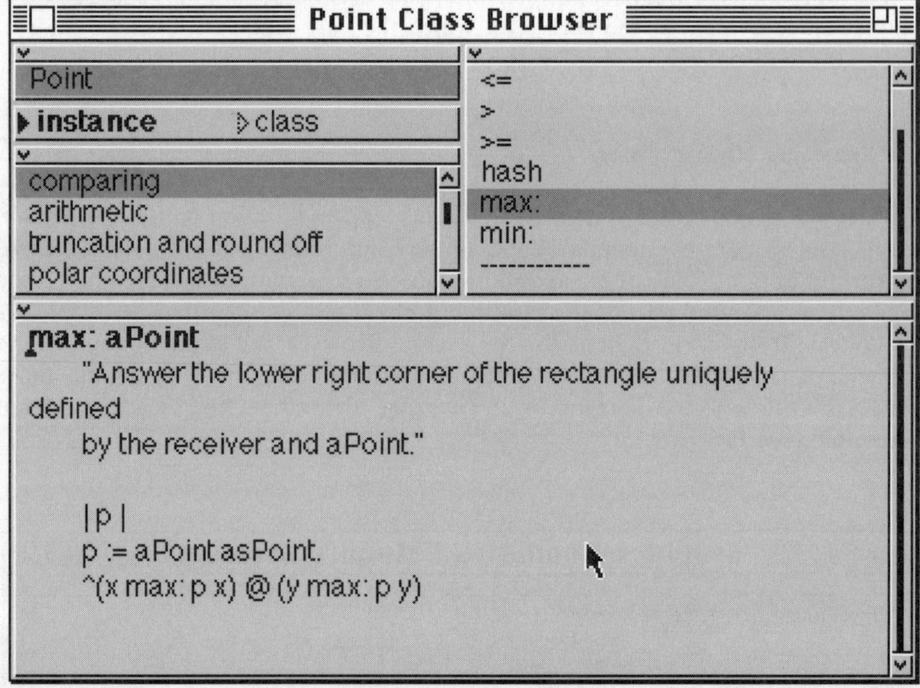

Figure 9.2 A Class Browser.

Two **spawn** options are available from the <operate> menu of the Class Names pane: **spawn** creates a Browser on only the selected class – a *Class Browser*, see Figure 9.2. (Other classes are not available.) Alternatively, **spawn hierarchy** creates a *Hierarchy Browser* on all classes in the hierarchy of the selected class (see Figure 9.3). A Hierarchy Browser provides the same information access, viewing and editing capabilities as a System Browser, except the information available is for a specified class and its superclasses and subclasses. This is a convenient way of browsing a 'vertical slice' of the hierarchy. (Note how the structure of the class hierarchy is reflected in the format of the list of class names.)

The **spawn** option from the <operate> menu of the Message Categories (Protocols) pane creates a Browser on only the methods in the selected protocol – a *Protocol Browser* (Figure 9.4). In the Message Selectors <operate> menu, **spawn** creates a Browser on only the selected method – a *Method Browser* (Figure 9.5).

Note that the underlying class structure is equally accessible and modifiable through any of these Browsers (subject to the limitations of what can be located with the particular Browser used). Also, the panes in each of these Browsers have exactly the same <operate> button menu as the corresponding pane in the System Browser.

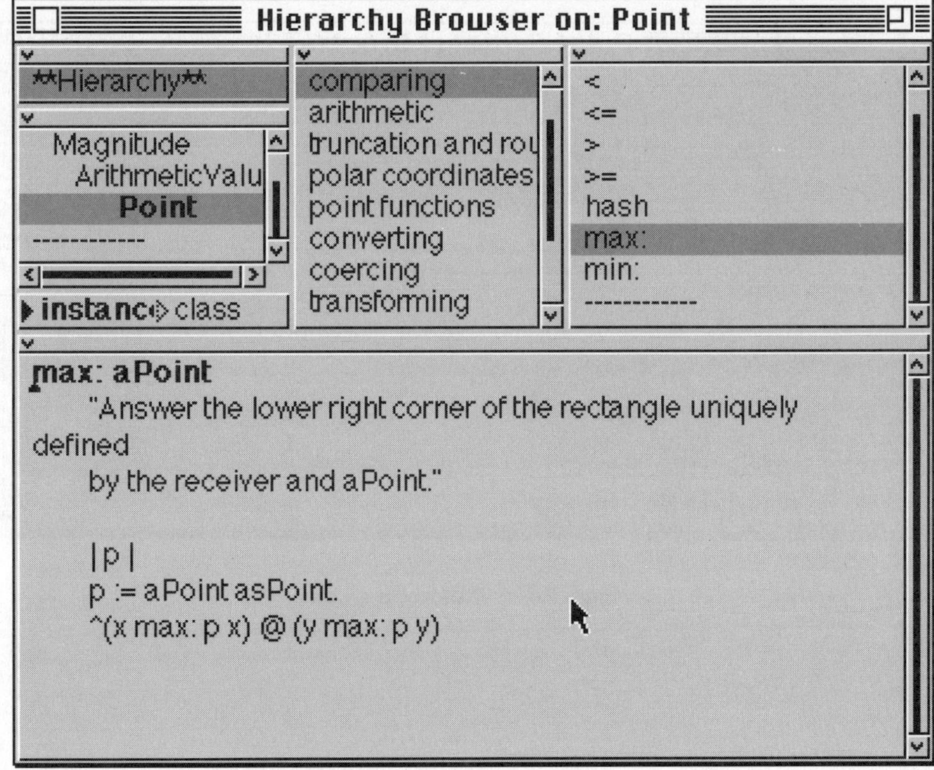

Figure 9.3 A Hierarchy Browser.

Finally, it is important to be aware of two consequences of spawning Browsers. If a new Browser is spawned from an existing Browser in which the method source code has been modified but not 'accepted', then the original Browser reverts to the original source code (as if the **cancel** option had been selected) and the new Browser contains the modified code. Second, note that the consistency of the representation presented to the user when multiple windows are in operation is not automatically managed. Changes made to a class or category in one Browser are not reflected in other Browsers until another selection is made, or the **update** option from the Class Categories <operate> button menu is used.

9.3 Alternative ways of opening Browsers

Frequently, we will wish to browse a particular class. Of course, we can always do this by finding the class in the System Browser, but there are two alternatives. The first is to use the **Browse** menu from the Launcher (Figure 9.6). (You have used

Point Protocol Browser

comparing

hash
max:
min:

```
max: aPoint
    "Answer the lower right corner of the rectangle uniquely defined
    by the receiver and aPoint."

    | p |
    p := aPoint asPoint.
    ^(x max: p x) @ (y max: p y)
```

Figure 9.4 A Protocol Browser.

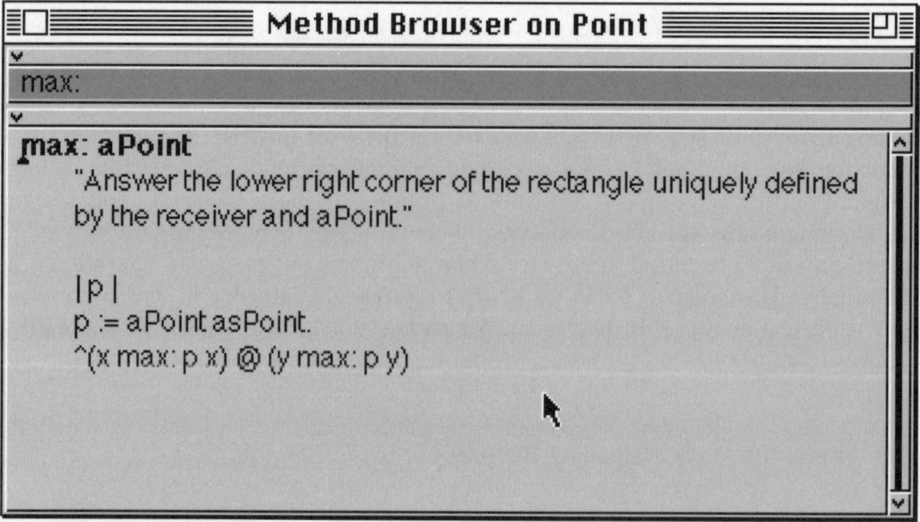

Figure 9.5 A Method Browser.

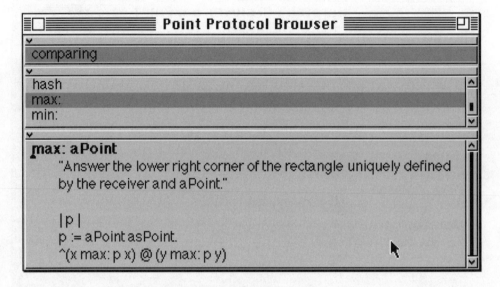

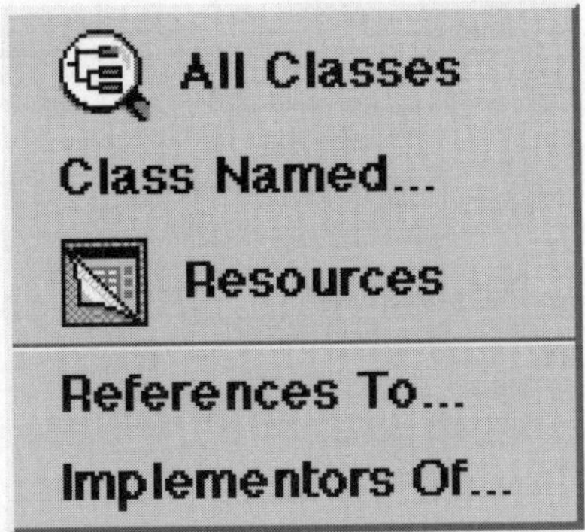

Figure 9.6 The **Browse** menu of the Launcher.

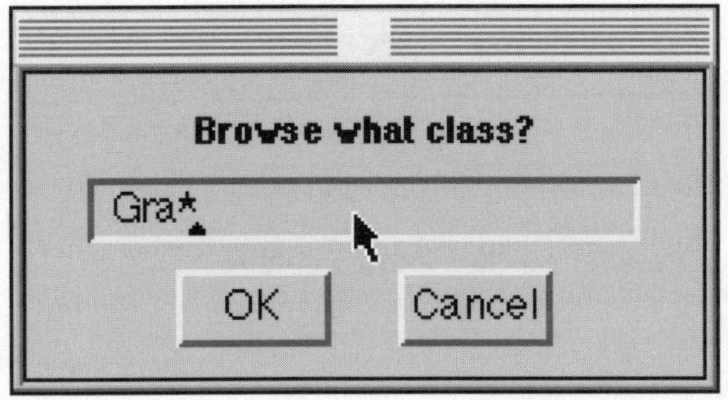

Figure 9.7 Entering a class name.

this menu before, to open a System Browser.) The menu also contains other options, and the one that is of interest here is the **Class Named . . .** option. When this menu is selected the user is presented with a request for a class. You may simply type the class name in full here, or, if you are unsure, use the wildcards described earlier in Chapter 6 (Figure 9.7). If the later approach is taken you will be presented with a list of matching classes (Figure 9.8), from which you may only select one.

The other alternative is to open a Class Browser directly from a Workspace. This can be done by sending the newOnClass: message to class Browser; for example, a Browser on class Point can be created by typing and evaluating the following expression in a Workspace:

```
Browser newOnClass: Point
```

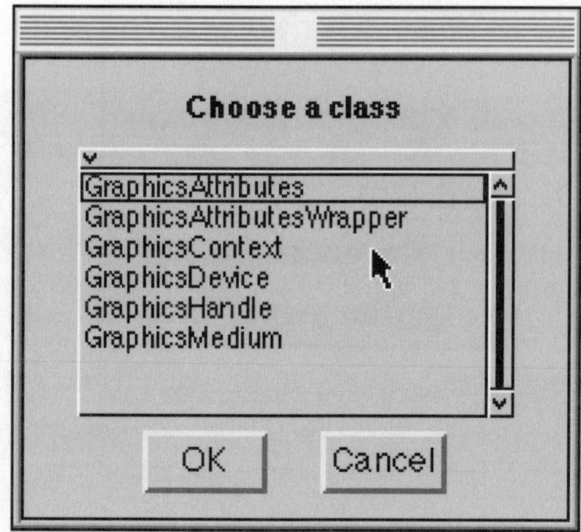

Figure 9.8 A Confirmer containing a list of classes matching those in Figure 9.7.

This is so useful that a shorthand way of opening a Class Browser is to send the message browse to that class or to any instance of that class. Therefore alternative ways of creating a Browser on class Point would be:

```
Point browse.
(3@4) browse.
```

The Class Browsers created in this way are identical to those created when the **spawn** option is used from the Class Names <operate> menu.

A complete System Browser can be opened using the expression:

```
Browser open
```

A Hierarchy Browser can also be created by evaluating an expression. For example, a Hierarchy Browser that includes class Point can be opened using:

```
HierarchyBrowser openHierarchyBrowserFrom:
                                    (Browser new onClass: Point)
```

Exercise 9.1

Experiment with creating various Category, Class, Protocol, and Method Browsers from existing Browsers. Include a hierarchy Browser.

Exercise 9.2

Experiment with creating various types of Browsers, by typing and evaluating expressions as suggested above.

Exercise 9.3

Browse the instance creation class methods of class Browser and try creating some other kinds of Browsers using the messages found there.

Exercise 9.4

Note how Browsers may be spawned from Browsers other than System Browsers.

Exercise 9.5

Modify a method (non-destructively or reversibly!) in one Browser.

Exercise 9.6

Verify that the changes are visible in other Browsers only after reselection or the use of the **update** menu option.

9.4 Summary

The System Browser not only provides a view of the whole VisualWorks image but also acts as a means of spawning other Browsers on selected parts of the image. Thus, the programmer can concentrate his or her attention on specific classes or method – making it easier to explore the image. One of the most useful Browsers is the Hierarchy Browser which clearly shows the inheritance path of a class. Although it's possible to open a Browser programmatically, in practice this is only useful when debugging. A comprehensive description of blocks is presented next, concentrating on their use in control structures.

10 Blocks and control structures (1)

This chapter returns to the notion of 'blocks' first introduced in Chapter 3, and illustrates how blocks can be used to implement a wide variety of control structures. Only conventional serial programming constructs are introduced here; more complex structures are discussed in Chapter 17 and parallel constructs (e.g. processes) are left to Chapter 25. We also consider block arguments and temporary variables.

10.1 Introduction

A block represents a deferred sequence of message expressions. A block is represented by a sequence of expressions (separated by full stops), surrounded by square brackets '[]'. For example:

```
[ans := Float pi / 2]
```

When a block is encountered in the evaluation of a method, the statements enclosed in the square brackets are *not* immediately evaluated.

When a block receives the message value, the expressions in the block will be evaluated in the context in which the block was defined which is not necessarily the current context. A block expression is an instance of BlockClosure and can therefore be assigned to a variable, e.g.:

```
testBlock := [this < that]
```

Thus, the following sequences of messages are identical:

```
testBlock := [this < that].
testBlock value
```

and

```
[this < that] value
```

The result returned from a block is the value of the last expression evaluated. Thus, for the expression:

```
ans := [3 even. 3 odd] value
```

the variable ans is set to true.

Exercise 10.1

Write a block expression which increments a temporary variable index by one. Assign the block to the variable addBlock. Send messages to addBlock to increment index.

Exercise 10.2

What is returned from an empty block? (Try [] value.)

Exercise 10.3

What is the effect of the sequence of expressions below? Try evaluating them to check whether you are correct. (The last exercise appears in the 'Blue Book', page 33.)

```
| incrementBlock sumBlock sum index |
incrementBlock := [index := index + 1].
sumBlock := [sum + (index * index)].
sum := 0.
index := 1.
sum := sumBlock value.
incrementBlock value.
sum := sumBlock value.
sum
```

10.2 Simple repetition

A very simple 'repetition' control structure using a block may be achieved using the timesRepeat: message sent to an Integer.

```
anInteger timesRepeat: argumentBlock
```

In this case, the message value is sent to the argumentBlock variable anInteger number of times. Examples include:

```
| this that |
this := 0.
that := 5.
4 timesRepeat: [this := this + that].
this

| a |
a := 1.
10 timesRepeat: [a := a * 2].
a
```

Exercise 10.4

Write a sequence of expressions to display the sum of the integers 1 to 100 in the Transcript.

10.3 Conditional selection

Blocks are also used as arguments in the conditional selection control structure. Conditional operations are achieved by sending one of the following messages to a Boolean object:

```
ifTrue: aBlock
ifFalse: aBlock
ifTrue: trueBlock ifFalse: falseBlock
ifFalse: falseBlock ifTrue: trueBlock
```

To get a Boolean object, just send any comparison message to an object. For example, send 4 the message > with the argument 2 and true will be returned (i.e. 4 > 2). Some useful comparison operators are:

=	<	>	<=	>=	~=
==	~~		(object identity and non-identity (Chapter 21 describes these terms in more detail))		

So putting this all together, an example *if* statement might look like:

```
a = b
  ifTrue: [a := b + 1.
    b := b - 2]
  ifFalse: [b := a]
```

or

```
| number parity |
number := 17.
(number \\ 2) = 0
  ifTrue: [parity := 'even']
  ifFalse: [parity := 'odd'].
parity
```

The value returned from ifTrue:ifFalse: is the value of the last block evaluated. So the above could also be written:

```
| number parity |
number := 17.
parity := (number \\ 2) = 0
            ifTrue: ['even']
            ifFalse: ['odd'].
parity
```

The keyword message ifFalse:ifTrue: is also provided.

Also provided are single-keyword messages, where only one consequence is useful:

```
a > b ifTrue: [a := b].
```

This statement would check to see if a is greater than b, and if so set the value of a to be the value of b. Other examples are:

```
a <= b ifFalse: [b := a].
```

```
index <= limit
    ifTrue: [total := total + (list at: index)]
```

If the condition is false, the block is not evaluated, and ifTrue: returns nil. Thus, it is equivalent to:

```
index <= limit
  ifTrue: [total := total + (list at: index)]
  ifFalse: [nil]
```

10.4 Conditional repetition

Simple conditional loops can be constructed using the whileTrue: or whileFalse: message selectors. Both the receiver and the message argument are expected to be blocks.

```
receiverBlock whileTrue: argumentBlock
receiverBlock whileFalse: argumentBlock
```

In the case of the whileTrue: message, the loop works as follows. The receiver block is sent the message value; if the response to this message-send is true, then the argument block is sent the message value. The loop repeats until the receiver block returns false. For example, to initialize an array list:

```
| list index |
list := Array new: 10.
index := 1.
[index <= list size]
  whileTrue:
    [list at: index put: 0.
    index := index + 1].
list
```

Equivalently, using the whileFalse: message:

```
| list index |
list := Array new: 10.
index := 1.
[index > list size]
  whileFalse:
    [list at: index put: 0.
    index := index + 1].
list
```

In some cases, all the 'useful' work may be done in the receiver block. In this case, the argument block may be omitted and the unary messages whileTrue and whileFalse used instead, for example:

```
| list index |
list := Array new: 10.
index := 1.
[list at: index put: 0.
index := index + 1.
index <= list size] whileTrue.
list
```

10.5 Block arguments

A block may take one (or more) arguments. The arguments are each represented by an identifier preceded by a colon (':'). They are separated from the expressions in the block by a vertical bar ('|'). For example:

```
[:each | total := total + each]
```

A block with a single argument is evaluated by sending it the keyword message value:. For example:

```
[:each | each degreesToRadians sin] value: 90
```

Blocks with more than one argument, e.g.:

```
[:x :y | (x * x) + (y * y)] value: 3 value: 4
```

use the corresponding keyword message, e.g. value:value:. Up to three arguments may be provided using this technique; any larger number of arguments can be handled by sending the message valueWithArguments:, which accepts an array of arguments. The same number of arguments must appear in the block and the message.

10.6 Block temporary variables

A block, like a method, can also define local (temporary) variables.

```
10 timesRepeat:
  [ | bTemp |
    bTemp := Rectangle fromUser.
    bTemp width > 100
      ifTrue: [Transcript show: 'Too Big!'; cr]
      ifFalse: [Transcript show: bTemp printString; cr]]
```

Here bTemp is local to the block.

Naturally, block arguments and temporaries can be used together. Here we create a block (called quadBlock) to resolve a quadratic equation, and then use it to solve the equation $y = 4x^2 + 5x - 6$:

```
| quadBlock |
quadBlock := [:a :b :c |
                | denominator root |
                denominator := 2 * a.
                root := ((b * b) – (4 * a * c)) sqrt.
                Array with: b negated + root / denominator
                        with: b negated - root / denominator].
quadBlock value: 4 value: 5 value: -6
```

Exercise 10.5

Rewrite the sum of integers example (Exercise 10.3) using (a) whileTrue:, and (b) whileFalse:.

Exercise 10.6

Write some expressions to find the maximum (or minimum) value in an array of numbers.

Exercise 10.7

Write some expressions to reverse the order of elements in an array.

Exercise 10.8

You might like to add a method reverse to the protocol of Array.

Exercise 10.9

Use a timesRepeat: loop to sum the odd integers from 1 to 100. (*Hint*: look in the testing messages of class Integer. Yes, this would be an inefficient way to do this calculation.)

Exercise 10.10

Use a whileTrue: loop to calculate the squares of the integers from 1 to 10. Print your answers in the Transcript.

Exercise 10.11

For all odd integers < 20 calculate the number which is (the factorial of twice the integer) divided by the square of the integer. Print your answer in the Transcript.

10.7 Summary

Blocks provide a very powerful programming mechanism. In this chapter we have been able to give only a taste of how and where they can be used. Starting with the fairly simple use of a block to provide repetition, the chapter shows how blocks may be used to provide conditional selection, conditional repetition and parameterizable algorithmic objects. We return to inheritance in the next chapter by giving examples to explore the way in which inheritance 'works'.

11 Use of inheritance

This chapter reviews message-sending and the method search mechanism, and considers the effect of messages to self and super. This very important aspect of using Smalltalk is illustrated with several small examples.

11.1 Methods revisited

A *method* describes how an object will respond to a *message*. It is made up of a *message pattern* and a *sequence of expressions* (separated by full stops). The names of arguments in the message pattern are accessible within the method. Temporary variables may also be used – they must be declared at the beginning of the method (just after the message pattern). Temporaries are initially nil, and are forgotten after the end of the method evaluation. The pseudo-variables self and super can also be used within methods to refer to the receiver itself. Once the method has finished evaluating, an answer is returned to the sender of the message. By default, the object returned is the receiver itself (i.e. self).

However, other objects can be returned by use of a return expression – an expression preceded by an 'up-arrow' ('^'). The return expression is the last expression evaluated in a method.

11.2 Review of message-sending

When a message is sent, the methods in the receiver's class are searched for one with a matching selector. If none is found, the methods in that class's superclass are searched. The search continues upwards until a match is found, or the top of the hierarchy is reached. (The superclass of Object is nil.) If a match is made, the corresponding method is evaluated. This will probably cause further messages to be sent.

If no match is found during the search, the message doesNotUnderstand: is sent to the receiver. The argument is the offending message. A method with selector doesNotUnderstand: is implemented in the instance protocol of Object, which causes an error message to be displayed in a Notifier.

11.3 Messages to self and super

When a method contains an expression that causes a message to be sent to self, the search for the corresponding method starts in the class of the instance *regardless of which class contained the method containing self*. It is just as if some other object had sent the message – the search starts exactly as described above.

The pseudo-variable super is also available for use within a method. It also refers to the receiver of the message (just like self). However, the search for the method does *not* start in the receiver's class. Instead, it starts in the *superclass of the class in which the method using super is located* (note that this is not necessarily the same as starting the search in the superclass of the receiver). The use of super allows methods to access other methods defined in classes further up the hierarchy, even if they have been *overridden* in subclasses. The following exercise demonstrates how the search proceeds.

Exercise 11.1

Type in the class descriptions and methods given below.

Class	One
Superclass	Object
Instance variables	*none*
Class variables	*none*
Pool dictionaries	*none*
Class category	Messages-example
Message protocol	tests

```
result1
    ^self test

test
    ^1
```

Class	Two
Superclass	One
Instance variables	*none*
Class variables	*none*
Pool dictionaries	*none*
Class category	Messages-example
Message protocol	tests

```
test
    ^2
```

Class	Three
Superclass	Two
Instance variables	*none*
Class variables	*none*
Pool dictionaries	*none*
Class category	Messages-example
Message protocol	tests

```
result2
    ^self result 1

result3
    ^super test
```

Class	Four
Superclass	Three
Instance variables	*none*
Class variables	*none*
Pool dictionaries	*none*
Class category	Messages-example
Message protocol	tests

```
test
    ^4
```

Evaluate the following expressions, one at a time:

```
| ex1 |
ex1 := One new.
ex1 test.

| ex1 |
ex1 := One new.
ex1 result1.

| ex2 |
ex2 := Two new.
ex2 test.

| ex2 |
ex2 := Two new.
ex2 result1
```

Explain what happens.

Exercise 11.2

Also, explain what happens with each of the following expressions (create the appropriate temporary variables, and evaluate each test and result expression in isolation):

```
ex3 := Three new.
ex4 := Four new.
ex3 test.
ex4 result1.
ex3 result2.
ex4 result2.
ex3 result3.
ex4 result3
```

These examples are from the 'Blue Book', pages 62–66.

Exercise 11.3

Show the sequence of message sends in the System Transcript by augmenting the above methods with extra expressions.

11.4 An example of inheritance

In Chapter 6 we introduced the class SpendingHistory as a simplistic model of a person's spending habits. Suppose we also want a class that is a more complete model of a person's overall finances – one that includes *income*. Rather than develop a class from scratch, we can subclass the existing SpendingHistory class, and consequently *inherit* both its behavior and data structure. The class description of the new subclass, called FinancialHistory, is specified below:[1]

```
SpendingHistory subclass: #FinancialHistory
    instanceVariableNames: 'incomes'
    classVariableNames: ''
    poolDictionaries: ''
    category: 'Financial Tools'
```

Add a new class category called 'Financial Tools' and edit the class template so that it appears as above. The class description introduces one extra instance variable incomes. Select **accept** from the <operate> menu.

The class FinancialHistory inherits the instance variables of its superclass SpendingHistory (i.e. cashOnHand and expenditures) and also its instance and class methods. Therefore, the class message initialBalance: is understood by class FinancialHistory as the corresponding method is implemented in its superclass. Let us revisit that method (in class SpendingHistory):

```
initialBalance: anAmount
^self new setInitialBalance: anAmount
```

We can see that the method creates a new instance of the receiver and sends it the message setInitialBalance;, hence we should implement the corresponding method in our new class as follows:

```
setInitialBalance: anAmount
  super setInitialBalance: anAmount.
  incomes := Dictionary new.
```

This method uses the pseudo-variable super as the receiver of the message setInitialBalance:. The consequence of sending this message is that the method setInitialBalance: in class SpendingHistory is evaluated, i.e. cashOnHand refers to anAmount, and expenditures refers to a new empty Dictionary. The only additional operation provided by the method above is that incomes refers to another new empty Dictionary. You should add this method to instance protocol private of class FinancialHistory.

The sequence of message sends that result from sending the message initialBalance: to class FinancialHistory now appears to be rather complex. We can number the stages as follows:

1. If you remembered to take a snapshot of your work in Chapter 6, you will find that class SpendingHistory is in your image. Otherwise, you may find that you need to revisit that chapter.

1 The class methods of FinancialHistory are searched for the selector initialBalance: – it is not found.
2 The class methods of SpendingHistory (the superclass of FinancialHistory) are searched for the selector initialBalance: – it is found.
3 The found method is evaluated, causing a new instance of the *receiver* (i.e. class FinancialHistory) to be created. This instance is then sent the message setInitialBalance:.
4 The instance methods of the class of the receiver (FinancialHistory) are searched for the selector setInitialBalance: – it is found.
5 The found method is evaluated, causing the expression super setInitialBalance: to be evaluated.
6 The search for the selector setInitialBalance: begins in the "superclass of the class in which the method using super is located" – i.e. the search begins in class SpendingHistory.
7 The instance methods of class SpendingHistory are searched for the selector setInitialBalance: – it is found.
8 The found method is evaluated, causing the instance variables cashOnHand and expenditures to be initialized as appropriate. The receiver is returned from the method (i.e. the instance of FinancialHistory is returned).
9 The remainder of the instance method setInitialBalance: in class FinancialHistory is evaluated, causing the instance variable incomes to be initialized. The receiver is returned from the method (i.e. the instance of FinancialHistory is returned).
10 There are no more expressions to evaluate in the class method initialBalance: in class SpendingHistory, and the return symbol indicates that the initialized instance (of FinancialHistory) should be returned.

Now, add the method totalReceivedFor: in protocol inquiries, the method receive:for: in protocol transactions, and the method printOn: in protocol printing. The code is:

```
totalReceivedFor: reason
    "return the amount received from reason. Answer
    0 if reason is not used for incomes"

    ^(incomes includesKey: reason)
      ifTrue: [incomes at: reason]
      ifFalse: [0]

receive: anAmount for: reason
    "Receive anAmount for a reason and increase the cashOnHand"

    incomes
      at: reason
      put: (self totalReceivedFor: reason) + anAmount.
    cashOnHand := cashOnHand + anAmount.
```

```
printOn: aStream
   "print a suitable representation of myself on aStream"

   super printOn: aStream.
   aStream space.
   incomes keysAndValuesDo: [:reason :amount |
      aStream cr.
      reason printOn: aStream.
      aStream tab.
      amount printOn: aStream]
```

Note how the printOn: method uses the pseudo-variable super to inherit behaviour from the superclass, so that all the programmer has to add are the message expressions necessary to print out details of income.

To test the new class, type the expressions shown below in a Workspace. Select and evaluate the code using **print it** (note that this example uses cascaded expressions).

```
| spendingHistory |
spendingHistory := FinancialHistory initialBalance: 800.
spendingHistory spend: 220 on: 'rent';
                spend: 30 on: 'food';
                spend: 45 on: 'drink';
                spend: 20 on: 'petrol';
spendingHistory receive: 300 for: 'salary';
                receive: 50 for: 'expenses';
                receive: 50 for: 'overtime'.
```

Exercise 11.4

Experiment with the class FinancialHistory, perhaps extending it with extra expressions that write to the System Transcript.

Exercise 11.5

Consider creating a class Griddedpoint, as a subclass of Point. Class GriddedPoint represents a two-dimensional point whose co-ordinates lie on some specified grid. What methods should class GriddedPoint re-implement so that its co-ordinates *always* lie on a 10×10 grid?

Before continuing, ensure that you take a "snapshot" of your image, by selecting the **Save As . . .** option from the **File** menu of the Launcher. We will return to this example later in the book.

11.5 Summary

To summarize, classes can inherit properties from other classes; this process is repeated to form a 'tree' of classes, rooted at Object.

- As stated above, a subclass inherits properties from its superclass.
- Subclasses are used to *refine* the functionality of the superclass, for either the external protocol or the internal implementation.
- Superclasses which should *not* themselves have direct instances are known as abstract superclasses. They are intended to support a partial implementation of features which are completed (differently) in subclasses.
- Each class is a (possibly indirect) subclass of class Object.
- The use of self or super can be used to control the methods selected in response to message-sends.

Having described the way in which inheritance can be used, the next chapter considers the different variables that can be shared by instances and classes.

12 Class variables and protocols

This chapter explores three types of variables not yet considered – the *class* variable, the *class instance* variable, and the *pool* variable. It goes on to explore protocol typically implemented in classes, including 'instance creation', 'class initialization' and 'examples'. These aspects are explored using class Date and class Time as examples. Other examples are taken from the VisualWorks classes LookPreferences, ScheduledWindow and FileBrowser.

12.1 Class variables

We have already seen one type of shared variable in Smalltalk – the global variable. Another type of shared variable is the *class variable*. This variable is only accessible by all instances of the class in which the variable is defined or any of its subclasses. Typical uses of class variables are:

- 'Constant' values used by all instances of the class and its subclasses, but which might need to be changed occasionally
- Private communication between instances.

In general, shared variables provide another mechanism for communication (as well as message passing). The over-use of shared variables is frequently an indication that a solution has not been well designed.

For example, class Date has five class variables, which are declared in the class definition as follows:

```
Magnitude subclass: #Date
  instanceVariableNames: 'day year'
  classVariableNames: 'DaysInMonth FirstDayOfMonth MonthNames
SecondsInDay WeekDayNames'
  poolDictionaries: ''
  category: 'Magnitude-General'
```

The instance variables (day, year) change with each instance, so they can only be accessed directly by the same object. The class variables, however, keep the same values across instances. So when an instance of Date wants to access the Array of Integers referenced by the DaysInMonth variable, for example, it does not have to send a message to itself. It can use the variable in its methods just as naturally as it would use an instance variable. Objects that are not in the inheritance chain would have to query Date for the information, for example, sending it the message nameOfMonth: Figure 12.1 demonstrates the use of a repeat structure to print the names of the months on the Transcript.

The initial value of a class variable is usually assigned in a class method (normally named initialize) and the corresponding message is typically sent as the final act of creating a class.

Exercise 12.1

Browse the class protocol of Date to discover where and how its class variables are used. Try some examples (e.g. Date today).

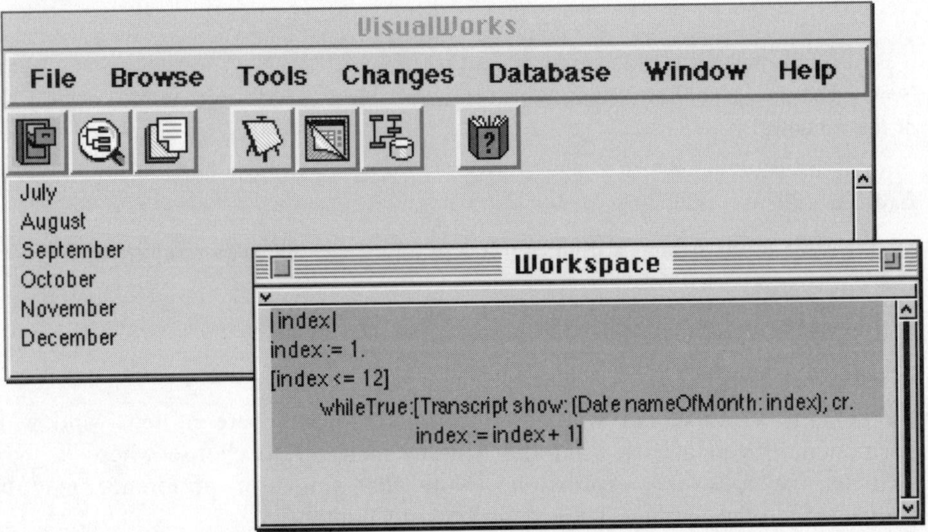

Figure 12.1 The class variable **DaysinMonth** holds on to a constant.

Exercise 12.2

Also explore the instance protocol of Date. Try some examples, including comparing and arithmetic. How would you subtract a number of days from an instance of Date?

Exercise 12.3

Create a new class protocol called 'examples'. Install some of your examples there. Remember to document your examples in method comments!

12.2 Examples

There are a number of examples of the use of class variables to control the appearance and behavior of the VisualWorks user interface. Here we describe three of them.

LookPreferences

Simple changes to the appearance of the user interface (the color of windows, menus, and so on) are managed by the class LookPreferences. Its class methods may be used to change the default settings; if you modify the current settings, you will have to re-initialize the class for the changes to take effect (i.e. evaluate the expression LookPreferences initialize).

Exercise 12.4

Browse the class LookPreferences. Which class variable is used to refer to the colour of the windows?

Exercise 12.5

Modify some of the default attributes of LookPreferences and then re-initialize the class.

ScheduledWindow

By default, VisualWorks will allow you to choose where a new window is positioned. If you always want the window manager to choose where it goes, evaluate the following expression. (Note that this user preference may be controlled via the Settings Tool, described in Chapter 5.)

```
ScheduledWindow promptForOpen: false.
```

Exercise 12.6

Use the browser to discover the name of the class variable that controls how a new window is positioned.

FileBrowser

The FileBrowser was described in Chapter 6. It's possible to specify an initial 'file pattern' (held by the class variable DefaultPattern) for retrieving the filename list by sending the message defaultPattern: to the class FileBrowser, supplying the (argument) pattern in the form of a string.

Exercise 12.7

Set the default file pattern of the FileBrowser so that, when opened, the file list contains the contents of the current directory. *Hint*: remember the use of 'wildcards'.

12.3 Class instance variables

The use of class instance variables is little understood, mainly because there are few examples of their use in VisualWorks. As its name suggests, a class instance variable is an instance variable for a class. At first this may seem a little confusing, but you should remember that every object is an instance of some class, thus every class is also an instance of some class. We have seen earlier that instance variables are inherited by classes, similarly, class instance variables are inherited.

It's important to distinguish between the use of a class variable and a class instance variable. For example, suppose class Persian inherits from class Cat. If Cat has a class variable, then Persian has the *same* class variable and value, i.e. if an instance of Persian modifies it, then instances of all subclasses of Cat will refer to that new value.

On the other hand, if Cat has a class instance variable, then all subclasses of Cat (including Persian) have their own copy of that variable and therefore can have their own private values.

Although there are not many examples of the use of class instance variables in VisualWorks, there is one which is a good example: class UILookPolicy. This class is an abstract superclass for classes that emulate the 'look and feel' of various window managers; its subclasses provide specific emulation for Macintosh, Windows, Motif or MS-Windows. It introduces three class instance variables: systemAttributes, systemWidgetAttributes and useSystemFontOnWidgets. Each of its subclasses initialize these variables in their respective class initialize methods to provide class-specific values. It is important to note that the class instance variables can only be accessed by class methods.

Exercise 12.8

Open a Hierarchy Browser on class UILookPolicy. Browse references to the class instance variables mentioned above. Where are they initialized?

Exercise 12.9

Open a Browser on all those classes that contain class instance variables. *Hint*: The following code returns *true* if the receiver has a class instance variable.

```
aClass class instVarNames isEmpty not
```

12.4 Pool variables

A *pool variable* is a variable whose scope is a defined subset of classes. Pool variables are stored in *pool dictionaries* (instances of PoolDictionary) – collections of name/value associations. The variables in a pool dictionary can be made accessible to any class by declaring the pool dictionary in the pool dictionary list of the class definition. Smalltalk, the dictionary of global variables, is itself a pool dictionary that is globally accessible. The class variables of a class are also stored in a pool dictionary that is accessible to the class, its subclass, and instances of the same. However, unlike class variables, pool variables can be referenced by classes outside the same subtree of the class hierarchy.

The purpose of a pool dictionary is to provide quick access to the contents of the dictionary, bypassing the usual dictionary lookup mechanism (see Chapter 14). One common use of pool variables is as a means of providing application-specific constants.

For example, the pool dictionary TextConstants is shared by all classes that deal with the display of text (including classes Text, ParagraphEditor and Composed-Text). It includes variables referring to basic character constants, providing the mapping from characters such as <tab>, <CR>, and <space> to their ASCII equivalents, allowing unprintable ASCII characters to be referenced by name.

For example, class Text declares the pool dictionary TextConstants in its class definition:

```
CharacterArray subclass: #Text
    instanceVariableNames: 'string runs'
    classVariableNames: ''
    poolDictionaries: 'TextConstants'
    category: 'Collections-Text'
```

The keys of the pool dictionary are referenced within Text methods as if they were global or class variables. For example, Figure 12.2 shows a method containing the

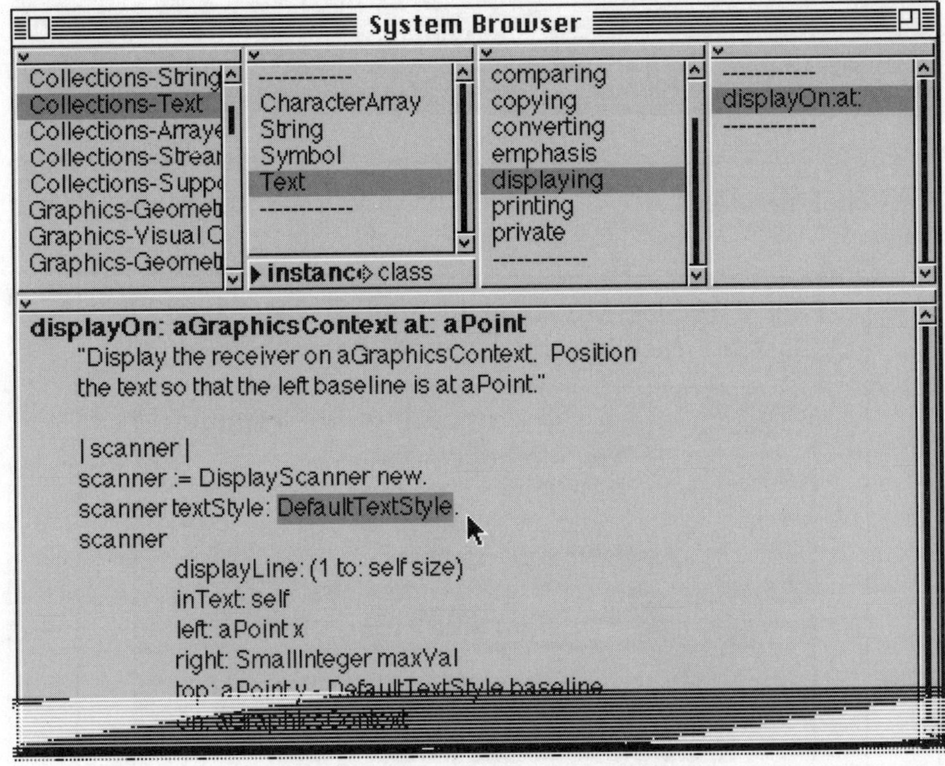

Figure 12.2 The pool variable **DefaultTextStyle** referenced in the method **displayOn:at:**in class **Text**.

pool variable DefaultTextStyle – one of the elements of the pool dictionary TextConstants.

Exercise 12.10

Inspect the pool dictionary TextConstants.

A new pool dictionary may be created by declaring the dictionary as a global variable. Pool variables may then be added to the dictionary using the message at: put:. For example:

```
Smalltalk at: #ExamplePoolDictionary put: PoolDictionary new.
```

(This creates a new global variable named ExamplePoolDictionary that refers to a new instance of PoolDictionary.)

```
ExamplePoolDictionary at: #ExamplePoolVariable put: someObject
```

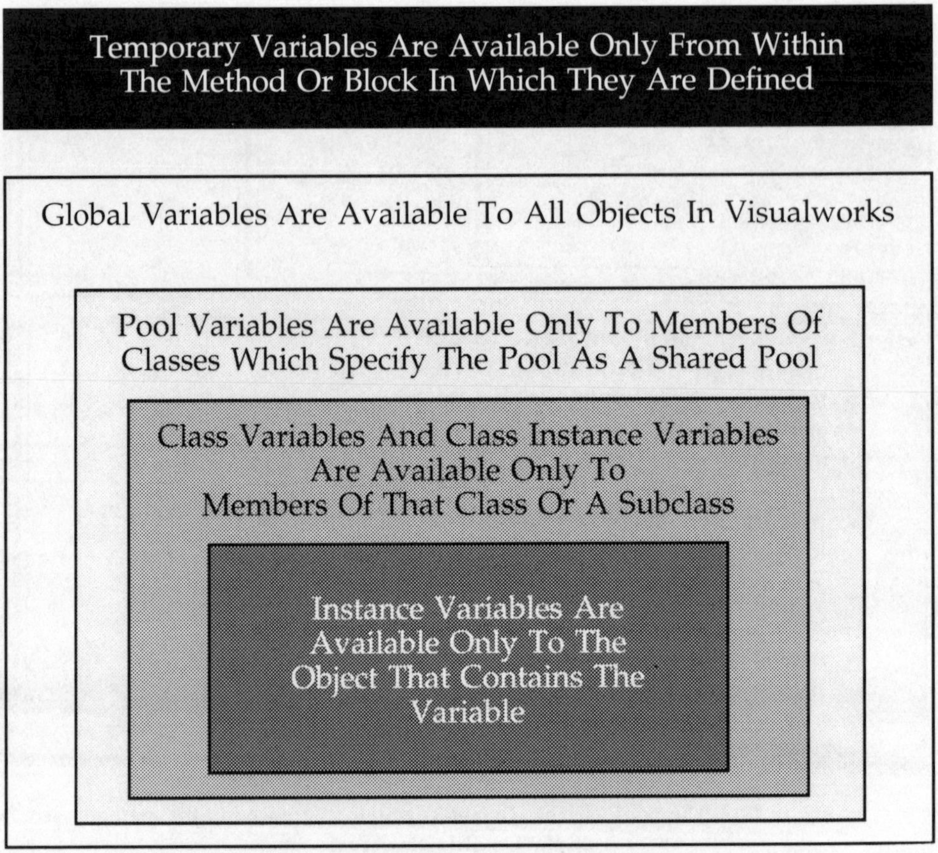

Temporary Variables Are Available Only From Within The Method Or Block In Which They Are Defined

Global Variables Are Available To All Objects In Visualworks

Pool Variables Are Available Only To Members Of Classes Which Specify The Pool As A Shared Pool

Class Variables And Class Instance Variables Are Available Only To Members Of That Class Or A Subclass

Instance Variables Are Available Only To The Object That Contains The Variable

Figure 12.3 The scope of the variables available in Smalltalk.

(This creates and adds a new pool variable named ExamplePoolVariable to the dictionary ExamplePoolDictionary.)

12.5 Summary of variable scope

We have now described all the types of variables available in Smalltalk: temporary, instance, class, pool, and global. Figure 12.3 provides a pictorial representation of variable scope.

Exercise 12.11

To see how scoping works, create a new class called Foo, and give it as many different variables of the same name as possible. (E.g. an instance variable named 'foo', a class variable named 'Foo'.) Also, add methods of the same name, perhaps including blocks which refer to their arguments by the same name!

12.6 Class protocol

When constructing a class, it is often difficult to arrive at a consistent naming convention for class protocols, but doing so is important so that your code structure is understandable to others. If you browse the VisualWorks image you will notice that some protocols become familiar. They are described below:

instance creation – This important protocol is very common. New instance creation methods to suit subclasses are frequently defined in order to initialize the new instance appropriately. Examples include those to create an instance from data in a stream (e.g. readFrom:).
class initialization – When a class has class variables, a class method (by convention, initialize) is required to set up the initial or default values of the variables.
examples – Helpful examples to explain the operation of a class are often provided. This is good practice.
documentation – Class methods solely for documentation are sometimes used. Generally, the class comment is a better place for this information. The method guideToDivision in class SmallInteger is an example of a class method provided solely as documentation (the documentation is in quotes and typically the last line of the method contains the expression ^self error: 'comment only').
accessing – Class methods to access class variables.
inquiries – General inquiries about information the class encapsulates are provided by many class methods. The method nameOfMonth: in class Date is an example (Figure 12.1).
instance management – A class may wish to provide some control over its instances, such as restricting the number or enforcing an ordering. The method currentWindow in class ScheduledWindow is an example.
private – Methods not for general use, provided to support the above protocols.

Exercise 12.12

Explore class Time. This class is a subclass of Magnitude. Note the class initialization and general enquires methods, and how they use the class variables. Try Time now.

12.7 Summary

Class variables, class instance variables and pool variables represent a group of variables whose access is shared by one or more classes. Of these variables, class variables are most often used, since they provide 'constants' shared by instances of a class and its subclasses. Because class instance variables are generally poorly understood – their scope is rather confusing – it's best to avoid them until you have more familiarity with Smalltalk. Pool variables, on the other hand, can be very useful as a means of providing access to constant values to a group of disjoint class hierarchies.

The grouping of class methods into protocols is generally a hit and miss affair – although most VisualWorks classes adhere to a common style (useful when searching for a class method in a Browser). We continue our examination of classes in the next chapter, paying close attention to two class hierarchies: headed by class Number and class Geometric.

13 Abstract superclasses

This chapter investigates the way in which common properties are held together in superclasses, and refined differently in subclasses. It also provides an introduction to the general notion of 'abstract superclasses', using examples from the Magnitude and Geometric hierarchies.

The chapter explores the Number hierarchy in some detail. The *coercion* mechanism for numbers is also outlined. The Geometric class hierarchy is also described, with class Rectangle receiving particular attention.

13.1 Introduction

An *abstract superclass* is a class with one or more subclasses, which itself does not have sufficient functionality to make instances of it useful. The intention is to capture some common aspects of its subclasses, rather than having the functionality duplicated in several (sub)classes. Subclasses that are not abstract are commonly called 'concrete'.

For example, note the way in which only some of the inequality tests are implemented in Date (look in protocol comparing); all others are implemented using methods in Magnitude (Figure 13.1). This mechanism makes extensive use of messages to self. You can also regard class Object as an abstract superclass for all classes in Smalltalk – instances of Object are seldom useful (except occasionally for testing purposes).

This chapter concentrates on two very important abstract superclasses: Number and Geometric.

13.2 The Number hierarchy

The numeric system of VisualWorks is quite extensive and flexible. It already possesses several useful number classes, and a general conversion mechanism to perform operations on disparate classes of number.

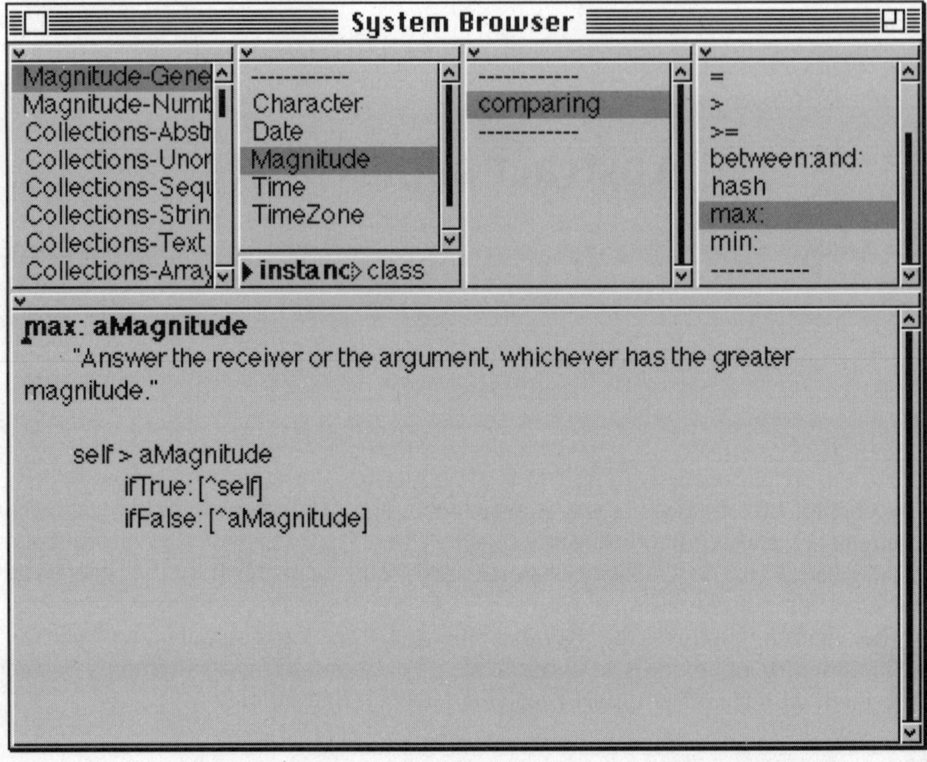

Figure 13.1 Class **Magnitude** captures common *comparison* aspects of its subclasses.

ArithmeticValue

Class ArithmeticValue represents the behavior necessary to perform arithmetic. It is a subclass of Magnitude and therefore inherits some equality/inequality properties. ArithmeticValue adds protocols such as arithmetic, mathematical functions, testing, and rounding. Nevertheless, the key methods respond with:

```
^self subclassResponsibility
```

The method named subclassResponsibility is implemented in class Object (Figure 13.2). This sets up a framework for the behavior of the class's subclasses, raising an error indicating that a subclass should have implemented this method.

The ArithmeticValue class hierarchy is as follows (abstract superclasses are underlined):

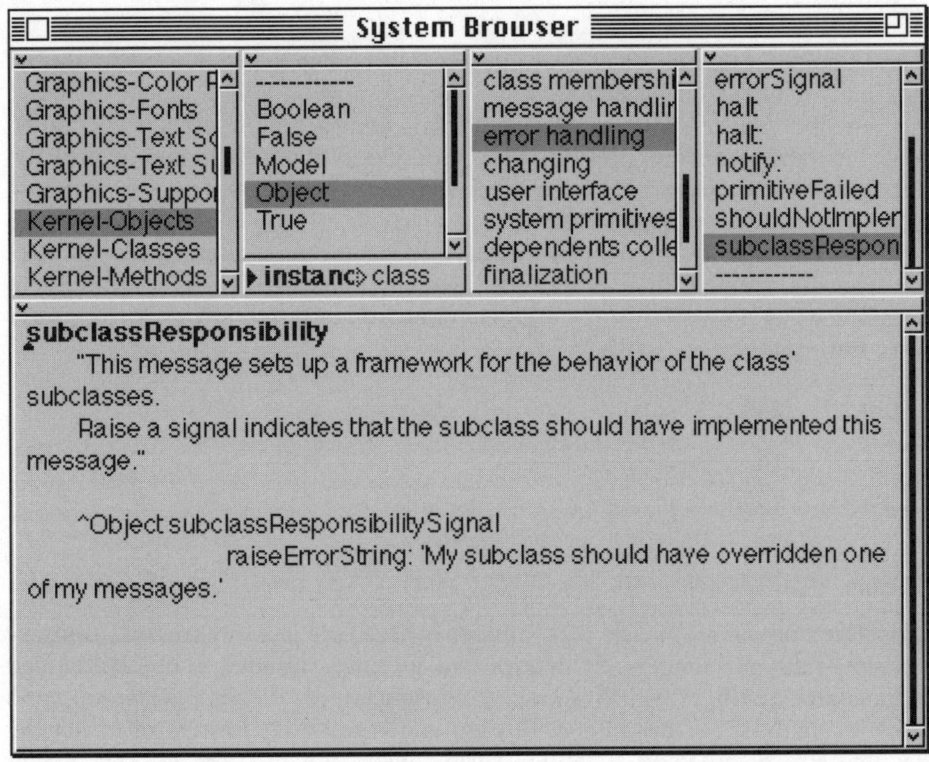

Figure 13.2 The implementation of the **subclassResponsibility** method.

```
Object
    Magnitude
        ArithmeticValue
            Number
                Fraction
                Integer
                    LargeInteger
                        LargeNegativeInteger
                        LargePositiveInteger
                    SmallInteger
                LimitedPrecisionReal
                    Double
                    Float
                FixedPoint
```

Number

Class Number represents scalar quantities, corresponding to real numbers. Number adds many mathematical functions which are only appropriate for scalar values. It also redefines arithmetic operators, and adds testing abilities (even and odd), truncation and rounding (ceiling, floor, rounded, truncated), and conversion messages both to convert to other classes of number and also to convert from degrees to radians and vice versa.

No specific methods are needed to create an instance of a number because they are typically created by calculations involving literals. However, there are occasions when it's useful to create a Number from a different base or in power form. For example:

```
16rff      255
2r1111     15
123e3      123000
```

Fraction

Class Fraction is a subclass of Number whose instances represent arbitrary precision rational numbers. It defines two instance variables – numerator and denominator (both of which should be instances of Integer subclasses), and redefines methods for arithmetic, testing, and truncation. Results of arithmetic functions are returned in fractional form, unless the message asFloat is sent explicitly. For example, evaluating the expression:

```
3 / 4
```

returns the result (3/4).

Integer

Class Integer is the abstract superclass representing integer arithmetic implementations. Methods in class Integer provide nearly all the functionality for integer operations, but the basic arithmetic operations are implemented in subclasses. The class redefines methods for arithmetic, testing and comparing, and adds factorization methods (factorial, greatest common denominator – gcd:, lowest common multiple – lcm:).

SmallInteger

Class SmallInteger represents integers sufficiently small to be represented directly by the virtual machine. Consequently, almost all of its methods are 'primitives' –

i.e. executed directly by the virtual machine. The boundaries between SmallInteger and larger integers occur at $2^{29}-1$ and -2^{29}.

LargeInteger

Class LargeInteger acts as an abstract superclass for classes LargePositiveInteger and LargeNegativeInteger to represent arbitrary precision integers. It is a subclass of Integer, and introduces little extra behavior. Large integers have no size limit (other than those imposed by memory constraints).

LimitedPrecisionReal

Class LimitedPrecisionReal is an abstract superclass for different kinds of 'floating-point' numbers.

Float

Class Float is a subclass of LimitedPrecisionReal and most of its methods for arithmetic, mathematical functions, comparing and truncating are implemented as primitives. Instances of Float represent 'short' (single-precision) floating-point numbers between 10^{38} and -10^{38}. Class Float also introduces Pi and RadiansPerDegree class variables as constants. Example instances of Float are:

```
123.456     10.0   -456.123
```

Double

Class Double is also a subclass of LimitedPrecisionReal, similar to class Float except that its instances represent 'long' (double-precision) floating-point numbers between 10^{307} and -10^{307}. Class Double also has class variables representing Pi and RadiansPerDegree. To force the compiler to recognize numbers as instances of Double, it is necessary to suffix the number with the letter 'd', for example:

```
123.456d
```

FixedPoint

Class FixedPoint represents numbers with arbitrary precision before the decimal point but limited precision after it (often used in business calculations). A prime example of their use is in representing currency values, which are always rounded off to the nearest hundredth, but which could easily have more digits than a Float (or a Double) could represent accurately. To create an instance of FixedPoint, it is necessary to suffix the number with the letter 'f', for example:

```
123.456f
```

Table 13.1

Class	Description
Magnitude	Linear Dimension
ArithmeticValue	Primitive Arithmetic
Number	Represents scalar quantities
LimitedPrecisionReal	Abstract superclass for various implementations of Real numbers
Float	Single Precision
Double	Double Precision
Fraction	A Rational number as a Fraction
Integer	Abstract superclass for integer implementation
FixedPoint	Represents 'business' numbers

In summary, the class hierarchy may be described as in Table 13.1. It is quite possible to add further subclasses to this hierarchy, for example Complex, Infinity and Infinitesimal.

Common messages

The typical arithmetic and mathematical operators of interest are described in Table 13.2. Most of the messages are understood by all number classes, those that aren't should be obvious. It is possible to optimize much of your 'number-crunching' code by careful selection of number classes. Techniques for optimization are considered briefly later in this chapter.

Coercion

If two objects involved in a mathematical operation are of different number classes, one must be converted to assure correct results. In Smalltalk, this process is called *coercion*. The coercion process has three steps:

1. The operation fails because of differing classes of operands.
2. Determine which operand is of the most general class (called *highest generality*).
3. Convert all operands to that class. (If one or more operands have to be coerced for the successful completion of the operation, then this is obviously compute-intensive.)

The generality of a number class is determined with the help of a method to which all numbers must respond, generality. This message returns an integer indicating a level of generality for that particular number class. SmallIntegers are of low generality, but Doubles are of high generality, since almost all numbers can be represented as a Double. Table 13.3 shows the subclasses of Number followed by their generality.

Exercise 13.1

Review the Magnitude, ArithmeticValue and Number hierarchy. There is a huge amount of functionality in this hierarchy, and you are advised to spend some time becoming familiar with these classes.

Exercise 13.2

Look at the different implementations of methods such as + and // in the hierarchy.

Exercise 13.3

Open an Inspector on an instance of Float. Send the message + 3.0 to self. What is the result? Try again, but use super rather than self.

Exercise 13.4

Why is raisedTo: implemented in the instance protocol of Number, even though it performs differently depending on the class of the receiver? How does raisedToInteger: work?

Exercise 13.5

Bit manipulation methods are defined for Integer (e.g. bitAnd:), and redefined in SmallInteger – why?

Exercise 13.6

Consider adding class methods to classes Float, Double or LimitedPrecisionReal to answer other (useful) constants when appropriate messages are received.

13.3 The Geometric hierarchy

The Geometric class hierarchy represents 'shapes' in two-dimensional space, such as line segment, circle, or rectangle. This notion is represented by the abstract class

Table 13.2

Message	Description	Examples	Result
+ - * /	Simple arithmetic	10 - 3 10/3	7 (10/3)
//	Integer divide	10 // 3	3
\\	Modulo	10 \\ 3	1
quo:	Truncated division, returns the integer portion of the quotient	10 quo: 3	3
rem:	Returns the remainder from a division	10 rem: 3	1
raisedToInteger:		10 raisedToInteger:3	1000
raisedTo:	Or use **	10 raisedTo: 1/3	(1/1000)
squared		10 squared	100
ln exp log	Power	10 ln 10 exp 10 log	2.30259 22026.5 1.0
sin cos tan	Trigonometric functions	10 sin 10 cos 10 tan	−0.544021 −0.839071 0.648361
arcSin arcCos arcTan	Transcendental	0.5 arcSin 0.5 arcCos 0.5 arcTan	0.523599 1.0472 0.463648
ceiling floor rounded truncated	Truncating	10 sin ceiling 10 sin floor 10 sin rounded 10 sin truncated	0 −1 −1 0
abs	Absolute	10 sin abs	0.544021
negated	Negate the receiver	10 sin negated	0.544021
reciprocal	Return the reciprocal of the receiver	10 sin reciprocal	−1.83816
positive	Test if receiver is >= 0	10 positive 0 positive	true true
strictlyPositive	Test if receiver is > 0	10 strictlyPositive 0 strictlyPositive	true false
negative	Test if receiver is < 0	10 negative	false
even	Test if receiver is even	10 even	true
odd	Test if receiver is odd	10 odd	false

Table 13.2 (cont.)

Message	Description	Examples	Result
isInteger	Test class of receiver	10 isInteger 10.0 isInteger	true false
isZero	Test if receiver is zero	10 isZero 0 isZero	false true
asInteger	Convert receiver to integer	10 asInteger 10.0 asInteger	10 10
asFloat	Convert receiver to float	10 asFloat 10.0 asFloat	10.0 10.0
asDouble	Convert receiver to double	10 asDouble 10.0 asDouble	10.0d 10.0d
asRational	Convert receiver to rational (fraction)	10 sin asRational	(−586822/ 1078675)
asCharacter	Convert receiver to character	65 asCharacter	$A
printStringRadix:	Print the integer in specified base	10 printStringRadix:2	'1010'

Table 13.3

Class	Generality
Double	90
Float	80
FixedPoint	70
Fraction	60
Integer	40
SmallInteger	20

Geometric, which provides almost all default behavior for its subclasses. In this respect the approach taken by the Geometric class hierarchy is different to that provided by the Number class hierarchy; most of the methods in class Geometric contain default (non-optimal) code for a *generic* shape (rather than subclassResponsibility). Subclasses of Geometric may provide their own (optimal) methods to override those provided by their superclass. However, for some methods it is not possible to provide a default method. In these cases, there is not an alternative to the use of the subclassResponsibility route.

It should be noted that these entities cannot be displayed directly, since they have no visual properties such as color or line thickness. However, as we shall see later (Chapter 20), it is possible to contain a Geometric in an appropriate 'wrapper', enabling it to play the role of a graphical object.

The class hierarchy is as follows:

```
Object
  Geometric
      Bezier
      Circle
      EllipticalArc
      LineSegment
      Polyline
      Rectangle
      Spline
```

Exercise 13.7

Compare the 'shape' of the Number and Geometric class hierarchies. Give at least two features that distinguish them.

We now briefly describe some of the Geometric classes.

Geometric

As an abstract class, class Geometric provides the minimum message interface to which all its subclasses must conform. It includes the following:

bounds	Answers a rectangle that bounds the coordinate region used by the receiver. Also commonly called its "bounding box".
outlineIntersects:	Answers whether the receiver's perimeter intersects the perimeter of the argument (a Rectangle).
regionIntersects:	Answer whether the receiver's area intersects the area of the argument (a Rectangle).
scaledBy:	Answer a new instance scaled by the argument, which can be a Point or a scalar.
translatedBy:	Answer a new instance translated by the argument, which can be a Point or a scalar.

Circles

Class Circle represents circular areas, and defines two instance variables: center (a Point) and radius (a Number). Instances can be created using:

```
Circle center: 100@100 radius: 50
```

Accessing methods allow the center, radius, diameter, and area to be returned. Otherwise, most methods provide an optimal re-implementation of those defined in the superclass.

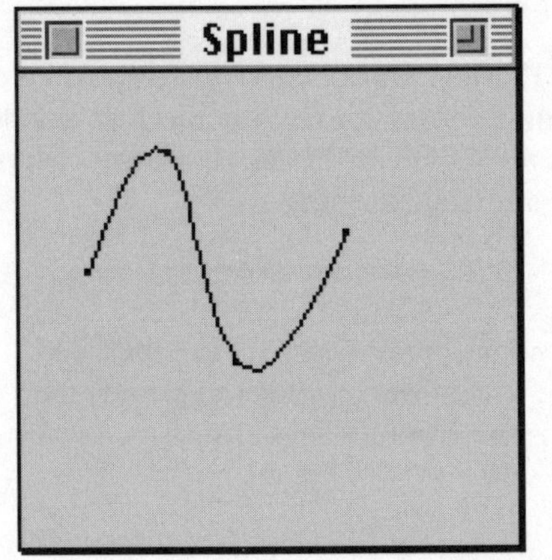

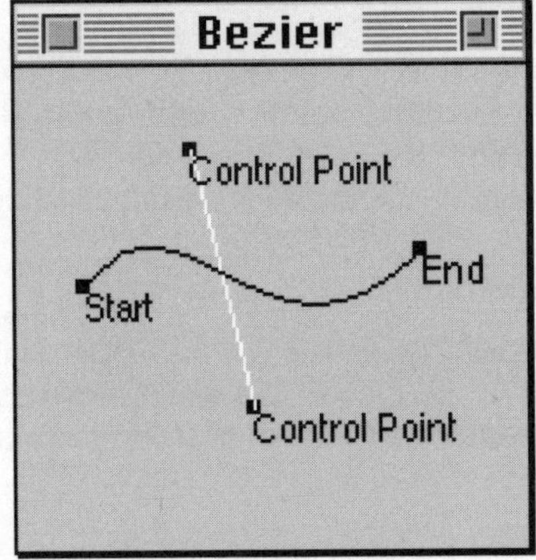

Figures 13.3 and 13.4 Comparison of a Spline and Bezier Curve.

Ellipses

Elliptical areas, and ellipses and circles, are represented by instances of EllipticalArc. Instance creation and accessing methods compatible with those of Circle are provided, but further methods allow the 'start' and 'sweep' angles to be defined. These angles, together with a Rectangle bounding the ellipse, are retained by instance variables.

Straight lines

Straight lines are represented by class LineSegment. This defines two instance variables start and end, both Points.

A LineSegment can be asked for its length which may then be compared to that of other LineSegments via usual operators (=, <). It can perform scaling (scaledBy:) and translation (translatedBy:). Instances can be created using:

```
LineSegment from: 10@10 to: 120@130
LineSegment with: 10@10 with: 120@130.
```

Methods for accessing the start and end Points are also provided.

Polygons

Arbitrary polygons and 'polylines' are represented by class Polyline. This defines a single instance variable vertices, which retains an Array of Points, of size three or more. Instances of Polyline can be created by:

```
Polyline vertices: (Array with: 10@10 with: 120@130 with: 120@10).
```

Curves

Two kinds of 'curve' are provided by the classes Spline and Bezier. A Spline is similar to a Polyline in that it connects a collection of vertices; the difference is that a Spline smoothes the corners (see Figure 13.3). A Bezier curve has a start, an end and two control points – each control point exerts gravity on the line segment connecting the start and end (see Figure 13.4). Both curve classes support comparison, intersection, testing, scaling, and transforming.

Exercise 13.8

Browse class Geometric and the subclasses mentioned previously. Try to understand how the concrete subclasses and the abstract superclass work together to provide the functionality.

Exercise 13.9

Try some examples of Circles and EllipticalArcs. Also, browse these classes, and look at the way in which the startAngle and sweepAngle methods are implemented. Why isn't one a subclass of the other?

Exercise 13.10

Try some examples of the transforming and testing methods for the various Geometric subclasses. Consider adding some more methods in the converting protocols of the classes, so that it is possible to convert from a Spline to a Bezier (for example).

Rectangles

Class Rectangle represents rectangular areas, with the sides always horizontal and vertical. Class Rectangle is the most widely used Geometric subclass. It is used in the user interface to indicate the sizes of windows and panes.

We have already seen how class Point (see Chapter 8) represents the abstract notion of a location in two-dimensional space. In just the same way, class Rectangle represents a rectangular area in two-dimensional space. Class Rectangle is a subclass of Geometric, and defines just two instance variables: origin and corner. These are instances of Point, and represent the top-left and bottom-right corners respectively. Since rectangles always have sides that are parallel to the horizontal and vertical axes, this is enough to completely define a rectangular area.

As with most classes, new instances of class Rectangle can be created by sending the message new to that class. However, this answers with a Rectangle with both instance variables nil; this is not very useful. To allow initialized Rectangles to be created, several instance creation messages are provided, some of which are:

```
Rectangle origin: aPoint corner: anotherPoint
Rectangle origin: aPoint extent: anotherPoint
Rectangle vertex: vertexPoint1 vertex: vertexPoint2
Rectangle left: leftNumber
      right: rightNumber
```

```
      top: topNumber
      bottom: bottomNumber
  aPoint extent: anotherPoint
  aPoint corner: anotherPoint
```

Thus we can see that it is possible to use a number of different expressions to create an initialized Rectangle. For example, the following three message sequences give rise to equal Rectangles:

```
| r |
r := Rectangle new.
r origin: 2@2.
^r corner: 30@30.

^2@2 extent: 28@28

^2@2 corner: 30@30
```

The instance protocol of Rectangle is exhaustive, some of the most frequently used messages are described in Table 13.4.

It's important to note the difference between intersects: and intersect:; the former returns a Boolean indicating whether the receiver and the argument overlap, and the latter returns a Rectangle describing the area of overlap. For example:

```
(3 @ 1 corner: 5 @ 6) intersect: (1 @ 2 corner: 7 @ 5)
```

returns (3@2 corner: 5@5) (see Figure 13.5).

Exercise 13.11

Browse class Rectangle (category Graphics-Geometry). Try some of the instance creation methods mentioned above, and any others you might discover in the class protocol.

Exercise 13.12

You may also like to consider how self is used in the instance creation methods. Where is the new message interpreted?

Exercise 13.13

What is returned from the expression rect1 intersect: rect2 if the areas of rect1 and rect2 do not overlap?

Exercise 13.14

Compare the effects of Rectangle fromUser with Rectangle fromUser: aPoint.

Table 13.4

Accessing	
origin: aPoint corner: anotherPoint	Set the origin and the corner of the receiver
origin: aPoint extent: anotherPoint	Set the origin and the extent of the receiver
origin: aPoint	Set the origin of the receiver
corner: aPoint	Set the corner of the receiver
origin	Return the origin of the receiver
corner	Return the corner of the receiver
left, right, top, bottom, etc.	Return the appropriate number
center	Return the center of the receiver
extent, width, height	Return the extent of the receiver (a Point), its width or height (respectively)
Testing	
= aRectangle	Returns a Boolean indicating whether the receiver is equal to the argument
contains: aRectangle	Returns a Boolean indicating whether the argument is contained in the receiver
containsPoint: aPoint	Returns a Boolean indicating whether the argument is contained in the receiver
intersects: aRectangle	Returns a Boolean indicating whether the argument intersects with the receiver
Functions	
scaledBy: aPointOrNumber	Returns a new Rectangle scaled by the argument
translatedBy: aPointOrNumber	Returns a new Rectangle translated by the argument
intersect: aRectangle	Returns a new Rectangle that is the intersection of the receiver and the argument
areasOutside: aRectangle	Returns a collection of Rectangles describing the difference between the receiver and the argument
merge: aRectangle	Returns a new Rectangle that is a merger of the receiver and the argument
insetBy: aRectangleOrPointOrNumber	Returns a new Rectangle that is inset by the argument
expandedBy; aRectangleOrPointOrNumber	Returns a new Rectangle that is expanded by the argument
area	Returns the area of the receiver
moveBy: aPointOrNumber	Moves the origin and corner of the receiver by the argument
moveTo: aPoint	Moves the origin and corner of the receiver to the argument

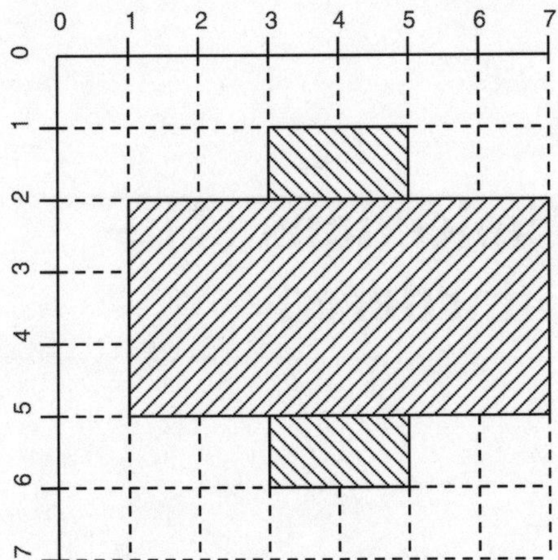

Figure 13.5 A visualisation of the expression (3@1 corner: 5@6) intersect: (1@2 corner: 7@5).

Exercise 13.15

We have already seen how class Point could have a different internal representation (Chapter 8), while retaining the same message interface. Consider the internal structure of class Rectangle in this light. Are alternative representations possible?

Exercise 13.16

You might like to try implementing a new class, NewRectangle, with a different internal representation (e.g. instance variable centre, height, width, or keep top-right and bottom-left corners), but which retains the same message interface as Rectangle.

13.4 Summary

Although Number and Geometric both act as abstract superclasses, the class hierarchies they head have very different patterns. The Number hierarchy appears as a fairly deep 'tree' containing intermediate abstract superclasses, whereas the Geometric hierarchy is completely 'flat'. The Number hierarchy, in particular, is crucial to VisualWorks – without the ability to represent numbers, VisualWorks would cease to function. However, of the Geometric hierarchy, only class Rectangle is really necessary (to represent the bounds of panes and windows).

In the following two chapters we continue our examination of 'crucial' Smalltalk classes: those that represent collections of one form or another. We begin by looking at collections in general and then describe specific classes and the behavior that they provide.

14 Collections (1) – unordered

This chapter describes the abstract superclass Collection, the root of a hierarchy of interesting classes that roughly correspond to the traditional data structures common in procedural languages. We demonstrate the behavior of Collections with examples that use class Set – a subclass of Collection. The examples demonstrate the creation of new instances, their access and enumeration.

We specifically describe *unordered collections* in this chapter, including classes Set, Dictionary and Bag, illustrating their use with examples. Subclasses of Dictionary, specifically IdentityDictionary and SystemDictionary, are also considered.

14.1 Introduction

A collection is simply a 'bunch' of objects. In most conventional languages, the *array* is the only sort of collection that is provided, and anything else must be implemented by the programmer. Additionally, most of these languages deal with collections containing only a single *type* of data.

In Smalltalk, the situation is different. A collection may be an instance of any of a number of available classes. Also, each Smalltalk collection may simultaneously contain objects of many different classes. For instance, a collection might contain Strings, Numbers, other collections, or even more complex structures as its elements. The behavior of the collection is independent of its elements.

There are two main kinds of collection: the first, called an *unordered* collection, does not refer to its elements based on a numeric index; the second, called a *sequenceable collection*, supports the notion of having an order associated with the elements and uses a numeric index to locate them. This chapter will examine unordered collections and Chapter 15 will concentrate on sequenceable collections.

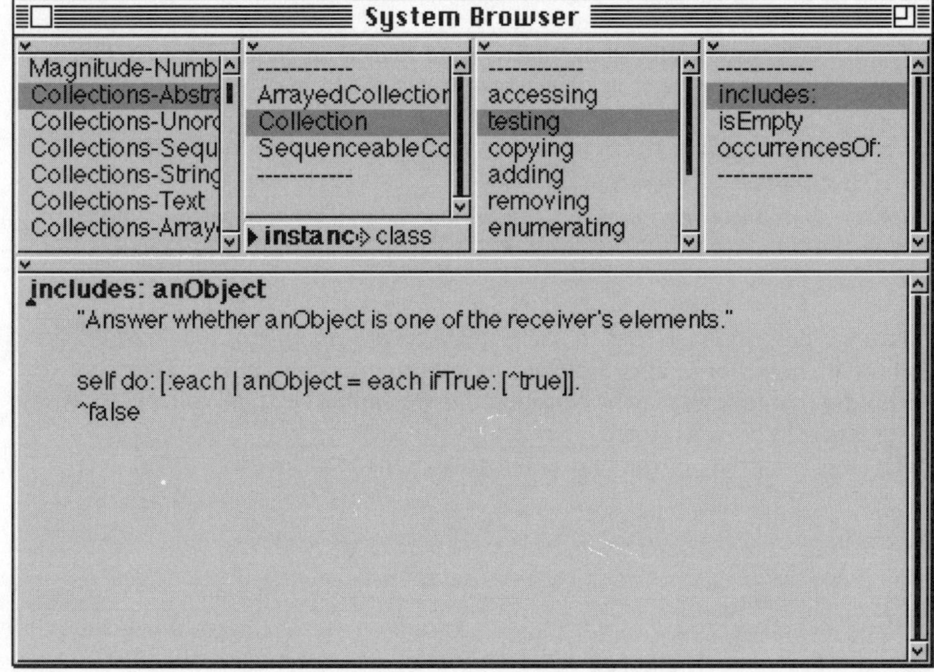

Figure 14.1 The **includes:** method implemented in class **Collection**.

14.2 Class Collection

The class Collection is an *abstract superclass* (see Chapter 13) of all the collection classes, and it therefore includes methods to provide the behavior shared by all its subclasses. For example, Figure 14.1 shows the implementation of the includes: method. Additional protocol is implemented by subclasses of Collection to support operations suitable only for that class (see later and Chapter 15). Class Collection is *unordered* – a property shared by its *concrete* subclasses (Table 14.1).

14.3 Unordered collections

There are three primary examples of unordered collections. The first, class Set, is of interest whenever membership information is of primary importance. The second, class Dictionary, is a subclass of Set whose elements are associations of two objects: a key and a value. The third, class Bag, is of interest whenever a tally of occurrences is required.

Table 14.1

Set	A Set contains all the objects put into it, in any order. Duplicates are not kept; adding equal objects many times results in only one such object in the Set.
Bag	A Bag contains all the objects put into it, in no particular order. Duplicate objects are permitted.
Dictionary	A Dictionary contains a Set of Associations between pairs of objects.

Here we describe class Set in some detail as *an example of a collection*, since much of its behavior is also provided by other collection classes. Therefore, the description that follows may be considered to be applicable to all collection classes, except where otherwise stated.

The class hierarchy of the unordered collections is as follows:

```
Object
    Collection
        Bag
        Set
            Dictionary
```

As mentioned earlier, a Set is a way of keeping information about simple groupings of objects. A Set keeps *exactly one copy* of any particular object in it. A Set can contain any number of objects, and the number can vary as needed. No explicit count need be kept by the programmer.

14.4 Creating instances of collections

We have already seen how to create instances of String and Array as literals (see Chapter 3). Other sorts of collections can be created by sending new or new: to the appropriate class. For example:

```
Set new: 5
```

creates a new Set of size five (all the elements are nil).

The new message by default creates a Set of size two; it will *grow* in size when necessary. (By default, most other collections have an initial size of 10.)

Initialized instances can be created using with:, with:with:, etc. For example:

```
Set with: 40 with: 2
```

creates a new Set with the two elements 40 and 2. This technique can be used to specify up to four arguments:

```
Set with: obj1
Set with: obj1 with: obj2
Set with: obj1 with: obj2 with: obj3
Set with: obj1 with: obj2 with: obj3 with: obj4
```

There are also several conversion messages (to convert a collection from one class to another) which are also useful when creating instances; these are considered in the next chapter.

14.5 Accessing elements of a collection

All subclasses of Collection behave in a similar way. For example, most provide mechanisms for adding, removing and testing.

Adding

Any object may be added to a collection using the add: message (Figure 14.2); its argument is the object to be added. It's important to note that the argument is returned from these messages, *not* the receiver. For example:

```
| set |
set := Set new.
set add: 'a'.
set add: 5.
^set
```

produces a Set containing 'a' and 5.

Often we wish to combine two collections; the addAll: message provides this functionality, adding the elements of the argument to the receiver. This is equivalent to *set union*. For example:

```
(Set with: 2 with: 3) addAll: (Set with: 4 with: 5)
```

produces a Set containing the SmallIntegers 2, 3, 4, and 5.

Removing

To remove an object from a collection, send the collection the message remove: – the argument is the object to be removed. An error will be raised if the argument is not present in the receiver. The message remove:ifAbsent: can be used to avoid this possible outcome; the second argument is a block which is evaluated if the first

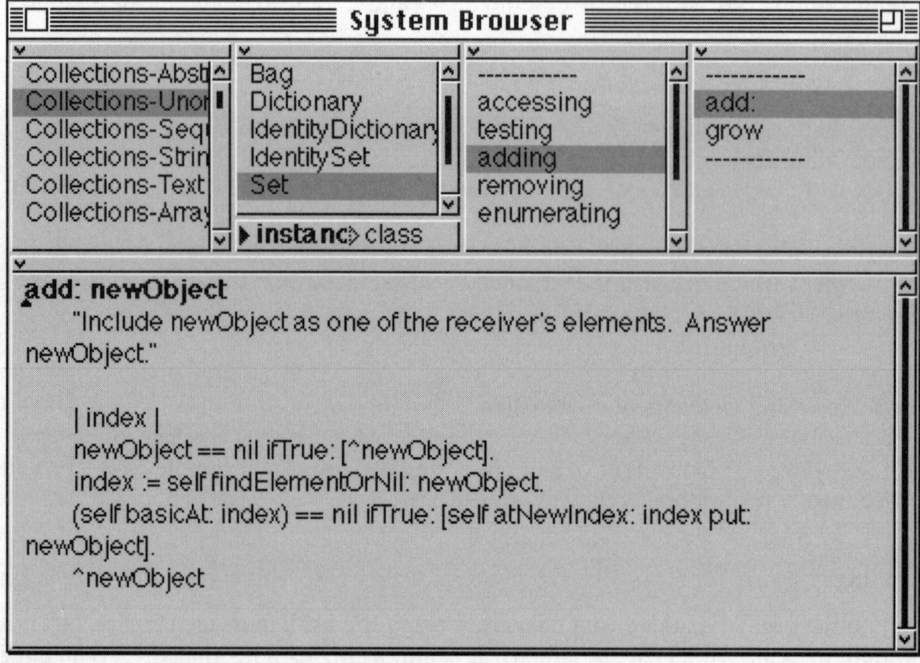

Figure 14.2 The **add:** method in class **Set**.

argument is absent. The two message sequences below use the remove: message to exemplify the difference between the add: and addAll: messages.

```
| set |
set := Set new.
set add: 'a'.
set add: 5.
set addAll: (Set with: 1 with: 3 with: 4).
set remove: 1.
^set
```

produces a Set containing the elements 'a', 3, 4, and 5 (i.e. Set ('a' 3 5 4)), whereas

```
| set |
set := Set new.
set add: 'a'.
set add: 5.
set add: (Set with: 1 with: 3 with: 4).
set remove: 1.
^set
```

causes an error because the temporary variable set refers to a Set containing three elements – Set ('a' 5 Set (1 3 4)) – one of which is another Set containing the element to be removed. The temporary variable set does not itself contain 1.

There are two messages which may be used to remove a *collection* of elements from another collection. The first, removeAll:, requires that all the elements of the argument be present in the receiver. Alternatively, the binary message (only applicable to class Set and its subclasses) answers those elements present in the receiver and absent from the argument – i.e. *set subtraction*. For example, the message sequence

```
| set |
set := Set new.
set add: 'a'.
set add: 5.
set addAll: (Set with: 1 with: 3 with: 4).
set removeAll: (Set with: 'a' with: 'b' with: 'c').
^set
```

results in an error, because not all the elements of the argument to the removeAll: message are present in the receiver. However, the similar message sequence

```
| set |
set := Set new.
set add: 'a'.
set add: 5.
set addAll: (Set with: 1 with: 3 with: 4).
set - (Set with: 'a' with: 'b' with: 'c').
^set
```

succeeds, returning a Set containing the elements 1, 3, 4, and 5 (i.e. Set (1 3 4 5)).

Enquiries

There are two general enquiry messages to which all collections will respond. The first of these is occurrencesOf:, which responds with the number of elements in the receiver which are equal to the argument. The second is size, which responds with the number of (non-nil) elements of the receiver. For example, the size of an empty set is 0, but the size of a Set containing an empty Set is 1.

Testing

Additionally there are two testing messages understood by all collection classes. The first of these, isEmpty, responds with a Boolean indicating whether there is at least one (non-nil) element in the receiver. The includes: message also responds

Table 14.2

collect: aBlock	Evaluates aBlock for each element. Answers with a collection of the same size, with the *result of the evaluation of the block for each element.*
select: aBlock	Evaluates aBlock for each element. Answers with a collection containing the elements of the receiver *selected when aBlock evaluated to true* (the collection may be empty).
reject: aBlock	Evaluates aBlock for each element. Answers with a collection containing the elements of the receiver *selected when aBlock evaluated to false* (i.e. the complement of select:).
detect: aBlock	Evaluates aBlock for each element. Answers with the *first element for which aBlock evaluates to true*. Alternatively, the message detect:ifNone: may be used; the second argument is a block which is evaluated if no elements of the receiver match the criteria specified in the first argument, otherwise detect: responds with an error.
inject: an Object into: aBlock	Accumulates a running value associated with evaluating the argument, aBlock, with the current value *and* the receiver as block arguments. The initial value is the value of the argument, anObject.
do: aBlock	Evaluates aBlock for each of the elements in the receiver.

with a Boolean, indicating that there is at least one element in the receiver that is equal to the message argument.

The includes: message may be used to reiterate the difference between the add: and the addAll: messages. Only the second of the following two message sequences returns true.

```
| set |
set := Set new.
set add: 'a'.
set add: 5.
set add: (Set with: 1 with: 3 with: 4).
^set includes: 1
```

```
| set |
set := Set new.
set add: 'a'.
set add: 5.
set addAll: (Set with: 1 with: 3 with: 4).
^set includes: 1
```

Enumerating

There are a number of messages that may be used to enumerate over a collection. The first three messages described in Table 14.2 answer with a new collection 'just

Table 14.3

(Set with: 1 with: 3 with: 4) collect: [:each | each factorial]	Set (1 24 6)
(Set with: 1 with: 3 with: 4) collect:[:each | each >=3]	Set (false true).
(Set with: 1 with: 3 with: 4) select:[:each | each >=3]	Set (3 4)
(Set with: 1 with: 3 with: 4) select:[:each | each > 4]	Set (), i.e. an empty Set.
(Set with: 1 with: 3 with: 4) reject:[:each | each >=3]	Set (1).
(Set with: 1 with: 3 with: 4) detect:[:each | each >=3]	3.
(Set with: 1 with: 3 with: 4) detect: [:each | each > 4] ifNone:['Not found']	'Not found'.
(Set with: 1 with: 3 with: 4) inject: 0 into:[:sum :each | sum + each]	8
(Set with: 1 with: 3 with: 4) inject: 0 into:[:max :each | max max: each]	4 1
(Set with: 1 with: 3 with: 4) do: [:each | Transcript show: each factorial printString; cr]	6 24
(Set with: 65 with: 66 with: 67) do: [:each | Transcript show: each asCharacter printString; cr].	$A $B $C

like the receiver'. The elements of this new collection depend on the criteria specified in the argument. The example expressions in Table 14.3 demonstrate the use of the messages in Table 14.2.

Exercise 14.1

Try creating instances of Set and adding the same object several times. Inspect the contents.

Exercise 14.2

Write a sequence of expressions to find the average (mean) of a collection of numbers. What is the minimum number of expressions required to achieve this?

14.6 Class Dictionary

Class Dictionary is a subclass of Set and represents a set of Associations. An Association is a pair of objects, a key and a value. A Dictionary stores a set of Associations in a manner that allows retrieval of the value when the key is known. This is occasionally known as *attribute-value* pairing.

Although the elements in a Dictionary are unordered, each has a definite name or *key*. Thus, a Dictionary can be regarded as an unordered collection of values with external keys (unique).

Adding

Although it's possible to send the add: message to a Dictionary, this is rarely done in practice since the argument is expected to be an instance of Association (see Figure 14.3). The conventional approach is to use the at:put: message which takes two arguments: a *key* and a *value*, each of which may be any object.

Accessing

The most commonly used accessing message is the keyword message at: which returns the *value* associated with the argument. If there is no *key* equal to the

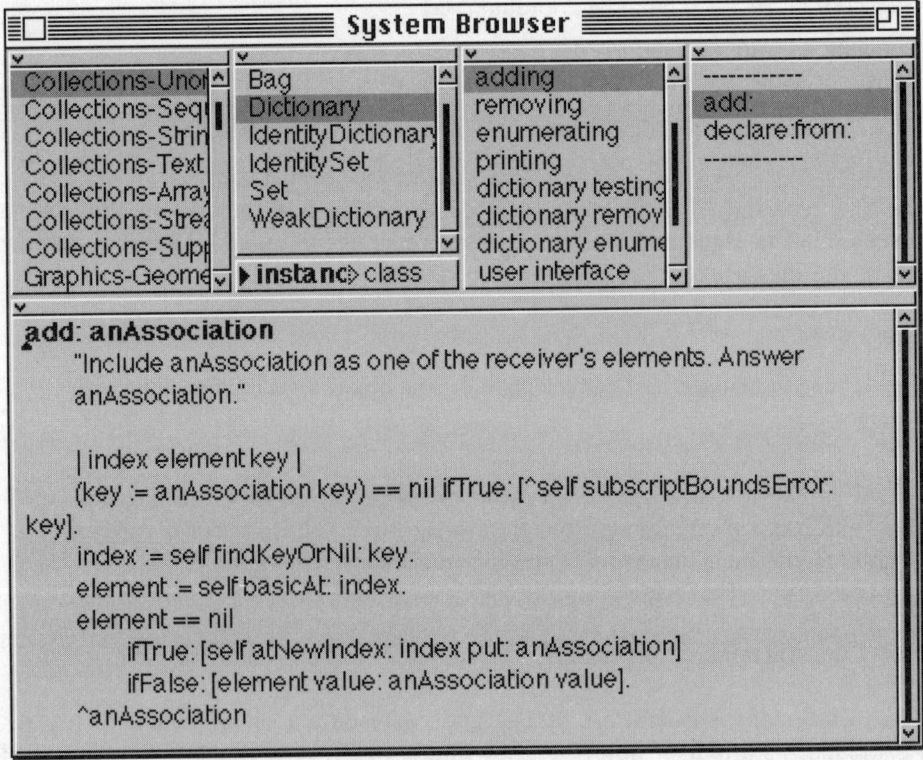

Figure 14.3 The **add:** method in class **Dictionary**.

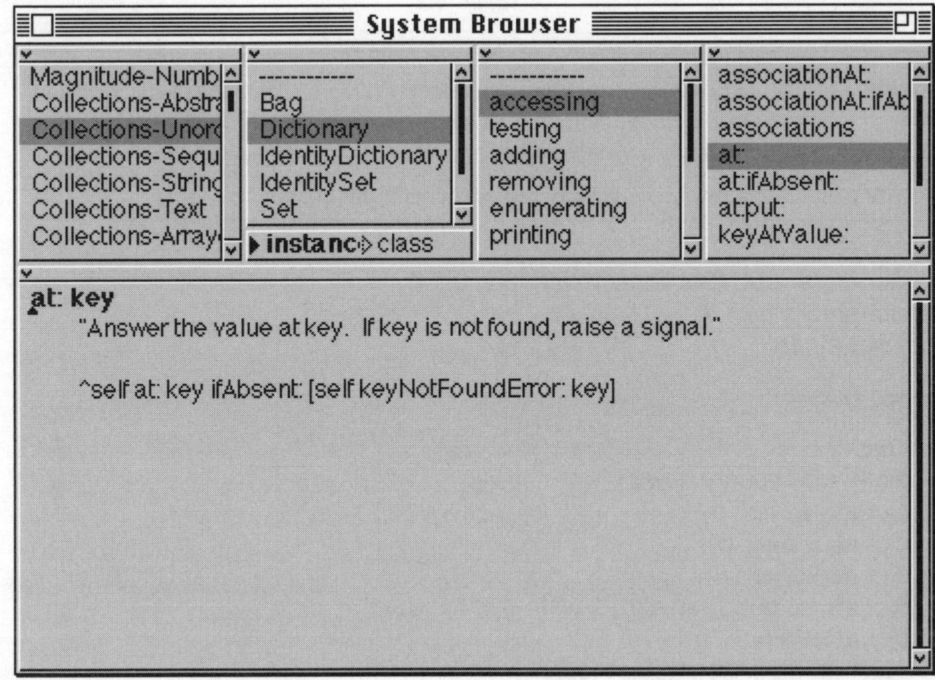

Figure 14.4 The implementation of **at:** in class **Dictionary**.

argument, then an error is raised. Alternatively, the message at:ifAbsent: may be used; the second argument (a block) is evaluated if no key is found

```
| dict |
dict := Dictionary new.
dict at: 'a' put: 1.
dict at: 5 put: 'b'.
dict at: $c put: 6.
dict at: 'a' put: (Set with: 1 with: 3 with: 4).
dict at: 3/4 put: 'b'.
^dict at: 'a'
```

returns Set (1 3 4).

```
| dict |
dict := Dictionary new.
dict at: 'a' put: 1.
dict at: 5 put: 'b'.
dict at: $c put: 6.
```

Table 14.4

keys	Answers with a Set of the keys from the receiver
values	Answers with an OrderedCollection (see Chapter 15) of the values in the receiver. Note that values are not necessarily unique
associationAt:	Answers with the Association given by the argument
keyAtValue:	Answers with a *key* associated with the argument

```
dict at: 'a' put: (Set with: 1 with: 3 with: 4).
dict at: 3/4 put: 'b'.
^dict at: $a
```

raises an error.

```
| dict |
dict := Dictionary new.
dict at: 'a' put: 1.
dict at: 5 put: 'b'.
dict at: $c put: 6.
dict at: 'a' put: (Set with: 1 with: 3 with: 4).
dict at: 3/4 put: 'b'.
^dict at: $a ifAbsent:['not found']
```

returns 'not found'.

Other Dictionary accessing messages are shown in Table 14.4. For example:

```
| dict |
dict := Dictionary new.
dict at: 'a' put: 1.
dict at: 5 put: 'b'.
dict at: $c put: 6.
dict at: 'a' put: (Set with: 1 with: 3 with: 4).
dict at: 3/4 put: 'b'.
^dict keys
```

returns Set ($c 'a' 5 (3/4)).

```
| dict |
dict := Dictionary new.
dict at: 'a' put: 1.
dict at: 5 put: 'b'.
dict at: $c put: 6.
dict at: 'a' put: (Set with: 1 with: 3 with: 4).
dict at: 3/4 put: 'b'.
^dict values
```

returns OrderedCollection ('b' 6 Set (1 3 4) 'b'). Class OrderedCollection is described in the next chapter.

```
| dict |
dict := Dictionary new.
dict at: 'a' put: 1.
dict at: 5 put: 'b'.
dict at: $c put: 6.
dict at: 'a' put: (Set with: 1 with: 3 with: 4).
dict at: 3/4 put: 'b'.
^dict keyAtValue: 'b'
```

raises an error because the Dictionary has two keys corresponding to the value 'b'.

Removing

The messages remove: and remove:ifAbsent: are not available for instances of Dictionary. Instead, the corresponding messages removeKey: and removeKey: ifAbsent: should be used. For example, the expressions:

```
| dict |
dict := Dictionary new.
dict at: 'a' put: 1.
dict at: 5 put: 'b'.
dict at: $c put: 6.
dict at: 'a' put: (Set with: 1 with: 3 with: 4).
dict at: 3/4 put: 'b'.
dict removeKey: 'a'.
^dict
```

returns a Dictionary containing these keys: (3/4), $C and 5.

Testing

Class Dictionary provides an extra testing message to determine the presence of a specified key – includesKey:.

Enumerating

The keyword enumerating message do: enumerates over the *values* of the receiver. Other enumerating messages are keysDo:, which enumerates the argument block with each of the receiver's *keys*; and keysAndValuesDo:. This last message takes a two-argument block as its argument, since both each *key* and its corresponding *value* are substituted for each enumeration. For example:

```
| dict |
dict := Dictionary new.
dict at: 'a' put: 1.
dict at: 5 put: 'b'.
dict at: $c put: 6.
dict at: 'a' put: (Set with: 1 with: 3 with: 4).
dict at: 3/4 put: 'b'.
dict do:[:each | Transcript show: each printString; cr]
```

```
| dict |
dict := Dictionary new.
dict at: 'a' put: 1.
dict at: 5 put: 'b'.
dict at: $c put: 6.
dict at: 'a' put: (Set with: 1 with: 3 with: 4).
dict at: 3/4 put: 'b'.
dict keysDo:[:each | Transcript show: each printString; cr]
```

```
| dict |
dict := Dictionary new.
dict at: 'a' put: 1.
dict at: 5 put: 'b'.
dict at: $c put: 6.
dict at: 'a' put: (Set with: 1 with: 3 with: 4).
dict at: 3/4 put: 'b'.
dict keysAndValuesDo:
    [:k :v | Transcript show: k printString; tab; show: v printString; cr]
```

Exercise 14.3

Browse the accessing, testing and removing protocols in Dictionary. Also, browse class Association.

Exercise 14.4

Create a Dictionary and insert a few associations. Test whether a particular value is associated with a key using at:.

14.7 Class IdentityDictionary

Instances of IdentityDictionary perform *key* lookup using object identity (==), rather than object equality (=), and are hence more efficient. Chapter 21 discusses this distinction in more detail.

You can see from the class definition in Figure 14.5 that the class is implemented with an associated collection of *values* (the instance variable valueArray), rather than as a single Set of Associations. For example:

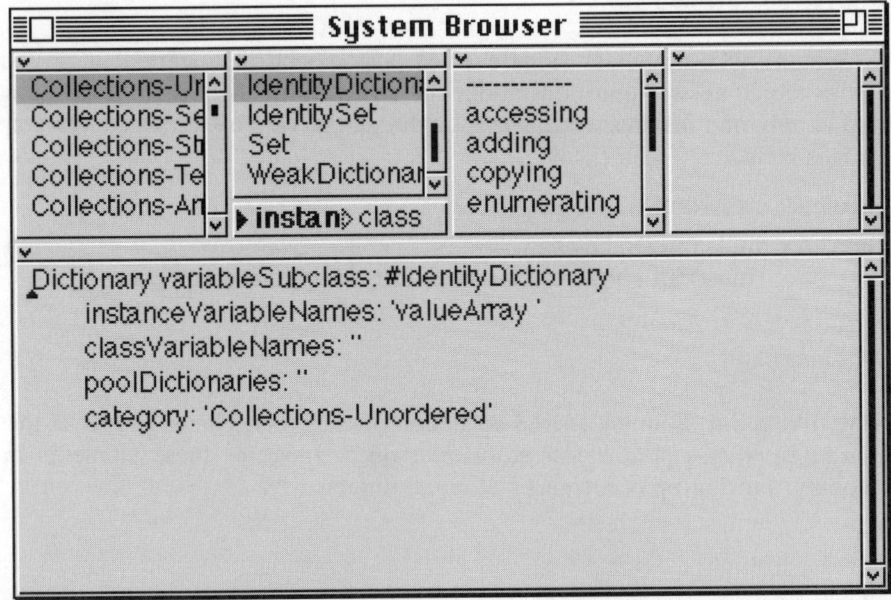

Figure 14.5 Class definition for **IdentityDictionary**.

```
| dict |
dict := IdentityDictionary new.
dict at: 'a' put: 1.
dict at: 5 put: 'b'.
dict at: $c put: 6.
dict at: 'a' put: (Set with: 1 with: 3 with: 4).
dict at: 3/4 put: 'b'.
^dict at: 'a'
```

raises an error, because the class uses object identity to look up 'a', which fails.

```
| dict |
dict := IdentityDictionary new.
dict at: 'a' put: 1.
dict at: 5 put: 'b'.
dict at: $c put: 6.
dict at: 'a' put: (Set with: 1 with: 3 with: 4).
dict at: 3/4 put: 'b'.
^dict at: $c
```

returns 6.

14.8 SystemDictionary

The SystemDictionary class (Figure 14.6) is a special dictionary that provides methods which answer questions about the structure of the VisualWorks image. There is only one instance of this class – the global variable Smalltalk. Example messages include:

```
Smalltalk classNames
Smalltalk allClassesDo:[:class |
        Transcript show: class name; tab; show: class category; cr]
```

14.9 Class Bag

A Bag, like a Set, is an unordered collection of elements. The difference is that a Bag *can store the same object more than once*. It stores these elements in a Dictionary, tallying up occurrences of equal objects.

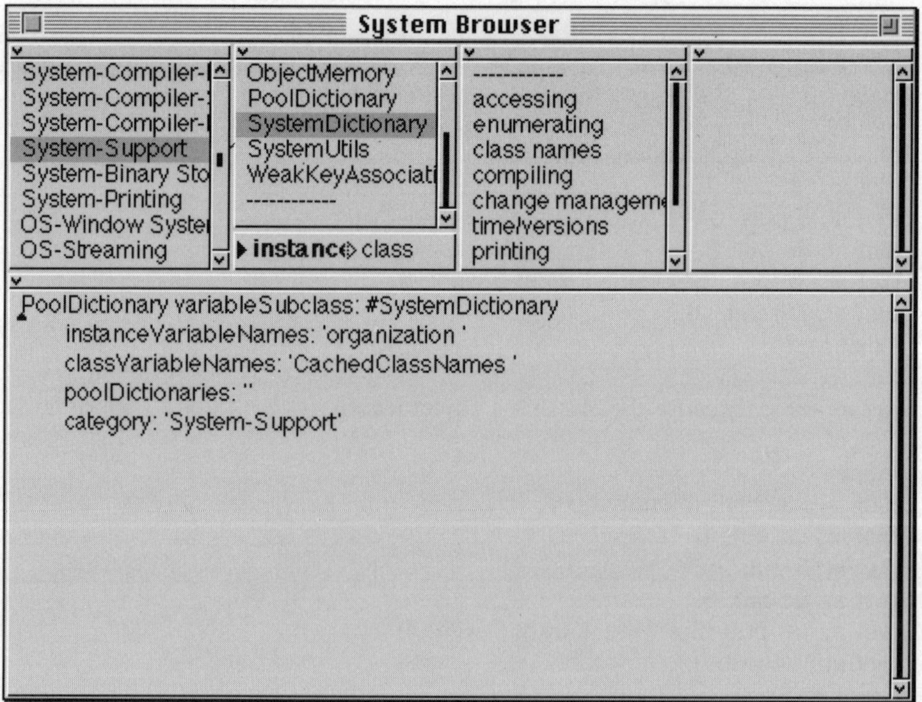

Figure 14.6 Class definition for **SystemDictionary**.

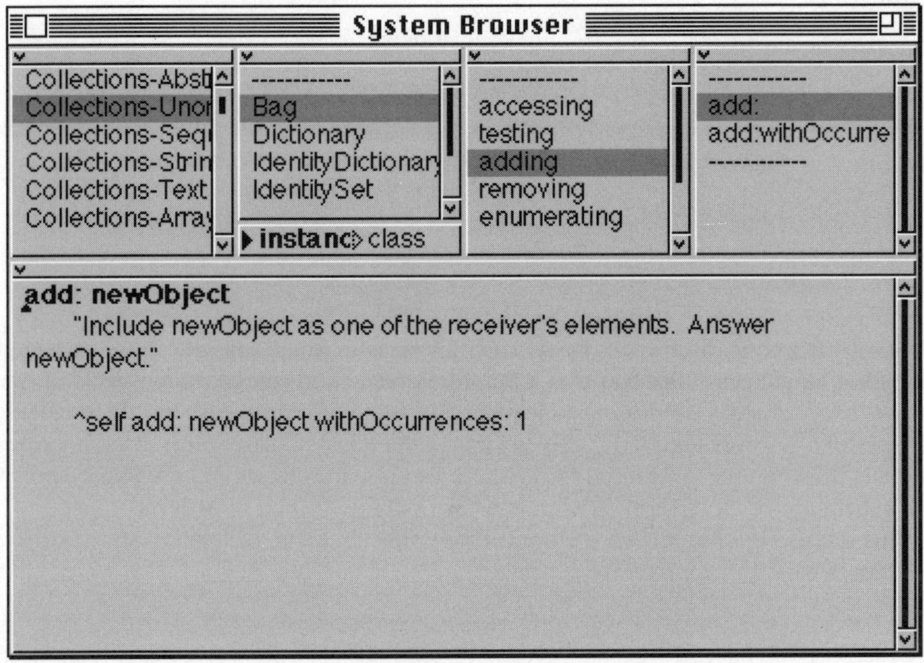

Figure 14.7 The **add:** method in class **Bag**.

Since a Bag can store the same object more than once, a specialized message add:withOccurrences: is provided for that purpose. Note that Bag overrides the default implementation of the add: method to ensure that one occurrence of the object is added (see Figure 14.7). The following two examples demonstrate the difference between classes Bag and Set:

```
| bag |
bag := Bag new.
bag addAll: (Set with: 1 with: 3 with: 4).
bag addAll: (Set with: 1 with: 3 with: 4).
^bag size
```

returns 6, whereas

```
| set |
set := Set new.
set addAll: (Set with: 1 with: 3 with: 4).
set addAll: (Set with: 1 with: 3 with: 4).
^set size
```

returns 3.

Exercise 14.5

Repeat Exercise 14.1, but using Bag rather than Set.

Exercise 14.6

Browse the implementations of Bag and Set. Why is Set not a subclass of Bag (or vice versa)?

14.10 Summary

One of the major differences between collections in Smalltalk and those provided by other languages is the fact that a Smalltalk collection can contain objects of *any* class, even objects of *different* classes. The behavior provided by all Smalltalk collections is represented by the abstract superclass Collection – its (concrete) subclass Set can be considered to be a representative example of how to use almost all subclasses of Collection. So far, we have only described unordered collections; in the following chapter we examine those subclasses of Collection that provide elements with an order or sequence.

15 Collections (2) – sequenceable

This chapter continues the discussion of collections, concentrating on sequenceable collections, as represented by abstract class SequenceableCollection and its subclasses, including classes Array and OrderedCollection. Other classes, including SortedCollection, String, and Symbol, are also considered here. Additionally, the chapter describes how to convert an instance of one class of collection to be an instance of another class.

15.1 Sequenceable collections

Unlike unordered collections, sequenceable collections access variables by a numeric index (a Dictionary can be used in this way in a limited sense). Class SequenceableCollection is an abstract superclass, of which class Array, and its superclass ArrayedCollection, may be considered to be typical sequenceable collections. Here we describe class Array as a *typical sequenceable collection*, since much of its behavior is applicable to all subclasses of SequenceableCollection. Therefore the description that follows may be considered to be applicable to all sequenceable collection classes, except where otherwise stated.

We then go on to consider classes OrderedCollection and SortedCollection, with their specialized protocol. The class hierarchy is as follows:

```
Object
        Collection
                SequenceableCollection
                        ArrayedCollection
                                Array
                        OrderedCollection
                                SortedCollection
```

15.2 Class Array

Arrays in Smalltalk are similar to one-dimensional arrays in many languages. Unlike all other collections, instances of class Array (and all other subclasses of ArrayedCollection) are *fixed size*. Once the size of an Array is declared it cannot be changed, and the Array cannot 'grow'. Consequently, class ArrayedCollection supports the notion of an externally defined ordering.

Creating

We have already seen how we can create instances of the Collection classes with the messages new, new:, with:, with:with:, etc. Class Array also responds to these messages, and in addition it provides the extra messages new:withAll: and withAll:. (It's also possible to use a literal array, e.g. #(1 3 4).) The following examples demonstrate their use:

```
Array new: 5 withAll: 'a'
```

produces #('a' 'a' 'a' 'a' 'a').

```
Array withAll: (Set with: 1 with: 3 with: 4)
```

produces #(1 3 4).

Adding

The add: messages should not be sent to instances of Array, since they may not grow in size (see Figure 15.1). To place objects in an array, the at:put: message is used; the first argument is the index which must be a positive integer within the bounds of the receiver, the second is the object to be placed. It is the object – not the array – that is returned from the at:put: message.

There are two additional messages that provide the ability to place more than one object. The first of these, atAllPut:, replaces each element of the receiver with the argument. For example, the expression

```
#(1 3 4) atAllPut: 5
```

produces an Array in which each element is 5, i.e. #(5 5 5). The message atAll:put: sounds similar but takes two arguments. The first argument is a collection of indices at which the second argument should be placed. For example, evaluating the expression

```
#(1 3 4) atAll: #(1 2) put: 5
```

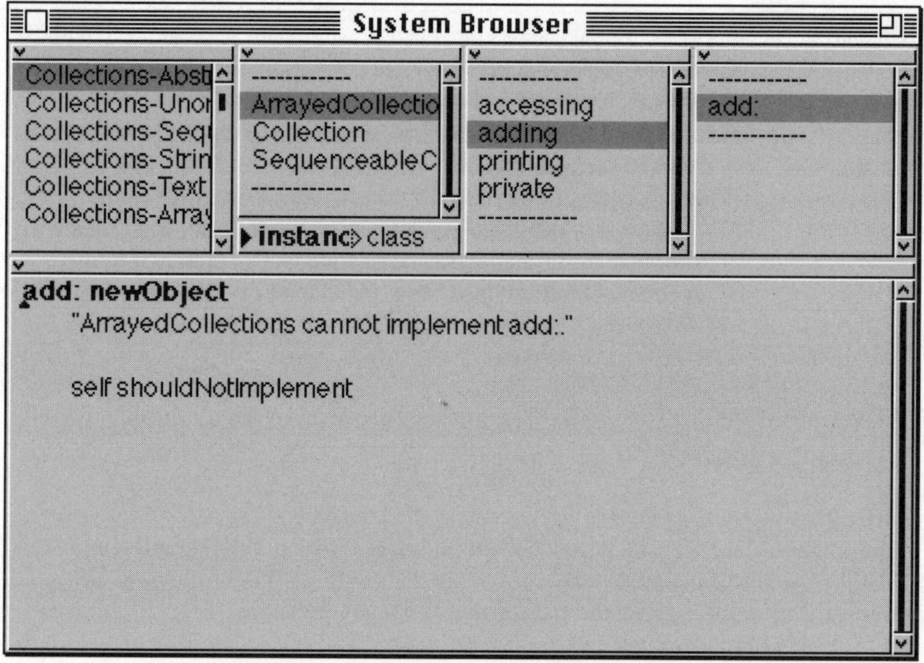

Figure 15.1 Elements cannot be added to instances of **Array**.

results in an Array whose first two elements are both 5, i.e. #(5 5 4).

Accessing

As you might expect, the message to access a particular element of an Array is at:. Thus the expression

```
#(1 3 4) at: 2
```

returns the second element, 3. There are, however, a couple of shortcuts provided: the messages first and last return the first and last elements of the receiver, respectively.

It's also possible to find the index of an element in an Array using the message indexOf:. However, this message is unusual in that if it fails to find an index corresponding to the argument; it returns 0, rather than raising an error. For example, the expression

```
#(1 3 4) indexOf: 3
```

Table 15.1

, (comma)	Create a new instance in which the argument is concatenated after the receiver.
reverse	Return a copy of the receiver in reverse order.
findFirst: (findLast:)	Return the index of the first (last) element of the receiver which meets the criteria specified in the argument block.
replaceFrom: to: with:	Specifies a range of elements in the receiver which are to be replaced with the elements of another sequenceable collection (the last argument of the message). The number of elements in the argument collection must equal the number of elements to be replaced.

returns 2, whereas

```
#(1 3 4) indexOf: 5
```

returns 0.

There are a number of other useful messages which fall broadly under the 'accessing' umbrella. These are shown in Table 15.1. The following are some examples that demonstrate the use of the messages in Table 15.1:

#(1 3 4), #(5 7 8)	#(1 3 4 5 7 8)
#(1 3 4) reverse	#(4 3 1)
#(1 3 4) findFirst: [:i | i >= 3]	2
#(1 3 4) findLast: [:i | i >= 3]	3
#(1 3 4), #(5 7 8) replaceFrom: 2 to: 5 with: #('a' 'b' 'c' 'd')	#(1 'a' 'b' 'c' 'd' 8)

Removing

Since the size of an Array cannot be modified, it is not possible to remove any of its elements. However, other subclasses of SequenceableCollection (notably those in the OrderedCollection hierarchy) *do* provide removing protocol (see later).

Copying

Rather than copying the whole of the collection, it's sometimes useful to copy some subcollection. There are several messages to support this requirement and the most common three are:

copyFrom: to: – return a new collection similar to the receiver containing the elements specified in the range indicated by the two numeric arguments.
copyWith: – return a new collection similar to the receiver, containing the extra element specified.
copyWithout: – return a new collection similar to the receiver, not including the element specified.

Examples are:

```
#(1 3 4), #(5 7 8) copyFrom: 2 to: 5     #(3 4 5 7)
#(1 3 4) copyWith: 5                     #(1 3 4 5)
#(1 3 4) copyWithout: 4                  #(1 3)
```

Enumerating

All the enumerating protocol described in Chapter 14 is applicable to sequenceable collections (e.g. do:). There are three additional messages which are of occasional use. The first of these, reverseDo:, simply enumerates across the receiver in reverse order. The keysAndValuesDo: message has the same selector as that provided for class Dictionary (Chapter 14), but substitutes each of the receiver's indices and its corresponding element for each enumeration. Finally, the message with:do: provides a mechanism of synchronizing the combined enumeration of two Arrays (the receiver and the first argument) in the evaluation of a two-argument block (the last argument).

The following examples demonstrate the messages described above:

```
#(1 3 4) do: [:i | Transcript show: i printString; cr]
#(1 3 4) reverseDo: [:i | Transcript show: i printString; cr]
#(1 3 4) keysAndValuesDo: [:k :v | Transcript show: (k * v) printString; cr]
#(1 3 4) with: #(4 5 6) do: [:i :j | Transcript show: (i * j) printString; cr]
```

Exercise 15.1

What's the difference between the following two message expressions?

```
#(1 3 4) reverse do: [:i | Transcript show: i printString; cr]
#(1 3 4) reverseDo: [:i | Transcript show: i printString; cr]
```

15.3 Class OrderedCollection

An OrderedCollection may be used as a multi-purpose data structure. It preserves the order in which things are added to it, and allows the elements to be accessed according to the order of entry. As such, it serves as a stack, queue, varying size array, and combinations thereof.

Adding

Unlike Arrays, OrderedCollections are not of fixed size. Therefore they may have elements added to them. There are several messages in protocol adding which provide the functionality to add single and multiple elements at various relative positions. Some of them are described below (remember that the argument is returned from these messages, *not* the receiver):

The following expressions demonstrate the messages in Table 15.2:

```
| coll |                                               OrderedCollection
coll := OrderedCollection with: 1 with: 3 with: 4.    (7 1 3 4 5 )
coll add: 5.
coll addFirst: 7.
^coll

| coll |                                               OrderedCollection
coll := OrderedCollection with: 1 with: 3 with: 4.    (1 7 3 5 4 )
coll add: 5 after: 3.
coll add: 7 before: 3.
^coll

| coll |                                               OrderedCollection
coll := OrderedCollection with: 1 with: 3 with: 4.    (5 7 8 1 3 4 9 11 12 )
coll addAllFirst: #(5 7 8).
coll addAllLast: #(9 11 12).
^coll
```

Table 15.2

add:	Add the argument to the receiver. This message is equivalent to addLast: (as shown in Figure 15.2).
addFirst:	Add (prepend) the argument to the receiver, putting it *before* all existing elements.
addLast:	Add (append) the argument to the receiver, putting it *after* all existing elements.
add:after:	Add the first argument to the receiver, placing it in the position after the second argument.
add:before:	Add the first argument to the receiver, placing it in the position before the second argument.
addAllFirst: (addAllLast:)	Add the argument collection to the receiver placing its elements before (after) any existing elements.

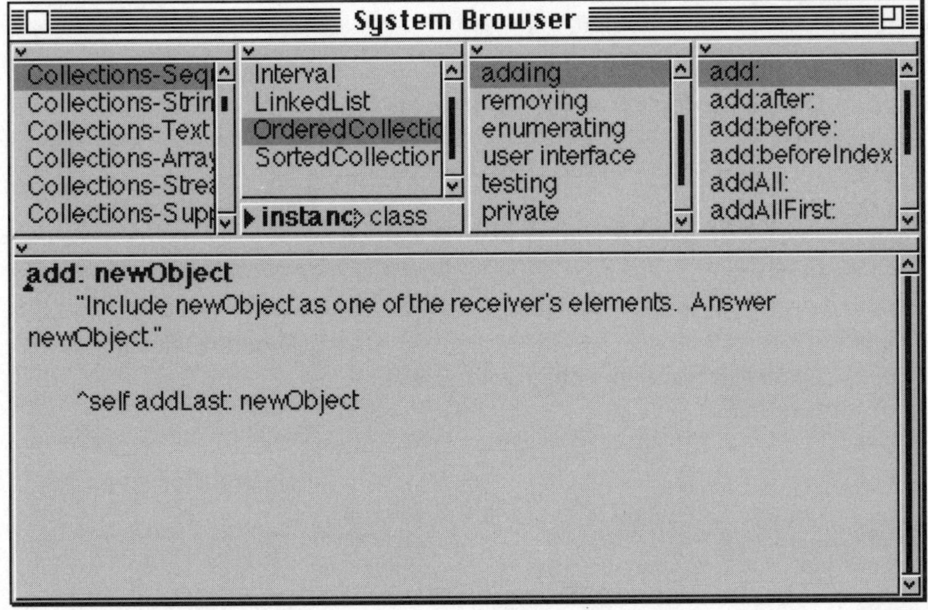

Figure 15.2 Adding an element to an **OrderedCollection** places it after any existing elements.

Accessing

In addition to the accessing messages described for class Array, there are two additional messages to retrieve elements of an OrderedCollection relative to some other specified element. These are after: and before:. The former returns the element in the collection whose index is one greater than the argument; similarly, the latter returns the object preceding that specified in the message.

Removing

Unlike class Array, OrderedCollection (and its subclasses) provide messages to remove elements. In addition to those mentioned for collections in general (Chapter 14), there are several other messages that are of interest. These are:

removeFirst (removeLast) – removes the first (last) element from the receiver.
removeFirst: (removeLast:) – the argument to this message is an integer which indicates how many elements should be removed from the front (rear) of the receiver.
removeAllSuchThat: – removes all those elements which meet the criteria specified in the block argument.

The following message sequences give examples of the above messages (in addition to the existing remove: message):

```
| coll |                                          OrderedCollection (1 4)
coll := OrderedCollection with: 1 with: 3 with: 4.
coll remove: 3.
^coll

| coll |                                          OrderedCollection (3 4)
coll := OrderedCollection with: 1 with: 3 with: 4.
coll removeFirst.
^coll

| coll |                                          OrderedCollection (1 3)
coll := OrderedCollection with: 1 with: 3 with: 4.
coll removeLast.
^coll

| coll |                                          OrderedCollection (4)
coll := OrderedCollection with: 1 with: 3 with: 4.
coll removeFirst: 2.
^coll

| coll |                                          OrderedCollection (1)
coll := OrderedCollection with: 1 with: 3 with: 4.
coll removeAllSuchThat: [:i | i >=3].
^coll
```

15.4 Class SortedCollection

Class SortedCollection is a subclass of OrderedCollection whose instances sort their elements according to some order. The order is determined by the expression contained in an instance variable called sortBlock. The block requires two arguments, and returns a Boolean, i.e. true or false (Chapter 21) – thus it acts as a 'function' for sorting the elements as each element is added. By default, all instances of SortedCollection use the class variable DefaultSortBlock (see Figure 15.3), which gives ascending order. Therefore any object that understands the message <= can be added to a SortedCollection.

Creating

In addition to the usual instance creation messages, SortedCollection provides two extra selectors to initialize the sortBlock to something other than the default. The sortBlock: message, when sent to the *class*, will create an instance of SortedCollection with its sortBlock initialized to that specified in the argument. Alternatively, the withAll:sortBlock: performs the same operation, with the additional benefit of providing some initial elements.

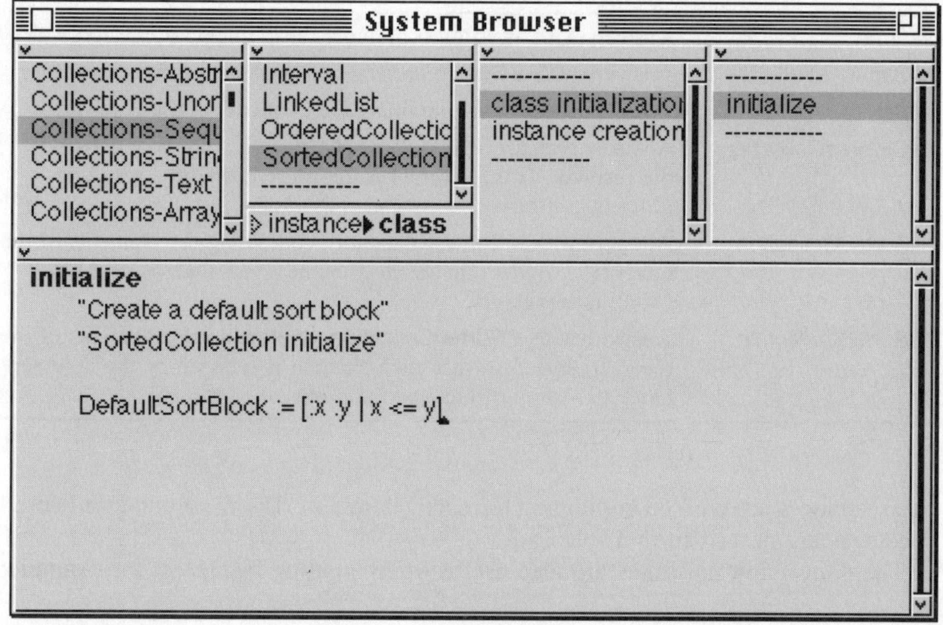

Figure 15.3 The class variable **DefaultSortBlock** is initialized to ascending order.

Accessing

Extra messages are provided to *get* and *set* the sortBlock of *instances* of SortedCollection via the messages sortBlock and sortBlock: respectively. The example below demonstrates the use of a SortedCollection.

```
| coll |
coll := SortedCollection new: 10.
coll sortBlock: [:x :y | x >= y].
#(1 3 4) do:[:i | coll add: i factorial].
^coll
```

Given that we are sorting in descending order, the result is SortedCollection (24 6 1).

15.5 Converting collections

There are many messages which can be used to *convert* an instance of one class of collection to another. Strictly speaking, the instances are not converted, instead

Table 15.3

asArray	Answers with an Array containing the elements of the receiver.
asBag	Answers with a Bag containing the elements of the receiver.
asSet	Answers with a Set containing the elements of the receiver.
asOrderedCollection	Answers with an OrderedCollection containing the elements of the receiver. If the receiver is unordered, then the resulting order is arbitrary.
asSortedCollection	Answers with a SortedCollection, containing the elements of the receiver, sorted so that each element is less than or equal to (<=) its successors.
asSortedCollection:	Answers with a SortedCollection, containing the elements of the receiver, sorted so that each element is ordered by the argument block (which must have two arguments).

new instances are created containing the same elements. The most commonly used messages are described in Table 15.3.

The conversion messages are also useful when creating instances, for example:

```
#(1 4 6 3 8 1) asSortedCollection
```

creates a SortedCollection containing the elements of the (literal) Array in ascending order. Other examples are:

```
(#(1 3 4), #(4 3 1)) asSet                                  Set (1 3 4)
(#(1 3 4), #(4 3 1)) asBag                                  Bag (1 1 3 3 4 4)
(#(1 3 4), #(4 3 1)) asOrderedCollection                    OrderedCollection
                                                            (1 3 4 4 3 1)
(#(1 3 4), #(4 3 1)) asSortedCollection                     SortedCollection
                                                            (1 1 3 3 4 4)
(#(1 3 4), #(4 3 1)) asSortedCollection: [:i :j | i > j]    SortedCollection
                                                            (4 4 3 3 1 1)
(Set with: 1 with: 3 with: 4) asArray                       #(1 3 4)
```

Exercise 15.2

Build a Binary Tree class as a subclass of Object. It should:

- Be able to add any object to the tree, as long as they are the same class and understand the '<' and '>' messages. Call the message which can perform this add: aValue;
- Be able to return a collection of the elements of the tree in ascending order.

Exercise 15.3

Make your binary tree class a subclass of class OrderedCollection. Build the following methods for your binary tree class, allowing it to act just like a collection.

do: aBlock
size (return the number of non-empty tree nodes in the tree)
remove: anObject ifAbsent: aBlock

Exercise 15.4

Verify that the following messages can be sent successfully to a member of your class (if you did everything correctly these should be available automatically):

asSortedCollection
printString
removeAll: aCollection

Exercise 15.5

Create an OrderedCollection of Integers. Convert it to a SortedCollection using the default sorting rule. Sort the collection so that they are in decreasing order of absolute value.

Exercise 15.6

Try converting an Array to a SortedCollection.

15.6 Strings

A String is a fixed-length sequence of Character objects. Class String and class Text are subclasses of CharacterArray. Strings are used in much the same way as strings in other languages. A String may be any length up to ~65K characters. Character objects can be obtained by placing a dollar symbol ($) in front of the desired character value. For instance, the Character object for lower-case 'c' can be obtained from $c.

It's important to note the difference between instances of Character and instances of String. For example, the String 'b' *contains* the Character $b, and is therefore *not equal* to it.

There are a few specialized Characters such as tab, or return. These may be obtained by sending the corresponding message to the class Character. For example, the expression Character tab returns a tab character.

There are many implementation-specific subclasses of String (e.g. MacString), corresponding to the way in which strings are handled in different operating systems. However, most of the behavior of String and its subclasses is implemented in its superclass CharacterArray. The protocol provided by CharacterArray is described below.

String manipulation

Since much of the computation of application programs is likely to center on the input and output of text, Smalltalk provides numerous messages to transform Strings. Some of the most useful ones are described in Table 15.4. Note that all these messages return a new instance, i.e. they are *non-destructive*. Examples of the messages in Table 15.4 are as follows:

```
'VisualWorks' chopTo: 9                              'Visuaorks'
'VisualWorks' contractTo: 9                          'Vis. . .rks'
'VisualWorks' dropFinalVowels                        'VslWrks'
'VisualWorks' dropVowels: 2                          'VisulWrks'
'VisualWorks' dropVowels: 4                          'VslWrks'
'VisualWorks' dropVowels: 5                          'slWrks'
'VisualWorks' findString: 'Work' startingAt: 1       7
```

Converting

Strings can also be case converted using asLowercase and asUppercase. For example:

```
'VisualWorks' asLowercase                            'visualworks'
'VisualWorks' asUppercase                            'VISUALWORKS'
```

Table 15.4

chopTo:	Combine start and end characters of the receiver in such a way that the final length of the string is equal to the integer argument.
contractTo:	Combine the start and end characters of the receiver, separated by an ellipsis, in such a way that the final length of the string is equal to the integer argument.
dropFinalVowels	Return a copy of the receiver missing all vowels, except for the first letter (if that was a vowel).
dropVowels:	The integer argument specifies how many vowels are to be removed from a copy of the receiver. If there are fewer vowels than the number specified then the difference is made up by removing characters from the beginning of the receiver.
findString: startingAt:	Search through the receiver searching for the (first) string argument, starting from the index specified by the (second) integer argument. Return the index at which the search string was found.

Comparing

Strings can be compared using the messages <, <=, >, and >=. The ordering is ASCII with case differences ignored. For example, the message < answers whether the receiver collates before the argument.

The match: method performs a pattern-matching operation. Case differences are ignored and 'wildcard' characters are matched only when in the *receiver*. A '#' character matches any one character, and a '*' character matches any sequence of characters, including no characters. Alternatively, the sameAs: message answers whether the receiver and the argument match precisely (ignoring case differences). For example:

```
'VisualWorks' match: 'VisualWorks' asLowercase        true
'VisualWorks' match: 'Vis*orks'                       false
'Vis*orks' match: 'VisualWorks'                       true
'VisualWorks' sameAs: 'VisualWorks' asLowercase       true
```

15.7 Symbols

A Symbol (see Chapter 3) is a label that conveys the name of a unique object such as a class name. There is only one instance of each Symbol in the VisualWorks image. Consequently, class Symbol overrides some of the protocol it inherits from class String. It's important to note the difference between testing for *equality* (=) and *identity* (==) between instances of classes String and Symbol (Chapter 21 describes the terms 'equality' and 'identity' in more detail):

```
'abc' = 'abc'          true
'abc' == 'abc'         false, Strings are not unique
#abc = #abc            true
#abc == #abc           true, Symbols are unique
```

Exercise 15.7

Create an instance of Array containing three Strings, in three different ways.

Exercise 15.8

Browse the CharacterArray and String protocols comparing and converting. Try some of these methods.

Exercise 15.9

Explore the CharacterArray methods match: and sameAs:. Try some example expressions.

Table 15.5

OrderedCollection	A collection where the ordering is given by the order in which elements are added. Can grow.
Array	A collection where the order is determined by an integer index, starting at 1. Cannot grow.
String	An indexed collection of Characters, with the index starting at 1. Cannot grow.
SortedCollection	A collection of objects, which is sorted according to an ordering defined in the instance of SortedCollection. Can grow.
Symbol	A subclass of String. (All Symbols are unique, while there can be two different Strings containing the same Characters.) Cannot grow.

Exercise 15.10

Investigate the CharacterArray method spellAgainst:, which is used in the spelling correctors.

Exercise 15.11

Investigate the effect of the replaceFrom:to:with: method (defined in SequenceableCollection) on instances of String.

Exercise 15.12

Write a method leftMost: in class CharacterArray whose argument is an integer, so that 'abcdef' leftMost: 3 returns 'abc'.

Exercise 15.13

Similar to above, write a method rightMost:, so that 'abcdef' rightMost: 3 returns 'def'. Ensure that both your methods work correctly when the integer argument is greater than the size of the receiver.

15.8 Summary

The preceding two chapters describe all the reader needs to know to understand how collections behave, and how to use them. Of the sequenceable collections, it is important to identify those that cannot *grow* (subclasses of ArrayedCollection), and thus should not be sent add: messages. Table 15.5 summarizes the sequenceable collections covered in the chapter.

In the following chapter we return temporarily to Browsers, completing the description of the options available from the many <operate> menus.

16 More on Browsers

In this chapter we describe the remaining Browser <operate> button menu options not yet explored. These options are demonstrated with examples drawn from previous chapters. Additionally, we conclude the description of the options available from the Launcher that are not covered elsewhere in the book.

16.1 Browser menus

Using the System Browser as an example we will consider each menu option from the available <operate> menus. The Browsers that may be spawned from the System Browser (or produced as a result of evaluating a message expression, from a Workspace for example) all share these menus. Some of the options have already been described (see Chapters 6 and 9) and the remainder will be described here.

Hardcopy

Before we examine each of the <operate> menus in turn, let us first describe the **hardcopy** option, since it is present in all the <operate> menus in the Browsers, and many of the other text-based windows. This option produces a file containing the source code for the selected method, protocol, class or category and sends it to the printer. (The format of the file is similar to that produced by the **file out as . . .** option, but doesn't contain any special characters recognized by the compiler – i.e. it may not be later filed-in.) After the operation has been successfully completed a notification is written to the System Transcript.

The Settings Tool (Chapter 5) should be used to select the appropriate form of printing for your platform. For example, in Figure 16.1, we have selected the options suitable for a Macintosh connected to a non-PostScript printer. For other platforms, please consult your VisualWorks 'User Guide' or 'Installation Notes'.

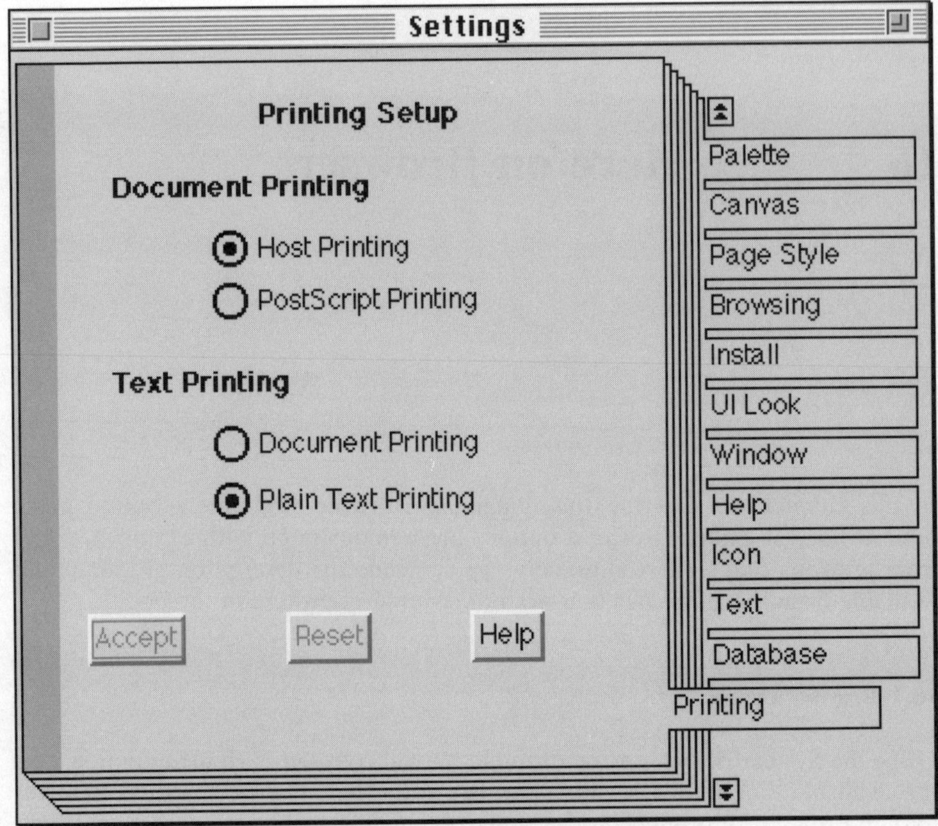

Figure 16.1 Setting the printing preferences.

The Class Categories menu

The Class Categories menu comes in two guises, according to whether or not a category is selected. Figure 16.2 shows the full menu, with those options always available indicated by a '†'. The numbers alongside the right-hand edge of the menu indicate the chapters in which an option has already been described.

rename as . . . – The user is prompted to provide a new name for the selected category. This option is often used when there is a conflict between category names or when correcting a typing mistake. All classes in the selected category are modified accordingly. The operation fails if the user provides a category name that already exists (unfortunately, no feedback is given to the user in these circumstances!).

remove . . . – This option removes the selected category *and the classes it contains* from the VisualWorks image. Not recommended, unless you are sure you know

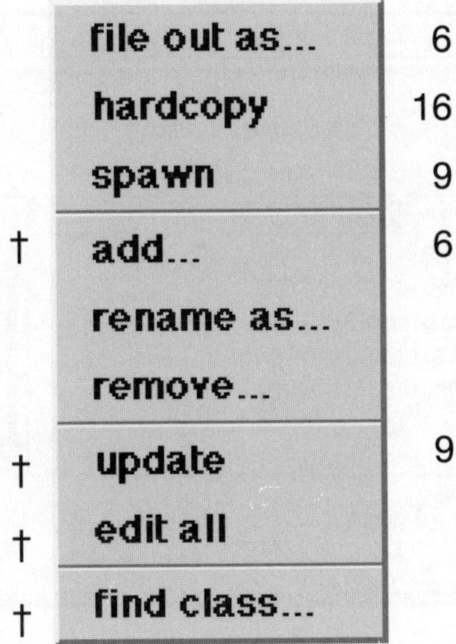

Figure 16.2 The Class Categories <operate> menu.

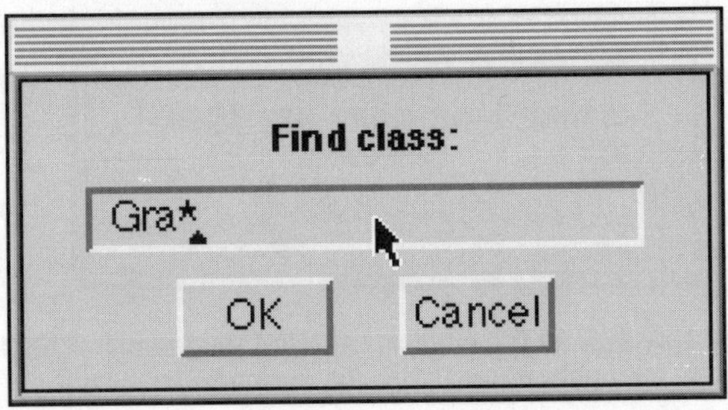

Figure 16.3 The **find class . . .** Prompter.

what you are doing – it is possible to remove classes which will prevent any further work being carried out in this image! The user is prompted to confirm the operation if the category contains any classes.

edit all – Prints the structure of all categories and their classes in the lower text pane. The order of the categories is the same as that in the class categories pane. By editing this list the user may change category names, category contents, and the

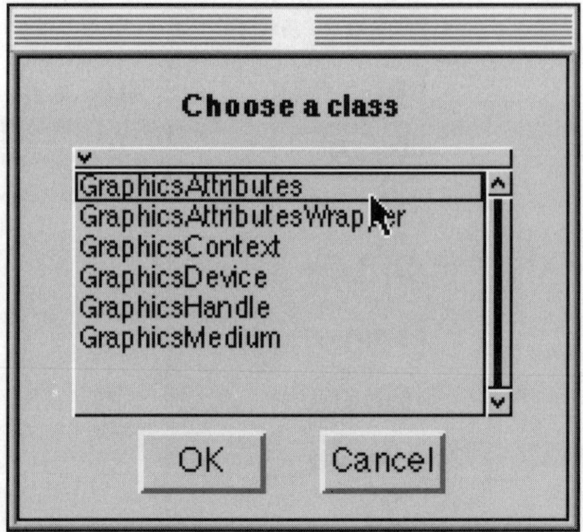

Figure 16.4 Possible class names beginning with 'Gra*'.

Figure 16.5 A Prompter to indicate that no class matches the name specified by the user (with the option to try again).

order in which the categories will appear. Although it is also possible to modify class names, all such changes are ignored. The user must select **accept** from the text pane <operate> menu to see the result of any changes that have been made. This option is seldom used, since other options exist by which the same modifications may be (more safely) carried out. Not recommended.

find class . . . – The user is prompted to specify a class name (possibly including the wildcards '*' and '#'). The category containing the specified class is selected in the category pane and the class is selected in the class pane. This mechanism is similar to that described in Chapter 9 for opening a Browser on a specified class, i.e. if more than one class matches the specified name, then the user is prompted to select the required class. For example, in Figure 16.3, the user specifies the name 'Gra*'; the resulting list is shown in Figure 16.4. If there is no class whose name matches the specified name, then a 'warning' Prompter appears (Figure 16.5)

The following exercises assume that you followed our recommendations in Chapter 11, and saved your work! (Otherwise, you will find it necessary to revisit that chapter.)

Exercise 16.1

Rename the class category Spending as Finance using the **rename as . . .** menu option

Exercise 16.2

Undo the modification in Exercise 16.1 using the **edit all** option.

Exercise 16.3

File out the class categories Spending and Financial Tools. Examine the files using the File Editor (Chapter 6).

Exercise 16.4

Remove the class category Financial Tools.

Exercise 16.5

File in the category Financial Tools from the file-out you created in Exercise 16.3.

Exercise 16.6

Experiment with the **find class . . .** option.

The Class Names menu

The Class Names menu (or 'Class Menu') is only available if a class is selected. Figure 16.6 shows the menu, with numbers alongside its right-hand edge indicating the chapters in which options have already been described.

inst var refs . . . – A menu is displayed listing the instance variables of the class and its superclasses. (The variables in each class are identified appropriately.) When the

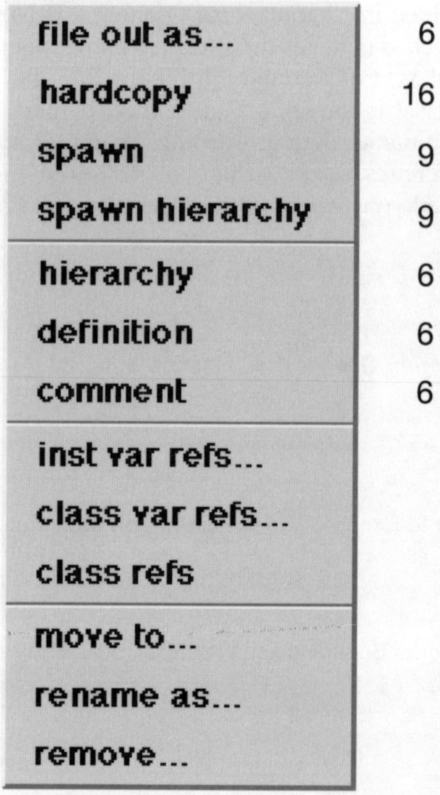

file out as...	6
hardcopy	16
spawn	9
spawn hierarchy	9
hierarchy	6
definition	6
comment	6
inst var refs...	
class var refs...	
class refs	
move to...	
rename as...	
remove...	

Figure 16.6 The Class Menu.

user selects a variable name, a Browser (called a 'Message-Set Browser' – see later) is opened on the methods in which the selected variable is referenced. For example, if the class FinancialHistory is selected, the **inst var refs . . .** option produces a list of its instance variable names (Figure 16.7).

class var refs . . . – Similar to above, except that the resulting menu contains a list of the *class* variable names for the class and its superclasses.

class refs – This option opens a Browser containing all those methods in which the *class* is referenced.

move to . . . – The user is prompted for a category name (which may be new or existing) into which to move the class. The System Browser is updated accordingly.

rename as . . . – The user is prompted to provide a new class name for the selected class. If appropriate, a Browser is opened containing the methods in which the class is currently referenced (using its old name); if necessary these methods should be amended. We recommend that you first check for references to this class (using the **class refs** option above) and make any necessary modifications *before* renaming the class.

Figure 16.7 A list of instance variable names for the class **FinancialHistory**.

remove . . . – The user is prompted to confirm this operation. It's easier to remove references to this class before you remove the class itself!

Exercise 16.7

Open a Browser which contains all methods referencing the class variable DefaultForWindows in class LookPreferences.

Exercise 16.8

Open a Browser which contains all methods which reference the class LookPreferences.

Exercise 16.9

Move the class SpendingHistory into the category called 'Financial Tools'.

Exercise 16.10

What will happen if you try to rename the class SpendingHistory as 'ExpendituresHistory? Go ahead and see if you are correct.

Exercise 16.11

What will happen if you try to remove the class SpendingHistory? Go ahead and see if you are correct. (This assumes that you didn't rename the class in Exercise 16.10!)

The Message Categories menu

The Message Categories menu (or 'Protocols Menu') is similar to the Class Category menu since it has two guises, according to whether or not a protocol is selected. Figure 16.8 shows the full menu, with those options always available indicated with a '†'. The numbers alongside its right-hand edge indicate the chapters in which options have already been described.

rename as . . . – Prompts the user for a new name for the selected protocol, then updates the protocol list in the Browser.
remove . . . – After prompting the user for confirmation, this option removes the protocol *and the methods it contains*. However, there is no attempt to discover if any other methods send messages corresponding to the methods contained in the selected protocol you are about to remove. (To determine all senders of a given message, see the **senders** option from the Message Selectors menu below.)
edit all – Prints the structure of the protocols and the methods they contain in the lower text pane. The order of the protocols is the same as that in the protocol pane. By editing this list the user may change protocol names, protocol contents, and the order in which protocols will appear. Although it is possible to modify message selector names, all such changes are ignored. The user must select **accept** from the

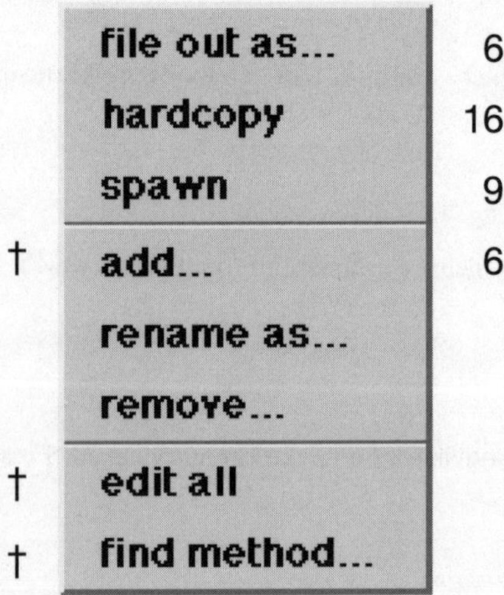

Figure 16.8 The Protocols Menu.

text pane <operate> menu to see the result of any changes that have been made. This option is seldom used, since other options exist by which the same modifications may be (more safely) carried out. Not recommended.

find method . . . – This option displays a list of the message selectors provided by the selected class. The instance/class switch on the Browser determines which group of selectors is displayed in the menu. Selecting a selector from the list causes its protocol to be selected in the protocol pane, itself to be selected in the message selectors pane, and its method to be displayed in the lower text pane. For example, Figure 16.9 shows the list of selectors in class SpendingHistory.

Exercise 16.12

In class SpendingHistory, rename the protocol private as initialize-release.

Exercise 16.13

Reverse the modification made in Exercise 16.12, by using the **edit all** menu option.

Exercise 16.14

File out the class protocol instance creation in class SpendingHistory. Examine the file using the File Editor (Chapter 6).

Exercise 16.15

Remove the class protocol instance creation from class SpendingHistory. File in the protocol from the file-out you created in Exercise 16.14.

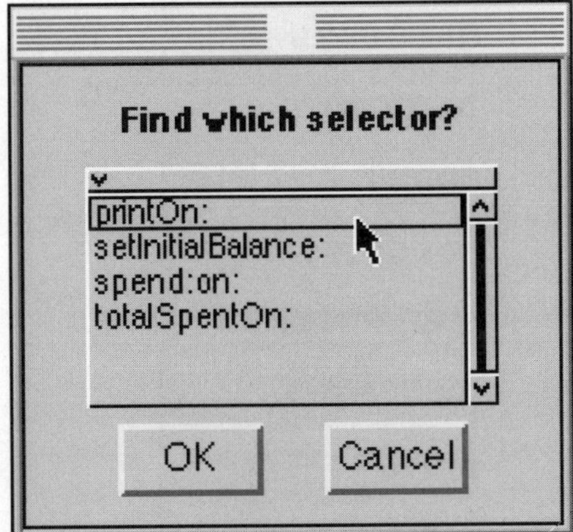

Figure 16.9 The list of message selectors defined for class **SpendingHistory**.

The Message Selectors menu

The Message Selectors menu is only available if a message selector is selected. Figure 16.10 shows the menu, with numbers alongside its right-hand edge indicating the chapters in which options have already been described.

The first three menu options are very useful in tracing message-sends (see also later for alternative ways of browsing the senders and implementors of a message):

senders – This option searches the VisualWorks image for all methods in which the message selector is sent. A Browser is opened. If the selected message selector is not sent by any method in the image, then the user is presented with a 'warning' Prompter.
implementors – This option opens a Browser containing all classes that implement a method corresponding to the selected message selector.
messages – This option displays a menu of the messages sent in the selected method. Selecting one of these messages opens a Browser containing the implementors of that message.
move to . . . – The user is prompted for the name of the destination protocol into which the selected method will be moved. If a protocol of that name does not exist then it is created. To *copy* the method to another class, the user must include both the class name and the message protocol, in the form *ClassName>selector*.
remove . . . – The method is deleted after confirmation from the user. It's advisable to ensure that there are no senders of the message (using the **senders** option above) before removing a method!

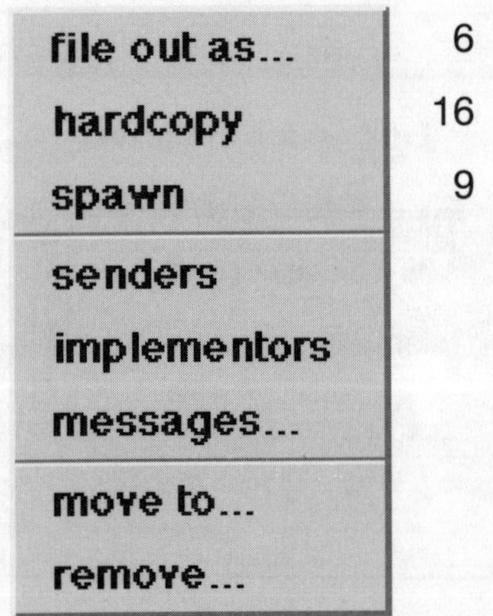

Figure 16.10 The Message Selectors menu.

find...	5
replace...	5
undo	5
copy	5
cut	5
paste	5
do it	5
print it	5
inspect	7
accept	6
cancel	6
format	
spawn	9
explain	
hardcopy	16

Figure 16.11 The Code menu.

Exercise 16.16

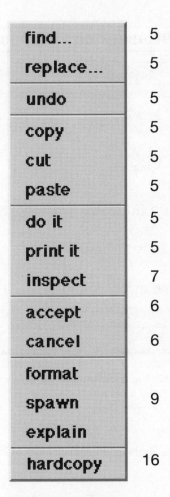

Select the message selector printOn: in class SpendingHistory. Open a Browser on all senders of this message.

Exercise 16.17

While having the same message selected, open a Browser on all implementors of printOn:.

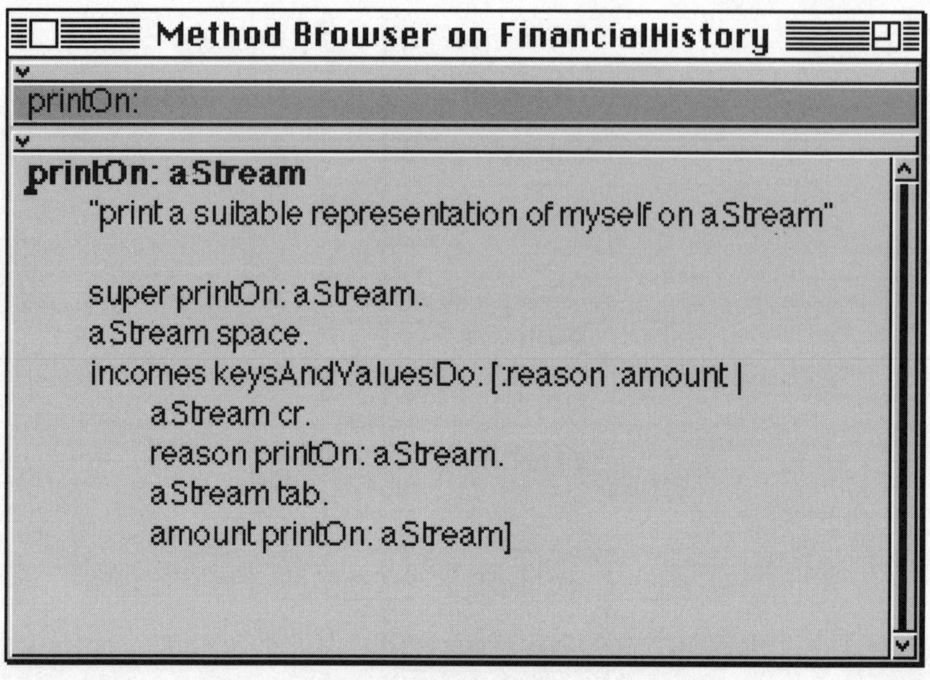

Figure 16.12 The **printOn:** method *before* formatting.

Exercise 16.18

Again from the same message, browse all implementors of keysAndValuesDo:.

The text pane menu

The text pane menu (or 'Code' menu) is always available, since the pane can also be used as a workspace for experimentation. Figure 16.11 shows the menu, with numbers alongside its right-hand edge indicating the chapters in which options have already been described.

format – This option modifies the layout of the method so that it adheres to the code indentation conventions. For example, Figures 16.12 and 16.13 display the original printOn: method in class FinancialHistory that we described in Chapter 11 before and after the use of the **format** option respectively.

explain – Used when a variable, literal or message selector is selected, this option appends an 'explanation' of the selection. The explanation usually includes some code which, when evaluated, opens a Browser on references to the selection. For example, in Figure 16.14 the Browser contains an explanation of the instance variable incomes.

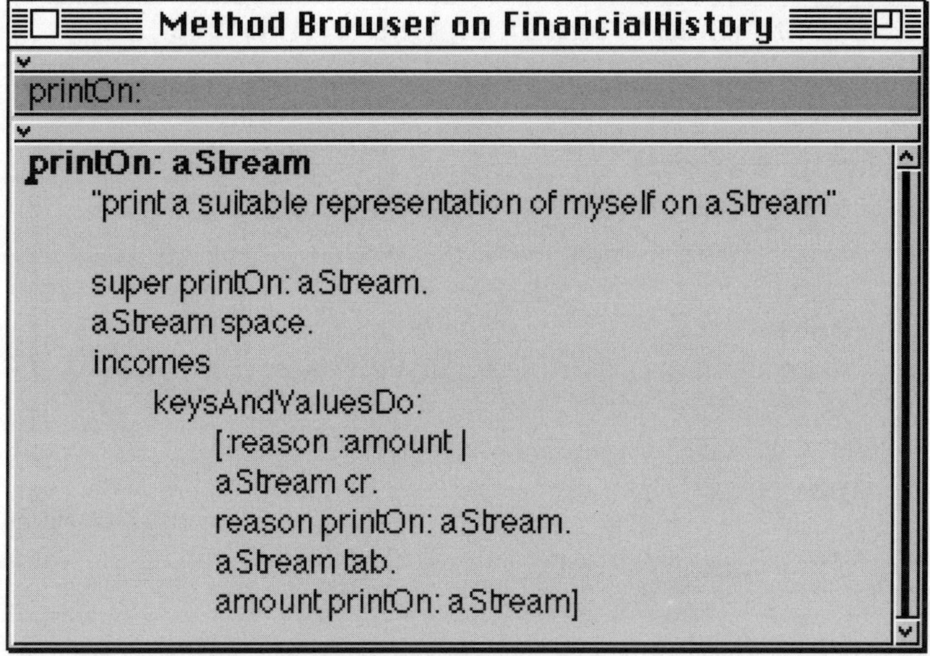

Figure 16.13 The **printOn:** method *after* formatting.

Exercise 16.19

Ensure that the methods in classes SpendingHistory and FinancialHistory adhere to the code formatting conventions.

Exercise 16.20

'Explain' the message space in the method shown in Figure 16.14.

16.2 Alternatives

You can also find all senders of a message by evaluating an expression of the form:

```
Browser browseAllCallsOn: #printOn:
```

This opens a new Browser containing all those methods that send the message printOn:. Alternatively, you can open a Browser containing all implementors of a method by evaluating an expression such as:

```
Browser browseAllImplementorsOf: #do:
```

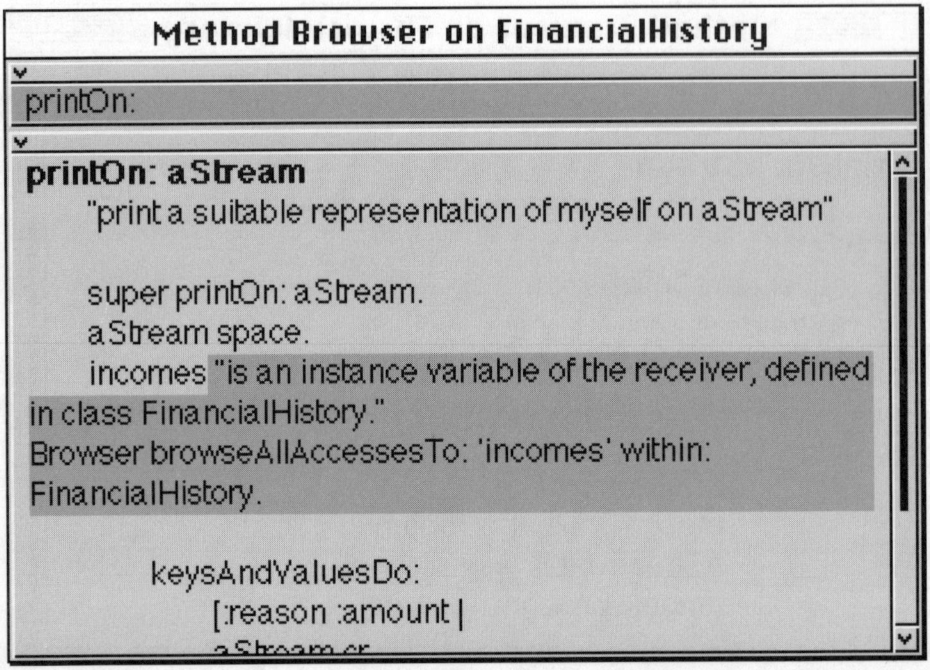

Method Browser on FinancialHistory

printOn:

```
printOn: aStream
	"print a suitable representation of myself on aStream"

	super printOn: aStream.
	aStream space.
	incomes "is an instance variable of the receiver, defined
in class FinancialHistory."
Browser browseAllAccessesTo: 'incomes' within:
FinancialHistory.

		keysAndValuesDo:
			[:reason :amount |
			aStream cr.
```

Figure 16.14 An 'explanation' of the variable **incomes**.

Finally, you can open a Browser containing all those methods that contain a reference to a specific class by evaluating an expression similar to:

```
Browser browseAllCallsOn: (Smalltalk associationAt: #Array)
```

16.3 Message-Set Browser

A Message-Set Browser is a special kind of Browser that gives access to a collection of methods with specific characteristics. For example, Figure 16.15 shows a Message-Set Browser containing all implementors of do:. You can see that the upper pane contains a list of class-selector pairs corresponding to the label of the Browser.

16.4 The Launcher

We have already described most of the operations available from the Launcher. The following sections describe the remainder, and identify those options already described.

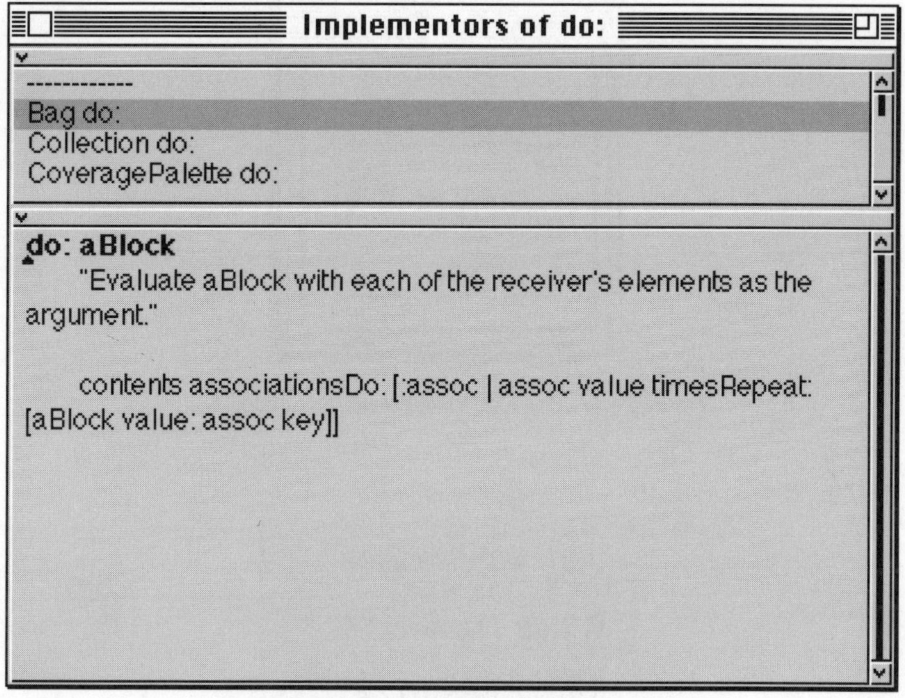

Figure 16.15 A Message-Set Browser.

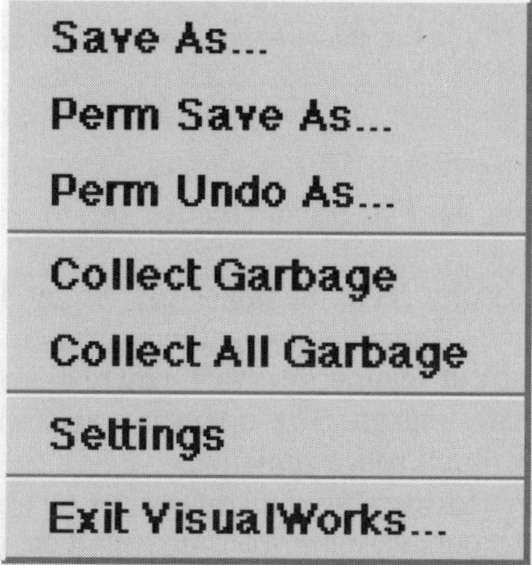

Figure 16.16 The **File** menu of the Launcher.

Figure 16.17 The **Exit Visualworks . . .** dialog box.

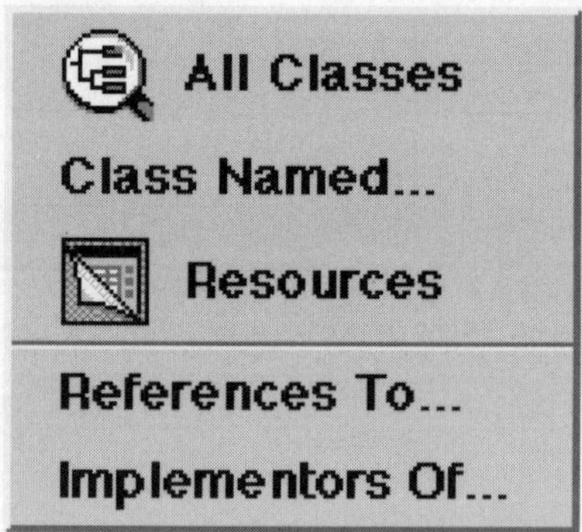

Figure 16.18 The **Browse** menu of the Launcher.

File

The options available from the **File** menu (Figure 16.16) are described below:

Collect Garbage – collects objects in the image that are no longer required (called *garbage*) and discards them, thus removing them from memory. Although this process occurs automatically at regular intervals, you may want to use this option to discard objects for a specific reason. The operation also writes a message to the Transcript indicating how much space remains.
Collect All Garbage – performs a similar operation to above. In addition, this operation searches for garbage in a memory zone called *Perm Space*. Consult your User Guide for more information on both options.
Settings – opens a window in which various options can be set. See Chapter 5.

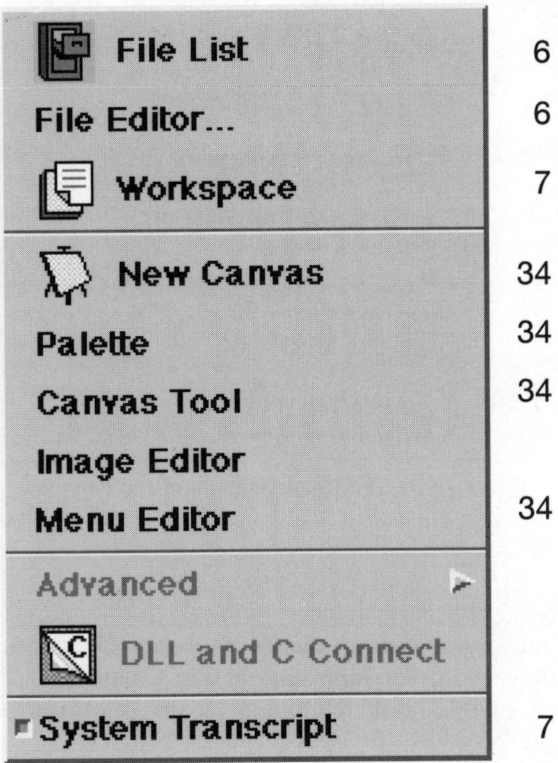

6
6
7
34
34
34
34
7

Figure 16.19 The **Tools** menu of the Launcher.

We have already described the **Save As . . .** option in Chapter 4. There are two other options for saving, **Perm Save As . . .** and **Perm Undo As . . .**. These more advanced options provide a means of using Perm Space; consult your User Guide for more information.

You should also be familiar with the dialog box that is produced when you select the **Exit VisualWorks . . .** option from the Launcher (Figure 16.17). This was described in Chapter 4.

Browse

The **Browse** menu of the Launcher (Figure 16.18) contains five options. By now you should be very familiar with the **All Classes** option. The **Class Named . . .** option was described in Chapter 9. The **References To . . .** and **Implementors Of . . .** options provide the same functionality as the **senders** and **implementors** options described earlier in this chapter. The remaining option, **Resources**, is described in Chapter 34.

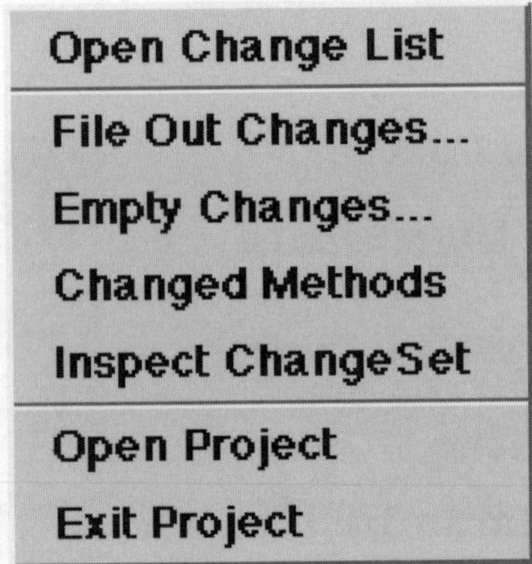

Figure 16.20 The **Changes** menu of the Launcher.

Tools

Four of the options available from the **Tools** menu (Figure 16.19) have all been described elsewhere and others are described in Chapter 34. The remainder are beyond the scope of this book. Numbers on the right-hand side of the menu indicate the chapter in which the option is described.

Changes

The options available from the **Changes** menu of the Launcher (Figure 16.20) are all described in Chapter 24.

16.5 Summary

This chapter completes the description of the Browsers available in VisualWorks. Hopefully, by now, the reader will feel completely at ease with the VisualWorks user interface, being able to navigate between class categories, classes, protocols and methods, using a combination of Browsers and the Launcher. We now return to blocks, examining how they are used to create 'looping' control structures.

17 Blocks and control structures (2)

This chapter considers further the construction of control structures using blocks. In particular, we describe class Interval and its use in a simple 'for' loop. Other constructions using blocks are also considered here, including the use of return expressions in blocks.

17.1 Class Interval

Class Interval is a special kind of sequenceable collection (see Figure 17.1) that represents a finite arithmetic progression or sequence. Such progressions are given by a starting number, a (finite) limit, and a method of computing the next number. The progression is specified at creation time and may not be changed or grown. Thus, it is logically a special class of array with a particularly efficient representation for the elements. Hence the usual at: message is available (but *not* at:put:, add:, or remove:) – i.e. once created, new elements cannot be added or removed from an Interval. Typically, Intervals are used for looping control (see later). However, they can also be manipulated as independent objects.

In general, Intervals are created by specifying start and end points along with an optional step-size. For example:

Interval from: *start* to: *stop*
Interval from: *start* to: stop by: *step*

Without the step-size, the Interval must be *non-decreasing* as in (1 to: 1) or (1 to: 10). Otherwise it denotes an empty Interval, i.e. an Interval without elements, e.g. (1 to: -10).

Intervals are more general than corresponding facilities in other programming languages because they can be constructed with arbitrary numbers. Consequently, it is legal to have Intervals such as:

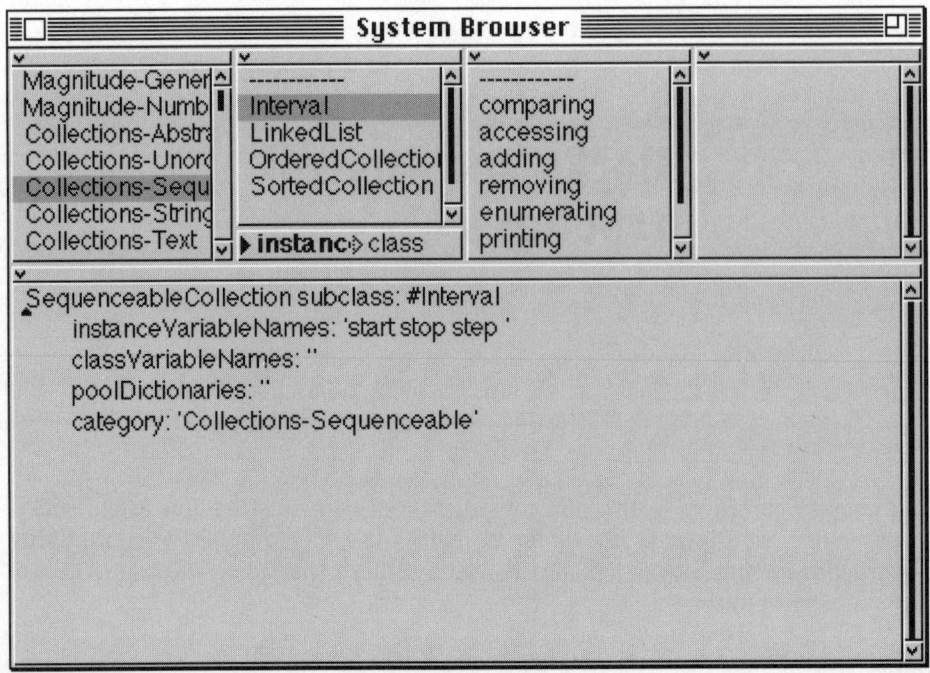

Figure 17.1 The class definition of **Interval**.

```
1 to: 10
(1/3) to: (8/3) by: (1/3)
1.5 to: 9.5 by: 0.5
1 to: 5.0 by: (1/3)
```

When accessed sequentially via the sequencing operations do:, collect:, and so on (see below) the elements obtained are not always of the same class. For instance, in the last example above, the elements accessed include 1 (a SmallInteger) and 4/3 (a Fraction).

Another way of creating an Interval is by sending to: or to:by: to a kind of Number. The following two expressions are equivalent:

```
Interval from: 10 to: 114 by: 4
10 to: 114 by: 4
```

As a subclass of SequenceableCollection, class Interval inherits lots of behavior (see Chapter 15). These messages include size, isEmpty, last, asArray, and so on. In addition, it provides access to its instance variable step via the increment message (see Table 17.1).

Table 17.1

(1 to: 10 by: 3) size	4
(1 to: -10 by: -3) size	4
(1 to: -1) size	0
(1 to: -10 by: 2) size	0
(1 to: 10 by: 3) isEmpty	false
(1 to: -10 by: -3) isEmpty	false
(1 to: -1) isEmpty	true
(1 to: 10 by: 3) last	10
(1 to: -10 by: -3) last	-8
(1 to: -10 by: 2) last	-11
(1 to: 5.0 by: (1/3)) last	5.0
(1 to: 3 by: 0.5) last	3.0
(1 to: 10 by: 3) asArray	#(1 4 7 10)
(1 to: -10 by: -3) asArray	#(1 -2 -5 -8)
(1 to: -10 by: 2) asArray	#()
(1 to: -1) asArray	#()
(1 to: 5.0 by: (1/3)) asArray	#(1 (4/3) (5/3) 2 (7/3) (8/3) 3 (10/3) (11/3) 4 (13/3) (14/3) 5)
(1 to: 3 by: 0.5) asArray	#(1.0 1.5 2.0 2.5 3.0)
(1 to: 10 by: 3) increment	3
(1 to: -10 by: -3) increment	-3

Exercise 17.1

Why does the expression (1 to: -10 by: 2) last return a nonsensical result?

Looping

Intervals respond to the message do: by evaluating the block argument for each of its values in sequence. Thus, an Interval can be used to construct the equivalent of a 'for' loop:

```
(10 to: 114 by: 4) do: [ :each Transcript show: each printString; cr]
```

This construction is so common that to:do: and to:by:do: are implemented in Number, so the initial parentheses can be omitted (see Table 17.2).

Table 17.2

I sum I sum := 0. 1 to: 10 do: [:i I sum := sum + (1 * 3)]. sum	165
I sum I sum := 0. 10 to: 1 by: -1 do: [:i I sum := sum + (i * 3)]. sum	165
I coll I coll := OrderedCollection new: 10. 1 to: 10 do: [:i I coll add: i factorial]. coll	OrderedCollection (1 2 6 24 120 720 5040 40320 362880 3628800)

Exercise 17.2

Try some examples using Intervals to control the repetition of a block.

Iterating

We have already seen that class Collection provides a protocol to iterate across elements of its instances. As instances of one of its (indirect) subclasses, Intervals also respond to these messages. For example:

```
(1 to: 3 by: 0.5) collect: [:eacheach factorial]
```

Exercise 17.3

Rewrite the first two examples in the section on Looping using the inject:into: message.

17.2 Instance behavior through blocks

We have already seen that blocks are a means of storing Smalltalk code as variables which can then be passed to other methods, evaluated, and so on. One particularly useful application of blocks is to provide 'instance behavior'. This means giving individual instances of a class some special behavior which is not common to all instances of that class. Generally this is accomplished by:

1. Setting aside one or more instance variables in the class for the block(s)
2. Implementing a method to set the instance variable(s)
3. Finally, creating some sort of 'execute' method to activate the behavior embedded in the block(s).

Examples in the VisualWorks image include SortedCollection (Chapter 15) and PluggableAdaptor (Chapter 33).

This technique also has applications in AI tools (setting individual responses for frames), in direct computing applications (such as spreadsheets, for cell formulae), and many other sorts of programs.

17.3 Return expressions in blocks

A method can have return expressions inside a block. For example, a method may contain the following code:

```
self someTest ifFalse: [“exit from method immediately” ^'Fail'].
“rest of method here”
```

This causes the method to return immediately if the test fails.

This behavior is frequently useful when expressing an algorithm with some special cases, or with exception conditions. It can also be used (together with the pseudo-variable self) to express recursive solutions.

However, a block is always evaluated in the *context in which it was defined*. This means that it is possible to attempt to return (using a return expression inside a block, i.e. '^') from a method which has already returned using some other return expression. This run-time error condition is trapped by the virtual machine, and an error Notifier displayed. For example, Figure 17.2 shows the method returnBlock which we have added to class Object. This method simply returns a block containing an expression to return self. Evaluating the expression

```
Object new returnBlock value
```

causes an error Notifier to appear.

17.4 Summary

The use of an instance of class Interval, when combined with a block, provides a simple 'for' loop. Additionally, because Interval is a subclass of SequenceableCollection, it inherits the ability to enumerate – using messages such as collect:, select:, etc.

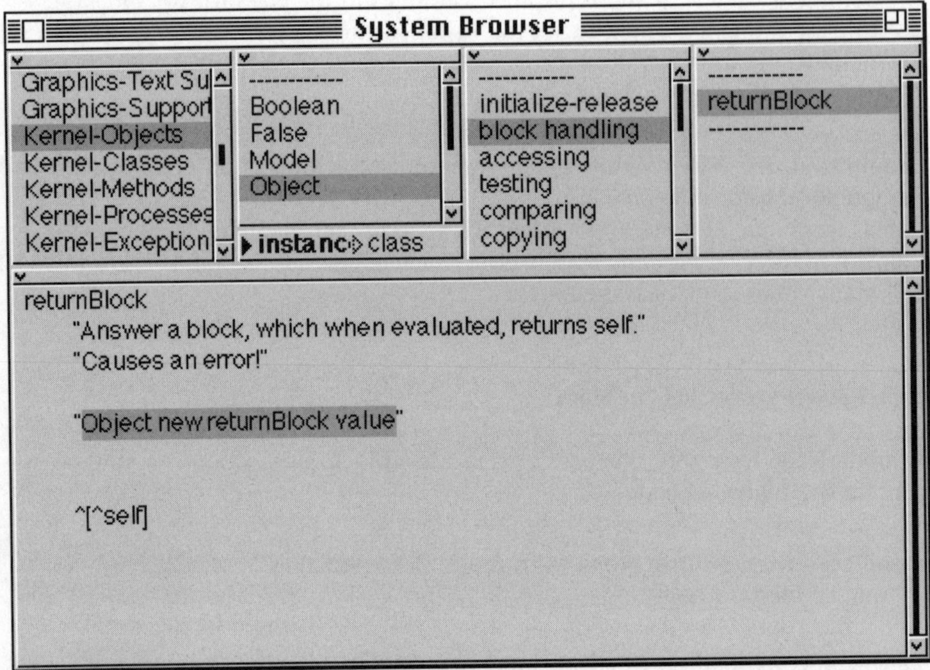

Figure 17.2 An example of the block expression that causes an error.

Blocks have access to the instance variables and temporary variables of the method in which they were first defined. Try to avoid using these variables in blocks that will be passed elsewhere, since side effects of the worst kind can be created. Therefore, if at all possible, use only those variables passed in as arguments, or temporaries declared local to the block.

The following chapter continues the theme of enumeration by looking at the use of 'streams' – a mechanism for controlling access to an underlying sequenceable collection.

18 Streams and files

The concept of 'streaming' over a collection of data – starting at the beginning, and going through it one element at a time – is such a useful one that special classes are provided in VisualWorks to support this kind of operation. This chapter starts by considering streams, and their relationship to subclasses of SequenceableCollection. (Streams do not themselves store the data items; instead they rely on some underlying storage – such as a sequenceable collection – to retain the items.) Examples of streaming over collections using subclasses of PositionableStream are given. Other types of streams, especially generators, are considered, using class Random as an example.

A major use of streams within VisualWorks is to provide a convenient mechanism for printing out objects. This mechanism is described here, with examples taken from existing VisualWorks classes.

This chapter goes on to consider file system access – how to read and write files from within VisualWorks – again with many examples.

18.1 Streams

Class Stream and its subclasses provide a convenient way of sequentially scanning a collection of objects. It supports a variety of operations for navigating within that stream of data: such as inserting, or searching. Class PositionableStream augments this mechanism by keeping track of your position in the stream. (Positioning in a Stream starts at 0.) There are a number of different classes of streams, but three are used most often. These are ReadStream, WriteStream, and ReadWriteStream. Generally, it's best to avoid ReadWriteStream; specify either a ReadStream or a WriteStream.

In the description that follows, we are essentially describing class PositionableStream. The (partial) class hierarchy is as follows:

```
Object
    Stream
        PeekableStream
            PositionableStream
                InternalStream
                    ReadStream
                    WriteStream
                        ReadWriteStream
```

The general operation of PositionableStream subclasses allows the use of the next message to access the 'next' object (and set the position after it), starting from the first one in the collection. Alternatively, the nextPut: message allows a new object (the argument) to be inserted into the underlying collection at the 'next' position (and set the position after it), replacing any object currently there.

The next and nextPut: messages in Stream subclasses are implemented using primitives, so they are particularly fast. Furthermore, Stream subclasses implement an efficient mechanism for making otherwise fixed-size collections, such as Array and String, larger on demand.

The usual way of creating a new instance of a Stream subclass is to use the class method on:. The argument should be the sequenceable collection over which you wish to stream. As a shortcut, it's possible to create an instance of ReadStream or WriteStream by sending the message readStream or writeStream (respectively) to a sequenceable collection. For example, the following expressions create new instances of a ReadStream (i and ii) and a WriteStream:

(i) ReadStream on: #(1 2 3 4 5)
(ii) ReadStream on: OrderedCollection new
(iii) #(1 2 3 4 5) writeStream

It is sometimes useful to discover the current position in the stream; the position message provides this. Alternatively, the message position: is provided to explicitly set the position within the stream. The messages reset and setToEnd may be used as shortcuts to setting the position to the beginning or end of the stream (respectively). We can also change the position implicitly by use of the skip message; this skips the 'next' object. To skip more than one object, use the skip: message – the argument should be an integer (negative to skip backwards).

As a convenient way to determine whether we have reached the end of the underlying collection, the message atEnd answers true if there are no further objects to be processed, false otherwise.

Class ReadStream

Class ReadStream is a concrete subclass of PositionableStream, and permits read-only access to the underlying collection. Thus, the nextPut: message is not supported, but the next message is available. In addition, we may use the next: message to access the number of objects specified in the argument. We can also use the contents message to retrieve the whole underlying collection. Alternatively, we may use the through: message to retrieve objects from the current position to a specified 'endpoint' object – the argument of the message, which should be an element of the collection. The upTo: message provides similar behavior, but doesn't retrieve the argument.

The example below creates a ReadStream on a (literal) Array containing five SmallIntegers:

```
| stream |
stream := #(5 4 3 2 1) readStream.
stream next; next; next.
^stream atEnd
```

The first three integers are accessed by the next messages; atEnd therefore answers false.

Class WriteStream

Class WriteStream is another concrete subclass of PositionableStream, and permits write-only access to the underlying collection. At first sight, this might be considered useless, but it turns out that, since we can still use the contents message to retrieve the (presumably) modified underlying collection, this class is in fact very useful.

In particular, WriteStreams are very useful for sequentially inserting objects into fixed-size collections such as Arrays and Strings. Very often, we don't know how large an Array or String will be required. However, WriteStreams have an efficient way of making collections larger – therefore, using a WriteStream to construct a String is likely to be very efficient, especially when compared with the concatenation message ','.

Furthermore, WriteStreams implement a number of useful variants on nextPut:, including nextPutAll:. The argument to the latter is a collection of objects, and all these objects are inserted into the WriteStream.

In the example below, an instance of WriteStream is created on an Array with ten elements, each of which are initially nil. First, some objects are added with nextPut:, then the individual elements of the (literal) String (i.e. the Characters in that String) are added to the stream, using the nextPutAll: message.

```
| stream array |
stream := (Array new: 10) writeStream.
stream nextPut: 6.
stream nextPut: $s.
stream nextPutAll: 'test,test, . . .'.
array := stream contents.
^array
```

Thus, the resulting Array, when extracted from the stream using the contents message, has the following elements:

#(6 $s $t $e $s $t $, $t $e $s $t $, $. $. $.)

Note that most, but not all, of the elements are Characters, and that the number of elements in the Array is now more than ten.

Finally, there are some additional messages that add particular characters to the stream. Especially useful are cr, tab and space. These insert the appropriate character into the stream.

Class ReadWriteStream

Class ReadWriteStream is a subclass of WriteStream, inheriting write-only access. It adds the capability of read access (like class ReadStream).

Exercise 18.1

Browse class PositionableStream and its subclasses.

Exercise 18.2

Try the examples above. Use an Inspector on the results.

Exercise 18.3

Write a whileFalse: loop which runs through a ReadStream, printing the contents individually on the Transcript.

Exercise 18.4

Try creating a ReadStream on an Interval. Experiment with next. What happens when you send it the message contents?

Exercise 18.5

Implement a subclass of ReadStream called CircularStream which, on reaching the end of the underlying collection, returns to the beginning. This would allow a collection to be streamed over repeatedly.

18.2 Printing

We have already discovered that we need to be able to print out any kind of object in a suitable fashion. For example, the **print it** option on many of the <operate> menus requires this. We have also seen the use of the printString message for this purpose.

The printString method is implemented in class Object (see Figure 18.1), and is therefore understood by *all* objects. The implementation creates a WriteStream on

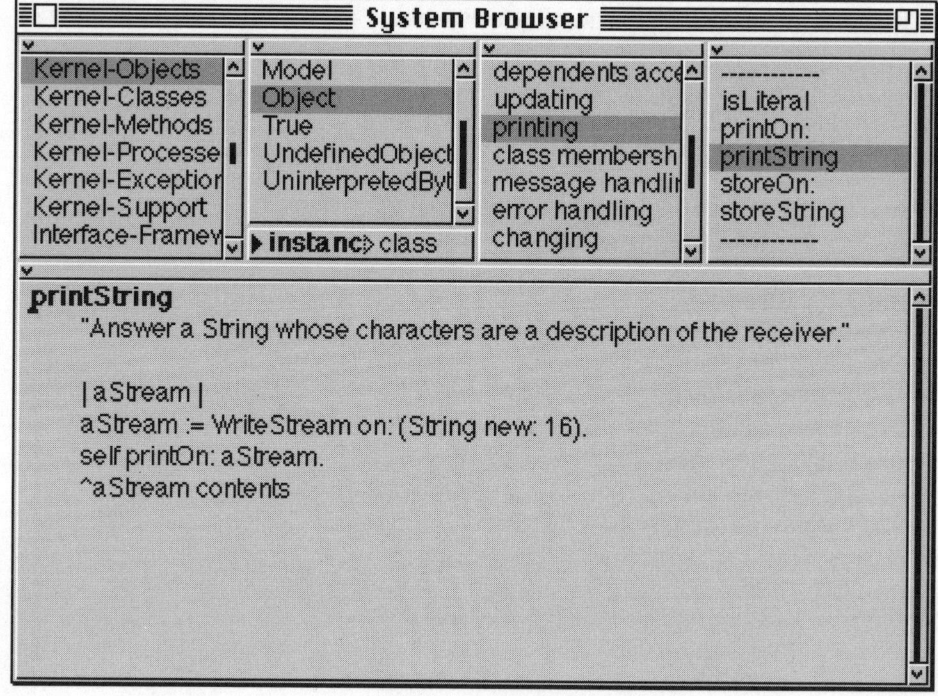

Figure 18.1 The implementation of the **printString** method (in class **Object**).

an uninitialized String, and uses this as the argument when sending the message printOn: to self. Once the printOn: message returns, the contents message is sent to the WriteStream to retrieve the 'completed' String.

The method printOn: has a default implementation in class Object, which uses nextPutAll: to add 'a' (or 'an') and the name of the class to the WriteStream. Many subclasses re-implement this method, to print out instances in a more attractive or comprehensible fashion. For example, Figure 18.2 shows the implementation of the printOn: method in class Point.

When you devise your own classes, you are encouraged to consider re-implementing the printOn: method, in order to assist testing, debugging and re-usability.

18.3 Accessing the file system

The need to access external files from VisualWorks is often surprisingly infrequent in practice, especially for stand-alone applications. However, several classes are provided to support the manipulation of files.

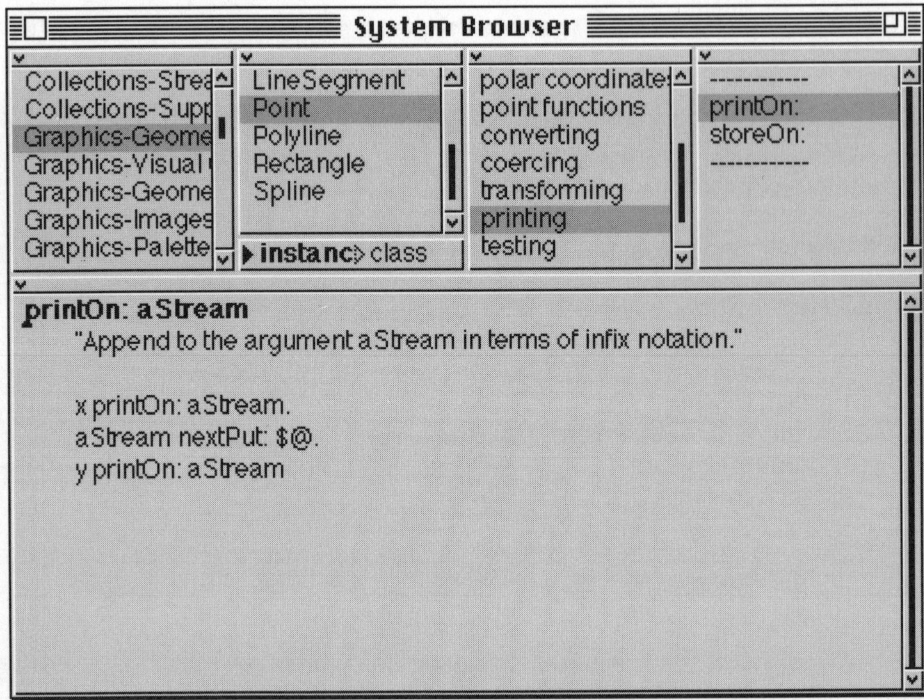

Figure 18.2 The implementation of **printOn:** in class **Point**.

Class Filename

Class Filename represents individual files and directories and provides a convenient mechanism for manipulating files. Class Filename is an abstract superclass; its platform-specific classes (MacFilename, PCFilename, and UnixFilename) provide most of the implementation. Always direct messages to Filename to maintain portability.

To create an instance of Filename, send the message named: to the class. The argument should be a String representing the name of the file in the usual way, possibly including directory names. Alternatively, the message asFilename may be sent to the String.

Class Filename contains many useful methods for the manipulation of files. For example, a file can be removed by sending the delete message to its Filename. (A run-time error occurs if the file does not exist.) The renameTo: message allows files to be renamed, the copyTo: message makes a copy of the file, and the moveTo: message moves a file from one location to another. The argument to each message is a String representing the name of the destination file. Other messages include:

exists – returns true if the file represented by the receiver exists, false otherwise
fileSize – size of the receiver (in bytes)
directoryContents – returns an Array of Strings (raises an error if the receiver is not a directory)
filesMatching: aString – as above, but uses *, #; and returns an OrderedCollection of Strings
contentsOfEntireFile – returns the contents of the receiver
edit – opens a FileBrowser on the receiver
makeDirectory – creates a new directory with the same name as the receiver

As well as messages which can be sent to instances of Filename, there are a number of useful messages that may be sent to the class itself. Some of these are described briefly below:

separator – return the Character used to separate components of the path name, e.g. one of $/, $:, $\ – for portability
maxLength – return the maximum allowed length for a filename on the current platform
volumes – return an Array of Strings identifying all disk volumes

Filestreams

It turns out that a convenient way of viewing the contents of a file is as a 'stream' of data (bytes, characters, etc.). This view is supported in VisualWorks by class ExternalStream, which is a subclass of PositionableStream. There are methods in Filename which return a stream on a named file; thus we can use all the methods inherited from PositionableStream and its superclasses to access the contents of the file. Hence, although there is no such class as Filestream, we refer to a *filestream* meaning a Stream attached to a Filename. The partial class hierarchy is shown below:

```
Object
    Stream
        PeekableStream
            PositionableStream
                ExternalStream
                    BufferedExternalStream
                        ExternalReadStream
                            ExternalReadAppendStream
                            ExternalReadWriteStream
                        ExternalWriteStream
```

The most convenient way of creating a filestream is to send the appropriate message to an instance of Filename. For example,

```
(Filename named: aFilename) readWriteStream
```

or

```
aString asFilename readWriteStream
```

It's often important to distinguish between those messages which create a *new* file and those that overwrite or append to an existing file. The examples below summarize:

aFilename readStream – read-only
aFilename appendStream – write-only – position is always at the end of the file
aFilename writeStream – write-only; empties the file first
aFilename readWriteStream – read and write access
aFilename newReadWriteStream – as above, but empties the file first

Class BufferedExternalStream is a Smalltalk representation of the data on an external file, which must be opened and closed. The creation of a stream on a Filename *opens* the file, but it must be closed explicitly. The close method first flushes the buffer, then closes the file. A common programming error is to omit to close files. This can lead to a number of possible outcomes: preventing other processes from accessing open files, losing data, or (on some platforms) running out of file resources.

Once a filestream has been created, then all the methods available in the superclasses are available for use. For example, the familiar messages next (for filestreams providing read-access) and nextPut: (for filestreams providing write-access) can be used. If the file contains Characters (the most common case), then obviously the argument to nextPut: should be a Character. Similarly, if nextPutAll: is used, the argument should be a String. As one would expect, by default filestreams are accessed one Character at a time (or a collection of Characters); the message binary causes the file to be accessed one byte at a time. To revert the filestream to 'character' mode, send it the message text.

The internal implementation of BufferedExternalStream does not actually perform a write to the disk for every character or byte written – this would be very inefficient. Instead, a buffering scheme is used. However, to ensure that data has been completely written to the disk, the method flush is provided.

Exercise 18.6

Browse the file system classes mentioned above.

Exercise 18.7

File out a class (e.g. Filename). Create a ReadStream on the file and inspect it. Try the effects of next and next:.

Exercise 18.8

Add a method to ExternalReadStream called nextLine, which will answer with a String containing all the characters up to, but not including, the next newline or carriage return Character.

Exercise 18.9

Using the answer from the exercise above, write some code that reads a character file and writes another with the lines *reversed*.

Storing Objects

Class Object contains two methods that are used when storing objects – storeString and storeOn:. These work in a similar way to the printString and printOn: messages described above. However, the intent is that the result of sending storeString to an object is a String, which, if compiled and evaluated, produces an *exactly similar* object. The same mechanism can also be used to produce a file (using a filestream rather than a String) which can readily be transferred between machines (on a diskette, or over a network, for example). This provides a simple way of transferring objects between VisualWorks images. There are, however, certain problems . . .

The storeOn: mechanism cannot cope with cyclic structures. Since almost all 'interesting' objects contain cycles, the storeOn: approach is rarely useful in practice.

Unfortunately, Smalltalk's compiler only allows methods which have less than 256 literals to be compiled. Since the general storeOn: messages ignore this fact, it is easy to get an object that was stored correctly, but cannot be retrieved.

Exercise 18.10

Browse the storeString and storeOn: methods in class Object.

Exercise 18.11

Use the **implementors** option from the <operate> menu of the protocols pane to browse other implementations of storeOn:.

A more successful alternative is to use the 'Binary Object Storage System' (BOSS) which stores objects in an encoded format. The protocol to BOSS is very similar to that of streams above. In the example below, we create an instance of FinancialHistory (see Chapter 11), and store it in a file using BOSS.

```
| spendingHistory fileStream storage |
spendingHistory := FinancialHistory initialBalance: 800.
spendingHistory  spend: 220 on: 'rent';
                 spend: 30 on: 'food';
                 spend: 45 on: 'drink';
                 spend: 20 on: 'petrol';
                 receive: 300 for: 'salary';
                 receive: 50 for: 'expenses';
                 receive: 50 for: 'overtime'.
"Open a stream on a file"
fileStream := 'spending.bos' asFilename writeStream.
"Open the storage
"storage := BinaryObjectStorage onNew: fileStream.
"Put the object into storage"
storage nextPut: spendingHistory.
"Close the storage (and thus the file)"
storage close
```

In the example below, we retrieve the object from the file created above, thus:

```
| fileStream storage spendingHistory |
"Open a stream on a file"
fileStream := 'spending.bos' asFilename readStream.
"Open the storage"
"storage := BinaryObjectStorage onOld: fileStream.
"Get the object from storage"
spendingHistory := storage next.
"Close the storage (and thus the file)"
storage close.
"Inspect the result"
spendingHistory inspect
```

Exercise 18.12

Create an object, such as a Point or a Rectangle, and store it in a file using BOSS.

Exercise 18.13

Retrieve the object you stored in the exercise above.

Exercise 18.14

Create a collection of objects, and store them on a file using BOSS; then retrieve them.

18.4 Class Random

Instances of class Random represent a 'stream' of randomly generated numbers – instances of Float in the range $0 \leqslant x < 1$. Thus, the following expression prints 10 random numbers in the Transcript:

```
| rand |
rand := Random new.
10 timesRepeat: [Transcript show: rand next printString; cr]
```

However, quite often there is a requirement to obtain random numbers within a range greater than or different from that offered by class Random. This requirement can be met easily via some simple arithmetic. For example, to produce a random number in the range 1 to 6, the following expression could be used:

```
| rand |
rand := Random new.
rand next * 5 + 1
```

Alternatively, to produce an *integer* random number in the range 1 to 6, the following expression may be used:

```
| rand |
rand := Random new.
(rand next * 6 + 1) truncated
```

Finally, we may also use an instance of class Random to produce a random element from a sequenceable collection:

```
| rand coll size |
coll := #('a' #b $c).
rand := Random new.
size := coll size.
5 timesRepeat: [| index |
                index := (rand next * size + 1) truncated.
                Transcript show: (coll at: index) printString; cr]
```

Exercise 18.15

Modify the last example above so that a random number may be returned from a specified Interval.

Exercise 18.16

Similarly, modify the example so that a random Character may be returned from a specified String.

Exercise 18.17

Consider implementing a subclass of Random (called BetterRandom, say) which takes responsibility for producing random numbers in a specified range.

18.5 Summary

The use of streams in Smalltalk provides an alternative mechanism for enumerating over a collection of objects. Although we can use the iterators described in Chapter 15, these are sometimes slightly awkward, especially if the collection is being simultaneously modified.

One of the more important uses of a stream is when it's necessary to create or edit a file. As we have seen, this may be achieved by using a stream opened on an instance of (some subclass of) Filename. The file may contain simple text, a representation of (one or more) classes, or Smalltalk objects.

In the following two chapters we begin to examine the graphical capabilities of VisualWorks. The first of these explores the 'media' that may be displayed on the screen.

19 Graphics (1) – media

Chapters 19 and 20 describe the graphical operations available in VisualWorks. This chapter considers the media that may be displayed on the screen and Chapter 20 describes the objects that may be rendered on those media. Additionally, this chapter describes the means by which the properties of the media may be modified – e.g. color, line width. Many examples are provided to introduce the reader to VisualWorks' graphics capabilities.

19.1 Introduction

There are basically three kinds of screen-based 'graphic media': *windows*, *pixmaps*, and *masks*. Collectively, they are known as *display surfaces*, since the classes that represent them are all subclasses of class DisplaySurface. The class hierarchy is as follows:

```
Object
        GraphicsMedium
                DisplaySurface
                        UnmappableSurface
                                Pixmap
                                Mask
                        Window
```

A window in VisualWorks corresponds to a window supplied by the host platform's window manager and is an instance of Window or one of its subclasses. It is a rectangular matrix of pixels, each pixel defining a color (via a palette – see later). Clearly, the range of colors available on any particular screen will be restricted by the display hardware (and perhaps the host window system). Each window also has a GraphicsContext on which objects may be drawn.

Windows do not retain their graphic contents automatically: certain operations produce 'damaged' regions in a window (e.g. moving, resizing, use of menus). The graphic contents of such regions are incorrect and must be regenerated by the Smalltalk code associated with the regions. (This is discussed in more detail in Chapter 30.)

A pixmap is similar to a window except that is *off-screen*. For the contents of the pixmap to be viewable, it must be drawn on the GraphicsContext of a window currently on the screen.

A mask is similar to a pixmap, except that its contents are based on 'coverage values' rather than 'color values' (this distinction is explored in more detail later). The area described by a mask therefore may be non-rectangular. Coverage values at mask pixels are either 0 (transparent) or 1 (opaque).

The abstract superclass DisplaySurface provides a mechanism to connect instances of its subclasses to the virtual machine, and hence to the screen. In addition, it provides many methods, including background: (which sets the 'background' color of its instances) and clear (which clears its current contents).

19.2 Class GraphicsContext

The abstract superclass GraphicsContext handles the displaying (rendering) of graphical objects, such as *Images* (see later) onto a graphic medium (much of the implementation of the rendering represented by GraphicsContext is directly supported by the virtual machine). (Specialized subclasses are responsible for output to the screen or a printer.) It is, as such, a repository of parameters affecting graphics operations; these parameters are retained as instance variables and accessible via instance messages (Figure 19.1). They include:

- The display surface on which to display.
- The coordinate system in which to interpret graphic operations. This may be different from the natural coordinate system of the graphic medium. (Coordinate values must lie in the range −32768 to 32767, i.e. $-(2^{15})$ to $2^{15}-1$.)
- The clipping rectangle – accessed via the message clippingBounds. The clipping rectangle is the area in which graphic objects may be displayed. If any region of a graphic object lies outside this region, it is said to be 'clipped'.
- The *paint* used to draw unpainted objects – black, by default.
- The width used to draw lines – one pixel, by default.

Using a GraphicsContext

There are two ways of displaying graphics. The simplest is to ask a graphic object to display itself on a GraphicsContext – for example, to display a String at a Point:

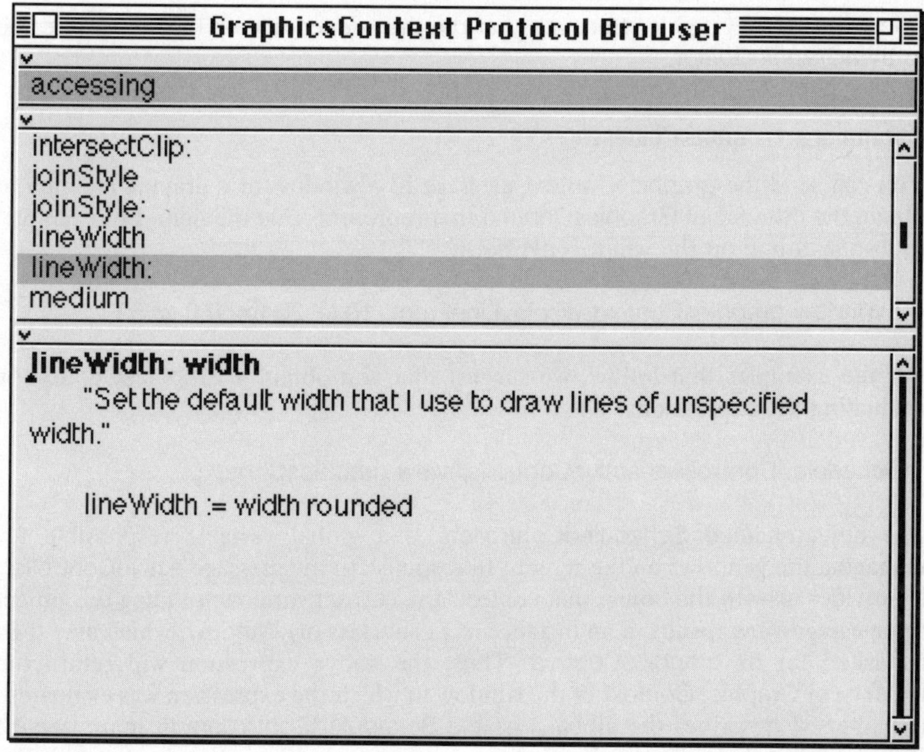

Figure 19.1 The **accessing** protocol of class **GraphicsContext**.

```
'Customer' displayOn: aGraphicsContext at: 100 @ 100
```

Similarly, a GraphicsContext can be requested to display a graphic object:

```
aGraphicsContext display: 'Customer' at: 100 @ 100
```

Both variants have exactly the same result.

The other way of displaying graphics is to send a message that specifies the type of graphic object to display – for example, to display a line:

```
aGraphicsContext displayLineFrom: 10 @ 20 to: 150 @ 50
```

Of these styles of graphics display, the first (asking a graphic object to display itself) is more flexible because it allows the creation of general display statements such as:

```
aGraphicObject displayOn: aGraphicsContext at: 10 @ 10
```

where the actual graphic effect varies at run time depending on the object referred to by *aGraphicObject*.

Obtaining a GraphicsContext

You can send the graphicsContext message to a window or a graphic medium to obtain the instance of GraphicsContext that represents that medium. For example, to display a line on the window *aWindow*:

```
aWindow graphicsContext displayLineFrom: 10 @ 20 to: 150 @ 50
```

For the examples that follow, we suggest that you obtain a GraphicsContext by evaluating the expression:

```
ScheduledControllers activeController view graphicsContext
```

The object named ScheduledControllers is a global variable responsible for managing the windows on the screen. In response to the message activeController, it provides us with the object that controls the current window; sending this object the message view results in an instance of (a subclass of) Window, which may then be asked for its graphicsContext. Thus, the above expression will return the instance of GraphicsContext of the window in which the expression was evaluated. (Chapter 31 describes the global variable ScheduledControllers in more detail.) So, to rewrite the example above:

```
ScheduledControllers activeController view graphicsContext
                displayLineFrom: 10 @ 20 to: 150 @ 50.
```

we may produce our first graphical display! (See Figure 19.2.)

GraphicsContext examples

Type and then evaluate the following example in a Workspace:

```
| gc |
gc := ScheduledControllers activeController view graphicsContext.
'A short, yet worthwhile string' displayOn: gc
                                 at: gc clippingBounds center
```

The following pages contain a number of examples for you to familiarize yourself with several of the available messages; there are more later in this chapter and in Chapter 20. Type each one of them in a Workspace and then evaluate it. You may

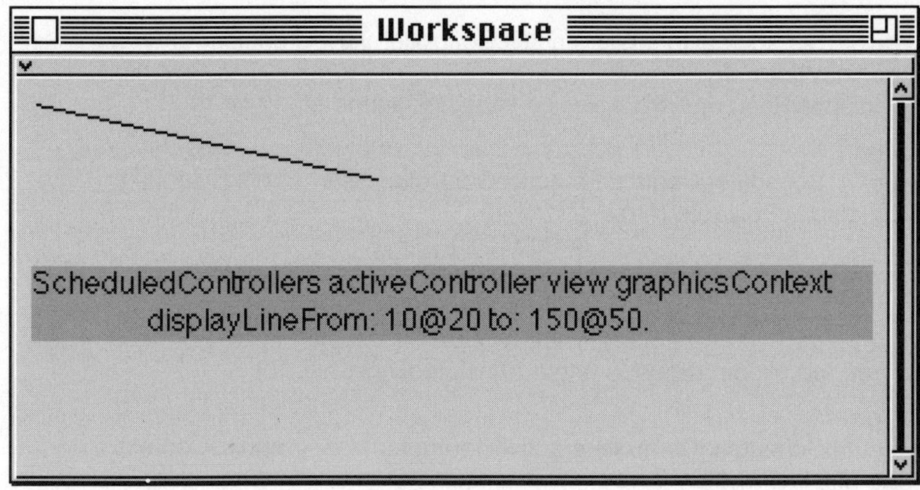

Figure 19.2 Producing a simple graphical display.

find it easier to use a large Workspace, and to refresh the window between examples.

```
| gc |
gc := ScheduledControllers activeController view graphicsContext.
gc displayString: 'A short, yet worthwhile string'
   at: gc clippingBounds center

| gc |
gc := ScheduledControllers activeController view graphicsContext.
gc displayString: 'A short, yet worthwhile string'
   from: 21
   to: 29
   at: gc clippingBounds center

| gc |
gc := ScheduledControllers activeController view graphicsContext.
gc displayRectangle: gc clippingBounds
| gc |

gc := ScheduledControllers activeController view graphicsContext.
gc displayRectangle: gc clippingBounds at: 10 @ 10

| gc |
gc := ScheduledControllers activeController view graphicsContext.
gc displayRectangularBorder: gc clippingBounds
```

```
| gc |
gc := ScheduledControllers activeController view graphicsContext.
gc lineWidth: 4;
  displayRectangularBorder: gc clippingBounds at: 10 @ 10

| gc |
gc := ScheduledControllers activeController view graphicsContext.
gc displayPolygon: (Array
                        with: 0 @ 0
                        with: 200 @ 0
                        with: 100 @ 100
                        with: 0 @ 0)
  at: (gc clippingBounds origin translatedBy: 10 @ 10)

| gc |
gc := ScheduledControllers activeController view graphicsContext.
gc displayPolyline: (Array
                        with: 0 @ 0
                        with: 200 @ 0
                        with: 100 @ 100
                        with: 0 @ 0)
  at: (gc clippingBounds origin translatedBy: 10 @ 10)

| gc |
gc := ScheduledControllers activeController view graphicsContext.
gc displayPolygon: (Array
                        with: 0 @ 0
                        with: 200 @ 0
                        with: 100 @ 100
                        with: 25 @ 50)
  at: (gc clippingBounds origin translatedBy: 10 @ 10)

| gc |
gc := ScheduledControllers activeController view graphicsContext.
gc lineWidth: 2;
  displayPolyline: (Array
                        with: 0 @ 0
                        with: 200 @ 0
                        with: 100 @ 100
                        with: 25 @ 50)
  at: (gc clippingBounds origin translatedBy: 10 @ 10)

| gc |
gc := ScheduledControllers activeController view graphicsContext.
gc displayArcBoundedBy: gc clippingBounds
  startAngle: 25
  sweepAngle: 60
```

```
| gc |
gc := ScheduledControllers activeController view graphicsContext.
gc displayWedgeBoundedBy: gc clippingBounds
  startAngle: 25
  sweepAngle: 60
```

```
| gc |
gc := ScheduledControllers activeController view graphicsContext.
gc lineWidth: 8;
  displayArcBoundedBy: gc clippingBounds
  startAngle: 25
  sweepAngle: 120
  at: (20 @ 20) negated
```

```
| gc |
gc := ScheduledControllers activeController view graphicsContext.
gc displayWedgeBoundedBy: gc clippingBounds
  startAngle: 25
  sweepAngle: 120
  at: (20 @ 20) negated
```

Exercise 19.1

Browse the examples class protocol of class GraphicsContext.

19.3 Class Paint

We mentioned above that a GraphicsContext has a *paint* as one of its parameters. Class Paint is an abstract class, and represents a *paint* that can be used for rendering a graphical object onto a graphic medium.

Paints can either be 'flat' colors, represented by the abstract superclass SimplePaint or a Pattern. A Pattern retains an Image (see Chapter 20) defining the pattern to be used.

Concrete subclasses of SimplePaint include ColorValue, representing 'real' colors, and CoverageValue, representing partially transparent areas (i.e. translucent). The above classes are structured in a class hierarchy, as follows:

```
Object
    Paint
        Pattern
            SimplePaint
                ColorValue
                CoverageValue
```

The class protocol of ColorValue has many methods for creating colors. For example:

```
ColorValue black.
ColorValue lightGray.
ColorValue darkGreen.
```

Alternatively, the color may be specified using one of the 'color models':

```
ColorValue red: 0.3 green: 0.4 blue: 0.05.
ColorValue cyan: 0.4 magenta: 0.4 yellow: 0.9.
ColorValue hue: 0.1 saturation: 0.7 brightness: 0.3.
```

Finally, we may also specify a degree of 'grayness':

```
ColorValue brightness: 0.5
```

CoverageValue has only one instance creation method:

```
CoverageValue coverage: aNumber
```

where $0 \leq aNumber \leq 1$.

Paint examples

Here are some more examples demonstrating how to use paint:

```
| win |
win := ScheduledControllers activeController view.
win background: ColorValue gray.
win clear

| gc |
gc := ScheduledControllers activeController view graphicsContext.
gc paint: ColorValue gray.
gc displayRectangle: gc clippingBounds

| gc |
gc := ScheduledControllers activeController view graphicsContext.
gc paint: ColorValue gray.
gc lineWidth: 4.
gc displayLineFrom: gc clippingBounds topLeft
   to: gc clippingBounds center
```

Exercise 19.2

Browse the Paint classes mentioned above.

Exercise 19.3

If you have a color screen, modify the examples to use colors other than gray.

19.4 Class Palette

In the description of graphic media above, we mentioned the concept of a *palette* – a *mapping* from a pixel value (a number) to a paint value (an instance of some subclass of Paint). Class Palette (a subclass of Collection) is an abstract superclass, and represents this mapping. The class hierarchy is as follows:

```
Object
    Collection
        KeyedCollection
            Palette
                ColorPalette
                    FixedPalette
                    MappedPalette
                        MonoMappedPalette
                CoveragePalette
```

Class ColorPalette is an abstract superclass for palettes that contain *only* ColorValues. Concrete subclasses include FixedPalette, where groups of the individual bits in the pixel values are interpreted directly as red, green and blue components.

Another useful subclass is MappedPalette, which allows an arbitrary mapping (a true lookup table) between pixel values and colors. Any of the Paint subclasses can be used as the color.

Class MonoMappedPalette handles palettes with exactly two colors – useful for monochrome screens. Useful Palette creation methods include:

```
MappedPalette whiteBlack.
MappedPalette blackWhite.
MappedPalette with: ColorValue red with: ColorValue green.
MappedPalette withColors: anArray.
```

Instances of CoveragePalette contain a *maximum pixel value* – this is used to determine the coverage value that corresponds to a pixel value (by dividing the value of a pixel by the maximum pixel value). Hence, each pixel value in a

CoveragePalette directly specifies a 'scaled' CoverageValue. To create an instance of CoveragePalette, a maximum pixel value must be supplied (represented by the argument *anInteger*):

```
CoveragePalette maxPixelValue: anInteger
```

Pixels in the range from zero to *anInteger* are mapped uniformly to coverage values in the range 0.0 to 1.0.

Examples in the creation and use of palettes are given when we describe class Image (Chapter 20), since they are most often used in conjunction with instances of that class.

Exercise 19.4

Browse class Palette (and its subclasses).

Exercise 19.5

Produce an example similar to those earlier which will:

1. Clear to gray a 250 × 250 pixel area in the top-left of the window.
2. Draw a border around the cleared area in white lines, four pixels wide.
3. Draw the diagonals of the area, in black lines, one pixel wide.
4. Display the string 'Origin' centered over the intersection of the two diagonals.

Exercise 19.6

Create a new example, based on the code from above, which will work for the *clipping bounds* of the window in which the expressions are evaluated.

19.5 Summary

The abstract superclasses DisplaySurface, GraphicsContext, Paint and Palette combine to provide VisualWorks' extensive graphics capabilities. First, the subclasses of DisplaySurface provide a representation of the screen-based graphics media in which objects may be displayed. Second, class GraphicsContext provides the behavior for displaying and rendering objects onto a graphic medium. Finally, subclasses of Paint and Palette are used to control the 'paint' at each pixel of the graphics medium.

In the following chapter we describe the graphic objects which may be displayed on a graphics medium.

20 Graphics (2) – objects

Much of the functionality in the VisualWorks image deals with graphical output, some of which was covered in Chapter 19. This chapter concentrates on the objects which may be displayed on the graphical media introduced in Chapter 19, which includes classes VisualComponent, Image, Text, and ComposedText. We also briefly examine ways in which instances of the Geometric classes (Chapter 13) may also be displayed.

20.1 Class VisualComponent

Class VisualComponent is an abstract class representing all sorts of graphic objects which might be displayed on the screen, and as such defines a standard protocol for all graphic objects. Most graphic objects are instances of some subclass of VisualComponent; however, there are also graphic objects that lie outside this class hierarchy. We have already seen some of these: for example, String, Pixmap, etc. It's important to note that although *all* graphic objects may be displayed (via the displayOn:at: message, for example), not all graphic objects may be a *component* of some other object – it is the behavior to act as a component, or to be contained, that is provided by class VisualComponent. We shall see later (in Chapter 30) how to create *nested* graphical structures whose elements are kinds of VisualComponent.

All VisualComponents also support a notion of a *bounds* – a Rectangle within which the graphic object will be displayed. Additionally, they can provide a *preferred bounds*, although they may be distorted away from this. These properties may be accessed via the bounds and preferredBounds messages, respectively.

20.2 Class Image

The abstract superclass Image is a subclass of class VisualComponent. It represents a rectangular array of pixels each of which in turn represent a particular color. Images commonly represent pictures captured by a scanner, etc. The size of an Image is retained by instance variables width and height that may be accessed via the corresponding messages.

A pixel can be represented by one or more bits. Subclasses of Image are provided to implement Images with pixels of different *depths*, e.g. Depth8Image. Pixels are mapped onto actual colors for display by a Palette, which is associated with an Image (see later).

Class Image supports many useful operations. An Image of one depth can be converted to an Image of a different depth (or with a different Palette). Pixels can be modified individually. Parts of one Image can be copied onto another. There are several useful Image manipulation methods provided. Images can also be used as *paint* for drawing and as a *mask* while rendering (see later).

There are many instance creation messages available for class Image. The most general message creates an 'empty' Image, i.e. one whose pixels are all zero. The template is:

Image extent: *aPoint* depth: *anInteger* palette: *aPalette*

Other messages are available to create an Image whose content is given by a ByteArray. For example, evaluating the message

```
Image parcPlaceLogo
```

will create a Depth1Image, shown in Figure 20.1. The parcPlaceLogo method (in class protocol examples) specifies a ByteArray containing the pixel arrangement that gives the Image's appearance.

There are two alternatives to the usual instance creation methods:

```
Image fromUser
Pixmap fromClipboard asImage
```

Figure 20.1 The ParcPlace logo **Image**.

The first of these waits for the user to 'grab' a rectangular region of the screen using the mouse, and then returns an Image (of the appropriate depth) whose contents are a copy of the pixels in that region. The second example creates an instance of Pixmap that is a representation of the graphics contents of the platform's clipboard and then converts this into an Image. (This operation only succeeds when using a window manager that provides a *graphic clipboard* – e.g. the Apple Macintosh.)

The examples below demonstrate the creation and display of instances of class Image. Some of the examples show how to use an Image as a *paint* and a *mask*. Also, note how the Images are constructed using a specified Palette (Chapter 19).

Displaying an 'empty' Image

First, we create an Image of depth one, whose extent is 100@50, with a 'whiteBlack' Palette. Then, we display it. (By default, the pixel values of a new Image are all zero. Hence the Image displays as a white rectangle, since we are using a whiteBlack Palette – 0 is mapped to white, 1 is mapped to black.)

```
| image gc |
gc := ScheduledControllers activeController view graphicsContext.
image := Image extent: 100@50
                depth: 1
                palette: MappedPalette whiteBlack.
image displayOn: gc
```

Displaying an existing Image

In an earlier example we referred to the parcPlaceLogo message. Here, we use the message again, and display the result. Note that, when displayed, the color of the text is red.

```
Image parcPlaceLogo displayOn:
    ScheduledControllers activeController view graphicsContext.
```

Magnifying an Image

By sending the message magnifiedBy: to an Image, we get a *new* larger Image:

```
(Image parcPlaceLogo magnifiedBy: 2@2) displayOn:
    ScheduledControllers activeController view graphicsContext.
```

Centering an Image

The displayOn:at: message is used in the example below to center the Image within the bounds of the window. The point at which the Image is displayed is its top-left corner (or *origin*). The point is determined by calculating the difference between the center of the bounds of the Image and the center of the bounds of the window (equivalent to the center of the clipping bounds of its GraphicsContext).

```
| gc image |
gc := ScheduledControllers activeController view graphicsContext.
image := Image parcPlaceLogo.
image displayOn: gc at: gc clippingBounds center – image bounds center
```

Changing the background color

This example is similar to the one above. However, we have introduced an extra statement to specify the color of the GraphicsContext, before displaying the Image.

```
| gc image |
gc := ScheduledControllers activeController view graphicsContext.
image := Image parcPlaceLogo.
gc paint: ColorValue gray.
gc displayRectangle: gc clippingBounds.
image displayOn: gc
        at: gc clippingBounds center – image bounds center
```

Creating a Pattern

We noted in Chapter 19 that a Pattern can be created from an Image. Here, we see another example, in which the paint of the GraphicsContext is specified to be a Pattern based on the ParcPlace logo. The effect of changing the paint is not visible until we display a filled rectangle:

```
| gc image |
gc := ScheduledControllers activeController view graphicsContext.
image := Image parcPlaceLogo.
gc paint: image asPattern.
gc displayRectangle: gc clippingBounds
```

Changing the tile phase

In this example we change the *tile phase* of the GraphicsContext, before displaying a filled rectangle. Note, also, that the argument to the displayRectangle: message is the result of a message expression which reduces the area by 20 pixels.

```
| gc image |
gc := ScheduledControllers activeController view graphicsContext.
image := Image parcPlaceLogo.
gc paint: image asPattern.
gc tilePhase: image extent //2.
gc displayRectangle: (gc clippingBounds insetBy: 2@2)
```

Changing the Palette

It's possible to change the Palette of an Image after it has been created. In the example below, we modify the color values to be light gray and dark gray (rather than black and red, as specified by the parcPlaceLogo method).

```
| gc image |
gc := ScheduledControllers activeController view graphicsContext.
image := Image parcPlaceLogo palette:
                    (MappedPalette with: ColorValue veryLightGray
                                   with: ColorValue darkGray).
image displayOn: gc
      at: gc clippingBounds center – image bounds center
```

Using CoverageValues (1)

In the two examples given below, we provide two mechanisms to produce a 'mask'. In the first example, we change the Palette of the Image so that it uses CoverageValues; in the second we use the modified Image as the 'shape' for an instance of Mask. Note how the background of the Image becomes transparent.

```
| gc image |
gc := ScheduledControllers activeController view graphicsContext.
image := Image parcPlaceLogo palette: CoveragePalette monoMaskPalette.
gc paint: ColorValue darkGray.
image displayOn: gc
    at: gc clippingBounds center – image bounds center
```

```
| gc image mask |
gc := ScheduledControllers activeController view graphicsContext.
image := Image parcPlaceLogo palette: CoveragePalette monoMaskPalette.
gc paint: ColorValue darkGray.
mask := Mask fromShape: image.
gc displayMask: mask
    at: gc clippingBounds center – mask bounds center
```

Using CoverageValues (2)

The following two examples mirror those given above. The only modification to the code is the expression which modifies the Palette of the Image, with the result that, when displayed, the text of the Image becomes transparent.

```
| gc image |
gc := ScheduledControllers activeController view graphicsContext.
image := Image parcPlaceLogo convertToCoverageWithOpaquePixel: 0.
gc paint: ColorValue darkGray.
image displayOn: gc
    at: gc clippingBounds center – image bounds center
```

```
| gc mask image |
gc := ScheduledControllers activeController view graphicsContext.
image := Image parcPlaceLogo convertToCoverageWithOpaquePixel: 0.
gc paint: ColorValue darkGray.
mask := Mask fromShape: image.
gc displayMask: mask
    at: gc clippingBounds center – mask bounds center
```

Exercise 20.1

Browse class Image and its subclasses. Pay particular attention to the image processing protocol.

Exercise 20.2

Try some examples of using Images. (Experiment with Images captured from the screen/clipboard.)

20.3 Class Text

Class Text is similar to class String (Chapter 15), except that class Text also provides its instances with style-based attributes or *emphasis*, such as font characteristics, size and color for each character of the string. For example:

'**Smalltalk-80**: An *Introduction* to Application Development'

To create a Text with *no* emphasis the message asText should be sent to an instance of String. Alternatively, the message fromString: may be sent to class Text, with a String as the argument.

The emphasis of a Text is represented by one or more of the Symbols below:

```
#bold          #italic
#serif         #sansSerif
#small         #large
#underline
#strikeOut
```

To create a Text with one of these emphases, the message string:emphasis: should be sent to class Text, with the Symbol representing the emphasis as the second argument; the String is the first. Some examples are:

```
'Smalltalk-80' asText
Text fromString: 'Smalltalk-80'
Text string: 'Smalltalk-80' emphasis: #bold
```

It's also possible to create a Text with multiple emphases, for example #large and #bold. In this case an Array of Symbols is used to represent the emphasis; for example:

```
Text string: 'Smalltalk-80' emphasis: #(#bold #large)
```

Once a Text has been created, its emphasis may be modified by sending it the message emphasizeFrom: start to: stop with: anEmphasis, where start and stop are indices of the underlying String and anEmphasis is a Symbol, or Array of Symbols, as described above.

There are also two shortcuts for the message emphasizeFrom:to:with:. These are emphasizeAllWith:, which uses the argument to change the emphasis for all the characters in the receiver; and allBold, which changes the emphasis of all the characters of the receiver to #bold. It's important to note that these messages are destructive – i.e. changing the emphasis of a sequence of characters *overrides* any existing emphasis for those characters. To retrieve the emphasis for a particular Character of the Text, send it the message emphasisAt: – the argument should be the index of the Character.

The code below gives an example of using Text. (The last line causes a 'warning' dialog box to appear, so that you may see the result of evaluating the code – see Figure 20.2.)

```
| aText index |
aText := 'Smalltalk-80: An Introduction to Application Development' asText.
index := aText findString: 'Smalltalk-80:' startingAt: 1.
aText emphasizeFrom: index
        to: 'Smalltalk-80:' size + index -1
        with: #bold.
index := aText findString: 'Introduction' startingAt: index.
aText emphasizeFrom: index to: index + 'Introduction' size with: #italic.
DialogView warn: aText
```

Figure 20.2 A **Text** with emphasis.

An Association (Chapter 14) may also be used as an emphasis, in which the *key* is #color and the *value* is a Paint. Some examples are:

```
| aText |
aText := 'Colourful' asText.
aText emphasizeAllWith: #color->ColorValue gray.
DialogView warn: aText

| aText |
aText := 'Colourful' asText.
aText emphasizeAllWith: (Array
                             with: #color->ColorValue gray
                             with: #italic).
DialogView warn: aText
```

Exercise 20.3

In a Workspace, modify the 'Smalltalk-80: An Introduction to Application Development' example to create the text 'The *Guardian*' in a large font. (For those of you unfamiliar with this British newspaper, the string 'the' is in a sans serif font, and the string 'Guardian' is serif, italic.)

20.4 Class ComposedText

As the class name suggests, class ComposedText (a subclass of VisualComponent) is a more sophisticated kind of text, offering control over its composition in terms of such characteristics as alignment and indentation. The easiest way to create a ComposedText is to send the message asComposedText to a String or Text. However, the class also provides several other class instance creation methods.

The simplest of these is withText:, which expects a Text as its argument. It's also possible to specify a *style* to be used when displaying; this is specified as the second argument in the class instance creation message withText:style:. The argument must be an instance of TextAttributes (see below). The final instance creation message withText:style:compositionWidth: expects a third (integer) argument that specifies the *composition width* of the resulting ComposedText in *pixels*.

Once created, instances of ComposedText may be modified in terms of their alignment, indentation, and composition width:

- The four messages leftFlush, rightFlush, centered and justified may be used to control the alignment of the text relative to its composition width. The default setting is leftFlush.
- Indentation and margin setting are achieved by the messages firstIndent: (first line), restIndent: (subsequent lines), and rightIndent: (all lines). Each has a corresponding message to retrieve the current setting. Use the clearIndents message to reset all three indents to zero.
- Finally, the messages compositionWidth and compositionWidth: may be used to access and set the width of a ComposedText. If a line of text is longer than the width of the ComposedText, then it will be wrapped around to the following line, if possible at a word boundary.

20.5 Class VariableSizeTextAttributes

The 'text attributes' or *emphases* described above (i.e. the symbols used to control character style) and others such as tab stops, line grid (the vertical distance between the top of one line of text and the next) and baseline (the vertical distance between the top of a line and the baseline of that line) are controlled by an instance of VariableSizeTextAttributes. (The baseline is the line from which a font's ascent and descent are measured – see also Figure 20.3.)

The VisualWorks image currently contains four instances of VariableSizeTextAttributes, named *default, small, large* and *fixed*. To access any one of these, send the message styleNamed: to the class with a Symbol as the argument. For example:

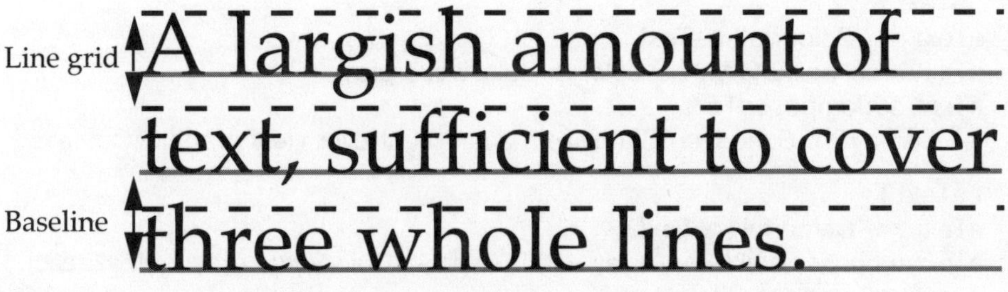

Figure 20.3 The difference between line grid and baseline.

```
VariableSizeTextAttributes styleNamed: #default
VariableSizeTextAttributes styleNamed: #large
VariableSizeTextAttributes styleNamed: #small
VariableSizeTextAttributes styleNamed: #fixed
```

One of the four is the *default* instance of VariableSizeTextAttributes – used as the default style for the display of all text in Browsers and other tools. The default may be accessed by sending the message default to the class. To change the default, send the message setDefaultTo: to the class, with the appropriate Symbol as the argument. (The 'Settings Tool' can also be used to change the default font; see Chapter 5 for more details.) You will also need to inform any open windows that they should redisplay themselves using the new default. This is achieved by sending the message resetViews to class VariableSizeTextAttributes. For example:

```
VariableSizeTextAttributes setDefaultTo: #fixed; resetViews
```

The examples below create instances of ComposedText and display them in the window in which the expressions are evaluated.

```
| gc composedText |
gc := ScheduledControllers activeController view graphicsContext.
composedText := 'A short, yet worthwhile string' asComposedText.
composedText
    displayOn: gc
    at: gc clippingBounds center – composedText bounds center

| composedText |
composedText := ComposedText withText:
            'Smalltalk-80: An Introduction to Application Development' asText
                                    style: (VariableSizeTextAttributes default).
composedText
    displayOn: ScheduledControllers activeController view graphicsContext

| aText |
aText := 'Colourful' asText.
aText emphasizeAllWith: #color->ColorValue gray.
aText asComposedText
    displayOn: ScheduledControllers activeController view graphicsContext

| aText |
aText := 'Colourful' asText.
aText emphasizeAllWith: (Array with: #color->ColorValue gray with: #italic).
aText asComposedText
    displayOn: ScheduledControllers activeController view graphicsContext
```

```
| composedText |
composedText := ComposedText withText:
'Smalltalk-80:\An\Introduction\to\Application\Development' withCRs asText
                            style: (VariableSizeTextAttributes styleNamed:#large).
composedText rightFlush
  displayOn: ScheduledControllers activeController view graphicsContext
```

Exercise 20.4

Browse classes ComposedText and VariableSizeTextAttributes.

Exercise 20.5

Experiment with creating your own instances of ComposedText.

Exercise 20.6

Modify the code from Exercise 19.5 to use an instance of ComposedText to display the word 'Origin'. Make sure the exact center of the word is over the center of the window.

Exercise 20.7

Change the default font for your VisualWorks image.

20.6 Displaying Geometrics

Although we haven't yet examined *wrappers* in detail in this book (see Chapter 30), it is worth mentioning them here in relation to the mechanism provided to display Geometric objects. As its name suggests, a wrapper encloses some other object – its *component*. A GeometricWrapper encloses a Geometric object and consequently allows it to behave as if it is a kind of VisualComponent.

Class StrokingWrapper allows a Geometric object to be displayed using lines, while class FillingWrapper allows a Geometric object to be displayed with its inside filled. Note that the latter form is not always sensible (e.g. a *filled* LineSegment!). The common properties of these classes are represented by the abstract superclass GeometricWrapper.

To create a GeometricWrapper, send the message on: to the appropriate class, with the Geometric object as the argument. For example:

```
StrokingWrapper on: (Circle center: 100@100 radius: 50)
```

As a shortcut, a Geometric object can be sent a message to return a GeometricWrapper with the receiver as the component. The messages are asStroker and asFiller. The example below creates a FillingWrapper containing a Rectangle.

```
| gc image |
gc := ScheduledControllers activeController view graphicsContext.
image := Image parcPlaceLogo.
gc paint: image asPattern.
gc clippingBounds asFiller displayOn: gc
```

Exercise 20.8

Browse the classes GeometricWrapper, FillingWrapper and StrokingWrapper.

Exercise 20.9

Modify the code from Exercise 20.6 to use Geometric objects.

20.7 Summary

This chapter completes our preliminary discussion of the graphics capabilities of VisualWorks. In later chapters we will introduce other important subclasses of VisualComponent. For the time being, we return to some aspects of Smalltalk, in particular the use of booleans, copying operations and the undefined object nil.

21 Logic operations and UndefinedObject

In this chapter we introduce several important facilities without which any programming system would be useless. Smalltalk's representation of boolean truth values and its implementation of comparisons and explicit copying are described. Finally, the properties of the undefined object nil are briefly investigated.

21.1 Class Boolean

In most computer languages some simple entities such as boolean values are built-in 'types'. However, in Smalltalk these types are represented as classes, just like any other kind of object. Here, we investigate the way in which Smalltalk represents truth and falsehood, and how logical operations can be performed.

In Smalltalk, 'truth' is represented by class True and 'falsehood' by class False. Since these two classes have much in common, a common abstract superclass Boolean (a subclass of Object) is introduced. The class hierarchy is shown below.

```
Object
    Boolean
        False
        True
```

Since we never need more than one instance of True (it never changes its value, after all!), the sole instance of True is referred to by the pseudo-variable true. Similarly, the sole instance of False is called false.

We have already seen (in Chapter 10) how keyword messages like ifTrue: and ifFalse: can be used together with blocks to form control constructs. These are implemented as methods in class Boolean and its subclasses.

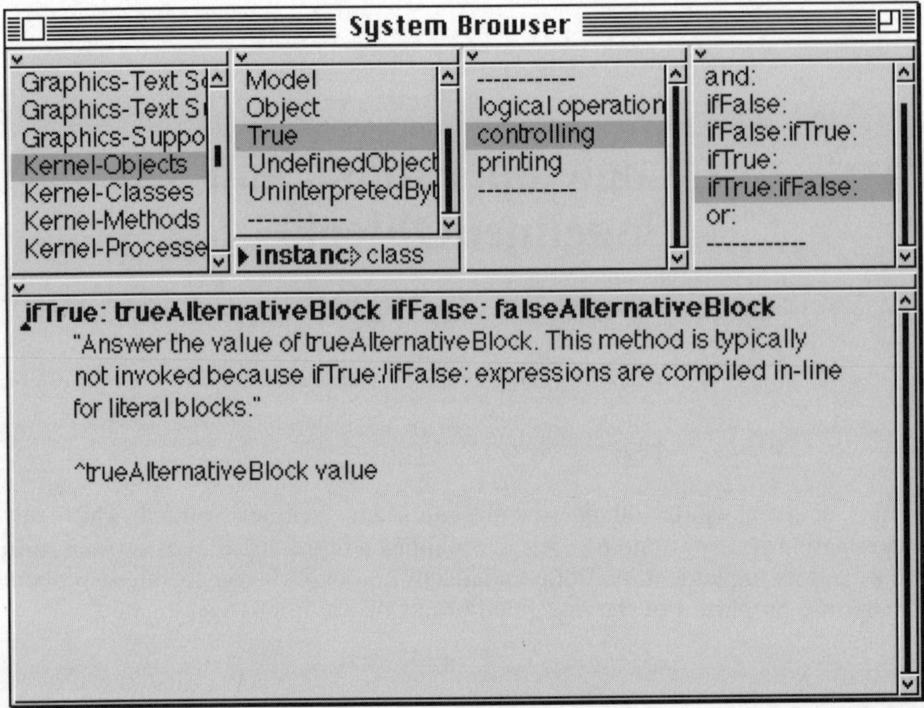

Figure 21.1 The implementation of **ifTrue:ifFalse** in class **True**.

Taking, for example, the message ifTrue:ifFalse:, this is implemented differently in classes True and False. In class True, the first argument (which is expected to be a block) receives the value message (Figure 21.1). Conversely, in class False, it is the second argument (also a block) which receives the value message. Thus, different blocks are activated depending on whether the receiver is true or false; in this way, an 'if-then-else' construct is implemented. Other similar control constructs (ifFalse:, ifTrue: and so on) are implemented in the same way.

You should note, however, that the ifTrue:ifFalse: method is used so frequently that it is recognized as a special case by the Smalltalk compiler. Therefore, specially optimized code is used, instead of an actual message being sent. This improves performance, but does reduce the flexibility; for example, it is difficult to extend the boolean classes to allow three-state logic (e.g. 'true', 'false' and 'unknown') without modifying the compiler.

Smalltalk provides the usual kinds of logical operations on truth-valued expressions. The following messages are supported in the logical operations protocol:

& – Evaluating conjunction (and function). A binary selector. Answers true if both receiver *and* argument are true, otherwise false. For example, the expression:

```
(3 < 4) & (5 < 6)
```

evaluates to true. You should note that the first pair of round brackets are redundant, but do help to make the intent clearer.

| – Evaluating disjunction (or function). A binary selector. Answers true if either the receiver *or* argument is true, otherwise false.

not – Negation. A unary selector. Answers true if the receiver is false, and vice versa.

eqv: – Logical equivalence. A keyword selector. Answers true if both receiver and argument have the same logic value, otherwise false. You should avoid confusing *logical equivalence* (the eqv: message) with *object identity* (==).

xor: – Logical not-equivalence. A keyword selector. Answers true if both receiver and argument have different logic values, otherwise false. For example, the following expression evaluates to true:

```
(3 < 4) xor: (5 > 6)
```

You should note that the *and* (&) and *or* (|) methods discussed above are *evaluating* forms: both the *argument* and the *receiver* are fully evaluated before the logic operation is performed. Evaluating both can be undesirable under some circumstances. In the following example, you should assume that *someInteger* is an argument to a message send, and can refer either to nil or to an instance of class SmallInteger. We want the code in the block to be evaluated only if *someInteger* is a positive integer.

```
someInteger notNil & (someInteger > 0)
        ifTrue: ["Code expecting positive integers only"]
```

This code is wrong. The problem is that the expression (someInteger > 0) is evaluated even if *someInteger* is nil. Thus, if *someInteger* is indeed nil, then nil will receive the > message, which it will not understand. The problem can be overcome by separating the two tests:

```
someInteger notNil
    ifTrue: [someInteger > 0
            ifTrue: ["Code expecting positive integers only"]]
```

However, this is rather ugly, and can become complicated if many tests are used. A better way is to use the method for non-evaluating conjunction called and:.

```
(someInteger notNil and: [someInteger > 0])
            ifTrue: ["Code expecting positive integers only"]
```

The argument to the and: message is a block, which is evaluated *only* if the receiver evaluates to true. Thus, in this example, if the variable *someInteger* does refer to nil, then the > message is never sent. A non-evaluating disjunction (or:) method is also provided.

Exercise 21.1

Browse classes Boolean, True and False. You should pay particular attention to the logical operations and controlling protocols.

Exercise 21.2

Try some examples using the logical operators described in this section. In particular, explore the difference between the evaluating and non-evaluating forms of logical operator.

21.2 Comparing objects

Any pair of objects can be compared with each other. However, we have already seen two different forms of comparison (see Chapters 14 and 15).The first comparison is *object identity*. Smalltalk expressions evaluate to objects; two expressions are identical in this sense *if and only* if they evaluate to exactly the same

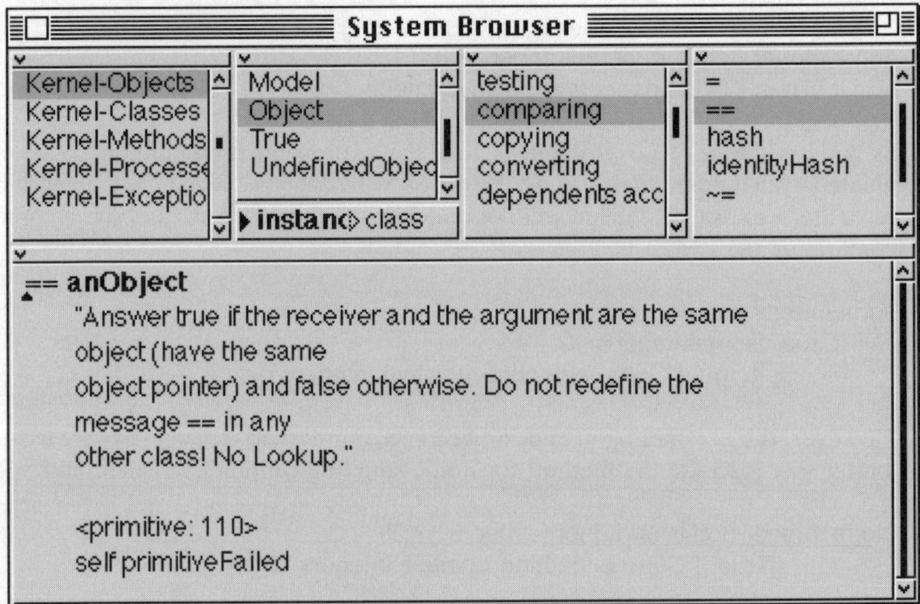

Figure 21.2 The implementation of == in class **Object**.

object. The message selector for this comparison is ==; the inverse test is ~~. The selectors == and ~~ are defined in class Object (see Figure 21.2).

The second comparison is *object equality*. Two expressions are equal if they evaluate to 'the same sort of thing'. Exactly what is meant by 'the same sort of thing' depends on the class of the object. For example, two Points can represent the same location in a plane, and thus be *equal*, but still actually be different objects, and therefore not *identical*. The message selector = is used for testing equality between objects; the inverse test is ~=.

The default implementation of = and ~= is in class Object (see Figure 21.3), and is the same as == and ~~ respectively. Therefore every object can be compared equal. However, many classes redefine = in a way appropriate to their function. Examples include class Point, class Rectangle (see Figure 21.4), and class Magnitude and its subclasses. Thus, class Float (a subclass of Number and thus Magnitude) defines = in a way appropriate for floating point numbers. Classes that *don't* redefine = include Symbol, Character, and SmallInteger – this is because instances of these classes are unique. In the case of Character and SmallInteger, instances are known as 'immediates', i.e. represented directly by the VM.

The internal implementation of several important classes which use equality, including Set and Dictionary, relies on *hashing* to achieve a high performance. The hash value is used to provide a starting point for a search for matching objects. The hash value must not change during the lifetime of the object, and it must be rapidly

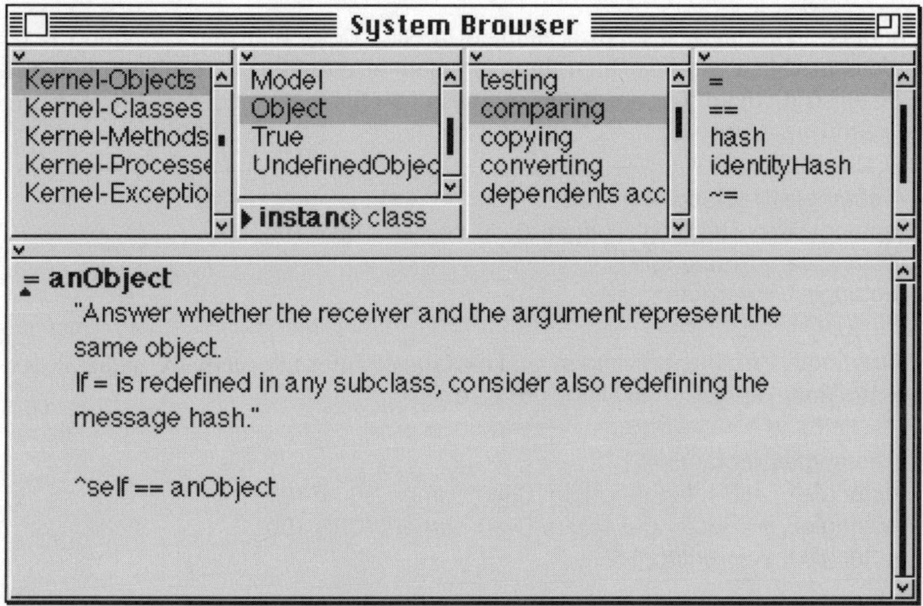

Figure 21.3 The implementation of = in class **Object**.

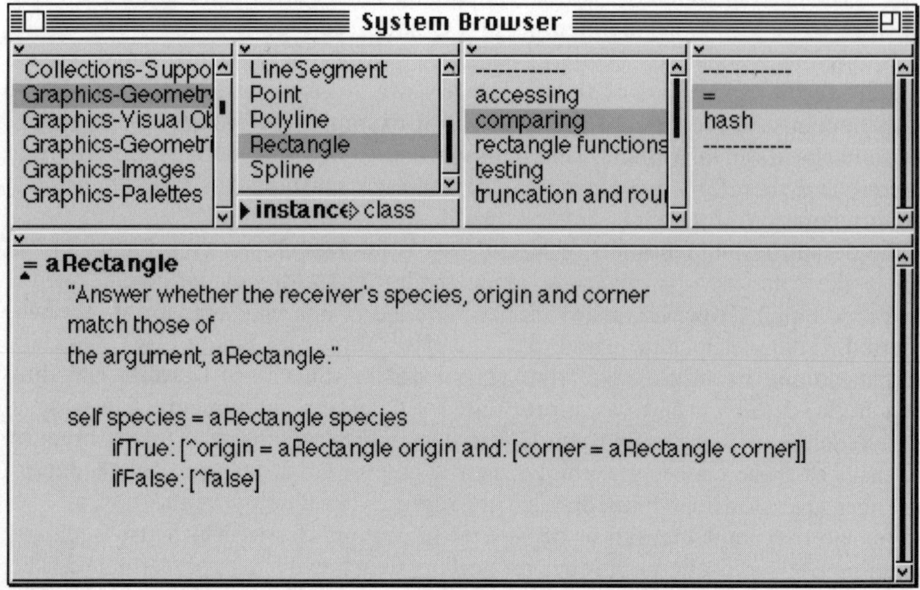

Figure 21.4 The implementation of = in class **Rectangle**.

generated. The method hash is defined in class Object; if the = method is re-implemented in a subclass, then the hash method should be re-implemented also.

To illustrate the difference between object identity and object equality, consider the following expressions:

```
| rectangle1 rectangle2 |
rectangle1 := Rectangle origin: 0@0 corner: 100@100.
rectangle2 := rectangle1.
rectangle1 == rectangle2.
```

Clearly, both variables *rectangle1* and *rectangle2* refer to exactly the same object, thus the final expression evaluates to true.

```
| rectangle1 rectangle2 |
rectangle1 := Rectangle origin: 0@0 corner: 100@100.
rectangle2 := Rectangle origin: 0@0 corner: 100@100.
rectangle1 == rectangle2.
```

In this case, however, *rectangle1* and *rectangle2* refer to different objects, even though they represent the same area and location. Thus, the last expression evaluates to false. However, the = method is redefined in class Rectangle (see Figure 21.4) to compare the origins and corners of rectangles. Thus, the expression:

```
rectangle1 = rectangle2
```

evaluates to true, as the two different rectangles clearly represent exactly the same area.

As another example of object identity, consider class IdentityDictionary. Its instances perform *key* lookup using object identity (==) rather than object equality (=), and are hence more efficient. (This distinction between 'identity' and 'equality' is also used in other symbolic programming languages, particularly Lisp.) For example, the following message expressions

```
| dict |
dict := IdentityDictionary new.
dict at: 'a' put: 1.
dict at: 5 put: 'b'.
dict at: $c put: 6.
dict at: 'a' put: (Set with: 1 with: 3 with: 4).
dict at: 3/4 put: 'b'.
^dict at: 'a'
```

raise an error, because the class uses object identity to look up 'a', which fails. However, the following code

```
| dict |
dict := IdentityDictionary new.
dict at: 'a' put: 1.
dict at: 5 put: 'b'.
dict at: $c put: 6.
dict at: 'a' put: (Set with: 1 with: 3 with: 4).
dict at: 3/4 put: 'b'.
^dict at: $c
```

returns 6.

Exercise 21.3

Browse the methods in protocol comparing in class Object (class category Kernel-Objects). You should note the comment in the == method. You might also like to browse the implementation of = in class Rectangle, and some of the other classes which redefine equality. *Hint*: use the expression:

```
Browser browseAllImplementorsOf: #=
```

to open a Message-Set Browser on all implementors of =.

Exercise 21.4

Try the examples using instances of Rectangle discussed above. Also, try similar examples with instances of class Point, or other classes that redefine the = (and hash) method.

21.3 Copying

Sometimes it is desirable to obtain a *copy* of an object. In Smalltalk, it is necessary to ask for a copy explicitly. The copy method is implemented in class Object, so that copies can be made of all objects in the image, except where copying is explicitly disallowed.

We can explore the copying of objects using the Rectangle example from above. Consider the following expressions:

```
| rectangle1 rectangle2 |
rectangle1 := Rectangle origin: 0@0 corner: 100@100.
rectangle2 := rectangle1 copy.
rectangle1 == rectangle2.
```

In this case, the variables *rectangle1* and *rectangle2* refer to different objects, and thus the last expression evaluates to false. However, the two rectangles are still equal.

In fact, two forms of copying are available in Smalltalk. The copy method makes a copy of the receiver object, and a copy of each object referred to by an instance variable, and so on recursively. The new object has no objects in common with the original object at all. Consider the example below:

```
| rectangle1 rectangle2 |
rectangle1 := Rectangle origin: 0@0 corner: 100@100.
rectangle2 := rectangle1 copy.
```

In this case, *rectangle1* and *rectangle2* refer to different instances of class Rectangle, and each of their instance variables (origin and corner) refers to different instances of class Point.

The shallowCopy method makes a copy of the receiver object, but does not make a copy of the objects referred to by any instance variables. Thus, the instance variables of both Rectangles refer to the same instances of class Point. In the following example:

```
| rectangle1 rectangle2 |
rectangle1 := Rectangle origin: 0@0 corner: 100@100.
rectangle2 := rectangle1 shallowCopy.
```

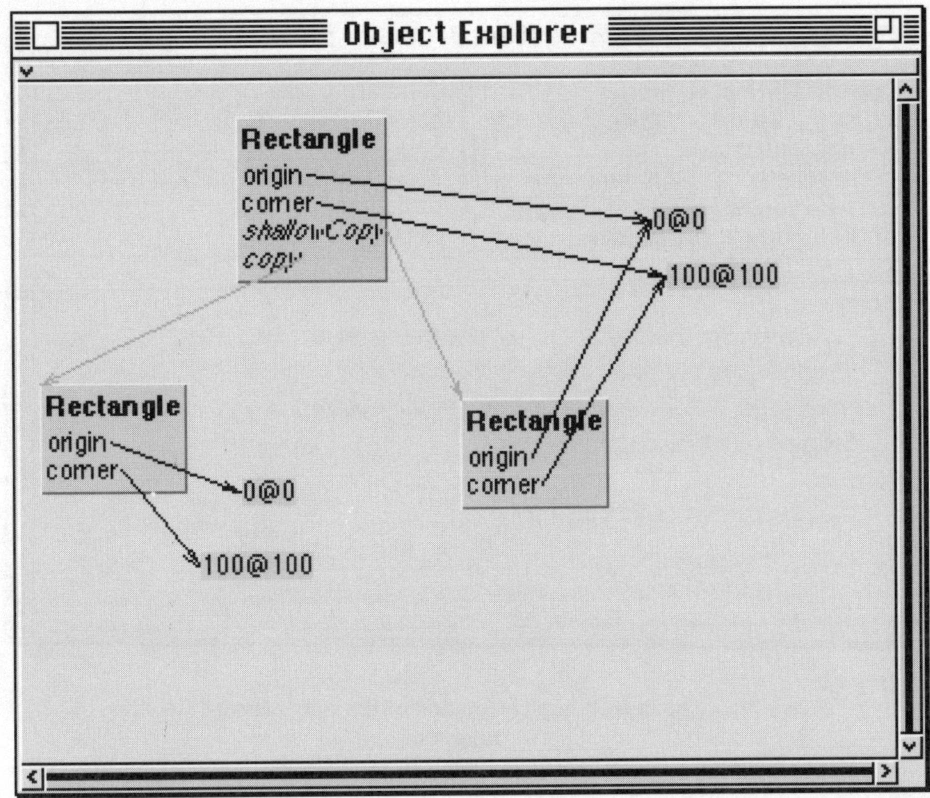

Figure 21.5 The difference between the **copy** and the **shallowcopy** messages. (This illustration was produced using 'Object Explorer' – a third-party addition to VisualWorks. See the Appendix for more details.)

the origin instance variable of both Rectangles refers to the same instance of Point. The distinction between the messages copy and shallowCopy is illustrated in Figure 21.5.

In the case of a shallow copy, if one of the Rectangles' Points is modified in some way, then both Rectangles are affected. The following expressions illustrate this.

```
| rectangle1 rectangle2 |
rectangle1 := Rectangle origin: 0@0 corner: 100@100.
rectangle2 := rectangle1 shallowCopy.
rectangle1 origin x: 42.
Transcript show: rectangle1 printString.
Transcript tab; show: rectangle2 printString; cr
```

This sort of code is a common cause of programming errors in Smalltalk.

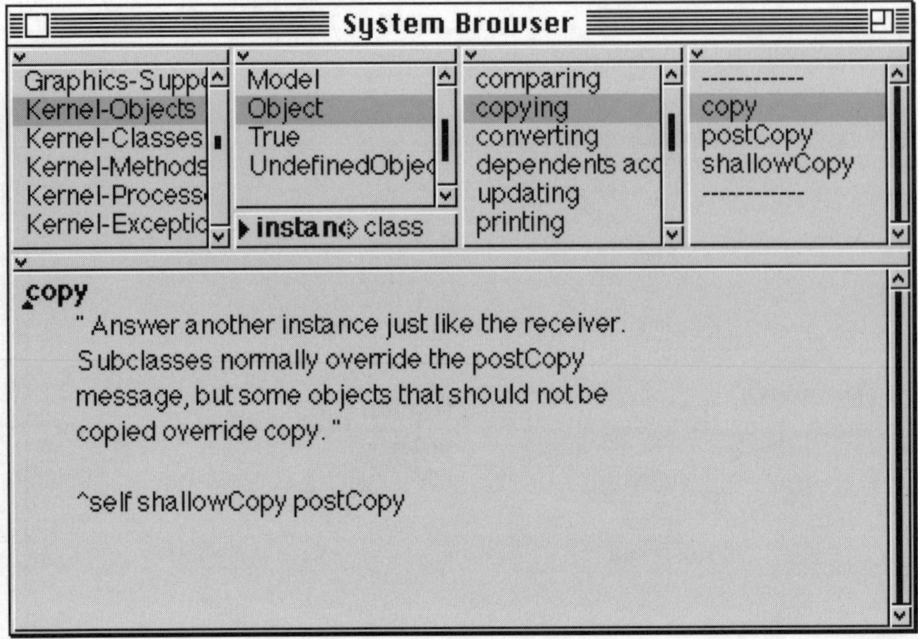

Figure 21.6 The default implementation of the **copy** message (in class **Object**).

Both copy and shallowCopy have default implementations in class Object. The default implementation of the copy method is shown in Figure 21.6.

Exercise 21.5

Browse the methods in protocol copying in class Object. Also, browse all implementors of the message selectors copy, shallowCopy and postCopy. You should be able to find some re-implementations where a copy is not made.

Exercise 21.6

Try some of the examples using copying described in this section. Also, try making copies of instances of other classes; for example, an OrderedCollection (see Chapter 15), an Image (see Chapter 20) or an Interval (see Chapter 18).

21.4 Class UndefinedObject

As we have already observed repeatedly, everything in the VisualWorks image is an object. However, we need an object to which, for example, instance

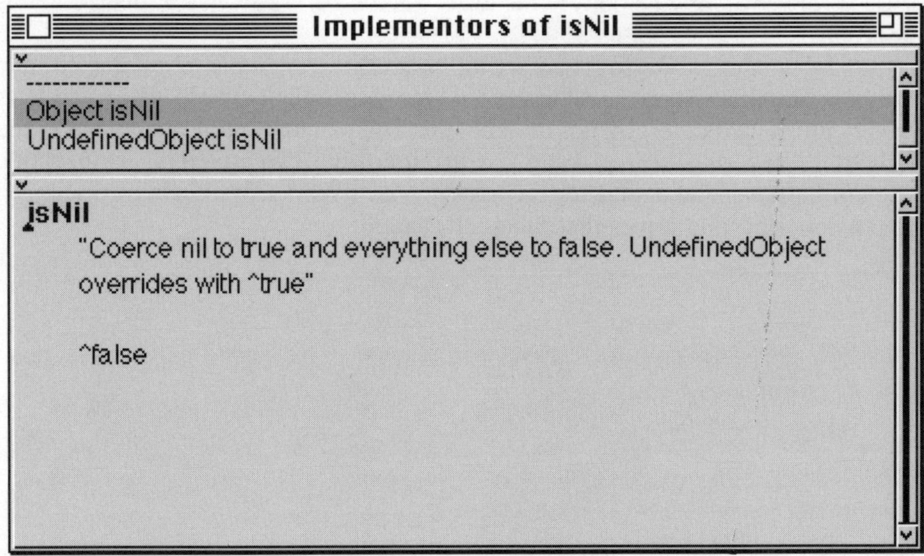

Figure 21.7 The implementation of **isNil** in class **Object**.

variables refer when we do not want to reference any particular object. Class UndefinedObject is provided for this purpose, and is a subclass of Object. Only one instance of UndefinedObject is ever required, and this sole instance is referred to by the pseudo-variable nil. Thus, uninitialized variables refer to nil.

Methods isNil and notNil are defined in class Object to answer false and true respectively, and are thus inherited by all classes. These methods are redefined by UndefinedObject to answer true and false respectively (see Figure 21.7).

Exercise 21.7

Browse class UndefinedObject. Why is shallowCopy redefined in this class?

21.5 Summary

Classes True and False are used to represent boolean truth values in Smalltalk, and provide logical operations. The conjunction and disjunction functions are available in two forms: evaluating and non-evaluating (&, | and and:, or:, respectively). We recommend using the non-evaluating forms where possible, as they are more efficient. Another efficient tip is to use the identity comparison message (==) where possible, as it is implemented by comparing object pointers in the virtual machine. When copying an object, it is important to choose the appropriate message, shallowCopy or copy – the latter should be used when a 'deep copy' is required.

The isNil and notNil messages are used frequently in Smalltalk to test if a variable has been initialized. Because nil is the only instance of UndefinedObject, the tests are very efficient. Therefore, it is unlikely that you would want to re-implement the methods in any class you develop. In the following two chapters, we examine the error handling and debugging facilities in VisualWorks. We begin by discussing the possible run-time errors that Smalltalk handles.

22 Run-time error handling

This chapter starts by considering the interpretation of the doesNotUnderstand: message from the virtual machine, and shows how this is used to create a *Notifier* of the suspended activity. Other ways of creating Notifiers are also considered. Useful features of Notifiers are described, with examples.

22.1 Interrupted message-sends

We have already seen (in Chapter 11) how the binding between a message selector and the corresponding method involves a search up the class hierarchy. If no method which matches the message selector is found, then the virtual machine sends a special message doesNotUnderstand: to the original receiver. The argument to the doesNotUnderstand: message is the message selector which was not found during the search.

When a corresponding method is found, however, this is evaluated, and a new *context* is created for this evaluation. This context contains the state of any temporary variables in the method, as well as information allowing the object answered by a method to be returned to the object that sent the message. This is analogous to a stack of activation records found with more conventional languages that support procedure or function calls. The Smalltalk activation stack is directly visible in the *Debugger* (see Chapter 23).

Interrupted message-sends can occur in a number of different ways. The most usual method is by sending a message to an object that does not understand that message; i.e. the object has no method in either its class or its superclasses that corresponds to the selector of the message. This is the typical response to a programming error. The default action (implemented in class Object) is to open an 'Error Notifier' window. Notifiers are discussed in a later section of this chapter.

Apart from messages that are not understood, message-sending can be interrupted in a number of other ways. The most useful of these is to interrupt deliberately, using the <control-c> key combination. This is useful in the case of runaway computations. It is also possible to stop a computation at predetermined points using a *breakpoint*. This is discussed in Chapter 23.

Another way in which a message-send can be interrupted is if recursion occurs in Smalltalk's error handling code. In other words, an error occurs when Smalltalk is already handling another error. This usually indicates that some method used when handling errors has been incorrectly modified.

There are also a number of other programming errors which are not, strictly speaking, interrupted message-sends, but will still cause a Notifier to appear. For example, you are not permitted to make new instances of certain classes; these include the boolean classes True and False (see Chapter 21), class UndefinedObject (Chapter 21), and class Character (Chapter 3). Also, some classes do not permit certain kinds of creation messages to be used; for example, the Number classes (Chapter 13).

Another common way of getting a run-time error is to try to evaluate a block (i.e. send a value message to an instance of class BlockClosure – see Chapter 10) with the wrong number of arguments. For example, the following expression generates an Error Notifier (Figure 22.1):

```
| result |
result := [ :arg | arg * 2] value.
```

The block requires one argument, but no arguments are supplied when the value message is sent. Also, sending a control message such as ifTrue: to an object which is not either true or false will generate an error, as will sending a loop message like whileTrue: to an object which is not a block.

There are a number of errors which are generated by inappropriate numeric expressions. These include attempting to divide a number by zero, or taking the square root of a negative number.

There are many error conditions associated with incorrect use of the Collection classes (see Chapters 14 and 15) – for example, trying to remove an element from a Set which is not actually in that set, or to add an element (using add:) to a collection which has a fixed length, such as an Array. Another common error is to send a message to an instance of an abstract superclass (see Chapter 13), which is not intended to have any instances of it created. Typically, an abstract superclass will implement its key methods as:

```
^self subclassResponsibility
```

to indicate that this method is overridden in a concrete subclass. Of course, in a partially complete new application, this error may indicate that a crucial method has been omitted in a subclass!

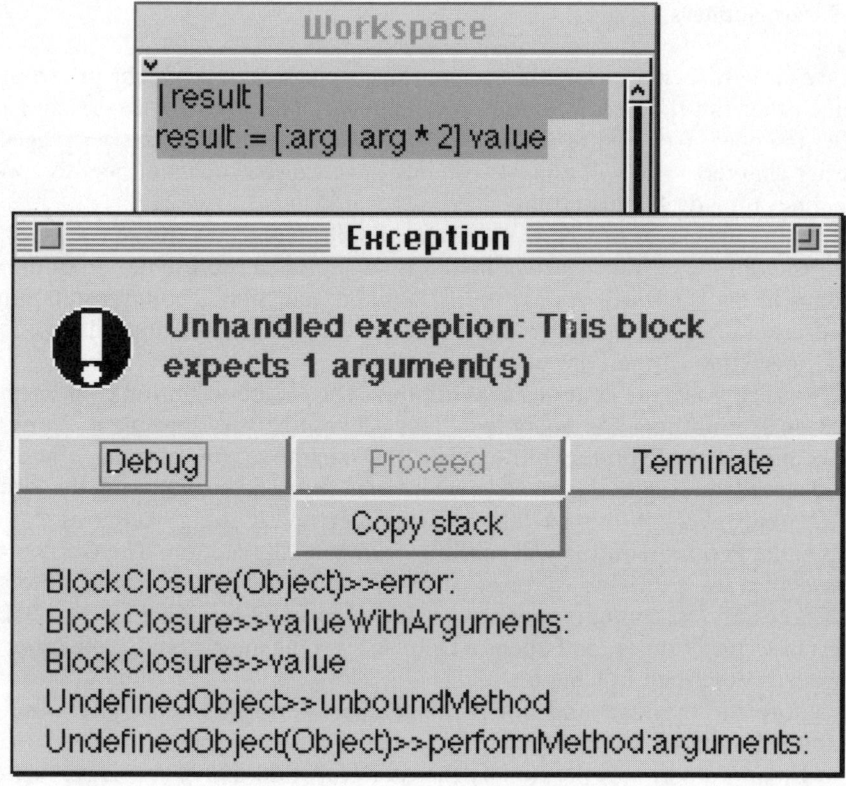

Figure 22.1 An Error Notifier.

Finally, you can add your own error indications as you develop applications. An error: method is implemented in class Object, so that you can insert expressions such as:

```
^self error: 'An error has occurred'
```

The argument to error: should be a string.

Exercise 22.1

Browse the error handling protocol of class Object. What is the difference between the error: and notify: methods?

Exercise 22.2

Find examples of the various error notifications discussed above. Try inserting your own error messages (using the error: selector) in some examples.

22.2 Error Notifiers

We have already seen a variety of ways in which a message-send can be interrupted, or some other run-time error condition can appear. This normally causes an Error Notifier to appear (see Figure 22.1). If you have been trying the exercises suggested in earlier chapters, you will almost certainly have caused such Notifiers to appear many times already by mis-typing.

The main purpose of this Notifier is to retain a reference to the activation stack associated with the currently active methods. A printable representation of the top five items in the stack will appear in the Notifier view area. The interpretation of this representation is discussed in Chapter 23. The Notifier's heading will give some general indication of the type of error.

The window normally contains four options. The **Proceed** button continues the evaluation as if nothing had happened. This may not be very sensible if a program error generated the Notifier, although in the meantime you may have added a method corresponding to the message which was not understood, using the System Browser. However, if the evaluation was interrupted using <control-c>, for example, the **Proceed** button will continue from the interruption. The **Copy stack** button copies the printable representation of the stack into the paste buffer (so that, if necessary, its contents may be transferred to an editor or a file). The **Debug** button closes the Notifier, and opens a Debugger on the interrupted evaluation; the Debugger is described in Chapter 23.

To ignore the message and not continue the interrupted activity, choose the **Terminate** button or the **close** item from the <window> menu.

If an Error Notifier is generated by the doesNotUnderstand: message, then the window has a fourth button, **Correct it. . .** . This invokes a run-time spelling corrector, which attempts to find the message selector nearest in spelling to the

Figure 22.2 The 'New Message' Prompter.

selector which was not understood. This is illustrated in Figure 22.2, where a misspelled message selector is sent to an instance of class Point. The compiler recognizes that the selector inpect is unknown but, for demonstration purposes, we use the **Proceed** button on the Prompter to persuade the compiler to go ahead anyway.

Naturally, when the inspect message is sent, it is not understood (Figure 22.3); an Error Notifier appears. If we invoke the spelling corrector using the **Correct it . . .** button, then a Confirmer appears suggesting a replacement, in this case, inspect (Figure 22.4). If we select the **yes** option, an Inspector will indeed appear (Figure 22.5).

You should note that the correction made by the run-time spelling corrector is not permanent in a method (unlike the case when the spelling corrector is invoked by the compiler – see Chapter 6). You will have to find and correct the error yourself, using the System Browser.

It is worth observing that the Notifier windows are scheduled; that is, they have independent activity within the user interface (just like browsers and Workspaces), and have the usual <window> button menu functions. In particular, this feature allows a computation to be stopped (using <control-c>) and restarted at a later

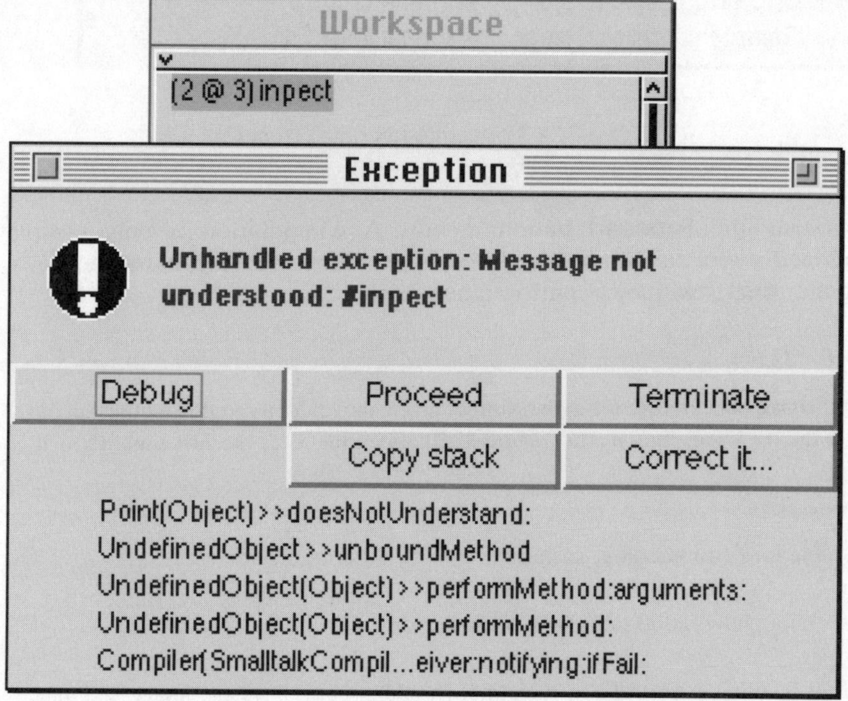

Figure 22.3 Correcting run-time errors (1).

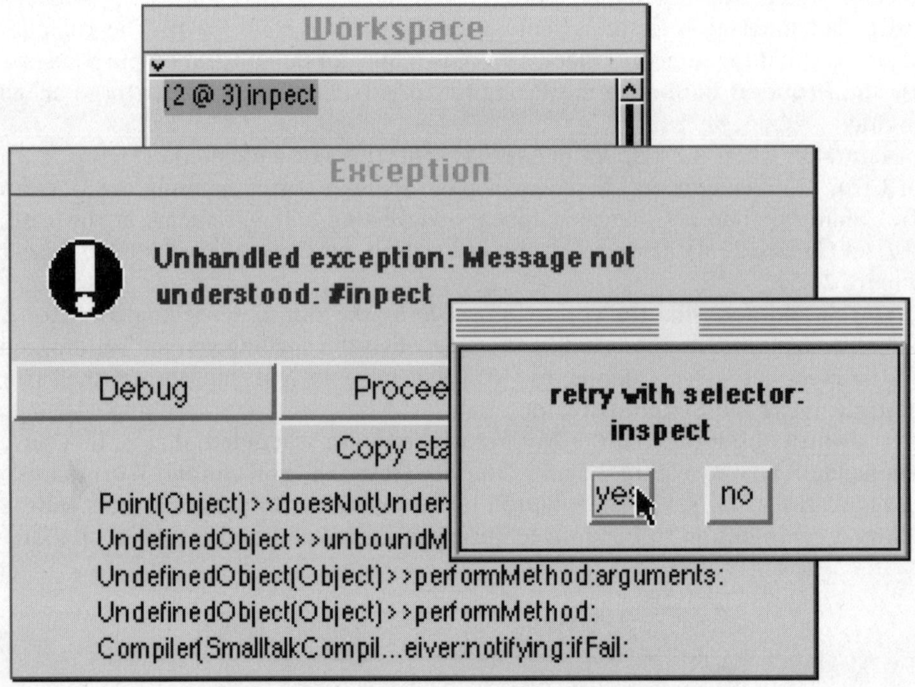

Figure 22.4 Correcting run-time errors (2).

time (using the **Proceed** button menu). A computation is only completely abandoned when the Notifier is closed by selecting the **Terminate** button or by using the usual <window> button **close** item.

Exercise 22.3

Work through the example using the Notifier given above. You should find that you do not get the 'new message' menu (Figure 22.2) appearing after the first time, though.

Exercise 22.4

Start some long computation, such as:

```
Transcript show: 2000 factorial printString; cr
```

Interrupt it, using <control-c>; a Notifier should appear. Save the image and quit. You should now be able to restart the VisualWorks image, and then complete the interrupted computation by selecting the **Proceed** button of the Notifier.

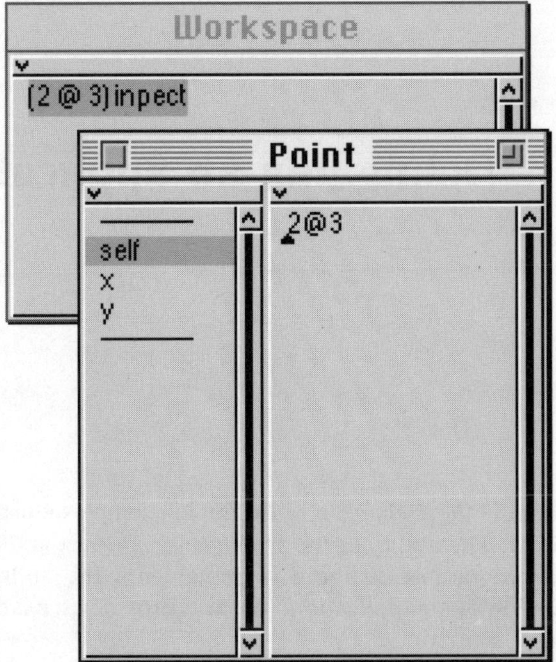

Figure 22.5 Correcting run-time errors (3).

22.3 Summary

There are many kinds of run-time errors that cause a Notifier to appear. The most common is the 'doesNotUnderstand' error – the result of sending an inappropriate message to an object. Once you are familiar with the potential cause of errors, you may find that you make less of them; alternatively, you'll need to use the Debugger, described in the next chapter.

23 Debugging an application

This chapter introduces the *Debugger*, with simple examples illustrating the power of the tools provided. The ability of the Debugger to inspect and modify variables in the suspended program is explored, together with the ability to single-step through the evaluation of an application. We also provide an example of using the Debugger to correct an error.

23.1 Introduction

When a program error occurs, a Notifier window appears displaying the last five message-sends (see Chapter 22). When you need to examine the conditions that led to the error, select the **Debug** button. The Notifier is replaced by a Debugger, which enables you to trace the program flow leading to the error (see Figure 23.1).

The primary functions of the Debugger allow the programmer to:

- Proceed with the evaluation step by step
- Examine a method in the activation stack
- Modify the method, and accept (recompile)
- Change the values of the variables in the activation stack
- Gain access to Inspectors on any object.

The Debugger window consists of six panes and two buttons. The upper two (larger) panes (separated by the buttons) are similar to the panes of a Message-Set Browser. The lower panes form two Inspectors.

The uppermost pane is a list of classes and messages; for each item, the class of the receiver and the message selector sent to the receiver is displayed, in the format className>>message. In brackets, the class where the method was found is shown (if it is different from the class of the receiver). This is exactly the format

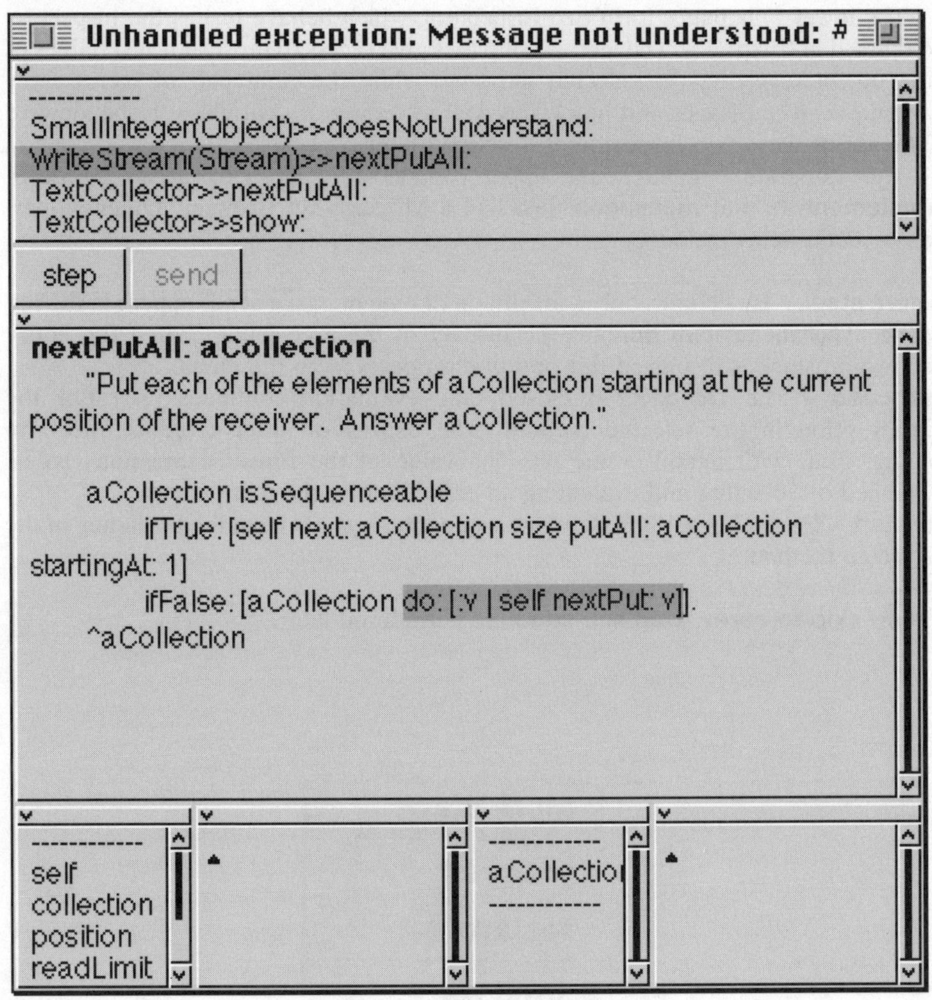

Figure 23.1 The Debugger.

that appears in the Notifier (see Chapter 22), except that in the case of the Debugger one of the message-sends can be selected. The text pane in the middle of the Debugger displays the source code for the method associated with the selected message. It has the usual <operate> menu. The displayed method can be edited and recompiled in the usual way. The message being sent to activate the next item up the stack of contexts is shown highlighted in the text pane, together with any arguments to that message. For example, in Figure 23.1, it is the message do: which is being sent to an object called *aCollection*; the argument to this message is a block.

The lower four panes form two Inspectors, which behave just as the Inspectors discussed in Chapter 8. The left pair of panes give access to the instance variables of the object receiving the selected message, while the right pair of panes allow arguments to messages and blocks, as well as temporary variables, to be viewed. The use of these two Inspectors is described later.

The <operate> menu in the upper pane (Figure 23.2) has items **senders**, **implementors** and **messages**, just like a Message-Set Browser. Other <operate> menu items include:

more stack – By default, only a maximum of nine message-sends appear in the top pane. This menu item doubles the display of message-sends. When the entire activation stack is displayed this option disappears from the menu.
proceed – The Debugger is closed, and evaluation continues just after the interruption in the selected method. The expression interrupted is forced to completion, with default value nil. The value of the forced expression can be changed by selecting and evaluating an expression in the text pane.
restart – The Debugger is closed, and evaluation restarts from the beginning of the selected method.

Items **skip to caret**, **step** and **send** are considered later.

Figure 23.2 The <operate> menu in the Debugger's top pane.

23.2 Breakpoints

Breakpoints are often useful in determining what is *really* happening inside Smalltalk. They simply provide a controlled mechanism for entering a Debugger at a known point.

Breakpoints may be placed in a method by editing the source text, inserting the expression:

```
self halt.
```

at the desired point, and recompiling the method. When this expression is evaluated, halt is sent to the receiver. The corresponding method is implemented in Object, so all objects respond to it. This opens a Notifier, with the heading 'Halt encountered'. You can proceed from this point, or select the **Debug** button. If many breakpoints have been inserted they can be identified by using the expression:

```
self halt: 'An identifying string'.
```

Exercise 23.1

Insert a self halt message into the diff: method in the arithmetic protocol of Number (that you created in Chapter 6) and evaluate an expression containing the message. Explore the activation stack shown in the uppermost pane. Does the **more stack** <operate> menu item do anything useful in this case?

Exercise 23.2

Try the **implementors** and **messages** <operate> menu items.

Exercise 23.3

Explore some other parts of the image by inserting breakpoints.

23.3 Message receiver context

The left Inspector panes in the Debugger give access to the *message receiver* of the selected message-send. Just like a normal Inspector, you can:

- Evaluate messages in the text pane, sending messages to self or
- Evaluate expressions which make assignments to instance variables or
- Select a variable, type a new value, and use **accept** to change the value.

You can then continue evaluation from the method containing the breakpoint, using **restart**.

23.4 Interrupted method context

The right Inspector panes in the Debugger give access to the state of the *method context* associated with the selected method. You have access to (and can change the values of):

- Arguments to the message
- Temporary variables
- Block arguments.

Again, you can continue the evaluation, using **restart**.

Exercise 23.4

Explore the effect of modifying instance variables, temporary variables and arguments within a Debugger.

23.5 Single-stepping through an evaluation

In the uppermost pane of the Debugger, three <operate> menu items are provided to permit single-stepping through an evaluation.

step – Performs a complete message-send in the selected method; i.e. the entire method corresponding to the message highlighted is evaluated. Any associated assignments are also carried out. (Warning: running in single-step mode can be quite slow, as the bytecodes are interpreted by Smalltalk code, rather than by the virtual machine itself.)
send – The highlighted message is 'sent', and *its* method is then displayed. Any assignments up to the highlighted message are also evaluated.
skip to caret – All message-sends and their corresponding assignments are carried out up to the point in the methods indicated by the caret.

Buttons corresponding to the **step** and **send** <operate> menu items are also provided.

Exercise 23.5

Trace the diff: example, using the **step** and **send** <operate> menu items.

Exercise 23.6

Experiment with the **skip to caret** <operate> menu item.

23.6 Debugging example

As a small example, let us modify the original version of the diff: method introduced in Chapter 6:

```
diff: aNumber
  "return the absolute difference between me and aNumber"
  | temp |
  temp := self - aNumber.
Transcript show: temp.
  temp < 0
    ifTrue: [^temp negated]
    ifFalse: [^temp]
```

Here, we have added the expression Transcript show: temp. to print out the result of the intermediate temporary variable on the Transcript. We will use this modified method to demonstrate the use of the Debugger.

Consider the following expression:

```
23 diff: -12
```

Evaluating this expression produces a Notifier window (Figure 23.3) indicating that there is an error. The window's heading informs us that an object has been sent a message that it does not understand. (The top line of the stack displayed in the Notifier also displays this information.)

The first line of the activation stack displayed in the Notifier shows that the receiver of the do: message is an instance of SmallInteger. At first this appears confusing because the original expression we evaluated sent a show: message to the Transcript (an instance of TextCollector), as displayed in the fifth line of the Notifier.

As an aside, it's worth noting two features of the activation stack as it's displayed in a Notifier:

- The first line usually shows the method that handled the error (e.g. doesNotUnderstand:), but often doesn't identify what *caused* the error.
- Other lines often contain information of marginal interest since they merely report messages that have been sent as part of the *mechanics* of Smalltalk.

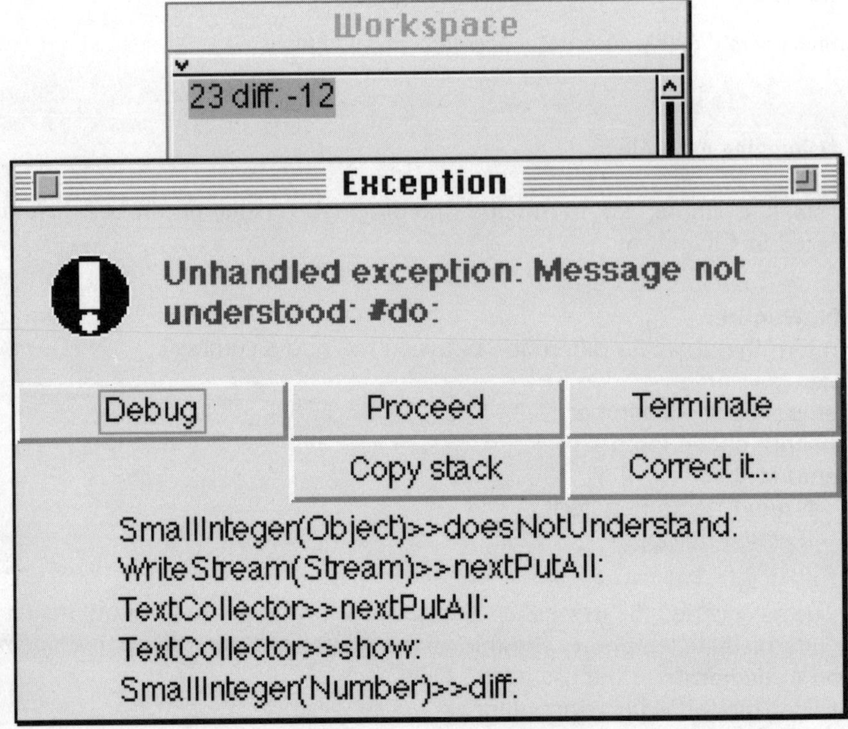

Figure 23.3 An Error Notifier.

Back to the example. We can see from the Notifier that an error occurred in the WriteStream>>nextPutAll: method. At this point we can either use the System Browser to examine that method or open a Debugger from the Notifier, as described below.

The label of the Debugger's window is identical to that of the Notifier from which it was created. In Figure 23.4 the line WriteStream(Stream)>>nextPutAll: has been selected, and the method is displayed in the text pane. Note that the *receiver* of the message is an instance of WriteStream, but the method is *implemented* in class Stream. The message-send that was being evaluated when the error occurred is automatically highlighted.

Here we find the explanation for the mysterious do: message. As you can see, it is the nextPutAll: method that sends the do: message. We have already seen in Chapter 14 that the do: method is implemented in the Collection classes, and therefore we would expect the receiver of the do: message to be an instance of one of the Collection classes. However, if we inspect the argument *aCollection* (from the right-hand Inspector in the Debugger), we see that it is an instance of

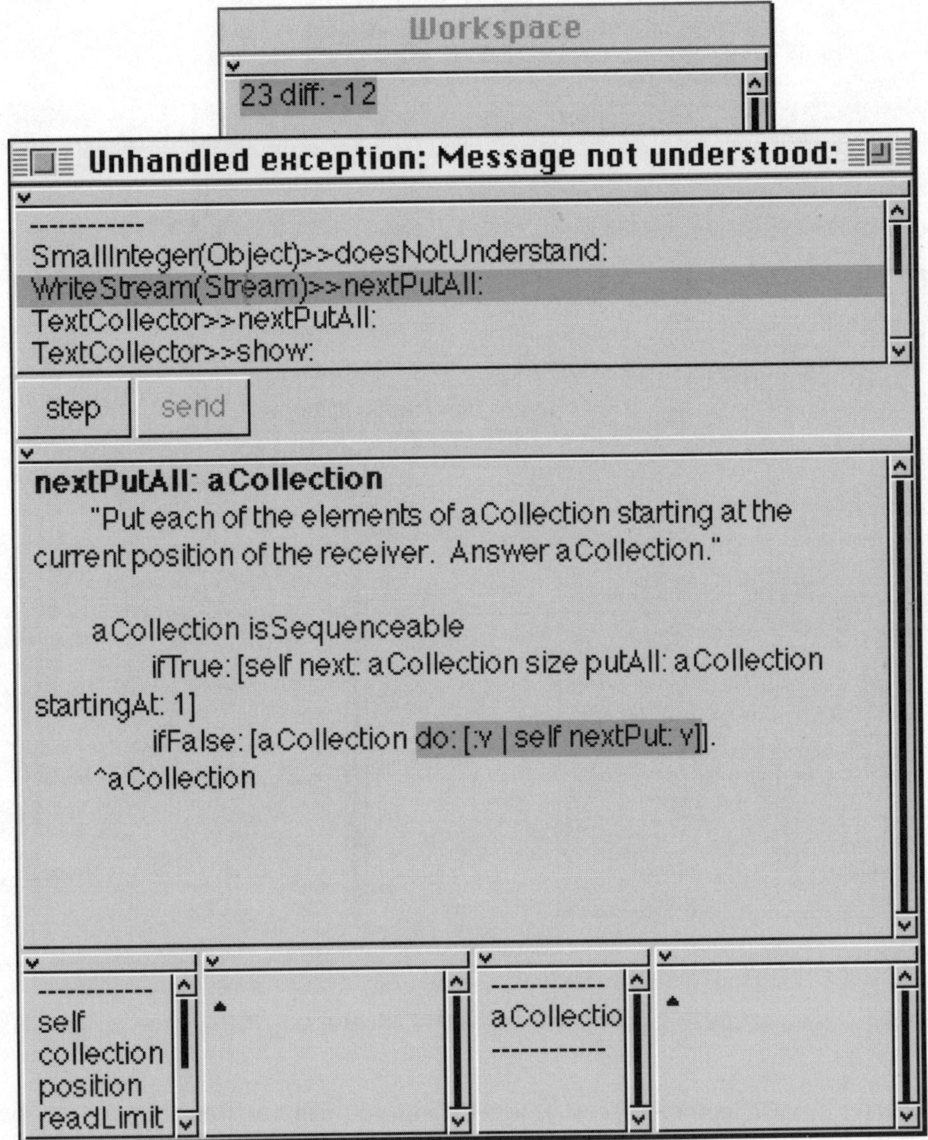

Figure 23.4 Debugging an error (1).

SmallInteger (Figure 23.5). In fact, as you may have already guessed, this is the result of the expression 23 diff: -12.

So where did the argument *aCollection* come from? As a clue, let us look a little further back in the activation stack. Figure 23.6 shows the Debugger with the

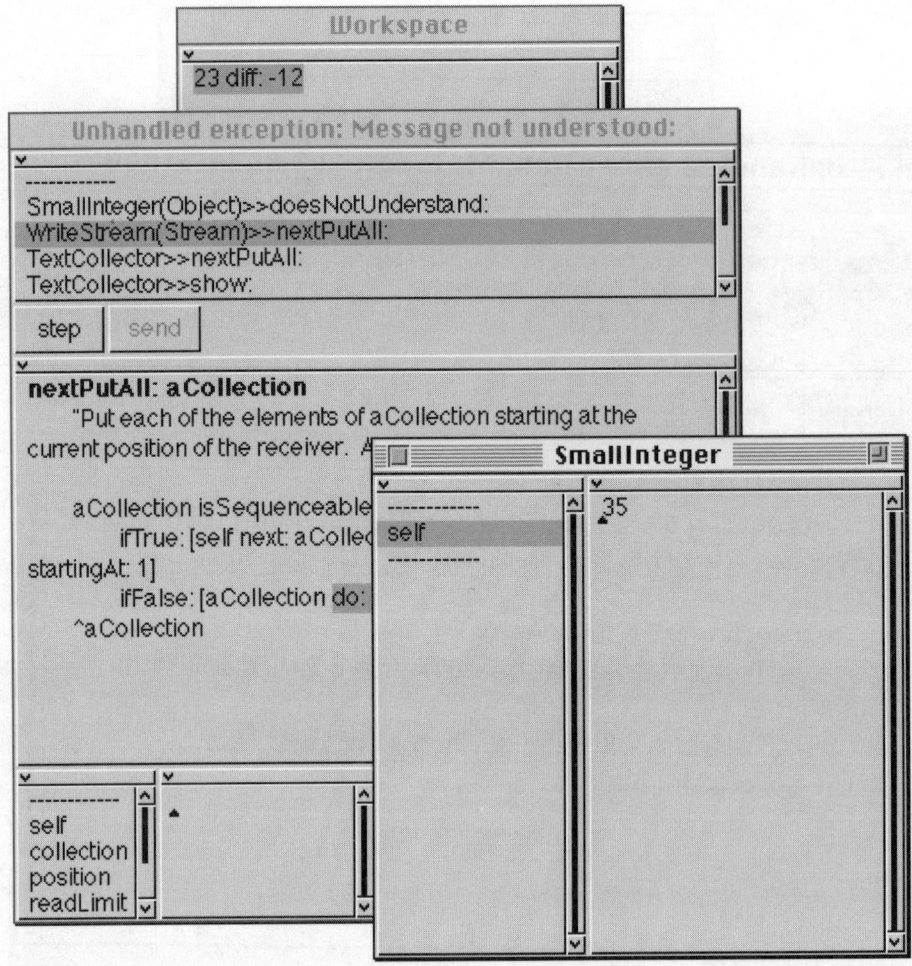

Figure 23.5 Debugging an error (2).

method TextCollector>>show: selected, and you can see from the text of the method that the argument is expected to be a String, not an integer!

To overcome the problem we should amend the diff: method. Rather than making this change in the System Browser, let us amend it in the Debugger. First select the method SmallInteger(Number)>>diff:, and modify the code according to Figure 23.7, then accept the change you have made.

Now select the **proceed** option from the <operate> menu of the top pane. The Debugger will close, evaluation of the (amended) expression will continue, and the result of 100 factorial will be printed on the Transcript (Figure 23.8).

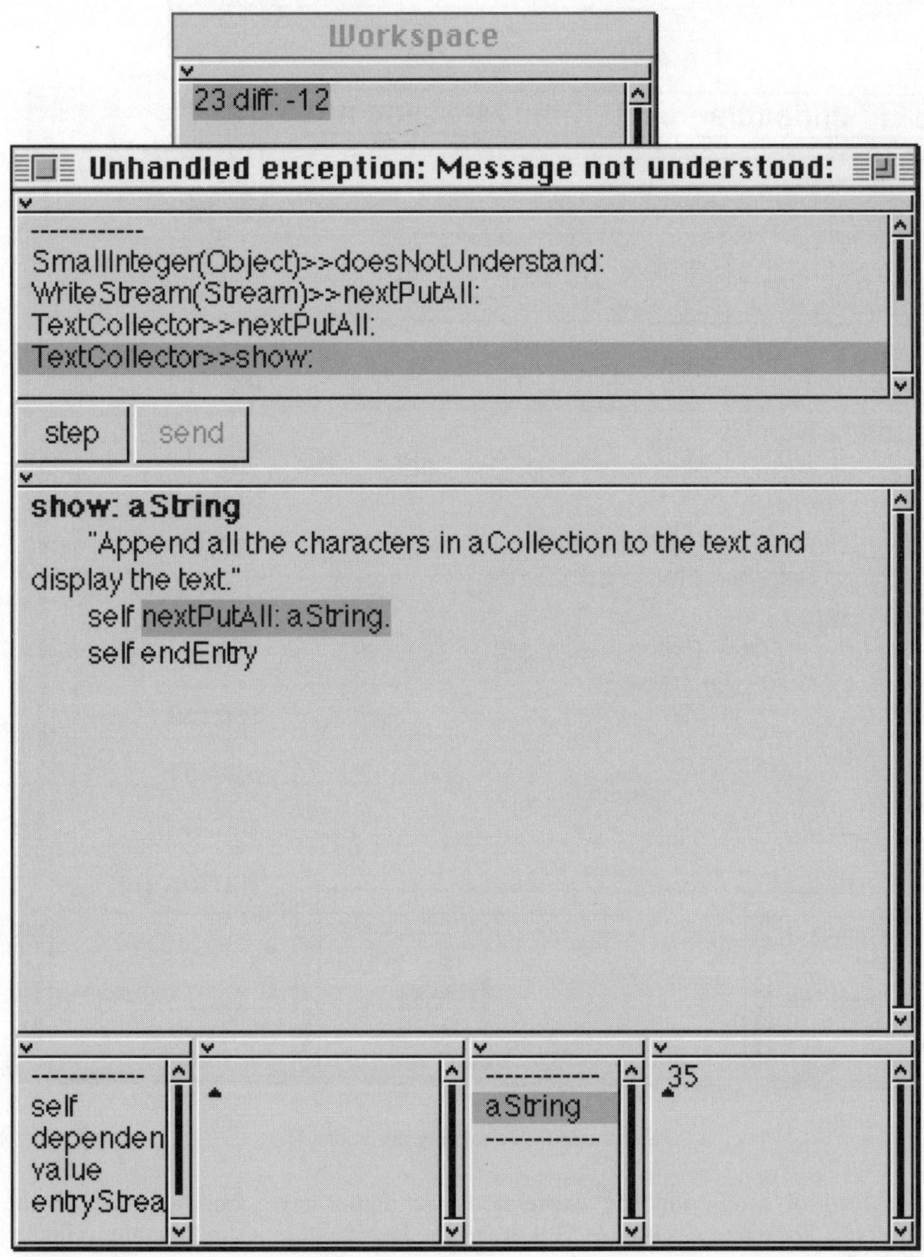

Figure 23.6 Debugging an error (3).

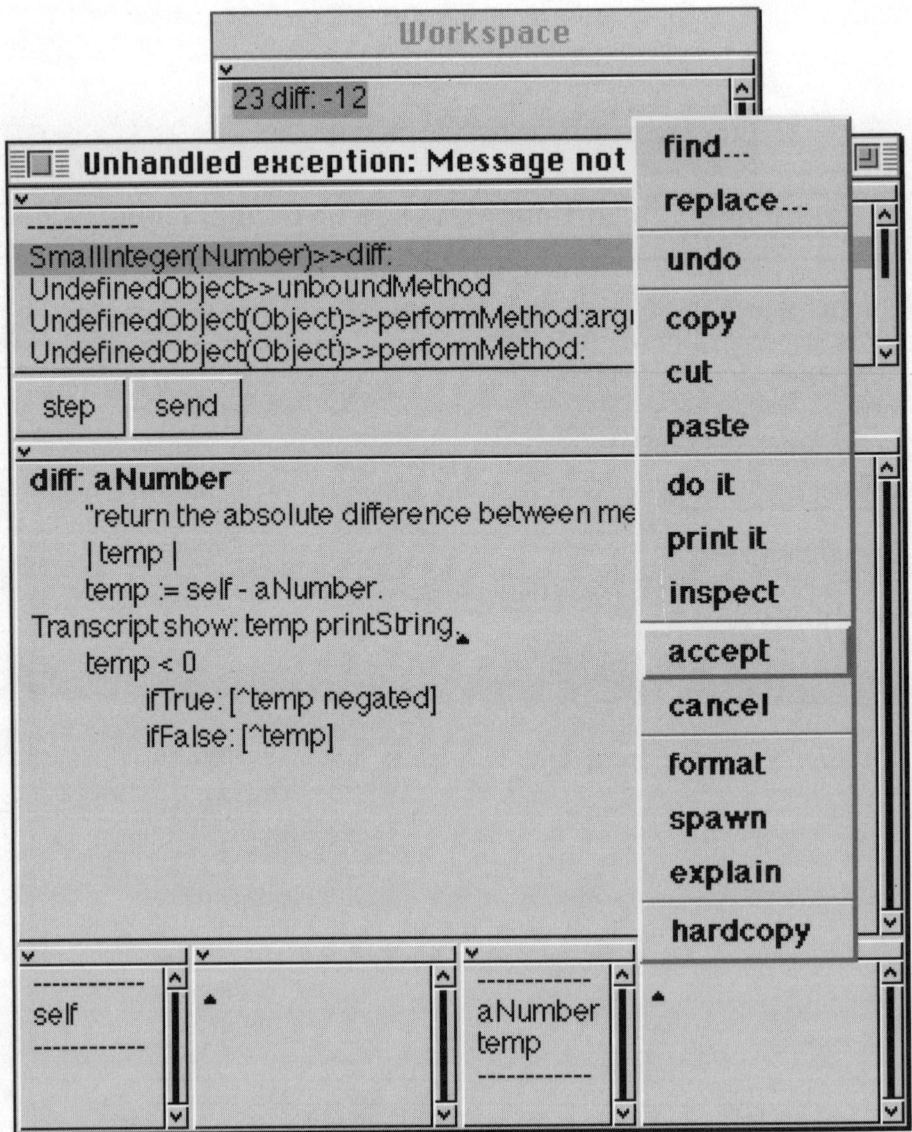

Figure 23.7 Debugging an error (4).

Instead of modifying the expression, we could have modified one of the variables. For example, Figure 23.9 shows the Debugger in a similar state to Figure 23.6. However, we have modified the argument *aString*, so that it refers to the (literal) String 'Hello, World!' by typing it and selecting the **accept** option from the <operate> menu.

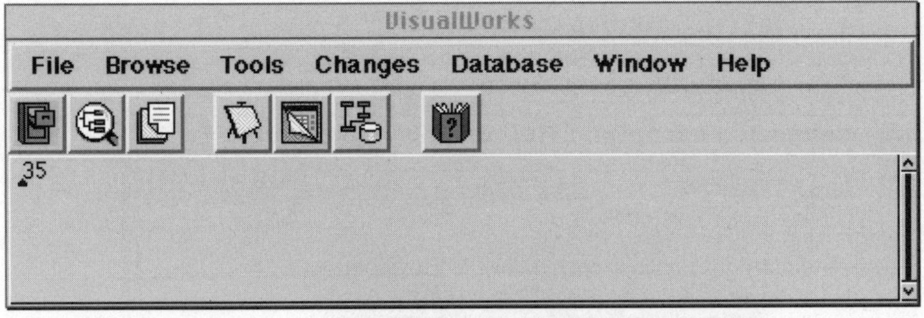

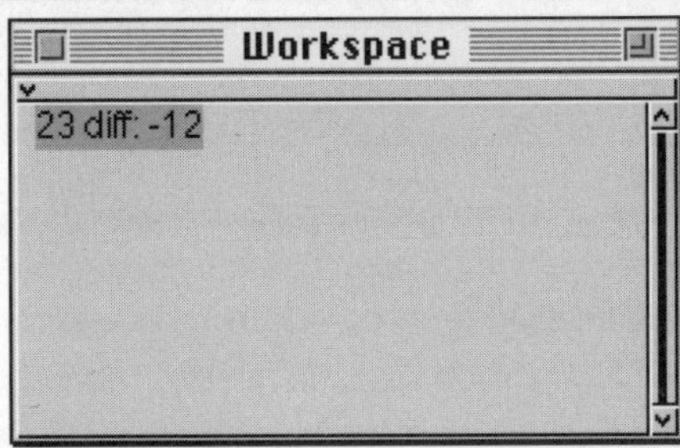

Figure 23.8 Debugging an error (5).

Now, if we restart the evaluation of the method with the **restart** option of the <operate> menu in the top pane, we will see the new result printed on the Transcript (Figure 23.10).

Exercise 23.7

Use the Debugger to follow the evaluation of the expression

```
'one' + 2
```

Exercise 23.8

Similarly, follow the evaluation of the expression

```
1 + 'two'
```

Why is the activation stack not the same as in Exercise 23.7?

23.7 Summary

In the example provided above, we described two ways of correcting errors. The first solution required the programmer to modify the code in the Debugger, then

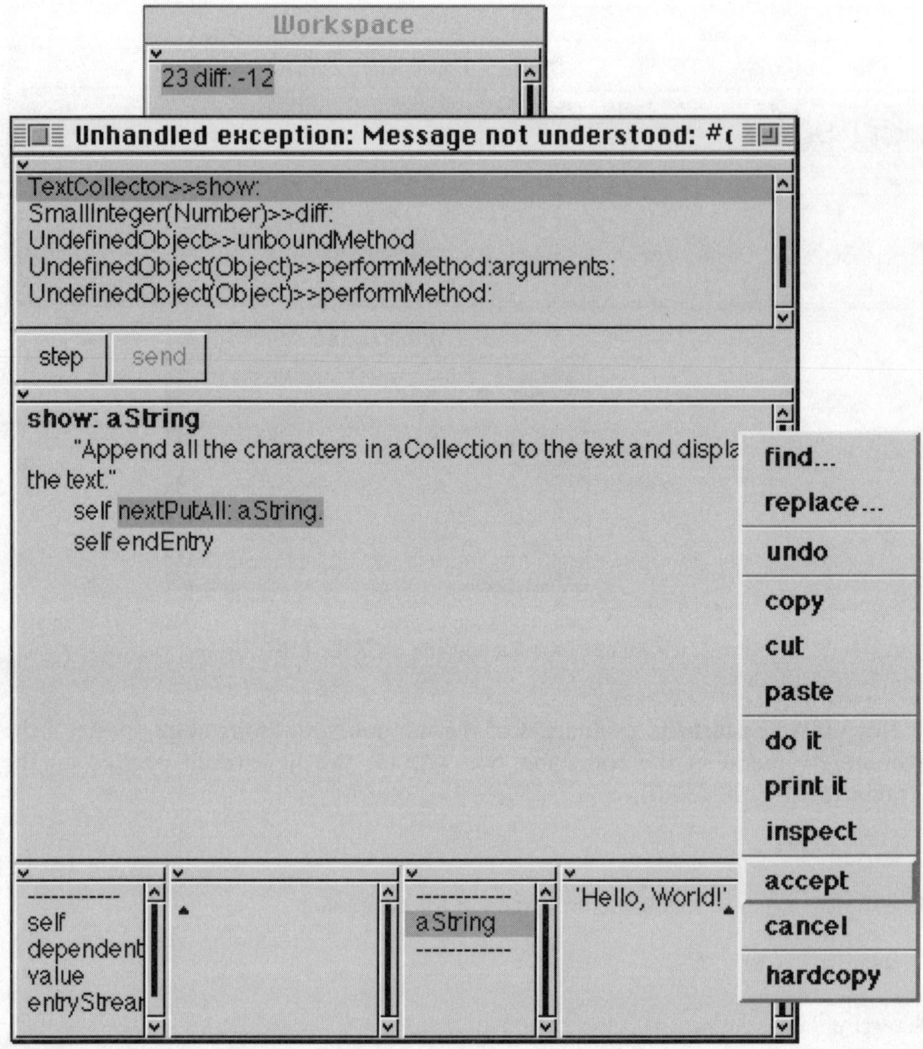

Figure 23.9 Debugging an error (6).

continue the evaluation; the second solution required the programmer to modify one of the variables used in the evaluation. The latter solution is only a 'stop-gap' approach – the problem is not really solved, we merely 'fixed' the variable so that computation could continue.

Once you have been using VisualWorks for some time, you will need to break up your software into manageable pieces. The next chapter explores VisualWorks' support for source code control.

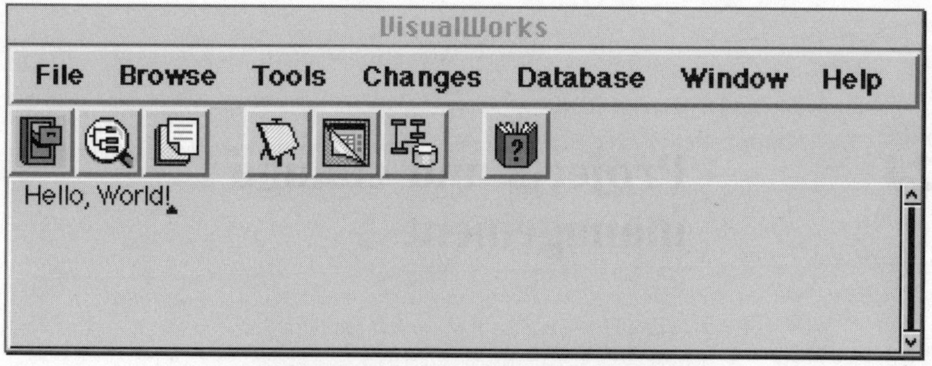

Figure 23.10 Debugging an error (7).

24 Projects and change management

In this chapter we explore the concept of Projects, which are used to separate different pieces of work within a single VisualWorks image. Also, techniques and tools to manage 'changes' within the image are discussed.

24.1 Projects

A Project separates different working environments within a single image. If you regard the VisualWorks screen layout as being a metaphor for a 'desktop', with the windows representing different pieces of paper, then Projects allow you to have several different desks! A Project maintains a separate collection of windows for display on the screen, as well as a separate record of changes made in each Project (recorded in *change sets*, see later). A Project can contain any number of 'sub-Projects'; this tree-like hierarchy can be extended to any depth.

When you first start using a VisualWorks image, you will have only one Project, which is at the top of the 'tree'. A new Project can be created by selecting the **Open Project** item from the **Changes** menu of the Launcher (you may be prompted for a rectangular area – for a window – in the usual way). You are advised to make this window fairly small, as it is only provided as a 'workspace' in which to keep comments about the contents of this new Project (see Figure 24.1). It is often useful to be able to keep a title and short description here, and to document changes made, things to do, and so on. All the usual <operate> menu options are provided. It's also useful to change the label of the window, so you can see the title of the Project even when the window is collapsed.

Once a new Project has been created, it can be 'entered' or accessed by pressing the **enter** button in the Project window. You will now be in the new Project, and the screen will be empty but for a Launcher. You may want to open a System Browser and a Workspace, by selecting the appropriate items from the Launcher

Figure 24.1 Creating a Project.

(see Chapter 4). You can return to the top-level Project by selecting the **Exit Project** option from the **Changes** menu on the Launcher; the windows associated with the top-level Project will be restored to the screen. If you re-enter your new sub-Project, you will see that each Project retains its own set of windows in their own positions. To close a Project permanently, select close in its <window> menu. (Note: You will lose any comments you have made if you close the Project window.)

A Project can contain any number of sub-Projects, and these can be nested to any desired depth. In general, however, it seems that two or three levels is enough for most purposes. However, it should be stressed that Projects do not provide a separate source code environment; a change made to (for example) the class hierarchy is visible in all Projects.

Exercise 24.1

Try creating a new Project as described above, and experiment with moving between them. Verify that changes made in one Project are visible in all Projects.

Exercise 24.2

What happens if you select the **Exit Project** menu item while in the top-level Project?

Exercise 24.3

Browse class Project in category Tools-Misc. In particular, see how the **enter** and **Exit Project** operations are implemented.

Exercise 24.4

Once you have become familiar with the class Menu (see Chapter 28), try implementing a new 'Project Browser'. The menu should display all Projects, and allow immediate access to any of them.

24.2 Managing change sets

Each Project maintains its own record of changes made to the VisualWorks image in a 'change set' associated with that Project. This change set can be manipulated in a number of ways; in particular, changes made can be reviewed, and selected changes can be *filed out* for use in other images. The change set retains information on the addition, modification and removal of methods and classes, the renaming of classes, and the movement of class and methods between categories.

Inspecting change sets

Either of the following expressions can be used to inspect the change set associated with the current Project. Figure 24.2 displays the change set for Chapter 6.

```
Project current changes inspect
ChangeSet current inspect
```

Fortunately, the **Inspect Changes** option from the **Changes** menu of the Launcher provides an easier route to access the same Inspector. The types of changes are listed in the left pane; select a type to display the changes in the right pane, or select self to see the entire list in formatted form. The change set can contain any of the following types of change:

- Added, deleted and changed classes
- Added, deleted and changed methods
- Changes in class categories (reported as 'Reorganized System') and message categories (reported as 'Reorganized Class')
- 'Special doIts', rarely encountered, involving a change such as renaming a global variable, that is effected via an evaluated expression (a *doIt*).

More usefully, the following expression opens a Message-Set Browser on the changes associated with the current Project. (Figure 24.3 shows the changed method in Chapter 6.)

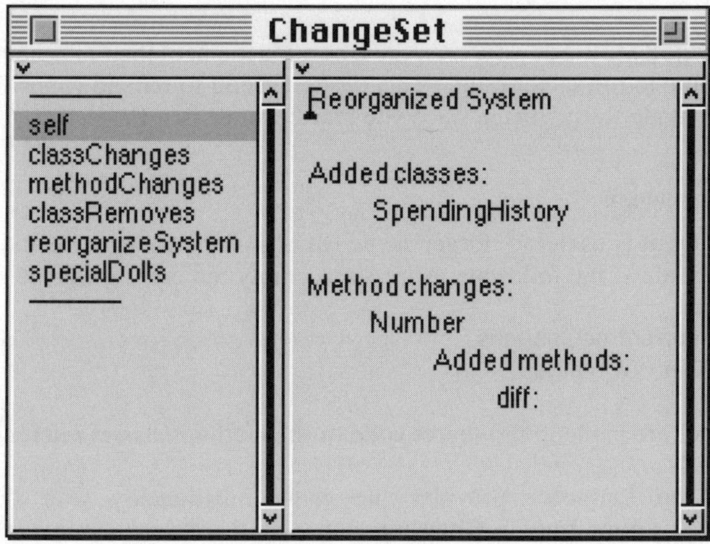

Figure 24.2 Accessing a change set.

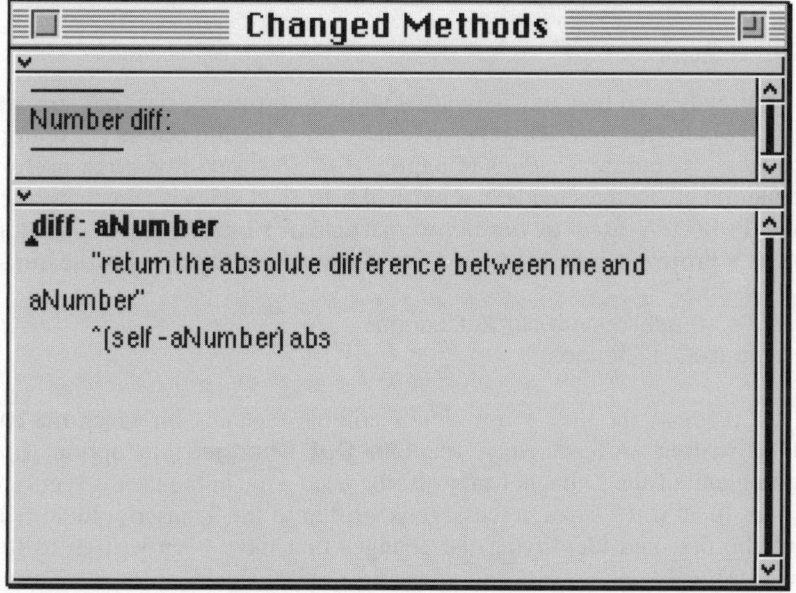

Figure 24.3 Browsing a change set.

```
Browser browseChangedMessages
```

(The **Changed Methods** option on the **Changes** menu of the Launcher provides a quicker route to the same result.) This is often useful to remind you what changes have been made to the image since you started work in a Project.

Forgetting changes

Occasionally, it is useful to 'forget' some (or all) of the changes associated with a Project. Either of the following expressions empty the current change set:

```
Project current noChanges
ChangeSet noChanges
```

(No changes are made to the source code or the methods/classes referenced by the change set.)

Again, the Launcher provides the same functionality with the **Empty Changes . . .** option from its **Changes** menu – in this case the user is requested to confirm the operation. Alternatively, just the changes associated with a particular class can be removed from a change set. In this example, all references to changes to class Integer are forgotten:

```
ChangeSet current removeClassChanges: Integer
```

Filing-out changes

We have already seen how any individual method, protocol, class or class category can be *filed out* to the underlying file system by using the **file out as . . .** option from the Browsers' <operate> menus (Chapter 16). However, it is often useful to be able to file out all changes made in a particular Project. This is especially attractive if a new Project is used to develop a particular VisualWorks application. All changes in a Project can be filed out using either of the following two expressions:

```
'someFile.st' asFilename fileOutChanges
Filename fileOutChanges
```

The latter requests the user to provide a suitable filename on which the changes should be written. Alternatively, the **File Out Changes . . .** option from the **Changes** menu of the Launcher may also be used – again the user is requested for a filename. In all three cases, a message is written to the Transcript identifying the name of the file, and identifying the changes that have been written to that file (Figure 24.4).

Alternatively, only those changes associated with a particular class (in this case, class Integer) may be filed out:

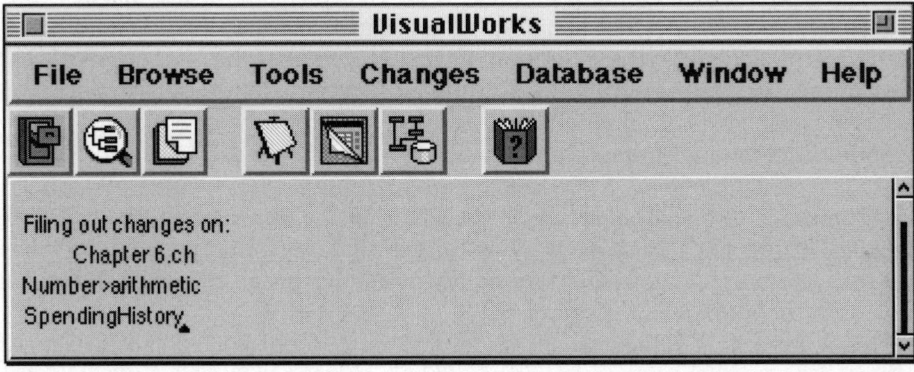

Figure 24.4 Messages written to the System Transcript when filing-out changes.

```
'someFile.st' asFilename fileOutChangesFor: Integer
```

To support the functionality discussed above, a ChangeSet class is provided. This class maintains separate records of changes made to whole classes and individual methods, within a particular Project.

Exercise 24.5

Experiment with accessing and browsing the change set, using the methods discussed in this section. In particular, you should experiment with 'filing-out' several changes in unrelated classes.

Exercise 24.6

Browse class ChangeSet in class category System-Changes.

24.3 The Change List Browser

The change set records changes to your VisualWorks image made in a particular Project, and saves this information within the image. The changes *file*, however, records all changes made in the entire image. This includes methods and classes changed or added to the image, as well as every **do it** selected from <operate> menus. Furthermore, since this information is stored in an external file, it is available even after a 'crash'. This file is called something like 'visual.cha'; in general, the suffix 'cha' will appear automatically.

Very occasionally, when developing new code, you may find that VisualWorks crashes. This may be due to a failure of the underlying platform (which is not your fault), or may be caused by some ill-advised change made in the image (which probably is your fault!). The simplest way of recovering the situation is to restart the image (which will restore the state to that recorded at the last snapshot), and use the following expression to look at the most recent change information:

```
SourceFileManager default recover: 5000
```

This copies the last 5000 characters in the 'changes' file into another file (called, by default, 'st80.recent'), and opens a File Editor window on it (see Chapter 6). You can then select expressions and reinstall them in your image by using the **file it in** option on the <operate> menu.

This approach is rather crude, and so a more sophisticated mechanism for browsing the changes file is provided. This is the 'Change List Browser'. This Browser allows one or more files, containing Smalltalk expressions in the 'filed-out' format, to be manipulated in various ways, including the ability to redo any expression of change and check for conflicting definitions of methods. A new Change List Browser can be opened by evaluating the following expression:

```
ChangeListView open
```

or by selecting the **Open Change List** option from the **Changes** menu of the Launcher. Both of these methods create an *empty* Change List Browser. Alternatively, a Change List Browser can be opened on *all* changes in the changes file made since the last snapshot (e.g. after a crash) using the expression:

```
ChangeListView recover
```

Figure 24.5 shows a Change List Browser containing all the changes that have been described so far in this book. The Browser is divided into two main panes, and eight switches. The upper pane is a fixed list, displaying changes and additions to methods and classes, and expressions directly evaluated from the user interface. In Figure 24.5, many items are available; several are doIts from Chapter 6, and two different versions of the diff: method in class Number. If an item is selected from the list, the corresponding method or expression is displayed in the lower pane.

The upper two switches in the Change List Browser affect the information displayed in the upper pane. If the **show file** switch is selected, then the name of the changes file which contains this item is displayed in brackets before the class and selector names. Similarly, if the **show category** switch is selected, then the list item is preceded in brackets by the name of the class category (for a change to a class), or the message protocol (for a change to a method) in which the change occurred. Empty brackets indicate a change that does not effect a class or method. The effect of these two switches is illustrated in Figure 24.6.

The lower six switches allow 'filtering' operations to be performed on the changes file. All these operations remove changes items from the upper pane that do not

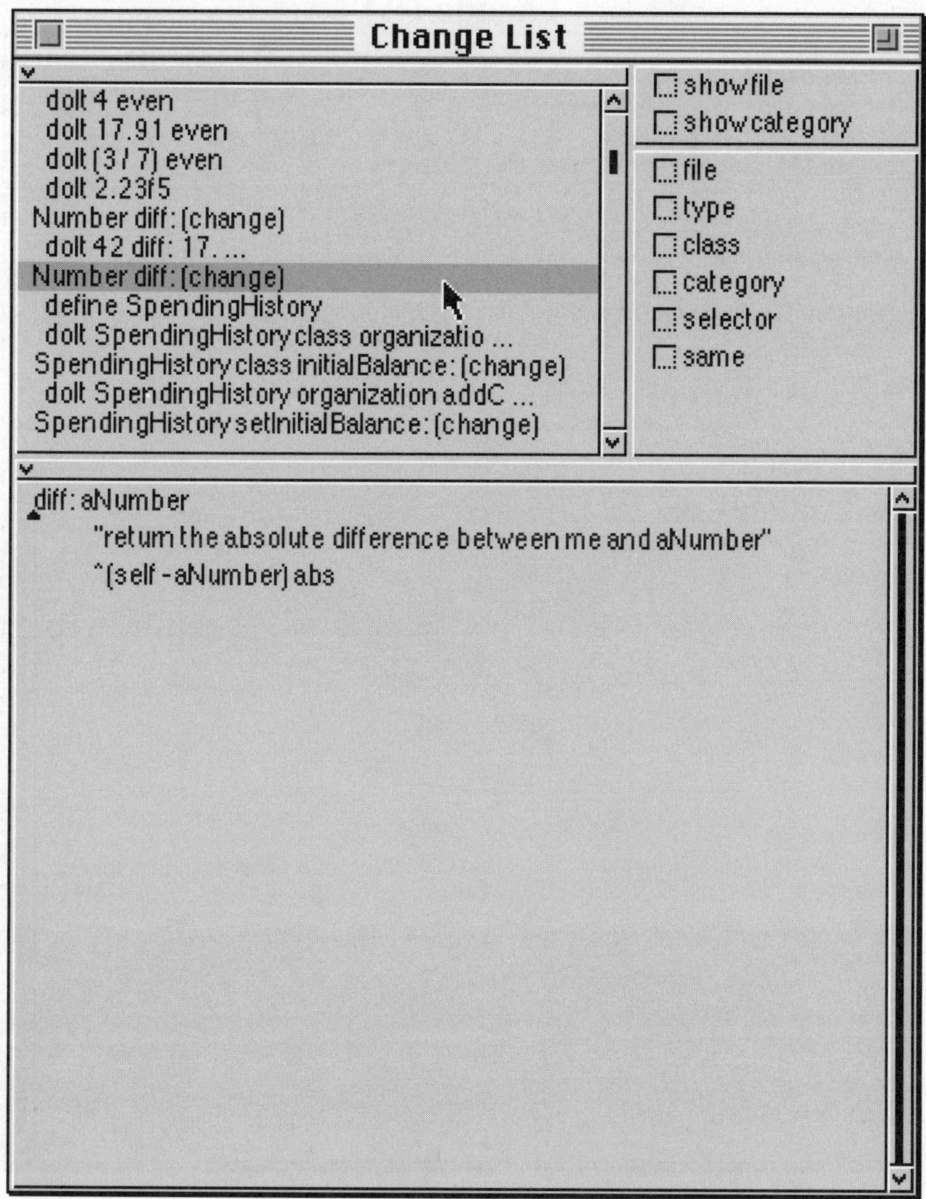

Figure 24.5 The Change List Browser.

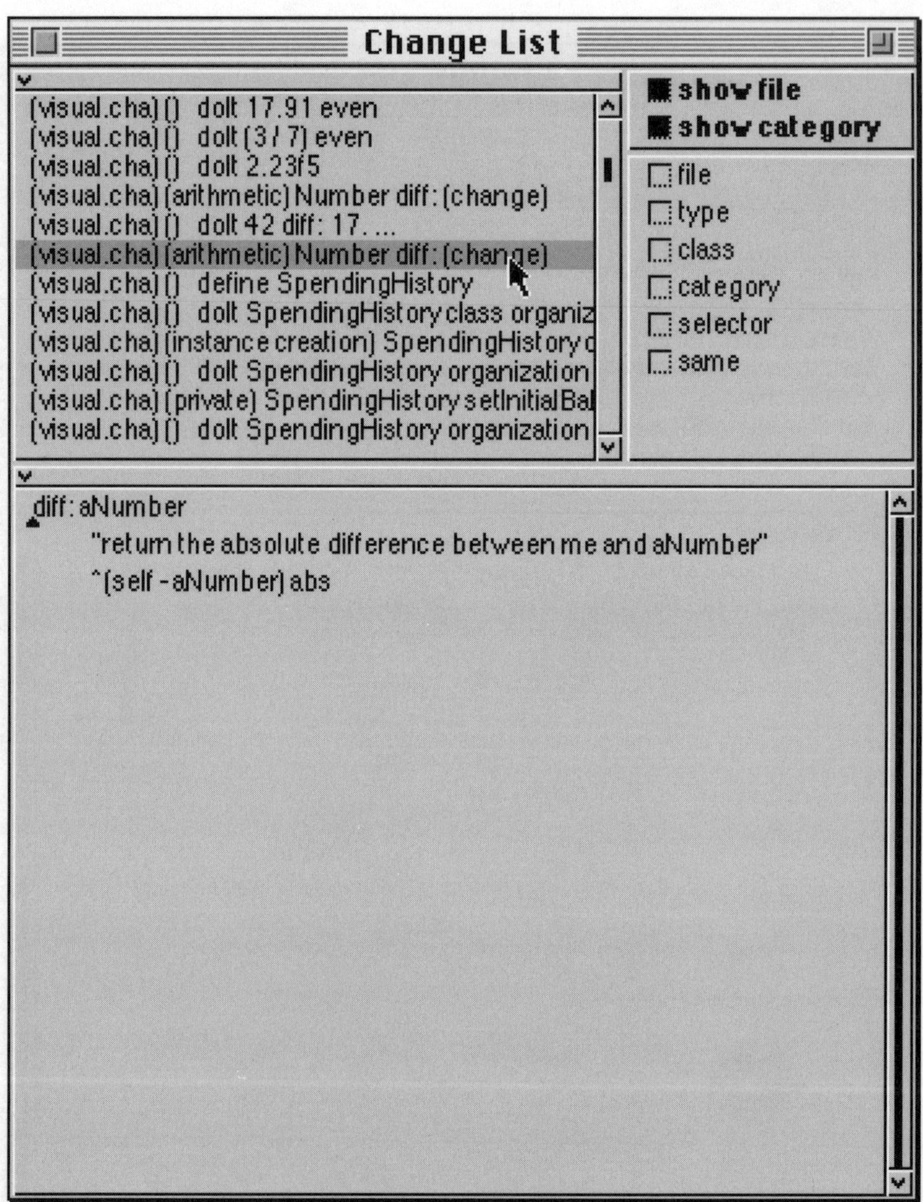

Figure 24.6 The Change List Browser (showing the file and category to which each change belongs).

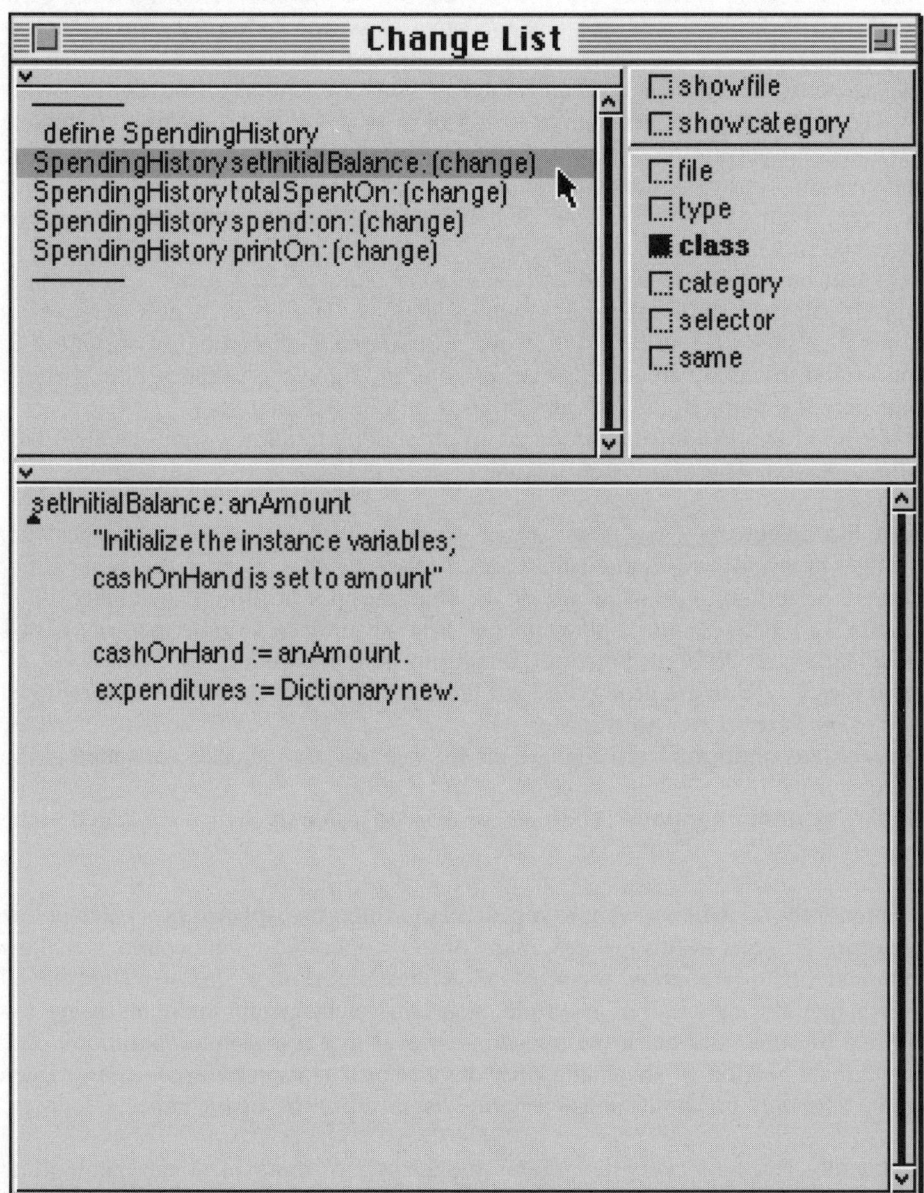

Figure 24.7 Filtering information in the Change List Browser.

correspond to the switch selected. The **file** switch removes all methods that do not come from the same changes file as the selected item. The **type** switch selects only items of the same type; i.e. doIt, class creation, or method definition items. The **class** switch displays only items of the same class, the **category** switch displays only items in the same message category (protocol) and the **selector** switch displays only items with the same message selector. Finally, the **same** switch displays only items that are identical; this allows (for example) possibly conflicting method definitions to be detected. The filter switch operations are independent, so that combinations of options are frequently useful when browsing change sets. For example, Figure 24.7 shows all changes made to class SpendingHistory first described in Chapter 6.

As can be seen from Figure 24.5, the lower pane in the Change List Browser supports all the usual <operate> menu functions. The upper pane's *hierarchical* <operate> menu (Figure 24.8), however, provides a large number of options. The options are divided into three sections: options handling changes files, options managing the items in the list, and options for conflict analysis.

The first item (**file in/out**) produces another menu to allow various changes files to be accessed. The options on this menu are as follows:

read file/directory . . . – You are prompted for the name of a changes file. Changes in this file are scanned and added to those already listed in the upper pane. You are permitted to use wildcards in the filename specification. (The ability of the Change List Browser to display changes from several files simultaneously allows modifications to different Smalltalk images to be compared.)
write file . . . – You are prompted for a filename. Changes not marked for removal (see below) are written to this file.
recover last changes – All changes made since the last snapshot are added to the changes list.
display system changes – All changes recorded inside the image are added to the changes list.

Frequently, we will not want to repeat all the changes displayed by a Change List Browser. To assist in this process, many of the <operate> menu commands allow change items to be *marked* for removal. An item marked in this way is displayed with a line through it. For example, you can select groups of items using the filtering buttons, and mark them all for removal in a few simple operations. The upper main section of the menu provides options to support this activity. Each option acts *only* on those items *currently* displayed in the upper pane.

replay all – Evaluate every item that is not marked for removal. A sub-menu offers the option of only replaying the remaining changes.
remove all – Mark every item for removal.
restore all – Remove the mark from all items.
spawn all . . . – Open a new Change List Browser on the items.

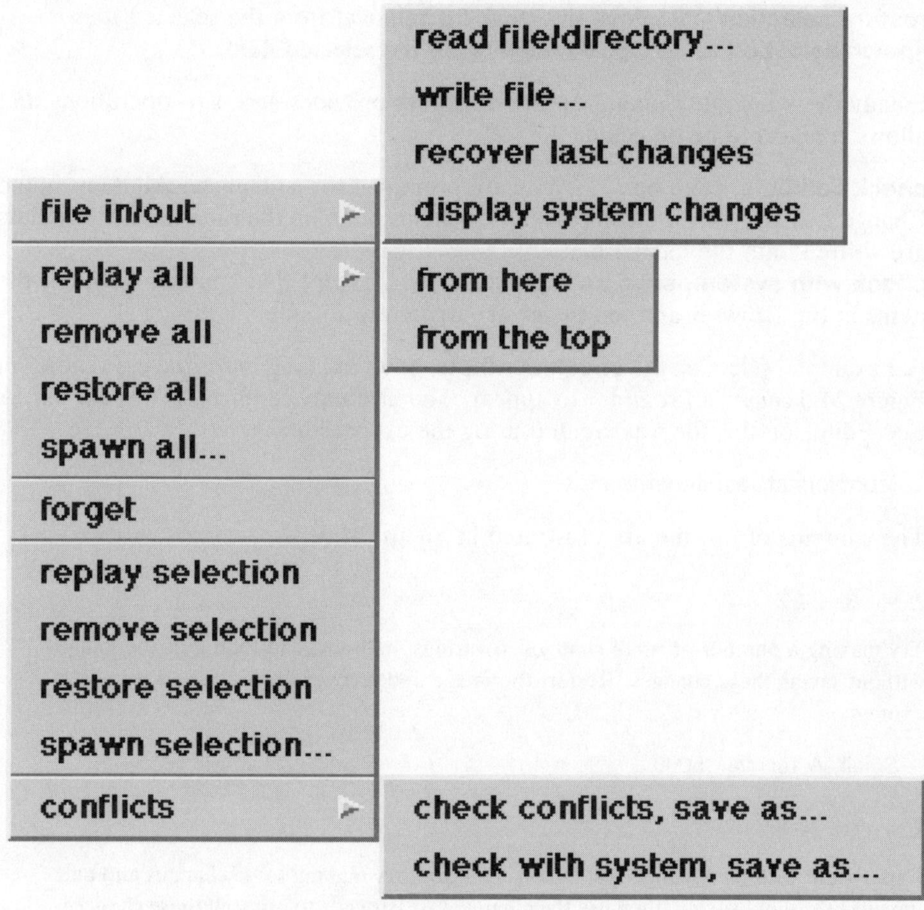

Figure 24.8 The <operate> menu in the top pane of the Change List Browser.

forget – Removes permanently from the list all items marked for removal.

A typical use of these operations for crash recovery would be to mark for removal all doIt items, and then evaluate all class and method items.

The lower main section of the menu contains options that operate only on the selected item.

replay selection – Evaluate the currently selected change item, even if it is marked for removal.
remove selection – Mark the selected item for removal.

restore selection – Remove the mark for removal from the selected item.
spawn selection . . . – Open a window on the selected item.

Finally the <operate> menu option **conflicts** provides access to operations that allows conflicts to be detected.

check conflicts, save as . . . – You are prompted for a filename. All items in the Change List Browser are compared. Any items defining the same method or class are written onto the named file.
check with system, save as . . . – As above, except that conflicts between the items in the Browser and the *image* are written to the file.

For example, selecting the **check conflicts, save as. . .** item for the case shown in Figure 24.5 causes a Prompter to appear. The filename 'conflicts.st' was chosen. A File Editor on this file was created using the expression:

```
'conflicts.st' asFilename edit
```

The contents of this file are illustrated in Figure 24.9.

Exercise 24.7

Try making a number of small changes to various methods, and then quit the image without saving these changes. Restart the image and recover these changes using the expression:

```
Smalltalk recover: 5000
```

Exercise 24.8

Experiment with the Change List Browser. Again, try making some changes and quit the image without saving, then use the Change List Browser to reinstall these changes.

Exercise 24.9

Create a new class, together with some new methods. Find out how this appears in the Change List Browser. Also, try moving a method from one protocol to another. Again, see how this is represented in the Change List Browser.

Exercise 24.10

Verify the operation of the display and filter buttons in the Change List Browser. To make this exercise effective, it is desirable to have a large number of different types of changes to explore. One way of achieving this is to use the **file in** option on the entire Smalltalk source code; this file will typically be named 'visual.sou'. You should therefore be able, for example, to browse every initialize method in the original source code. (*Warning:* it will take quite a long time to parse and display the entire source file!)

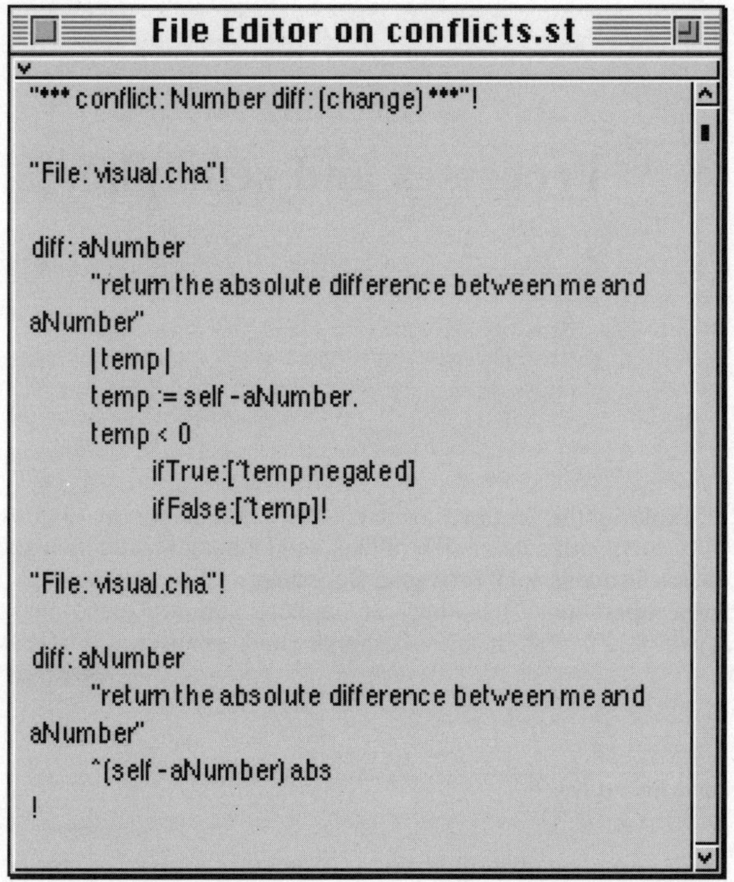

Figure 24.9 A 'conflicts' file.

24.4 Summary

VisualWorks provides Projects as a means of organizing the changes made to an image. Each Project maintains its own set of changes in an instance of ChangeSet. The changes in a ChangeSet may be inspected, forgotten, or filed out. Files containing the changes made in a Project may be filed in to another image – providing a method of sharing code in a workgroup environment. In the next chapter we discuss the classes in VisualWorks available to provide multiprocessing and concurrency control.

25 Processes and semaphores

This chapter explores the features available in Smalltalk for the expression of *concurrency*. It starts with a discussion of Link and LinkedList, and then goes on to introduce classes Process and ProcessorScheduler. Classes to support various synchronization operations, including Semaphore, SharedQueue and critical sections, are explored though the use of examples and exercises. Class Delay is also considered.

25.1 Links and linked lists

We have already seen a number of different Collection classes where the objects in that collection are ordered in some way (Chapter 15). These classes are always ultimately subclasses of SequenceableCollection. Instances of these classes have a definite order, which may in some cases be externally defined (instances of Array, for example); in other cases, the order is implicit, such as instances of OrderedCollection.

Here, we introduce another subclass of SequenceableCollection called LinkedList, instances of which behave something like a 'list'. Class LinkedList defines two instance variables: firstLink which is a reference to the first item in a list, and lastLink which is a reference to the last item (see Figure 25.1). If the list is empty, both instance variables are nil. Since LinkedList is a Collection class (see Chapter 14), it inherits much protocol for accessing (at:), removing (remove:) and enumerating (do:, select:) its elements. Additional methods are provided to support adding and removing items at the beginning of the list (addFirst:, removeFirst) and at the end of the list (addLast:, removeLast). However, instances of class LinkedList represent collections whose elements are *all of the same class*: they are special 'link items', instances of class Link, or of a subclass.

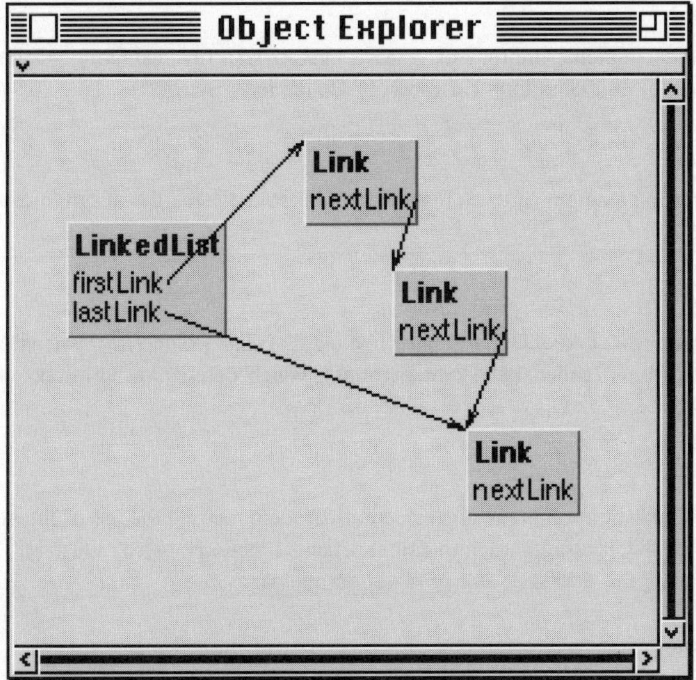

Figure 25.1 A linked list.

Class Link is a subclass of Object, and defines just one instance variable (nextLink). This is a reference to the next *link* in the list, or nil if there are no further items. Thus, Link may be described as an abstract superclass which provides its instances with the ability to refer to another instance of Link. However, an instance of Link does not have a way to keep a reference to the actual *object* in the collection; instead, subclasses of Link are used. Useful subclasses of Link would define one or more additional instance variables, to refer to the actual objects *in* the linked list.

You should note that classes Link and LinkedList are primarily provided to support *multiprocessing* in Smalltalk. The structure implemented by these classes is sufficiently simple that the virtual machine can directly manipulate a collection of objects representing *runnable* processes. For more general use, other concrete subclasses of SequenceableCollection such as OrderedCollection (Chapter 15) should be used; instances of OrderedCollection can contain any kind of object, rather than only instances of Link (or a subclass).

Exercise 25.1

Browse the implementation of class LinkedList (in category Collections-Sequenceable) and class Link (in category Collections-Support).

Exercise 25.2

Why is inserting elements into an instance of LinkedList using the at:put: message not permitted?

Exercise 25.3

Try constructing a LinkedList containing instances of class Point. *Hint*: you will require a subclass of Link (called LinkPoint perhaps), which defines an additional instance variable point.

Exercise 25.4

Using a linked list of points (as suggested above), demonstrate the use of the addFirst: and removeFirst messages to implement 'stack' functions. Also, illustrate 'queue' functions using the addLast: and removeLast messages.

Exercise 25.5

You might like to try implementing a subclass of LinkedList called Stack, which implements methods called push: and pop. Would class Stack be more useful if it was implemented as a subclass of OrderedCollection instead?

25.2 Processes

Smalltalk supports *multiple independent processes*. These are *lightweight* processes, as they share a common address space (object memory). Each instance of class Process represents a sequence of actions which can be performed by the virtual machine.

We have already seen how blocks are used to implement a wide range of control constructs (see Chapters 10 and 17). Blocks are also used as the basis for creating Processes in Smalltalk. The simplest way to create a Process is to send a block the message fork. For example, selecting and evaluating the expression:

```
[Transcript cr;
        show: 100 factorial printString] fork
```

creates an instance of class Process containing a block that will display the factorial for 100 in the System Transcript. The new Process is added to the list of scheduled Processes. This Process is runnable (i.e. scheduled for evaluation) immediately, and will start evaluating as soon as the current Process (one controlling the window manager) releases control of the processor.

We can create a new instance of class Process which is *not scheduled* by sending the newProcess message to a block:

```
| aProcess |
aProcess := [Transcript cr;
                        show: 100 factorial printString] newProcess
```

The Process is not actually *runnable* until it receives the resume message:

```
aProcess resume
```

A Process can be temporarily stopped using the suspend message. A *suspended* Process can be restarted later using the resume message. The terminate message is used when a Process is no longer required. Once a Process has received the terminate message, it cannot be restarted.

It is also possible to create and execute a Process containing a block with any number of arguments.

```
| aProcess |
aProcess := [:first :second |
            Transcript cr;
                        show: (first raisedTo: second) printString]
                newProcessWith: (Array with: 2 with: 20).
aProcess resume.
```

The example above creates a Process which, when it runs, will display 1048576 (2^{20}) in the System Transcript.

Priorities

In fact, Smalltalk supports *prioritized* Processes, so that we can create Processes of high priority which run before other Processes of lower priority. Eight priority levels are supported, with level 1 being the lowest. The priorities have names assigned to them, described in Table 25.1.

We can create a *runnable* Process with specified priority using the forkAt: message. The argument is an integer, but should be derived as a result of evaluating an expression, for example (the global variable Processor is described later in this chapter):

```
[Transcript cr;
        show: 100 factorial printString]
                    forkAt: Processor userBackgroundPriority.
```

Table 25.1

Priority	Name	Purpose
100	timingPriority	Used by Processes that are dependent on real time. For example, Delays (see later).
98	highIOPriority	Used by time-critical I/O Processes, such as handling input from a network.
90	lowIOPriority	Used by most I/O Processes, such as handling input from the user (keyboard, pointing device, etc.).
70	userInterruptPriority	Used by user Processes desiring immediate service. Processes run at this level will pre-empt the window scheduler and should, therefore, not consume the processor forever.
50	userSchedulingPriority	Used by Processes governing normal user interaction. Also the priority at which the window scheduler runs.
30	userBackgroundPriority	Used by user background Processes.
10	systemBackgroundPriority	Used by system background Processes. Examples are an optimizing compiler or status checker.
1	systemRockBottomPriority	The lower possible priority.

Alternatively, we can use the priority: message to change the priority of an existing Process. For example, in the code below we create two Processes: *process1* and *process2*, which are given priorities 10 and 98 respectively. Note that *process1* is resumed before *process2*. The result on the Transcript is shown in Figure 25.2.

```
| process1 process2 |
Transcript clear.
process1 := [Transcript show: 'first'] newProcess.
process1 priority: Processor systemBackgroundPriority.
process2 := [Transcript show: 'second'] newProcess.
process2 priority: Processor highIOPriority.
process1 resume.
process2 resume.
```

The *default Process priority* (and the priority at which expressions are evaluated using the user interface) is 50 (userSchedulingPriority). The scheduling algorithm used is described in detail later in this chapter.

As we have already indicated, Processes in Smalltalk are represented by instances of class Process. This class is a subclass of Link, for reasons we shall see later. Class Process defines four additional instance variables: these include

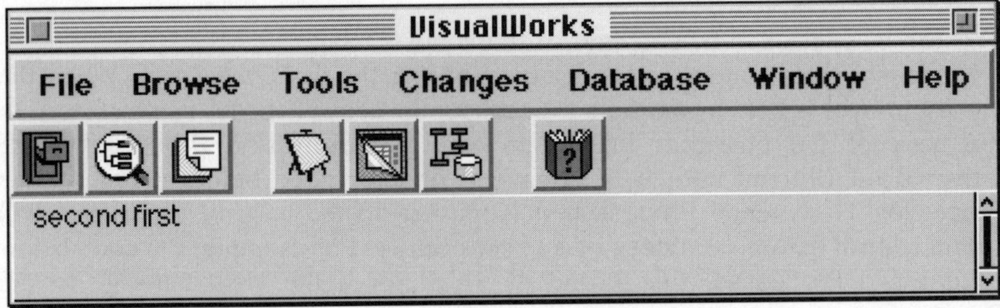

Figure 25.2 The result of evaluating the message expressions.

priority, which retains an integer representing the priority of a Process, and suspendedContext which is the context that is currently being evaluated by this Process.

Exercise 25.6

Try some examples of creating simple Processes using the fork and newProcess messages sent to blocks. You may like to display trace messages in the System Transcript.

Exercise 25.7

Browse class Process (in category Kernel-Processes). Try sending the resume, suspend and terminate messages to a Process created using the newProcess (or newProcessWith:) message sent to a block.

Exercise 25.8

Browse class BlockClosure to see how the fork and newProcess methods are implemented.

25.3 Scheduling processes

Class ProcessorScheduler manages the runnable Processes. As the virtual machine has only one processor, its single instance is represented by a single global variable Processor. We have already come across the use of the variable as the receiver of messages to return an appropriate priority.

Note that Process is a subclass of Link, and that ProcessorScheduler has an instance variable representing a LinkedList of 'quiescent' Processes. The active Process (the one actually running) can be identified by the expression

```
Processor activeProcess
```

This can be controlled by suspend or terminate messages.

Processor gives control to the Process having the highest priority. When the highest priority is held by multiple Processes, the active Process can be forced to the back of the quiescent Processes with the expression Processor yield. Otherwise it will run until it is suspended or terminated before giving up the Processor. However, a Process that is 'pushed to the back of the queue' will regain control before a Process of a lower priority. For example, the code below creates two Processes, the second of which sends the yield message to the Processor:

```
| process1 process2 |
process1 := [Transcript show: 'Process 1'; cr] newProcess.
process2 := [Transcript show: 'Process 2, first part'; cr.
             Processor yield.
             Transcript show: 'Process 2, second part'; cr] newProcess.
process2 resume.
process1 resume
```

The result on the Transcript is shown in Figure 25.3.

Apart from the two messages activeProcess and yield, most application programmers will never use ProcessorScheduler directly.

The scheduling is actually performed by the virtual machine. Note that the scheduling algorithm interrupts Processes with a low priority to run Processes with a higher priority, but will not run several Processes at the same priority concurrently.

Exercise 25.9

Browse the classes Process and ProcessorScheduler. Note the instance protocol in ProcessorScheduler which answers various scheduling priorities.

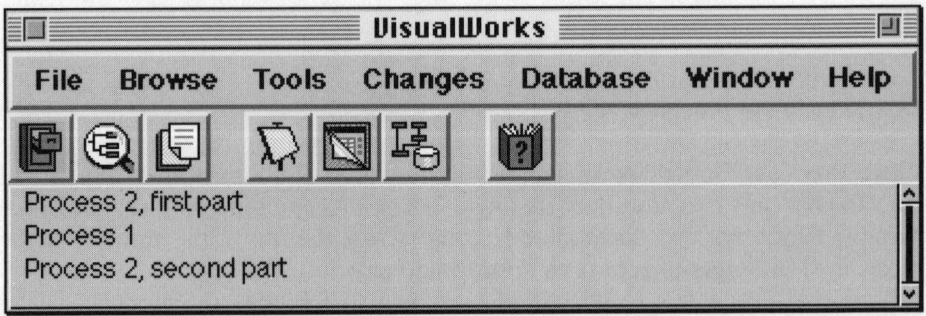

Figure 25.3 Two **Processes** writing to the Transcript.

Exercise 25.10

Try altering the priority of your Processes created earlier. You may need to include Processor yield expressions to prevent one Process from blocking others at the same priority level. Try not to create Processes that run forever at high priority levels – such Processes are very difficult to stop!

25.4 Synchronization using semaphores

So far, we have shown how we create independent Processes using Smalltalk. However, for realistic applications, we expect that there will be some interaction between Processes: these Processes will have references to some objects in common, and such objects may receive messages from several Processes in an arbitrary order. This may lead to unpredictable results.

To illustrate this, consider a class Counter, with one instance variable value:

```
Object subclass: #Counter
   instanceVariableNames: 'value'
   classVariableNames: ''
   poolDictionaries: ''
   category: 'Processes-Experiments'
```

On creation, the value instance variable is set to 0, by an initialization method in the instance protocol:

```
initialize
   value := 0
```

The 'instance creation' class protocol method used is:

```
new
   ^super new initialize
```

Instance protocol methods are also provided to read and set the value instance variable, and to increment this variable.

```
value
   ^value

value: anInteger
   value := anInteger

increment
   value := value + 1
```

Now, suppose we create two Processes, which can both send messages to the same instance of Counter. The first Process repeatedly sends the message increment; the other Process is of a lower priority and sends the message value, checks whether the result is 9 or greater, and if it is then prints it on the Transcript and resets the value to zero (using the value: message). Note that the two Processes are *not* synchronized.

```
| counter |
counter := Counter new.
Process1 :=[| delay |
            delay := Delay forMilliseconds: 40.
            [counter increment.
            delay wait] repeat] newProcess.
Process2 := [| delay |
            delay := Delay forMilliseconds: 40.
            [| currentValue |
            currentValue := counter value.
            currentValue >= 9
                ifTrue:[Transcript cr;
                            show: currentValue printString.
                    counter value: 0].
            delay wait] repeat] newProcess.
Process2 priority: Processor userBackgroundPriority.
```

Process1 and *Process2* are global variables. The use of class Delay is described later in this chapter. The two Processes may be started using:

```
Process1 resume.
Process2 resume.
```

The result may appear as in Figure 25.4 (depending on the amount of user interface activity). The Processes may be terminated by evaluating the following expressions.

```
Process1 terminate
Process2 terminate
```

In the example above, the sequence of numbers displayed in the Transcript appears non-deterministic. Fortunately, in Smalltalk there is a class called Semaphore which is used to synchronize multiple Processes.

Exercise 25.11

Implement the class Counter and type in and evaluate the example code above. Start both Processes and examine the Transcript. Explain its behavior.

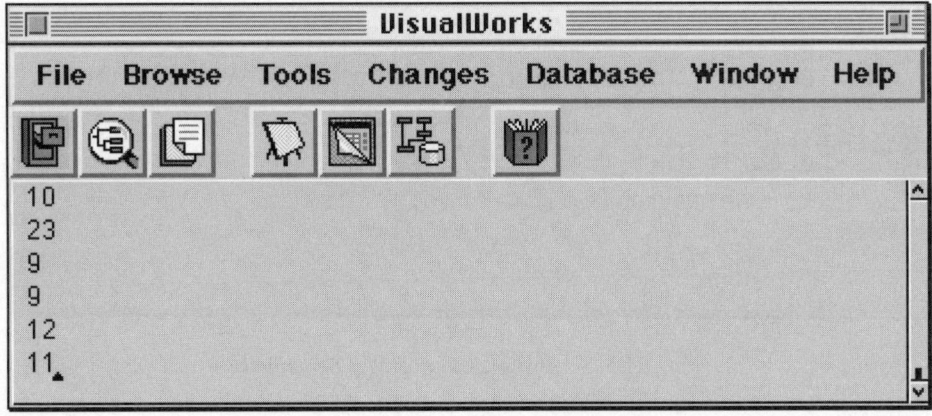

Figure 25.4 Two **Processes** sharing one object.

25.5 Semaphores

A Semaphore is an object used to synchronize multiple Processes. A Process can wait for an event to occur by sending the message wait to a Semaphore. A Process can signal that an event has occurred by sending the message signal to a Semaphore. For example,

```
| sem |
Transcript clear.
sem := Semaphore new.
[Transcript show: 'The '] fork.
[Transcript show: 'quick '.
sem wait.
Transcript show: 'fox '.
sem signal] fork.
[Transcript show: 'brown '.
sem signal.
sem wait.
Transcript show: 'jumps over the lazy dog'; cr] fork
```

gives the result in Figure 25.5.

A Semaphore will only return from as many wait messages as it has received signal messages. When a Semaphore receives a wait message for which no corresponding signal has been sent, the Process sending the wait is suspended. If a Semaphore receives a wait message from two or more Processes, it resumes only one Process for each signal message it receives from the Process it is monitoring.

Figure 25.5 Synchronization using a **Semaphore**.

Unlike a ProcessorScheduler, a Semaphore pays no attention to the *priority* of a Process.

A Semaphore is frequently used to provide mutual exclusion from a *critical region* of code. This is supported by the instance method critical:. The block argument is only evaluated when no other critical blocks sharing the same Semaphore are evaluating.

A Semaphore for mutual exclusion must start out with one extra *signal*, otherwise the critical section will never be entered. A special instance creation method is provided:

```
Semaphore forMutualExclusion
```

Exercise 25.12

Browse class Semaphore, paying particular attention to the method critical:.

Exercise 25.13

Repeat Exercise 25.11 so that the two Processes are synchronized.

25.6 Shared queues

When it's necessary to match the output of one Process with the input of another, it's important to ensure that the Processes are synchronized. This synchronization may be achieved using an instance of class SharedQueue, which provides synchronized communication of arbitrary objects between Processes. (SharedQueue uses Semaphores to achieve its synchronization.)

An object is added to a SharedQueue from a Process by sending the message nextPut: (with the object as argument) and retrieved by another Process sending the message next. If no object has been added to the queue when a next message is sent, the Process requesting the object will be *suspended* until an object is available.

25.7 Delays

Class Delay represents a *real time* delay in the evaluation of a Process. An instance of Delay will respond to the message wait by *suspending* the active Process for a certain amount of time. The time for resumption of the active Process is specified when the Delay is created.

The resumption time can be specified relative to the current time with the messages forMilliseconds: and forSeconds:; both messages expect a numeric argument. A Delay created in this way can be sent the message wait again after it has resumed. For example, the expression:

```
| minuteWait |
minuteWait := Delay forSeconds: 60.
minuteWait wait.
```

suspends the active Process for a minute. This could also be expressed as:

```
(Delay forSeconds: 60) wait
```

The resumption time can also be specified as an absolute time with respect to Smalltalk's millisecond clock with the message untilMillisecond:. A Delay created in this way *cannot* be sent the message wait repeatedly.

Exercise 25.14

Use a Delay to implement a simple clock which prints the current time in the Transcript every few seconds. You may want to use the expression:

```
Transcript clear; show: Time now printString
```

Exercise 25.15

Browse classes Delay and SharedQueue (both in category Kernel-Processes). Explain how Semaphores and critical regions are used to implement these classes.

Exercise 25.16

(Hard) Attempt a Smalltalk representation of 'Dijkstra's Dining Philosophers problem'. Five philosophers spend their lives eating and thinking. The philosophers share a common circular table surrounded by five chairs, each belonging to one philosopher. In the center of the table there is a bowl of rice and the table is laid with five chopsticks. When a philosopher thinks, he or she does not interact with any colleagues. From time to time, a philosopher gets hungry and tries to pick up the two chopsticks that are closest (the chopsticks that are between the philosopher and his or her left and right neighbors). A philosopher may only pick up one chopstick at a time. Obviously, a philosopher cannot pick up a chopstick that is already in the hand of a neighbor. When a hungry philosopher has both chopsticks at the same time, he or she eats without releasing the chopsticks. After eating enough, the philosopher puts down both chopsticks and starts thinking again.

The suggested solution represents each chopstick as a Semaphore, using the wait and signal messages. This guarantees that no two philosophers use the same chopstick simultaneously. The suggested solution is also asymmetric; an odd philosopher picks up the left chopstick first, then the right chopstick, while an even philosopher picks up the right chopstick first.

It is suggested that each philosopher is represented by an instance of class Philosopher. The problem could be a class DiningPhilosophers, with the philosophers and the chopsticks maintained in instance variables.

You may want to display tracing messages in the System Transcript. How could you introduce some indeterminacy into the solution, given the way the Smalltalk scheduler handles Processes of the same priority? (The problem presented here is loosely based on the one originally proposed for Little Smalltalk, presented in Tim Budd's book *A Little Smalltalk*, pp. 116–121.)

25.8 Summary

Class Process provides a sophisticated mechanism for the scheduling of processes in VisualWorks. However, we should raise a note of caution – without careful programming, Processes can be difficult to control. The problems of concurrency can be overcome by the use of Semaphores, which (among other things) provide a means of specifying 'critical regions' – message expressions that can be evaluated by only one Process at a time.

In the next chapter we return to the description of classes. Smalltalk is unlike many other object-oriented languages because a class is itself an instance of some other class – termed its 'metaclass'.

26 Classes and metaclasses[1]

This chapter considers the implementation of the class structure within Smalltalk, and introduces the *Metaclass* concept. Classes such as ClassDescription and Behavior are explored. The concepts here are widely misunderstood, possibly because of the tongue-twisting terminology used; an attempt is made to clear away the confusion in this chapter. (It's also worth saying that some of the ideas presented here can be difficult to understand, and are irrelevant to everyday application programming.)

26.1 Introduction

In this chapter we will consider the way in which classes are implemented within the VisualWorks image. As we have already noted, *classes are themselves objects*, and can respond to messages. Typically, messages (such as new, new: and so on) are used to create new instances of that class. The idea of *metaclasses*, which are the *classes of classes*, is introduced from a historical perspective, and the useful properties of this approach are outlined.

Be warned that the terminology used when discussing classes and metaclasses is extremely tongue-twisting: at the end of this chapter, you will appreciate the veracity of statements like: 'The class of class Metaclass is class Metaclass class'! (You should recall that the names of classes start with upper-case letters, as they are global variables, and that words which are defined within Smalltalk are reproduced here in a sans serif font.) Fortunately, in practice you need to know almost nothing about metaclasses to use VisualWorks effectively; the user interface hides most of these details from you.

[1] This chapter is based on an article written by Mario Wolczko, when at the University of Manchester, with permission.

26.2 Classes and metaclasses

There are two kinds of objects in Smalltalk: those which can create new objects and those which cannot. The former kind are called *classes* and can create new instances of that class. We already know that every object is an *instance* of some *class*, and that every class (except class Object) has a superclass. So, for example, we know that (3@4) is an *instance* of class Point (see Chapter 8), and that class Point is a *subclass* of class ArithmeticValue. To define things more precisely: an object is a class *if and only if* it can create instances of itself.

There are just two fundamental mechanisms which can create objects: they are the primitive methods new and new: which are defined in a class called Behavior. Class Behavior also defines the basicNew and basicNew: methods, which have the same functionality, but subclasses are not supposed to override them. Any object that understands these messages (and thus evaluates the methods in class Behavior) is a class.

In the earliest versions of Smalltalk developed at Xerox Palo Alto Research Center (Xerox PARC), such as Smalltalk-72, classes were not objects. The users found that this was a problem: it was impossible to handle classes in the same way as other entities. For example, it was not possible to send messages to a class, and other ways of creating objects had to be used. This situation also made it difficult to create new classes.

In Smalltalk-76, classes became objects. Since every object must be an instance of a class, every class was an instance of class Class. Thus, this class contained the methods corresponding to messages that were understood by all classes, including messages allowing new instances of a class to be created, such as new and new:. In addition, class Class understood messages to create new classes, and therefore must be an instance of a class itself. In fact, in Smalltalk-76, class Class was an instance of *itself!* Some simpler variants of Smalltalk available today also use this approach (for example, Little Smalltalk).

As the researchers at Xerox PARC used Smalltalk-76, they found that initializing objects was a little painful and prone to error. Since all classes are instances of Class, they all behave identically, and there is no way of creating instances of a class with specialized instance creation or initialization methods. This means that there is no class/instance distinction in the Browser, and that the only way to create initialized objects is to first send new (or new:) to the appropriate class, and then send an initialization message to the created instance. For example, creating and initializing an instance of class Point was done by:

```
Point new x: 4 y: 5
```

A common source of bugs was to forget to initialize the newly created object, or to initialize it incorrectly. Clearly, it is desirable that the instance creation messages either perform the correct initialization automatically or insist that appropriate parameters be supplied. For example, you will find that in the instance creation protocol of class Point, only the x:y: and r:theta: creation methods are provided, not new or new:.

If class Point is to be able to respond to the x:y: message while class ArithmeticValue is not, then it is clear that classes Point and ArithmeticValue cannot be instances of the same class. The solution adopted in Smalltalk-80 is to have every class the *only* instance of another class, which is termed its *metaclass*. Every metaclass is, of course, an instance of a class, but as all metaclasses behave identically they are instances of the same class, which is called Metaclass.

Metaclasses are in one-to-one correspondence with classes, and are generated when the class is defined. Since each class is the sole instance of its metaclass, there is no need for a special name for every metaclass. Consequently, they are named via their related class. Thus, the name of the metaclass which is the class of Point is Point class.

We have already seen that every object is an instance of a class, and class Metaclass is no exception. Noting that Metaclass is a class with multiple instances, it follows that Metaclass is an instance of its metaclass, called Metaclass class. Furthermore, Metaclass class, like all the other metaclasses, is an instance of Metaclass itself. This relationship between metaclass and metaclass class is a point of circularity in Smalltalk-80.

The relationship between classes and their metaclasses is summarized in Figure 26.1. Instance–class relationships are represented by gray arrows, while class–superclass relationships are shown with black arrows.

As an aside, all objects can be sent the message class to discover their class. So, for example, the expression:

```
(3@4) class
```

answers with Point. Similarly, we would expect the expression:

```
Point class
```

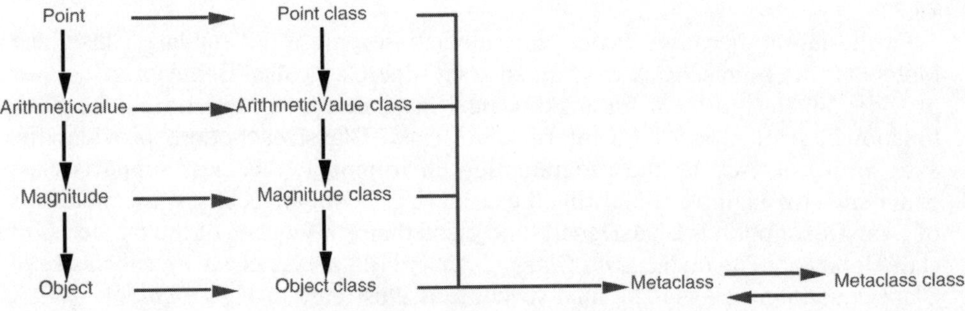

Figure 26.1 Class–instance relationships.

to respond with its metaclass. Of course, this actually prints as Point class! We can summarize the instance relationships between classes and metaclasses as follows. All the following expressions answer true:

```
(3@4) class == Point
Point class == Point class. "Point class is a metaclass, the class of Point"
Point class class == Metaclass.
Metaclass class class == Metaclass. "Circularity"
```

You may well be asking: just what is the significance of the class–metaclass relationship? For almost all application development in Smalltalk, these aspects need not concern you. The creation of metaclasses is hidden so well by the programming environment that you need not be aware of it. The only thing you need be aware of is that just as a class specifies the behavior of its instances in its instance methods, the behavior of the class itself (the class methods) is specified by its metaclass.

So far, we have only been considering *instance* relationships. However, earlier we observed that all classes (except Object) have a superclass. We know already that the superclass of Point is ArithmeticValue, but what is the superclass of its metaclass (Point class), class Metaclass and its metaclass Metaclass class? (You can find out the superclass of a class by sending it the message superclass.) The general rule is that, if x is a subclass of y, then x class is a subclass of y class. Thus, the superclass of Point class is ArithmeticValue class. While it would have been perfectly feasible to build Smalltalk in such a way that every metaclass was a direct subclass of Object, building it this way means that class methods are inherited using a *parallel hierarchy*. This means that there are two, parallel hierarchies: one for classes and one for their metaclasses.

As the *only* class that has no superclass is Object, we need a superclass for Object class. We know that all the instances of the metaclasses are classes, and thus it makes sense to concentrate the general notion of 'classness' into one class called Class, and make that the superclass of Object class. Naturally, the metaclass of class Class is called Class class. Our hierarchy of classes now appears in Figure 26.2.

Furthermore, because classes and metaclasses are very similar, Class and Metaclass are both subclasses of an abstract superclass called Behavior. This class provides all the protocol for making new instances, and supports all the basic functionality for classes. An intermediate class, ClassDescription, provides the extra protocol used by the programming environment; this class supports class comments, for example. Following the usual rules about metaclasses, the metaclass of ClassDescription is ClassDescription class that is a subclass of the metaclass of class Behavior. The metaclasses Class class and Metaclass class are subclasses of ClassDescription class. The final structure is illustrated in Figure 26.3.

We can make a number of interesting observations about the class–metaclass structure. All objects, including classes and metaclasses, are instances of classes

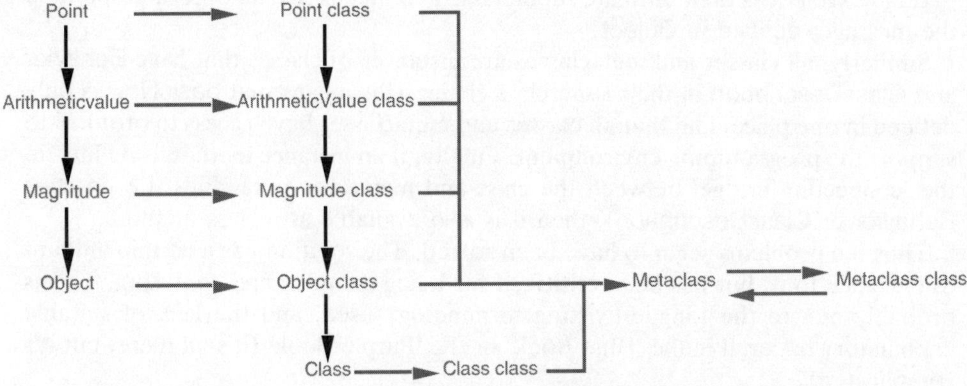

Figure 26.2 Class–superclass relationships for classes.

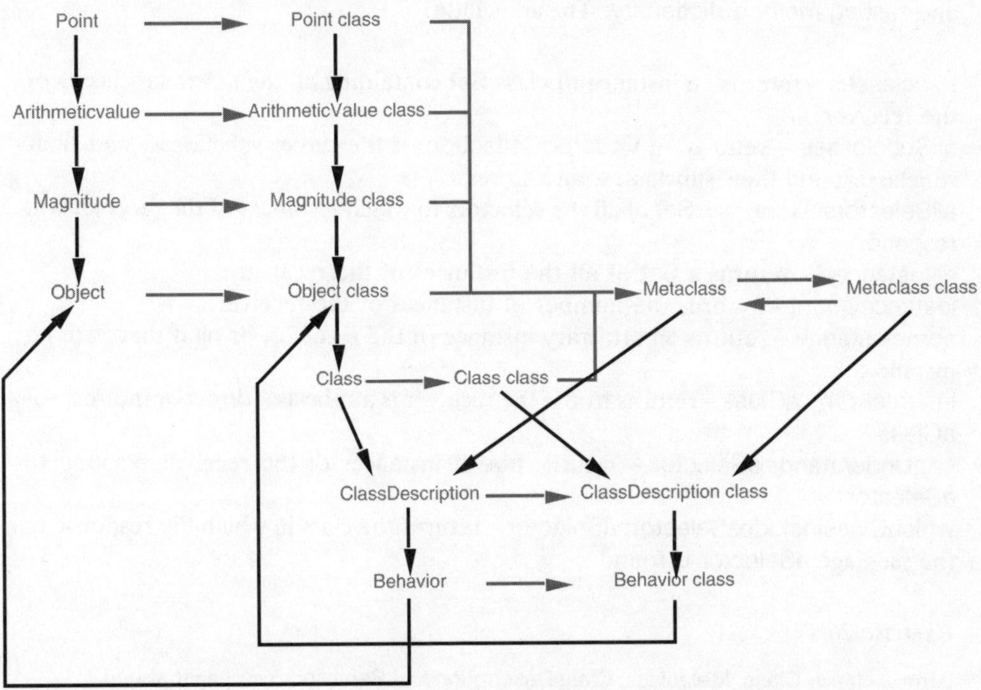

Figure 26.3 Classes **Behavior** and **ClassDescription**.

that have Object as their ultimate superclass. This means that *all* objects respond to the messages defined in Object.

Similarly, all classes and metaclasses are instances of classes that have Behavior and ClassDescription in their superclass chain. This means that basicNew is only defined in one place, and that all classes and metaclasses have access to protocol to support the programming environment. Finally, if an instance method is defined in the 'connecting bridge' between the class and metaclass hierarchies (i.e. in class Behavior or ClassDescription), then it is also available as a class method.

Thus the problems seem to have been solved. The solution has a certain amount of elegance to it, but has been criticized for being complex and confusing. This is probably due to the tongue-twisting terminology used, and the lack of suitable explanatory material in the 'Blue Book' or the 'Purple Book' (it's all there, but it's complicated).

Various authors have proposed going back to the situation in Smalltalk-76 (i.e. all classes are instances of Class), and alternative schemes are also in the works (not at Xerox). It is doubtful that the former will be adopted, but it remains to be seen whether anyone can come up with a better solution.

There are many methods defined in class Behavior, but the most useful ones are to be found in the following protocols: accessing class hierarchy, accessing method dictionary, accessing instances and variables, testing class hierarchy, and testing method dictionary. These include:

subclasses – returns an instance of class Set containing all the *direct* subclasses of the receiver.
allSubclasses – returns an OrderedCollection of the direct subclasses, and their subclasses, and their subclasses, and so on.
allSelectors – returns a Set of all the selectors to which instances of the receiver will respond.
allInstances – returns a Set of all the instances of the receiver.
instanceCount – returns the number of instances of the receiver.
someInstance – returns an arbitrary instance of the receiver, or nil if there are no instances.
inheritsFrom: aClass – returns true if the receiver is a subclass (direct or indirect) of aClass.
canUnderstand: aSelector – returns true if instances of the receiver respond to aSelector.
whichClassIncludesSelector: aSelector – returns the class in which the response to the message aSelector is found.

Exercise 26.1

Browse classes Class, Metaclass, ClassDescription and Behavior. You might also like to try inspecting an instance of a metaclass (i.e. a class), by sending the inspect message to a class of your choice. For example:

```
Point inspect

Metaclass inspect
```

Exercise 26.2

You might also like to try exploring the class and metaclass hierarchies using the class and superclass messages. For example, what is the result of the following expressions?

```
42 class superclass class class superclass

Metaclass superclass class superclass superclass class
```

You should be able to work out the expected result from Figure 26.3.

Exercise 26.3

Try some of the methods defined in class Behavior.

26.3 Summary

The metaclass concept is central to Smalltalk, but for most readers it is of no importance. If, however, you wish to change how classes behave, and how new classes are defined, then an understanding of the class–metaclass relationship is essential.

In the following chapter we return to mainstream application development. We describe the Smalltalk dependency mechanism and in Chapter 29, examine its use as the foundation of the VisualWorks user interface.

27 The dependency mechanism

The dependency mechanism is widely used when constructing interactive graphical applications using the 'MVC' structure (Chapter 29), but has many other uses as well. The implementation and use of the dependency mechanism is explored with examples, and some of the problems with its use are considered.

27.1 Introduction

We have already seen several ways in which activities can be coordinated within Smalltalk. For example, we have seen how one object can *send a message* to another object, thereby requesting an action to be performed. This can be regarded as two objects coordinating their roles. We have also seen various types of *shared variables* (class variables, for example), although their use for communication has been denigrated. The *dependency* mechanism provides another way in which controlled communication can take place, by allowing one object to *depend* on another.

The major use of the dependency mechanism in VisualWorks is to provide the links between a 'model' (the application data) and its 'view' (a visible representation) in a Model–View–Controller (MVC) application (see Chapter 29). However, here we will consider the dependency mechanism in isolation.

27.2 Operation of dependencies

The basic mechanism provided allows one object (objectB in Figure 27.1) to *depend* on another object (objectA). Alternatively, we could say that objectA has a *dependent*, objectB. Naturally, objectA can have as many dependents as necessary, and objectB can depend on as many objects as necessary.

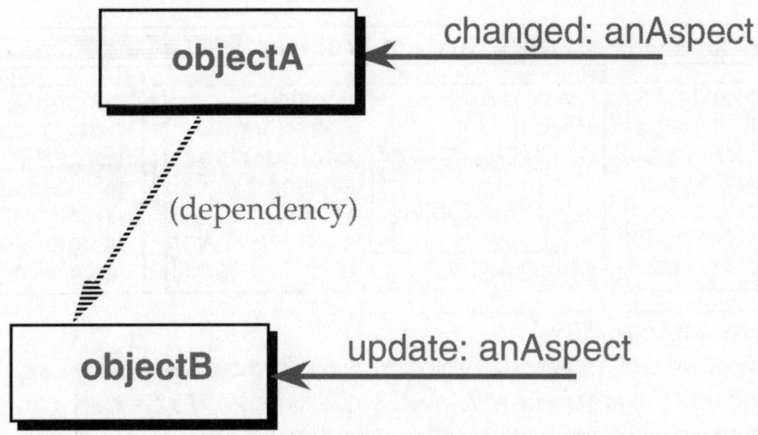

Figure 27.1 The **changed:** and **update:** messages.

In this book, dependencies will be represented diagrammatically by a 'fuzzy' arrow, as illustrated in Figure 27.1. This should be distinguished from references made by variables (solid black arrows) and messages sent to objects (gray arrows).

27.3 Changing and updating

When a particular object *changes*, any of its dependents may need to *update* themselves. In our example, if objectA changes, objectB will be updated. This mechanism is provided by two groups of messages: 'changed' messages and 'update' messages.

To indicate a change, an object must receive a 'changed' message. Usually, this message is sent to self as part of the method which actually makes the changes, using an expression like:

```
self changed: anAspect
```

The change information is propagated to any dependents, each of which receive an update: message, whose argument is the same *aspect* supplied to the corresponding changed: message. Thus, the dependent object can perform appropriate actions based on the aspect provided. The aspect is often a Symbol, which can be tested by the object receiving the update: message.

Consequently, if you wish a class of objects to perform some specific action when an object on which they depend changes, you should re-implement its update: method accordingly. The default implementation, defined in Object, performs no action (Figure 27.2).

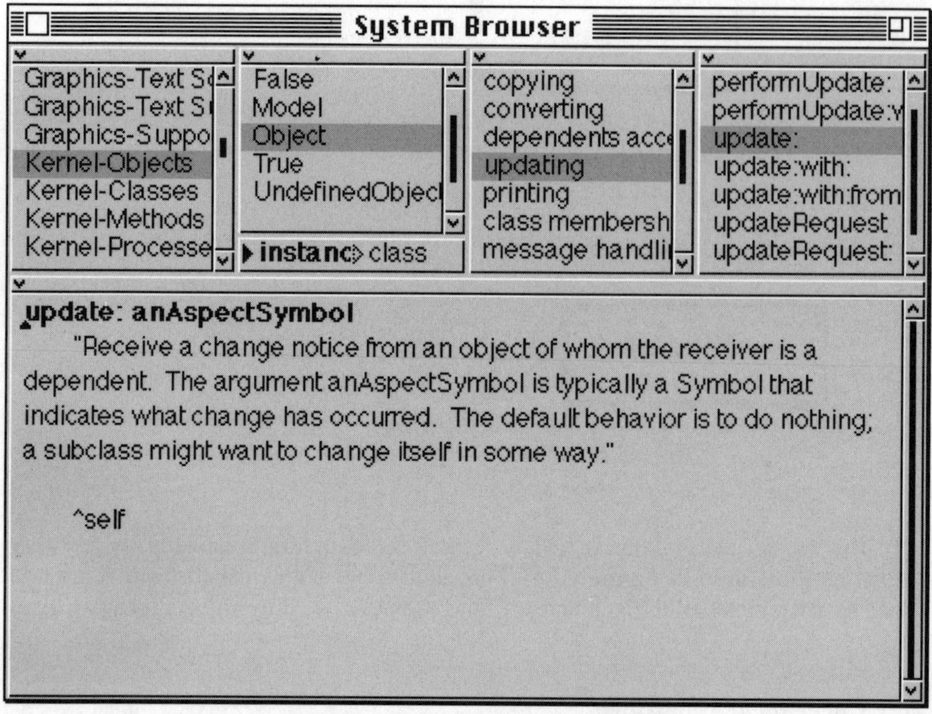

Figure 27.2 The default implementation of **update:** (in class **Object**).

There are also two other 'changed' messages, which provide different levels of parameterization. The simplest is the changed message, which is equivalent to the message changed:nil. The most complex is the message changed:with:; this variant provides dependent objects with even more information with which to discriminate available actions.

The extra 'update' messages are update:with: and update:with:from:. In both cases, the second argument is the same object as the second argument of the changed:with: message above. In its most complex form, the last argument of the 'update' message corresponds to the receiver of the 'changed' message.

In some cases, an object may wish to check with its dependents before making a change, to ensure that changes are made consistently (see Exercise 27.4 for an example). The changeRequest message should be sent to an object that wants to change. This checks with all its dependents, by sending the updateRequest message to each dependent in turn. The default implementation of updateRequest is to answer true; subclasses should re-implement this method to perform appropriate checks.

27.4 Broadcasting

Another facility using dependencies is the *broadcast* mechanism, which permits an arbitrary message to be sent to each of an object's dependents in turn. For example, in Figure 27.3, objectA has two dependents, objectB and objectC. When objectA receives the message:

```
broadcast: #someMessage
```

someMessage is sent to each of the dependents in turn. There is also a form that permits messages with one argument to be broadcast; for example:

```
broadcast: #someMessage: with: aParameter
```

This broadcast mechanism can be useful when dependencies are used in simulations (see the example in Exercise 27.6), but it is not used anywhere within the standard VisualWorks image.

27.5 Maintaining dependents

Clearly, some way of creating and removing dependencies is required, and messages to support this are provided. The addDependent: message allows a dependency to be constructed, so that:

```
objectA addDependent: objectB
```

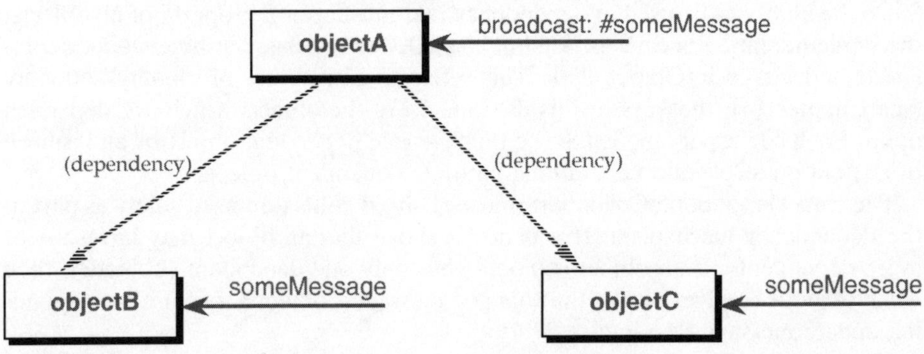

Figure 27.3 The **broadcast:** message.

installs the dependency illustrated in Figure 27.1. Similarly,

```
objectA removeDependent: objectB
```

removes this dependency link. To find out which objects depend on a particular object, the dependents message may be used. For example:

```
objectA dependents
```

will answer either with one dependent object (objectB in the case above) or an instance of DependentsCollection (see later) containing multiple dependent objects.

Finally, one very useful method is provided to dismantle dependency relationships. The release message can be sent to any object; this removes any links to objects which depend on the receiver. Taking the example in Figure 27.3, sending release to objectA would remove all its dependents (here objectB and objectC). This message should be compared with the removeDependent: method discussed previously, which removes just one object (the argument) as a dependent of objectA.

The release message is widely used in VisualWorks applications to ensure that dependency structures are deleted when no longer required. If the release message is not sent, objects may remain in object memory only because they are dependents, and will not be removed by the garbage collection processing. This can result in much wasted space in the image. Any application that creates explicit references to dependents should override the release method to remove such references. It should also include the expression super release in the new method to ensure that all the dependents are correctly deleted.

27.6 Dependency implementation

Since the ability to be used in dependency relationships is a property of all objects, the implementation is concentrated in class Object. A class variable DependentsFields is declared in Object class. This refers to an instance of IdentityDictionary (see Chapter 14); the *keys* in this dictionary are the objects which are depended upon. Each corresponding *value* is either the sole dependent object or an instance of DependentsCollection containing multiple dependent objects.

The class DependentsCollection is a specialized collection used solely as part of the dependency mechanism. It was noted above that an object may have one or more dependents. If an object (objectA) has only one dependent (objectB), then when objectA receives one of the changed messages, objectB is sent a corresponding update message (see Figure 27.4).

However, if objectA has two or more dependents (for example, objectB and objectC) then those are contained in an instance of DependentsCollection (Figure

DependentsFields	
key	*value*
objectA	objectB

Figure 27.4 An object with only one dependent.

DependentsFields	
key	*value*
objectA	DependentsCollection (objectB objectC)

Figure 27.5 An object with more than one dependent.

27.5). Consequently, when objectA receives a changed message, the instance of DependentsCollection is sent the corresponding update message, which it then *forwards* to each of its elements (objectB and objectC).

Most of the methods discussed above are implemented in the instance protocols changing, updating, dependents access, and initialize-release of class Object (in category Kernel-Objects). Associations in the dependency dictionary are created automatically when a dependent is added to an object currently without dependents. Similarly, when the last dependent to an object is removed, that object is also removed from the dependency dictionary.

This implementation of the dependency mechanism has the advantage that there is no overhead associated with objects in order to use this feature. There are only associations in the DependentsFields dictionary for the objects involved in a relationship at the present time. However, the implementation is somewhat inelegant and can exacerbate problems in faulty applications that do not correctly release dependents. Under these circumstances, objects no longer required are still referred to by the dependency dictionary, and are not garbage-collected. This can lead to excessive wasted space. Also, as a dictionary access is required every time an object receives a changed: message, this mechanism is potentially inefficient when very large numbers of dependency relationships exist.

An alternative implementation would be to have an instance variable in *every* object (including all numbers, characters and strings). This would be nil if an object had no dependents, a reference to the sole dependent object (if there were only one) or a reference to a DependentsCollection containing multiple dependents, when such existed. However, since this would require space for an instance variable in every object, and there are many tens of thousands of objects in a typical VisualWorks image, this approach would waste a lot of space.

As a compromise, a subclass of Object, called Model, can be used as the abstract superclass of all objects that are expected to be depended upon. Typically, Model is used as an abstract superclass for classes of objects used as the 'model' in a Model–View–Controller application (see Chapter 29). Instances of class Model have an instance variable (called dependents) which may refer to one or more dependents, as discussed above. This permits a more efficient implementation to be used.

The Model implementation for the dependency mechanism also reduces the problems with certain faulty applications. It is possible to leave dependency links set up accidentally when an application is no longer required. With the original implementation, unwanted objects could be referenced only by the DependentsFields dictionary. Thus, they would not be recovered by a garbage-collection process, and would waste space in the virtual image. With the Model implementation, leaving dependency links installed merely results in the creation of 'circular' (indirectly self-referential) garbage, which can be recovered by the garbage collector. However, not all objects can use this improvement; in these cases, careful use of the release message is required to overcome this problem.

Exercise 27.1

As DependentsFields is a class variable of class Object, it is accessible from all methods in the image. Try inspecting DependentsFields using an expression like:

```
DependentsFields inspect
```

You should then be able to inspect the various dependency relationships in your image.

Exercise 27.2

Use the System Browser to view the implementation of the dependency mechanism. In particular, browse the methods addDependent: and breakDependents.

Exercise 27.3

Browse the re-implementation of the dependency mechanism in class Model.

Exercise 27.4

The changeRequest and updateRequest messages are used to ensure that when some text has been edited but not recompiled (accepted), an appropriate prompter is used to ensure this is what the user really wanted. Browse the use of these messages in the image. (*Hint*: Use the **senders** and **implementors** menu items from the Browser <operate> button menu, or the Launcher **browse** menu.)

27.7 Example: clocking flip-flops

As mentioned previously, the dependency mechanism is most usually used as part of the Model–View–Controller mechanism (see Chapter 29). Here, however, we will explore dependencies using an example that avoids the complexities of MVC. This example also illustrates the way in which *simulations* of 'real world' systems can be constructed using VisualWorks.

We will construct a simple simulation of digital logic circuits, particularly *flipflops*, which make up a large part of the hardware of all computer systems. Such digital circuits represent logic values as *true* or *false*, although these states are often called 1 and 0 respectively. We will model these states using the Smalltalk Boolean classes (see Chapter 21).

A flipflop (see Figure 27.6) is a digital logic circuit which 'remembers' the logic state of its **D** input when a clock signal (**Clk**) is applied. In this case, the **D** input state is recorded at the instant that the **Clk** signal changes from logic level **0** to **1**. This transition is normally referred to as a 'positive edge'. You should note that the **D** input is ignored at all other times, and this input may change as often as it pleases. (Strictly speaking, an approximation to a positive-edge triggered, master–slave D-Type flipflop is being modelled here.)

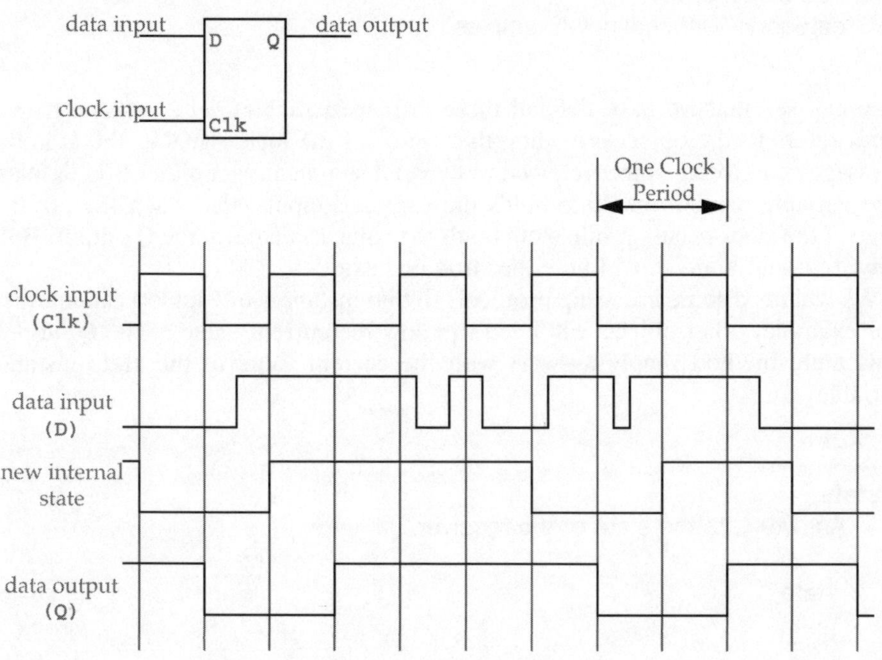

Figure 27.6 Basic flipflop operation.

However, the new state captured by the **Clk** signal is not available at the output (Q) until a later time. In this model, point Q does not change until the **Clk** signal changes from a 1 to a 0 (a 'negative edge'). This feature has the advantage that the **Q** output from one flipflop can be fed directly into the **D** input of another, with both flipflops being controlled by the same clock. Consequently, various useful circuits, such as *shift* registers, can be constructed easily.

In typical synchronous digital systems such as computers, large numbers of flipflops (often many thousands) are controlled from the same clock. While it would be possible in our simulation to arrange for every flipflop to 'know about' its clock source, this is quite inconvenient. As an alternative, we will make each flipflop a *dependent* of the clock, so that all timing information is distributed using the dependency mechanism. More generally, when constructing simulations using Smalltalk, distributing 'global' knowledge (such as time) using dependencies is frequently very useful.

To illustrate the dependency mechanism, we will create two new classes. The first of these new classes is FlipFlop which has the following class definition:

```
Object subclass: #FlipFlop
    instanceVariableNames: 'input state newState'
    classVariableNames: ''
    poolDictionaries: ''
    category: 'Dependency-Examples'
```

You can see that we have defined three instance variables. The variable named input refers to the object providing the source of the logic signal at the **D** input. Messages sent to the object referred to by input should answer either true or false. The variable named newState holds the captured input value when the positive edge of the clock occurs, while state holds the value available at the **Q** output. Both newState and state should be either true or false.

We will need some accessing protocol, so that instances of FlipFlop can interact. For example, other objects will need to know the current value at the **Q** output. This state method simply answers with the current value of the state instance variable.

```
state
    "Answer with the state of the receiver."

    ^state
```

We will also want to install the link between the **D** input and the (simulated) digital device to which it is connected.

input: aLogicUnit

```
"Set the input to be aLogicUnit"

input := aLogicUnit
```

Most real flipflops have some additional inputs for setting the internal state to a known value without using the clock input, for initialization purposes. To model this, we will provide two methods for setting the **Q** output to **1** (preset) and to **0** (clear).

preset

```
"Set the state to true, immediately."

state := true.
newState := true
```

clear

```
"Set the state to false, immediately."

state := false.
newState := false
```

For our purposes, we will assume that flipflops are always created with the **Q** output set to **0** so our initialize message in instance protocol initialize-release is simply:

initialize

```
"Initialize the receiver."

self clear
```

The initialize method is used by the instance creation method in class protocol 'instance creation' as follows:

new

```
"Create a new initialized instance of the receiver."

^super new initialize
```

The actions of the flipflop when clocked are captured by the following two methods in instance protocol clocking:

positiveClock

```
"Copy the input value into the receiver's new state."
newState := input state
```

```
negativeClock
    "Copy the remembered input state into the receiver's state."

    state := newState.
```

The positiveClock method simply copies the logic value from the input device into the newState variable, while the negativeClock method transfers the captured value to the state variable. This corresponds exactly to the operation of the abstract flipflop discussed previously.

As we are going to use the dependency mechanism to provide the clock information, we must add our own update: method (in protocol 'updating') to override that provided by class Object.

```
update: anAspect
    "Perform the clocking action on a rising edge."

    anAspect == #risingEdge ifTrue: [self positiveClock].
    anAspect == #fallingEdge ifTrue: [self negativeClock]
```

You should note that the *aspect* is expected to be one of two symbols, to indicate which clock action is to be performed. This use of an aspect symbol to the update: message is often useful when using dependencies.

Finally, we will override the release message inherited from Object, so that we can break up any (potentially) circular structures created.

```
release
    "Reset any references to remove possible cycles."

    input := nil.
    super release
```

This removes any reference to other objects, and then uses the release method in class Object to break up the dependency links.

We need some way of generating the clock signals. For this purpose, we can create a class Clock with very simple functionality.

```
Object subclass: #Clock
    instanceVariableNames: ''
    classVariableNames: ''
    poolDictionaries: ''
    category: 'Dependency-Examples'
```

No instance variables are required. Only one instance method is needed (in protocol cycling); this simply indicates that a whole clock cycle (both positive and

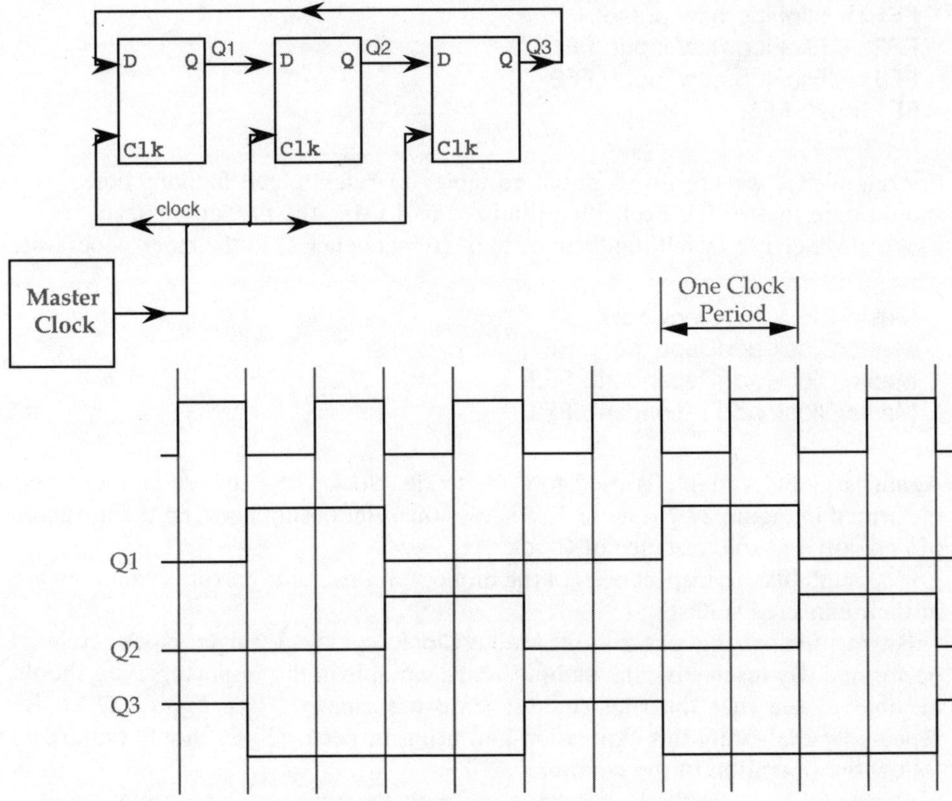

Figure 27.7 Ring counter using flipflops.

negative edges) has taken place, and that any dependents should change appropriately.

```
cycle
    "Perform one clock cycle."

    self changed: #risingEdge.
    self changed: #fallingEdge
```

As an example using the simulations of flipflops and clocks developed here, consider the circuit shown in Figure 27.7. This circuit has three flipflops connected in a circle to form a ring counter. If one flipflop is initialized to a **1** and the others to a **0** then, as the system is clocked, the **1** shifts around the ring of flipflops. The circuit therefore has three different states and can be used as a simple counter.

We can construct a simulation of the ring counter using the following expressions:

```
FF1 := FlipFlop new preset.
FF2 := FlipFlop new input: FF1.
FF3 := FlipFlop new input: FF2.
FF1 input: FF3.
```

For simplicity, we are using global variables to refer to the flipflops here. You should note that FF1 is explicitly initialized to 1 using the preset message.

We also need to install the 'connections' (dependencies) to the clock generator.

```
MasterClock := Clock new.
MasterClock addDependent: FF1.
MasterClock addDependent: FF2.
MasterClock addDependent: FF3.
```

Again, a global variable is used to refer to the clock. This completes the circuit illustrated in Figure 27.7. Figure 27.8 shows the relationship between the instances of FlipFlop and sole instance of Clock.

You might like to inspect each of the flipflops at this point, to verify that they are in their expected states.

By evaluating the expression MasterClock cycle, a single clock cycle is performed. By reselecting the state instance variable in the Inspectors, you should be able to see that the ring counter state has changed (see Figure 27.9). By repeatedly evaluating this expression and using Inspectors, you should be able to follow the operation of the counter.

Once you have finished experimenting with the ring counter simulation, it is essential to ensure that the circular structures constructed are dismantled, so that the space taken by the objects can be recovered by the garbage collector.

```
MasterClock release.
FF1 release.
FF2 release.
FF3 release.
FF1 := FF2 := FF3 := MasterClock := nil.
```

These expressions remove the dependency links between the flipflops and the clock. References from the global variables are removed by assigning nil to these variables. You can verify that the flipflops have disappeared using the expression FlipFlop instanceCount.

Exercise 27.5

Try out the example used in this section. Verify that the number of true and false states in the shift register does not change, regardless of the initial configuration. (You

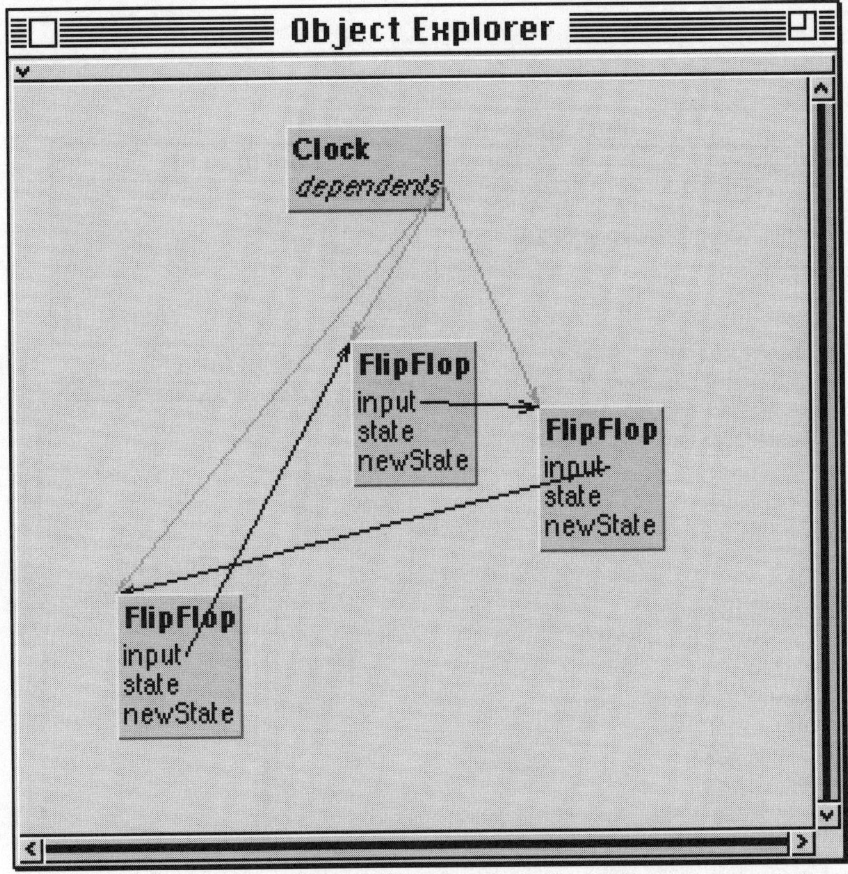

Figure 27.8 The instances of **FlipFlop** and **Clock**.

might also like to implement a cycle: method, which performs the *cycle* action a number of times given by a numeric argument.)

Exercise 27.6

Try re-implementing the cycle method in class Clock using the broadcast mechanism.

Exercise 27.7

You might like to try implementing a more complex example using flipflops. For example, try building a twisted-ring counter, where the **Q** output from the last flipflop is inverted (negated) before being fed into the **D** input of the first flipflop. In this case, there is no need to 'preset' any of the flipflops – why is this?

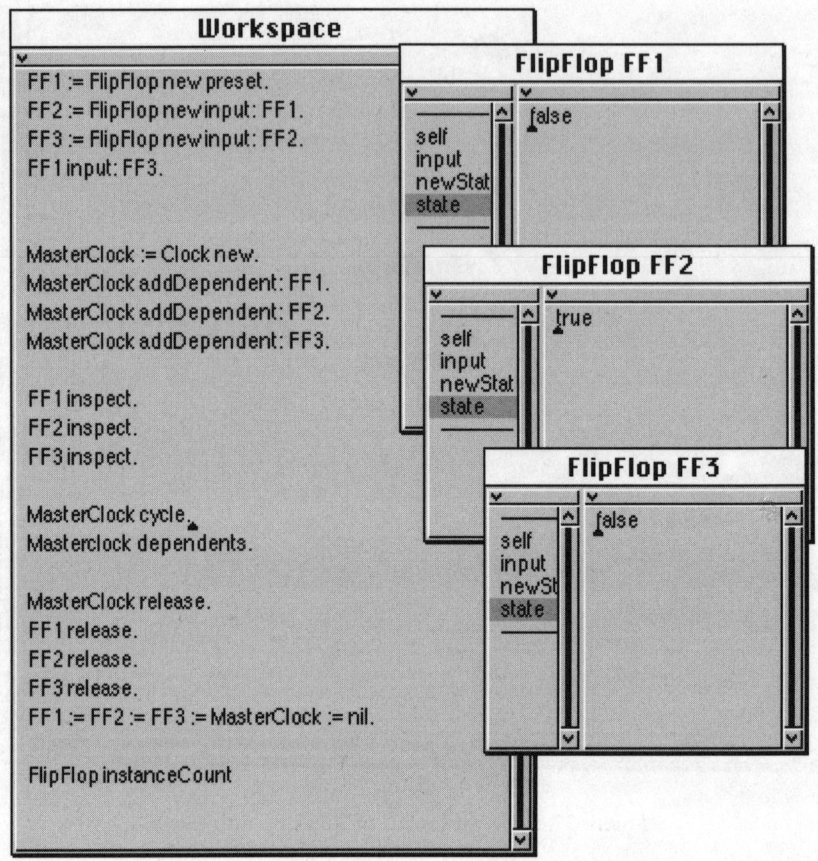

Figure 27.9 Ring counter implementation in operation.

(*Hint*: Implement a class Inverter, which answers with the negated logic value obtained from the device at its input.)

Exercise 27.8

There is plenty of scope for constructing much more sophisticated simulations of synchronous digital systems using the techniques outlined here. You might like to consider the problems of developing a wider range of digital components, including logic gates (such as AND and OR gates) and other types of flipflops (such as J–K flipflops).

27.8 Summary

The Smalltalk dependency mechanism is widely used throughout VisualWorks. At its simplest, it may be used as a mechanism to inform one object of a change in another object. For example, in the financial industry, one often models 'Derivatives' – a financial product whose value is dependent on the share price of some equity. By modelling a Derivative as a dependent of its underlying equity, changes in equity share price can be easily propagated. We now begin our exploration of programmatic control of the VisualWorks user interface, first by using 'Dialogs', before continuing to describe the use of the 'Model–View–Controller' mechanism and the classes provided to support it.

28 Dialogs – menus, Prompters and Confirmers

This chapter considers the use of the three main interaction 'Dialogs' widely used in applications. These include menus, 'Prompters', and 'Confirmers'.

28.1 Using menus

Menus are widely used to support interactive input in VisualWorks, for example to get commands from the user. A list of textual items is presented on the screen; one of these may be selected using the mouse or keyboard. The result is an object corresponding to the menu item selected. Menus are objects, just like everything else in VisualWorks, and are frequently used in conjunction with controllers, especially ControllerWithMenu (see Chapter 31) and its subclasses.

Individual menus are instances of class Menu. Instances may be created in several ways, but one of the most common is by using the labels: message, which takes as its argument a String (or a Text) containing embedded 'carriage return' characters. The carriage return characters indicate the separation between each menu item. For example:

```
Menu labels: 'Coffee
Tea
Chocolate'
```

It is often convenient to send the String argument the message withCRs, which answers with a new String in which the 'backslash' characters ('\') are replaced by carriage return characters. Thus, the above example could be written:

```
Menu labels: 'Coffee\Tea\Chocolate' withCRs
```

You will have seen that some menus have lines between selected items. A Menu with this property can be initiated using the labels:lines: instance creation method, as follows:

```
Menu labels: 'Coffee\Tea\Chocolate\Donut\Cookie\Brownie' withCRs
        lines: #(3)
```

When the labels:lines: message is used, lines are drawn under the menu items indicated by the integers in the second argument.

Once created, an instance of Menu can be made to appear by sending it the message startUp. The example shown in Figure 28.1 displays a Menu with six items.

Once the Menu is active, the item on the menu under the cursor (the selection) is highlighted. Unless otherwise specified, when the mouse button is released, the Menu will answer with an integer corresponding to the selected item. In the above example, if **Coffee** was selected, then 1 would be answered. If no item was selected when the button was released, then 0 would be answered.

As a variation, a Menu can also answer with an item from a sequenceable collection of 'values' (corresponding to the items in the menu) specified via an alternative instance creation method. This example uses an Array of Strings, one of which is selected according to the menu item chosen.

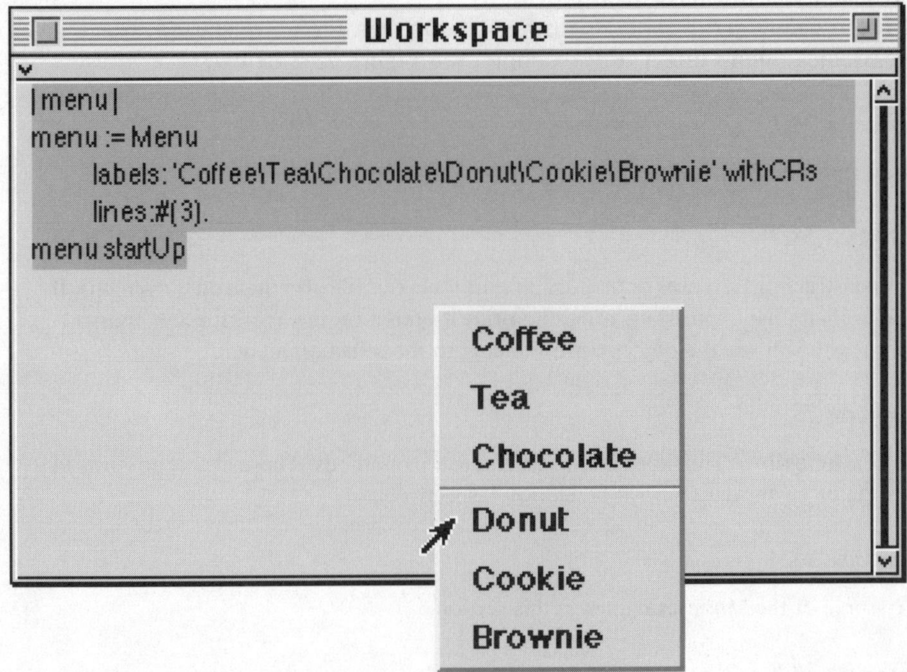

Figure 28.1 **Menu** example.

```
| aMenu |
aMenu := Menu
        labels: 'Coffee\Tea\Chocolate\Donut\Cookie\Brownie' withCRs
        lines: #(3)
        values: #('$0.30' '$0.40' '$0.45' '$0.55' '$0.15' '$0.30').
aMenu startUp
```

A typical use of 'values' is to select a message to send to another object. For example:

```
| aMenu |
aMenu := Menu
        labels: 'Time\Millisecond Clock\Total Seconds' withCRs
        values: #(#dateAndTimeNow #millisecondClockValue
#totalSeconds).
Transcript cr; show: (Time perform: aMenu startUp) printString
```

This example sends one of three messages to class Time, depending on which menu item is selected. The result of this message-send is displayed in the System Transcript. This use of the Menu is common in the implementation of the various Browsers you will have seen previously.

If the *values* array contains further Menus then these are started, which gives a hierarchical menu effect. For example, see Figure 28.2 below.

Exercise 28.1

Browse the implementation of Menu in category Interface-Menus.

Exercise 28.2

Try constructing instances of Menu, and start them (i.e. display them on the screen). If you evaluate the expressions using the **print it** option on the Workspace <operate> menu, you will see the object corresponding to the selection made.

Exercise 28.3

Try the labelArray: and labelList: instance creation methods. These expect an Array of Strings or an Array of Arrays of Strings respectively.

Exercise 28.4

Try some of the Menu examples in this section.

Exercise 28.5

Try creating a hierarchical menu.

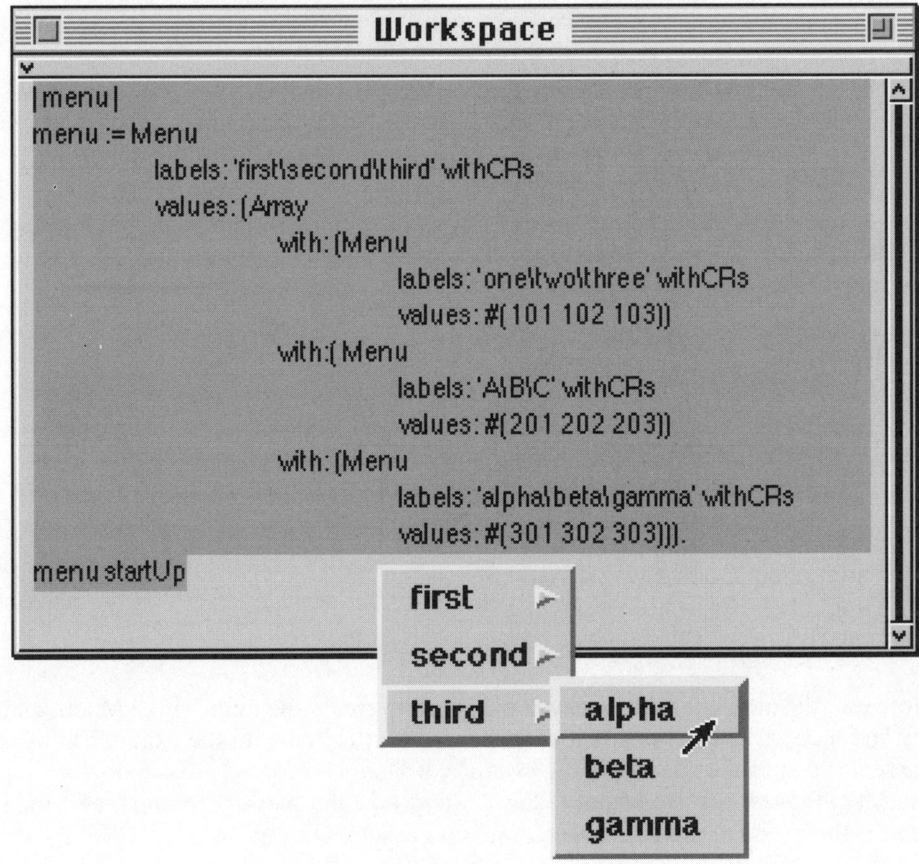

Figure 28.2 Hierarchical **Menu** example.

Exercise 28.6

In the example using perform: above, what happens if no item is selected from the menu? Modify the code to overcome this problem.

Exercise 28.7

Browse references to class Menu in the image, and the class examples.

Exercise 28.8

Build a method for class SequenceableCollection named elementFromUser. This method should allow the user to get a Menu containing all the elements in the collection (the receiver), select one, and have it returned from the method. Test your method on the following code:

```
#('b' 1 3 (4 5 6) 22) elementFromUser
```

Alternative ways of creating a menu

Rather than using the mechanisms described above, it is possible to use an instance of MenuBuilder to create a Menu. In the example below, we send messages to an instance of MenuBuilder to create the Menu described earlier in the chapter.

```
| mb |
mb := MenuBuilder new.
mb addLabel: 'Coffee' value: '$0.30';
   addLabel: 'Tea' value: '$0.40';
   addLabel: 'Chocolate' value: '$0.45';
   line;
   addLabel: 'Donut' value: '$0.55';
   addLabel: 'Cookie' value: '$0.15';
   addLabel: 'Brownie' value: '$0.30'
mb startUp
```

Note that the message addLabel:value: is used to create the items in the Menu, and the line message is used to add a divider between the items. In the example above, we sent the message startUp to the instance of MenuBuilder, whereas below we ask the MenuBuilder for the Menu it has created (via the message menu), and then send *it* the message startUp, to recreate an earlier example.

```
| mb menu |
mb := MenuBuilder new.
mb addLabel: 'Time' value: #dateAndTimeNow;
  addLabel: 'Millisecond Clock' value: #millisecondClockValue;
  addLabel: 'Total Seconds' value: #totalSeconds.
menu := mb menu.
Transcript cr; show:(Time perform: menu startUp) printString
```

Exercise 28.9

Browse class MenuBuilder, paying particular attention to the building instance protocol.

Exercise 28.10

Experiment with the MenuBuilder class examples.

Exercise 28.11

Try creating a hierarchical menu using the MenuBuilder class.

Exercise 28.12

Modify your solution to Exercise 28.8 to use class MenuBuilder.

28.2 Using Prompters

In VisualWorks, Prompters are the usual way to request the user for typed input (often called 'Fill-in-the-Blank'). When input is required, a small window appears, usually under the cursor. This window typically has three sections: an upper section that contains an explanatory message; a middle section, into which the user is expected to type a response; and a lower section containing buttons labeled **OK** and **Cancel**. An <operate> menu supporting editing functions is available, and the usual typed input mechanisms are supported. (Shortcuts to the **OK** and **Cancel** buttons are provided by the <CR> and <esc> keys, respectively.) You will already have seen many examples of their use in the image (see Chapter 4).

Prompters are instances of class Dialog which can be found in class category Interface-Dialogs. The basic instance creation method for a Prompter is to send the message request: to the class. The argument is expected to be a String, Text or ComposedText representing the title of the Prompter, which can have embedded carriage return characters. (The withCRs message is often useful.) For example, the expression in Figure 28.3 produces the Prompter shown in Figure 28.3.

Figure 28.3 A Prompter.

There are two alternative instance creation methods:

```
request:initialAnswer:
request:initialAnswer:onCancel:
```

The second argument is also a String which is initially displayed in the middle section of the Prompter. This String is normally the default input value. If the last form of instance creation is used, then the third argument is a block containing expressions that will be evaluated if the user presses the **Cancel** button.

The following example expressions might be used to read in a grid size for a graphical drawing package:

```
| answerString aGridSize |
aGridSize := 50. "Initial Grid size."
answerString := Dialog
                    request: 'New Grid Size?'
                    initialAnswer: aGridSize printString.
answerString isEmpty ifFalse:
  [aGridSize := Number readFrom: (ReadStream on: answerString)]
```

You should note that, in this case (Figure 28.4), the instance creation method request:initialAnswer: answers with a String typed by the user. This example also illustrates the use of a ReadStream (see Chapter 19) to create a number from a String. This approach means that the grid size can be entered using any of VisualWorks' number formats.

Alternatively, we may wish to indicate to the user via the Transcript that the **Cancel** button was pressed (see also Figure 28.5):

```
| answerString aGridSize failed |
failed := false. "Flag to test for success"
aGridSize := 50. "Initial Grid size."
answerString := Dialog
            request: 'New Grid Size?'
            initialAnswer: aGridSize printString
            onCancel: [failed := true.
                 Transcript show: 'No grid size'; cr].
failed ifFalse:
  [aGridSize := Number readFrom: (ReadStream on: answerString)]
```

Exercise 28.13

Try some of the Prompter examples given above. You might also like to construct your own.

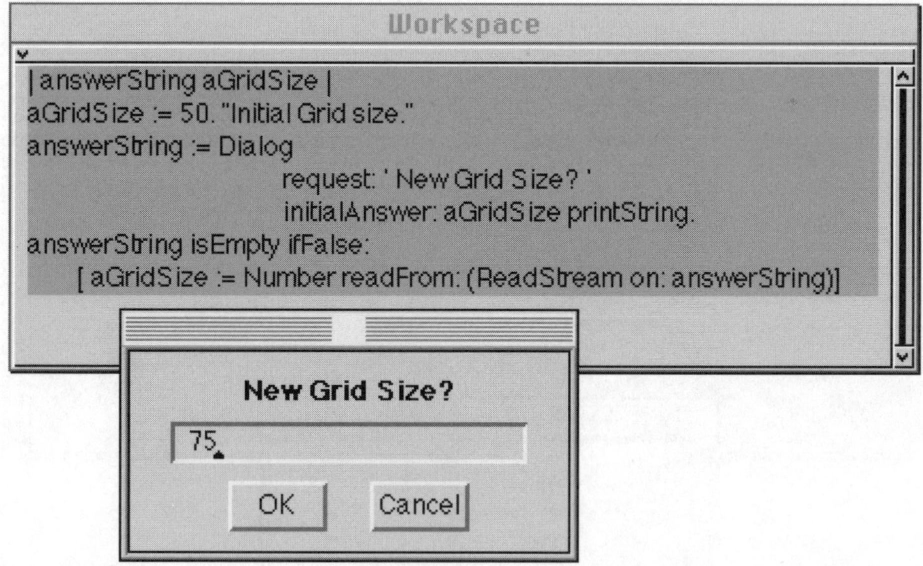

Figure 28.4 Returning a number from a Prompter.

28.3 Using Confirmers

Confirmers are VisualWorks' way of asking for an answer from a collection of options (most commonly a 'yes/no' answer). A Confirmer is a window which has two parts: an upper section containing a message and a lower part containing one or more buttons (e.g. buttons displaying **yes** and **no** – see Figure 28.6). One of the buttons in the dialog box will have an inset border; this is the default. This means that if you press the <CR> key, that option will be selected. The user is expected to click the <operate> mouse button over one of the buttons. You will already have seen several examples of Confirmers in action (see Chapter 4).

Confirmers are also instances of class Dialog. The basic instance creation method for a 'yes/no' Confirmer is confirm:. The argument is expected to be a String, Text or ComposedText representing the 'question'. In this case the Confirmer will present **yes** as the default option and answer with true or false (depending on the user's selection).

As an example of the use of a 'yes/no' Confirmer, consider the code below:

```
(Dialog confirm: 'Do you understand this?')
    ifTrue:[Transcript cr;
                    show: 'Good. Carry on to the next exercise.']
    ifFalse:[Transcript cr; show: 'Oh, dear. Try again.']
```

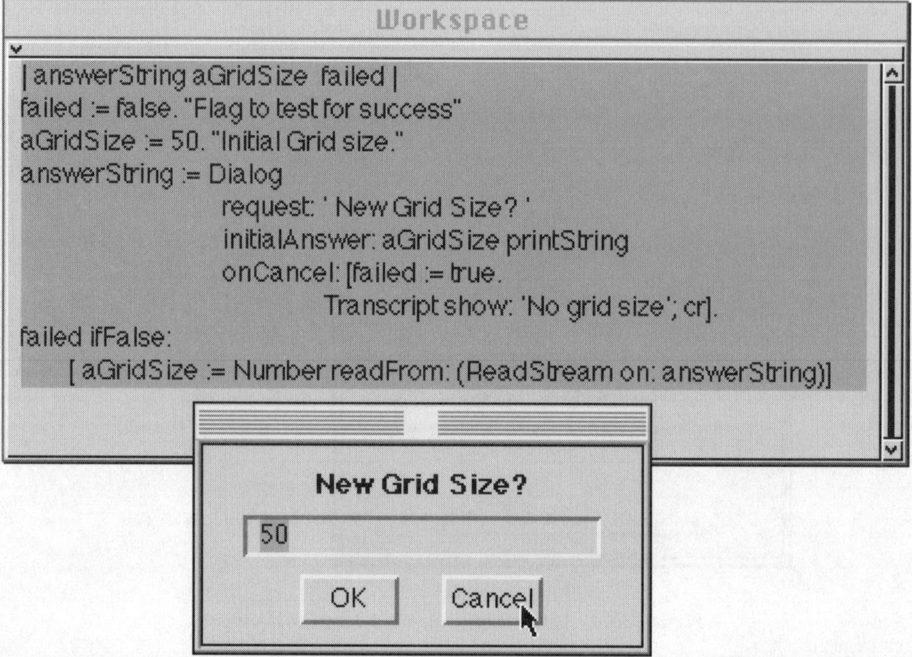

Figure 28.5 Providing a Prompter with a 'cancel' block.

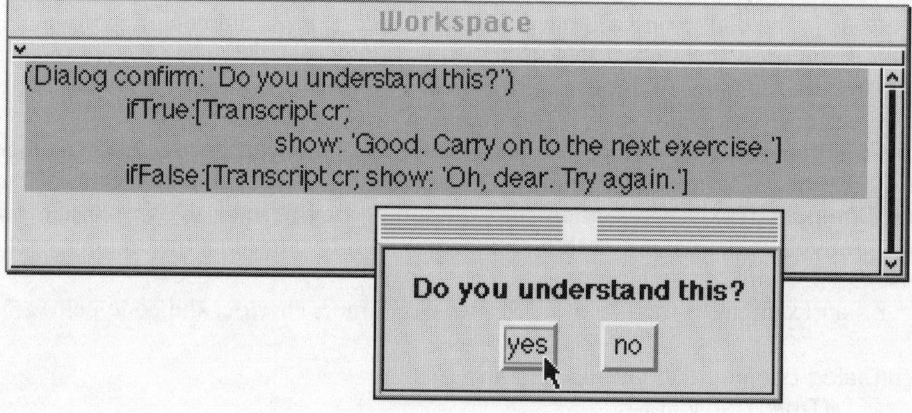

Figure 28.6 A Confirmer.

This creates a Confirmer (Figure 28.6) and, depending on the user's response, displays one of two different phrases in the System Transcript.

Alternatively, the programmer may present **no** as the default option by using the message confirm:initialAnswer:, as in the code below:

```
Dialog confirm: 'Confirmation needed?' initialAnswer: false
```

The programmer may alternatively specify that only one button is to be presented to the user – as a 'warning' (you will already have seen many examples of this kind of dialog). The message to achieve this is simply warn:; the argument is a String, Text or ComposedText containing the warning. For example:

```
Dialog warn: 'You have been warned!'
```

Exercise 28.14

Try some of the Prompter and Confirmer examples given above. You might also like to construct your own.

28.4 Other dialogs

Other dialog styles are available (see the class messages in Dialog for more details), while many more can be created.

Exercise 28.15

Try out some of the other kinds of dialogs available. Browse the class protocol examples in class Dialog.

28.5 Summary

Dialogs provide a relatively simple means of obtaining user input. It's often possible to provide the user with a constructed menu, or pre-built Prompter or Confirmer, rather than building a complex window. It's important to note that all the dialogs rely on the Model–View–Controller mechanism, described in the following chapter.

29 Introduction to models, views and controllers

The Model–View–Controller paradigm is an important part of Smalltalk. This chapter introduces the concepts involved in general terms, and indicates how a *view* communicates with its *model*, and with its corresponding *controller*. Some idea of the complexity of applications which can be constructed is illustrated.

Additionally, we give some examples of models, and finish by giving a summary of the stages in building an interactive application.

29.1 Introduction

Building a new window in VisualWorks is a complex exercise, but not as complex as in other languages. The basic concept of a VisualWorks window depends on three elements, the *model*, *view*, and *controller*. Each of these is a specialized type of object that combines with the others to produce a working window. This method of building windows is called 'MVC'. We will examine how the elements work and how they can be created.

The MVC mechanism is used throughout VisualWorks. It provides a general structure for the construction of interactive applications with graphical user interfaces. The programming interface and tools which you have already seen throughout this book are all constructed in this way. In this chapter, we will outline the basic features of MVC, and suggest how they might be used to construct graphical user interfaces.

29.2 MVC basics

The basic idea behind MVC is the separation of a graphical interactive application into two parts: the abstract application (or *model*) which can perform the necessary computations without reference to any form of input/output (I/O), and the user interface part, which has the responsibility for all I/O functions. This separation allows the application designer to concentrate on one aspect of an application at a time, thus simplifying the design and development process. It may even allow different people to implement these two parts. Also, it is quite possible that different applications may be able to use the same user interface components, or that different user interfaces may be supplied for a single application.

In Smalltalk, the *user interface* part of an application is itself split into two parts: the *view*, which handles all display (output) operations and manages some part of a window; and the *controller*, which handles user input from the keyboard and mouse. The view and controller can communicate between themselves without interacting with the model. You should note that, in Smalltalk, any object can be used as the model. This object may be very simple (an instance of class Boolean, for example). Frequently, however, the model is an instance of a specially constructed class (like the Browser, for example) with many instance variables; consequently, the model can be as complex as required.

As might be expected, the functions of views and controllers are represented by classes within the VisualWorks image. In general, a view used by an application is an instance of a subclass of VisualPart (see Chapter 30). This class supports general mechanisms to display a visual representation of some aspect of a model in a pane of a window.

Similarly, the controllers used in a graphical application are instances of a subclass of class Controller (see Chapter 31). A controller may also provide input prompts (menus, Prompters, Confirmers). Instances of this class have a reference to a *sensor* representing the mouse and keyboard, so that it can process user input. A controller handles mouse clicks, menu interactions, keystrokes, and any other user input. In MVC applications, we frequently see two distinct types of actions initiated from a controller:

1. Communications from controller to model, causing a change of state in the application in some way
2. Communications from controller to view, causing a change in the visible representation *without* affecting the state of the model.

This division of labor among three objects makes for a very flexible and extensible window system. It also has the following benefits:

- It separates the user interface code from the underlying structure. (We want to avoid giving the model intimate details about its views that would make it difficult to be separated from them.)
- Views present some aspect of the model to the user. The same model may have different views presented to the same user simultaneously.

29.3 Communications in MVC

The communications between the model, view, and controller in a VisualWorks application can be summarized as in Figure 29.1. As in previous chapters, the communication between various objects is illustrated by a 'boxes and arrows' diagram. Objects are shown by rectangles, and instance variables referring to other objects are illustrated by solid black arrows. Communication by the dependency mechanism is shown by a fuzzy arrow. The view has references to its controller and model (using instance variables), and the controller has references to its view and model. Thus, the model can be sent messages from the controller, perhaps informing it of user actions; and from the view, typically enquiring about the model's current state. You should note, however, that the model has no explicit knowledge of any user interface, and that the only form of communication from a model to its views is by the dependency mechanism (see Chapter 27). This is used to inform the view that the model has changed in some way. In this manner, the model is isolated from any knowledge of its visible representation.

You can see that the separation of model and view/controller fits nicely into the object-oriented programming model, as the interface between them is defined in terms of messages understood by the model and the answers returned to the view and controller in response to such messages. Thus, the internal operation of the model is hidden from the view and controller, and only a well-defined external interface is used.

In normal use, a particular controller will become *active* under certain conditions, such as the mouse cursor being placed over its corresponding view. (The

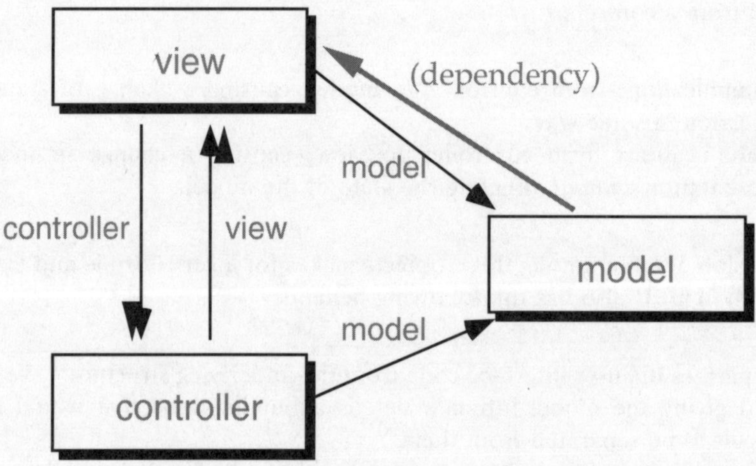

Figure 29.1 Basic model–view–controller triad.

way in which controllers become active is discussed in Chapter 31.) Once active, the controller will process user input from the keyboard or mouse, providing responses (such as menus, see Chapter 28) as necessary. The controller can send messages to the model, perhaps based on a selection made from a menu. The model may change some part of its state, and use the dependency mechanism to inform the view that a change has been made, typically using an expression such as:

```
self changed: anAspect
```

(This message is described in Chapter 27.)

Any view that is a dependent of the model will subsequently receive an update: message, with *anAspect* as its argument. The view can then send messages to the model to discover its new state, and can redisplay the visual representation accordingly. It is also possible for the controller to send messages directly to the view, so that (for example) the visible representation can be changed under user control, without changing the application (for example, to change the position of an object in a pane). Also, there is normally no communication from the model to the controller, although the controller can be made a dependent of the model if necessary.

29.4 Multiple views

It is important to emphasize that a particular model can have more than one view at a time, each of which with its own controller. The manner in which information is presented to the user need not be the same in each view, so that aspects of the same model need not be presented in the same way. Figure 29.2 shows how this can be arranged, with two view/controller pairs interacting with the same model. User input via any of the controllers may cause messages to be sent to the model. When the model changes, all dependents receive one of the *update* messages, so that all views have the opportunity to update their visible representation.

To illustrate the use of multiple views displaying the same aspects of their model in different ways, consider the example in Figure 29.3. You will already have seen how methods are provided in ObjectMemory to answer with the current amount of free memory, and the current number of object unused pointers (see Chapter 5). In the application model for this example, a Process (Chapter 25) is created, which runs at regular intervals (using a Delay, see also Chapter 25). When the Process runs, it samples the current level of activity within the image, and stores those values in an OrderedCollection. Different subclasses of View are used (to produce different visual representations) of the model, so that when the model signals a change using the dependency mechanism, the views send messages to the model to get the current sampled values, and then display these values in various ways.

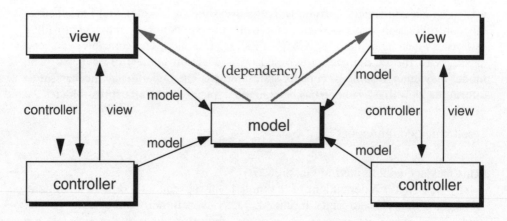

Figure 29.2 Multiple view–controller pairs on the same model.

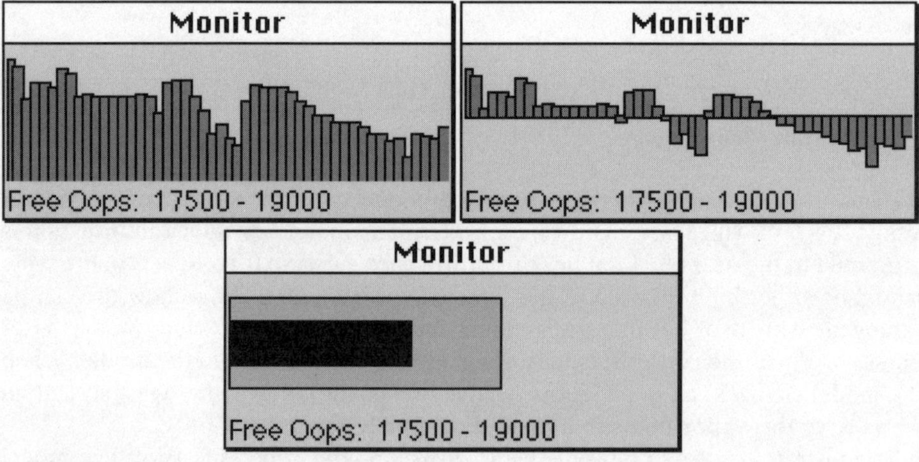

Figure 29.3 Different views of the same model – System Monitoring.

29.5 Models

Chapters 30 and 31 describe the classes that are available to be used as views and controllers (respectively). In this section we concentrate on classes used to fill the role of *model*.

When designing an application, it's useful to distinguish two kinds of model:

1. A *domain* model: Consists of behavior required for some application domain along with information needed to carry out the behaviour. This model often persists beyond the lifetime of the users' interaction and typically includes a complex object structure that may be used by a number of different applications. For example, in a financial application, the model may contain objects pertaining to securities or trades.
2. An *application* model: Consists of behavior that is required to support the user's interaction along with information needed to carry out the behavior. For example, the information in the model may represent a selection in a list, or the contents of a paste buffer.

It is relatively straightforward to create a new domain model, since an instance of any Smalltalk class may take the role, although it will usually be a subclass of Model. In the case of an application model, however, it's almost always necessary to create a bespoke class. The internal structure of the class – in terms of its instance variables – is usually represented by instances of those classes in the ValueModel class hierarchy described below. These are the objects that represent the selection in a list, the entry in a text field, the value of a slider, or the boolean value of a button, and so on.

29.6 Class ValueModel

The abstract class ValueModel epitomizes the idea of a *holder* class – one that references a value of some sort. ValueModel provides its subclasses with default behavior for accessing an object (via the value message) and a means of specifying an object (via the corresponding value: message). In the VisualWorks image there are two major subclasses of ValueModel, called ValueHolder (described below) and PluggableAdaptor (described in Chapter 33). (Chapter 34 describes other subclasses of ValueModel used primarily by the Canvas mechanism.) When an instance of some subclass of ValueModel receives a value: message, its dependents are sent the message update: #value.

Class ValueHolder provides an instance variable (called value) to reference the object received as the argument to a value: message. An instance of ValueHolder is often used to act as an intermediary for another object, such as a Boolean or a String, that does not behave like a model.

To create an instance of ValueHolder, send the class the message with:, passing the initial value as its argument. For example:

```
ValueHolder with: (FinancialHistory initialBalance: 800)
```

Additionally, for your convenience, three other instance creation messages are available:

newBoolean (when the value is to be initialized to false)
newFraction (when the value is to be initialized to 0.0)

newString (when the value is to be initialized to an empty String, i.e. '')

An instance of ValueHolder is the typical model for each component of a free-standing dialog box. (See Chapter 33 for examples.)

29.7 Building an MVC application

In general, the MVC mechanism is a good idea, but it is sometimes badly used. There are some examples of quite poor coding techniques, and (worse) poor design of the separation between the view, controller and model. Historically, because of the lack of adequate documentation, MVC has not been widely appreciated, although it is a very powerful general mechanism.

Chapter 32 contains a worked example of an MVC application. In order to provide you with a complete overview of the stages involved in the construction of an MVC application, we feel it is worth presenting a 'recipe' for you to follow.

1. Build your *domain model* – i.e. some object or objects that represent your domain. This model may be as simple as a Boolean or a collection but is more likely to be quite complex. Simulate any operations that may be performed later as a result of user interaction by the use of Inspectors and the Transcript.
2. Build your *application model*. In reality, this model may be same object(s) that you created in (1) above, but typically it is a specialized object designed to handle user interaction and redirect messages to the domain model if necessary. Ensure that the application model provides the required functionality by simulating operations via Inspectors and the Transcript. In addition, make sure that you have appropriate 'changed' messages in place. Implement the methods needed to allow the user to manipulate the model.
3. Build your view(s). If you are lucky you will be able to use one of the existing views (see Chapter 30) or one of the 'pluggable' views (see Chapter 33); but you may have to develop your view class(es) yourself. Most of the work in a view is done by the displayOn: method, which takes an instance of GraphicsContext as its argument (an example is given in Chapter 30). Implement a displayOn: method if you can't inherit it. Remember that each view should display a particular visual representation of some aspect of the model. If you are planning to use multiple views on your model, as part of a multiple-paned window, then it's a good idea to test each view in turn before arranging them in a window. At this stage it's best not to provide any controller functionality; a specialized class – called NoController – is available to fill this role.
4. Arrange your view(s) in a window (see Chapter 30) and by manipulating your application via an Inspector, ensure that the content of each pane is modified according to the corresponding 'changed' messages.
5. Build a controller for each view (see Chapter 31), if necessary providing a menu (Chapter 28) of options via a class variable (see Chapter 12). If you have defined new menu messages, implement them as instance methods in the controller

class. If there is something special about *selection* in the controller's corresponding view then create a new redButtonActivity method for that controller. If something special should happen when the pane becomes *active* (such as the cursor changing shape) or *inactive*, then create a new controlInitialize or controlTerminate method (respectively). Connect each controller to its view and test that you can manipulate your model and the changes reflected in changes to the view(s).

6. Create an *opening* method for your application (possibly on the class side of your main view) that creates an instance of ScheduledWindow (see Chapter 30), creates each of the panes (each is itself an MVC triad), arranges it in a *layout specification* (see Chapter 30), and then sends the message open to the ScheduledWindow instance.
7. Iterate stages 1 to 6 until 'cooked'.

Exercise 29.1

Consider the possibilities of an alternative abstract structure to MVC, which would fit within Smalltalk's object-oriented programming paradigm. Is the separation between user input and user output necessary and/or desirable?

Exercise 29.2

Once you are more familiar with models, views and controllers, and have read right through to the end of the book, you might like to consider implementing a System Monitor similar to that shown in Figure 29.3. Among other things, you might want to monitor the amount of memory remaining to the image (ObjectMemory current availableFreeBytes) and the number of object pointers ('oops') remaining (ObjectMemory current oopsLeft). You could also count the number of mouse button and keyboard operations since the last sample and the number of file input/output operations. You will probably want to have menu options allowing the style of display, the parameter to be displayed, the sampling rate and the number of samples displayed to be changed. You should also arrange for the displays to scale themselves appropriately, and to change the scale as necessary. *Hint*: you will probably want to have a special class of 'monitor' objects, to use as the model in this application.

29.8 Summary

All VisualWorks windows rely on the MVC mechanism. Thus, it is important that readers have a good understanding of how the mechanism operates. Whether you will be creating new applications or maintaining existing ones, unless you feel familiar with the relationships between the objects that combine to form an MVC triad, you'll make little progress. Having introduced MVC in abstract, the following two chapters describe the Smalltalk classes corresponding to views and controllers.

30 The VisualPart class hierarchy and class ScheduledWindow

This chapter explores the VisualPart class hierarchy, concentrating on the general mechanisms it provides. The way in which panes can be arranged is also described, and examples of the transformations managed by the *wrapper* mechanism are given. The invalidation mechanism is also described.

The additional functionality provided by class ScheduledWindow is considered and, again, many examples are provided. By the end of this chapter you should be able to create your own windows on the screen.

30.1 Introduction

You will be familiar by now with the user interface provided by VisualWorks and, in particular, the way in which windows are provided to permit you to manipulate objects within the image. This chapter explores the notion of a VisualWorks window and its component panes, some of which may be *views*.

Views are part of the MVC mechanism introduced in the previous chapter. They are responsible for communication from an underlying data structure (the *model*) to the user, usually by displaying in a window. In typical MVC applications, specialized view classes – frequently subclasses of VisualPart – are constructed especially for the application. Often, these views contain much code to convert the internal structure of a model into a form easily comprehended by the user.

30.2 Class VisualPart

We have seen in earlier chapters how it is possible to display directly to a pane in a window from within VisualWorks (see Chapters 19 and 20). However, the mechanisms we have seen so far provide very little control over the way in which the content of a pane is dynamically modified. The basic function supported by class VisualPart is a controlled way of updating some portion of a window.

The abstract class VisualPart is a subclass of VisualComponent, and is itself the top of three class hierarchies, rooted at DependentPart, Wrapper, and CompositePart. In fact, the hierarchy of classes based at VisualPart is one of the largest and most complicated parts of VisualWorks (see Figure 30.1). In this book we cannot hope to describe every one of these classes, but we can at least consider some of the basic behavior provided.

Exercise 30.1

Browse the protocol of class VisualPart. There is quite a lot of it, and it is worth getting to be familiar with the methods provided.

The abstract class DependentPart simply adds the ability to invalidate instances of its subclasses when they receive an update: message from one of the objects on which they depend. This causes instances to redraw themselves and means that instances of subclasses of DependentPart can be used to graphically represent dynamic aspects of a model.

The only direct subclass of DependentPart in the VisualWorks image is View. Class View is the abstract superclass for new, application-specific panes. From Figure 30.1 you can see that there are already a very large number of View subclasses in the image, for example text views, list views, buttons, and switches (described in Chapter 33). Class View introduces an instance variable named controller, so that each of its instances can be associated with an instance of a subclass of Controller (see Chapter 31) to manage user input.

It's important to distinguish between two different uses of the word 'view'. So far, we have used it to describe an area of a window, similar to 'pane', in which some visual aspect of a model may be displayed. This meaning should not be confused with View, the name of the abstract class (note the sans serif font), that provides its subclasses with suitable behavior to display in a window. There is no implication intended that all views should be instances of class View.

30.3 Arranging panes in a window

Frequently, we will wish to arrange panes in a window. To support this, a *framework* structure of panes can be created: a pane can have one or more *components*. Conversely, we can say that a pane may have a *container*. For example, in a System Browser, each of the panes is a separate component within a single container. A component will always display in part of the *bounds* of its container. The uppermost container in a framework is called the *top component*; the top component has no container.

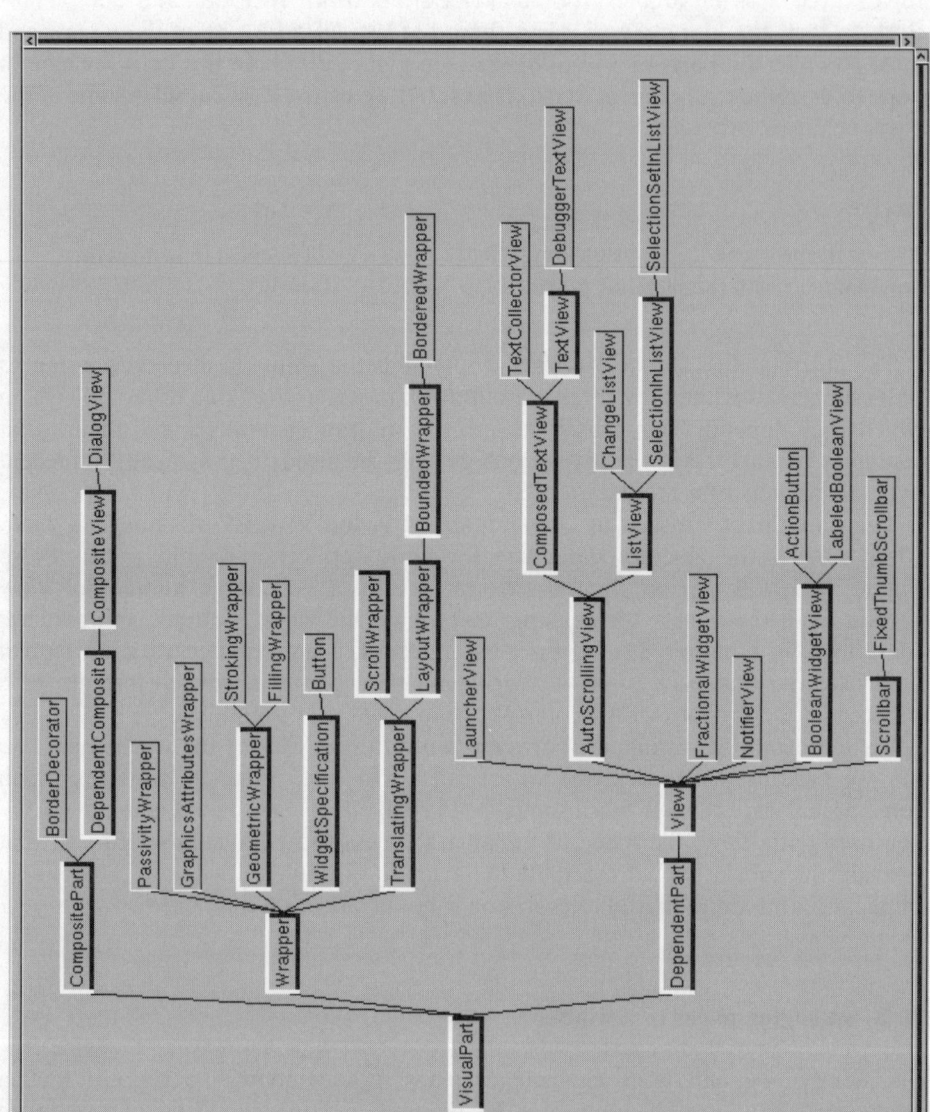

Figure 30.1 Part of the **VisualPart** class hierarchy.

Each pane in a framework structure has its own two-dimensional coordinate system, independent of the coordinates of its container or the screen. For example, an application-specific view can work in a coordinate system convenient for the application that is independent of the size and location of the window on the screen. Transformation methods are available to convert from a pane's private coordinate system to that of its container, or to the coordinate system of the screen.

30.4 Class ScheduledWindow

As mentioned in Chapter 19, an instance of class Window represents a graphic medium. For constructing applications, a Window is not very useful as it does not know how to participate in a framework of panes. This is the role of ScheduledWindow, the main subclass of Window.

A ScheduledWindow is the top component in a visual parts framework, with connections to the display screen and window manager. Although not part of the VisualPart class hierarchy, an instance of ScheduledWindow participates in an MVC structure, since it always has a controller (an instance of StandardSystemController, – see Chapter 31 – or a subclass), and may have a model. It can also have a label, an icon (the icon is ignored on the Macintosh), and a minimum and maximum size. However, it can have only a single component (which may be an instance of DependentPart, CompositePart, or Wrapper, or their subclasses). Additionally, each ScheduledWindow has its own instance of LookPreferences (see Chapter 12) to dictate its internal appearance.

We noted above that a ScheduledWindow may have a reference to a model. However, it's unlikely that a ScheduledWindow will want to be dependent on a model, since there are very few occasions in which the window will want to change according to a change of state of its model. However, there are a few occasions in which this dependency is useful. We have already seen some examples of this:

- *Closing a text window* – for example, you may have already noticed that if you attempt to close a System Browser which contains source that has not been 'accepted', you will be prompted to confirm that you wish to discard the changes you have made. This behavior relies on the changeRequest/updateRequest mechanism described in Chapter 27.
- *Changing the label of a window* – for example, when using the FileBrowser, if you modify the path you wish to search, the label of the window is updated to reflect the new path name. This behavior relies on the FileBrowser sending itself a changed:with: message in which the first argument is the Symbol #label and the second argument is a String representing the new label of the window.

When a window is opened on the screen, the platform's window manager gives it some form of *decoration* – a border and some widgets to provide access to window manager operations such as quit, and collapse. A VisualWorks window – an

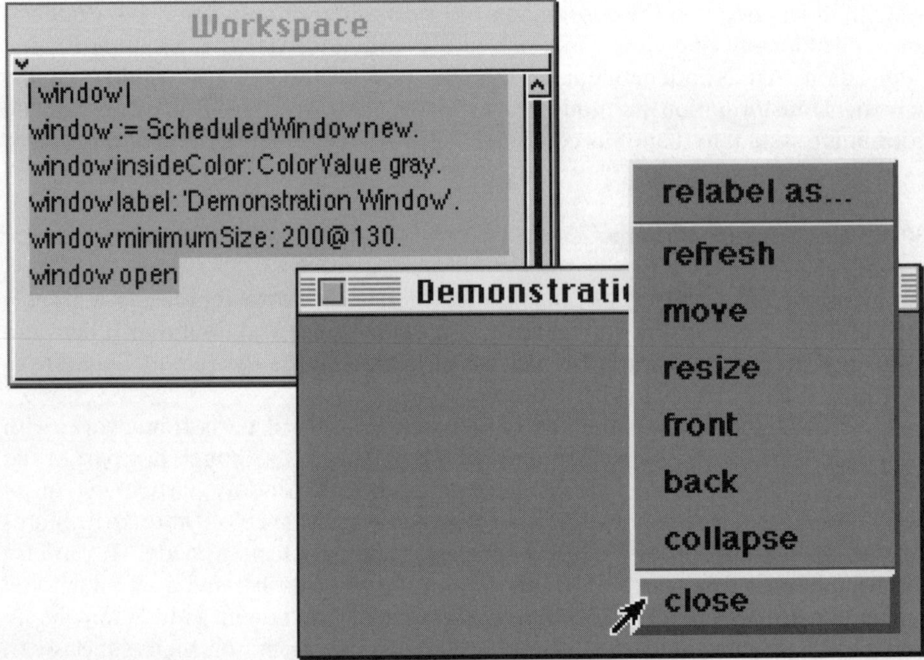

Figure 30.2 An example **ScheduledWindow**.

instance of (a subclass of) ScheduledWindow – may have one of three decorations, known as 'normal', 'dialog' and 'popUp', corresponding to the following characteristics:

- Normal – so-called 'full' decoration, including a border and widgets providing access to window manager operations (for example, a Browser)
- Dialog – a (less obvious) border and usually widgets (for example, a Prompter)
- PopUp – no decoration (for example, a menu)

By default, an instance of ScheduledWindow is opened with 'normal' decoration. This is achieved by sending it the message open, thus:

```
ScheduledWindow new open
```

This creates a window with a default inside color, no label and few restrictions on its size. Nevertheless, this window will understand all the normal resize and repositioning messages. Furthermore, it will automatically have an instance of StandardSystemController attached to it (see Chapter 31), so that the usual <window> menu is available. Normally, however, we will want a more interesting window, so further messages will be sent to the newly created instance of ScheduledWindow before the open message is sent. An example is shown in the workspace in Figure 30.2.

Exercise 30.2

Browse class ScheduledWindow. Try further examples creating ScheduledWindows, as in Figure 30.2. You might like to experiment with some of the other messages understood by ScheduledWindow such as maximumSize:.

Exercise 30.3

Add a method to class ScheduledWindow called fixedSize: which may be used to fix the size of the window, preventing the user from resizing it.

30.5 Adding a component to a window

A window without a component isn't particularly useful. In the example below we give the window a component (an Image) before opening it (see Figure 30.3):

```
| window |
window := ScheduledWindow new.
window label: 'Example One'.
window component: Image parcPlaceLogo.
window open
```

Because the Image is a component of the window, whenever the window is resized or refreshed its contents will be redisplayed. In Chapters 19 and 20 we saw that when we displayed directly onto a window its contents were not retained. This property of redisplaying after a *damage* event is part of the invalidation mechanism which is described later in this chapter.

Exercise 30.4

Experiment with the example above.

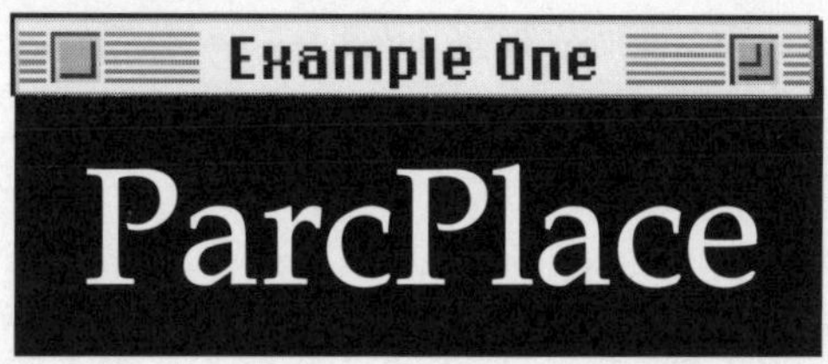

Figure 30.3 An **Image** displayed in a **ScheduledWindow**.

Exercise 30.5

Substitute an instance of ComposedText for the Image in the example.

Exercise 30.6

Try to substitute a Geometric object such as a Circle as a component in the example; see Chapter 20 for a description of displaying Geometrics.

30.6 Wrappers

Class Wrapper is another subclass of VisualPart. Instances of class Wrapper contain a single component, retained by the instance variable component. VisualParts assume that their containers are wrappers. (We have already seen use of wrappers for displaying Geometrics in Chapter 20.) Wrappers support the relative positioning of components, when these components are contained in an instance of CompositePart. Although Wrapper is not an abstract class, instances of it are seldom used. The preferred approach is to use instances of Wrapper's subclasses as shown in Table 30.1.

Instances of VisualPart are normally contained within a BoundedWrapper (if no border or coloring is required), or in a BorderedWrapper otherwise.

30.7 Class CompositePart

The (non-abstract) class CompositePart is yet another subclass of VisualPart. (It is the composite equivalent of VisualPart.) Instances of this class can be included in a

Table 30.1

Class	Description	Example creation expressions
TranslatingWrapper	Adds to Wrapper the ability to translate its component by an offset. Instances are typically used to hold a visual component of a fixed size, such as an Image.	TranslatingWrapper on: Image parcPlaceLogo at: 40 @ 40
BoundedWrapper	Adds the notion of a definite *bounds*. It also supports a *layout specification* (typically, a Rectangle).	BoundedWrapper on: Image parcPlaceLogo in: (20 @ 20 corner: 100 @ 200)
BorderedWrapper	Adds the notion of a colored border (an instance of Border), together with an inside color.	BorderedWrapper on: Image parcPlaceLogo in: (20 @ 20 corner: 100 @ 200)

framework structure to hold many components, all of which are assumed to be instances of a subclass of Wrapper. Each of these components will be a container of some other instance of a subclass of VisualComponent.

A subclass of CompositePart is DependentComposite. This class allows for the construction of a framework of parts, all of which depend on the same model. CompositeView subclasses DependentComposite to add an overall controller; as its name suggests, it is the composite equivalent of View.

Several messages are provided by class CompositePart which may be used to add a visual component to an instance of CompositePart (or one of its subclasses). A typical example is add:at:, in which the first argument is any VisualComponent and the second argument is a Point. In the method that corresponds to this message, the VisualComponent is first enclosed in a TranslatingWrapper (using the Point as its offset) before being added to the collection of components. The full set of messages (and the wrappers they create) is presented in Table 30.2.

Exercise 30.7

Browse the messages in Table 30.2.

In the example below, we install a CompositePart as the component of a ScheduledWindow, and add a ComposedText to the CompositePart at an offset point (Figure 30.4):

```
| window composite |
window := ScheduledWindow new.
window label: 'Example Two'.
composite := CompositePart new.
window component: composite.
composite add: 'Example Two' asComposedText at: 40@40.
window open
```

Table 30.2

Message	Creates Wrapper
add: aVisualComponent at: aPoint	TranslatingWrapper
add: aVisualComponent in: aLayoutObject	BoundedWrapper
add: aVisualComponent borderedIn: aLayoutObject	BorderedWrapper
add: aVisualComponent in: aLayoutObject borderWidth: anInteger	BorderedWrapper
addWrapper: aWrapper[a]	

[a] The argument must be an instance of one of the Wrapper classes.

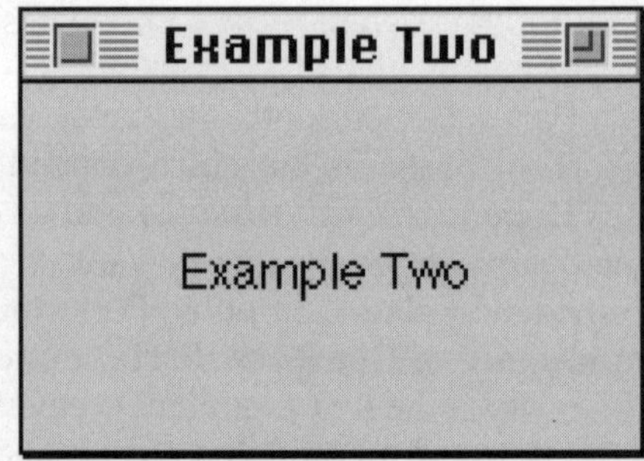

Figure 30.4 A **ComposedText** displayed in a **ScheduledWindow**.

Exercise 30.8

Using an instance of TranslatingWrapper, write a sequence of message expressions to produce the same result as the example.

Alternatively, we could specify the Rectangle in which a component should be located, thus (Figure 30.5):

```
| window composite |
window := ScheduledWindow new.
window label: 'Example Three'.
composite := CompositePart new.
window component: composite.
composite add: (Circle center: 100@100 radius: 100) asFiller
        in: (0.25@(1/3) corner: (2/3)@0.75).
window open
```

Exercise 30.9

Using an instance of BoundedWrapper, write a sequence of message expressions to produce the same result as the example.

Continuing in the same vein, we can modify an earlier example to enclose the component in a Border, as follows (Figure 30.6):

```
| window composite |
window := ScheduledWindow new.
window label: 'Example Four'.
composite := CompositePart new.
window component: composite.
composite add: 'Example\Four' withCRs asComposedText
        borderedIn: (0.25@(1/3) corner: (2/3)@0.75).
window open
```

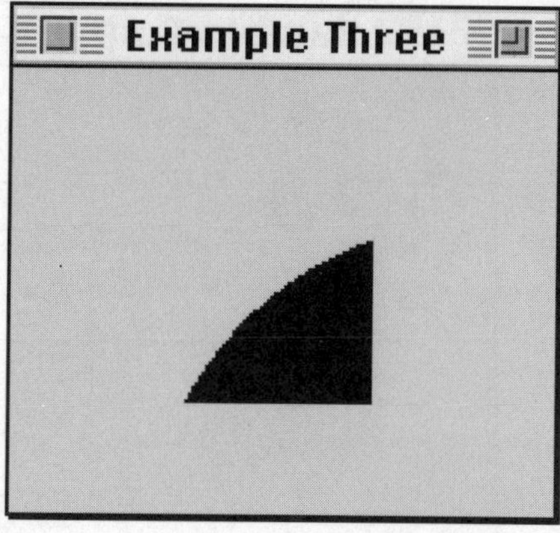

Figure 30.5 Displaying a **Circle** in a **ScheduledWindow.**

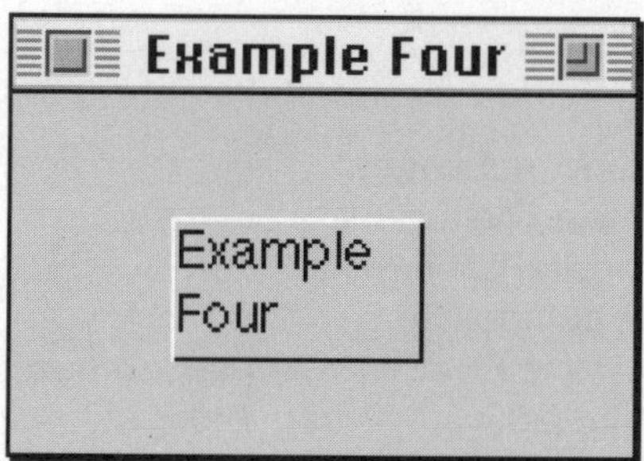

Figure 30.6 Displaying a **ComposedText** (enclosed in a border) in a **ScheduledWindow**

Exercise 30.10

Using an instance of BorderedWrapper, write a sequence of message expressions to produce the same result as the example.

Exercise 30.11

Modify your answer to Exercise 30.10 to give a three-pixel-wide yellow border.

In the last two examples above, the Rectangle gives the *relative* dimensions of the component – its *x* and *y* coordinates lie between 0 and 1. Alternatively, we

Figure 30.7 Specifying the layout using a **Rectangle**.

could use a Rectangle to specify the absolute position of the component, as follows (Figure 30.7):

```
| window composite |
window := ScheduledWindow new.
window label: 'Example Five'.
composite := CompositePart new.
window component: composite.
composite add: 'Example\Five' withCRs asComposedText
            borderedIn: (20@30 corner: 120@130).
window open
```

Exercise 30.12

Modify your answers to Exercises 30.9, 30.10 and 30.11 to use a Rectangle that specifies the absolute position of the component.

30.8 Layout specification

We have seen how a Rectangle may be used to specify the layout of one component within another. There are occasions, however, when a more complex layout specification is required. For example, it's sometimes necessary to position a component at the right-hand edge of a variable-sized window. In these cases, we use a *layout object* such as an instance of LayoutOrigin or LayoutFrame. Both are subclasses of the abstract class Layout.

A LayoutOrigin is used when you are only concerned about the position of the *top-left* of an object (when it cannot stretch or shrink, such as an Image). The LayoutOrigin contains a leftFraction and a topFraction (quantities between 0 and 1). These specify a relative point inside the container's bounds, as a fraction of the size of the area. The absolute point is obtained by adding a leftOffset and topOffset – measured in pixels. A LayoutFrame is like a LayoutOrigin, but additionally has a rightFraction, bottomFraction, rightOffset and bottomOffset. (Note that the right and bottom fractions are measured from the left and top!) By default, all these parameters are zero – i.e. occupying no space.

The two examples below demonstrate the use of a LayoutOrigin and LayoutFrame to position a component (Figures 30.8 and 30.9).

```
| window composite text layout |
window := ScheduledWindow new.
window label: 'Example Six'.
composite := CompositePart new.
window component: composite.
text := 'Example\Six' withCRs asComposedText .
"Position the text at the right-hand edge of its container, one third down, no
matter what the size of the window"
layout := LayoutOrigin new
            leftFraction: 1;
            leftOffset: text bounds width negated;
            topFraction: 1/3.
composite add: text borderedIn: layout.
window open
```

```
| window composite layout text textBounds |
window := ScheduledWindow new.
window label: 'Example Seven'.
composite := CompositePart new.
window component: composite.
text := 'Example\Seven' withCRs asComposedText.
textBounds := text bounds expandedBy: 2@2.
"Position the text one quarter along and half way down its container, ensure
that its bounds don't change when the window is resized"
layout := LayoutFrame new
            leftFraction: 1/4;
            rightFraction: 1/4;
            rightOffset: textBounds width;
            topFraction: 1/2;
            bottomFraction: 1/2;
            bottomOffset: textBounds height.
composite add: text borderedIn: layout.
window open
```

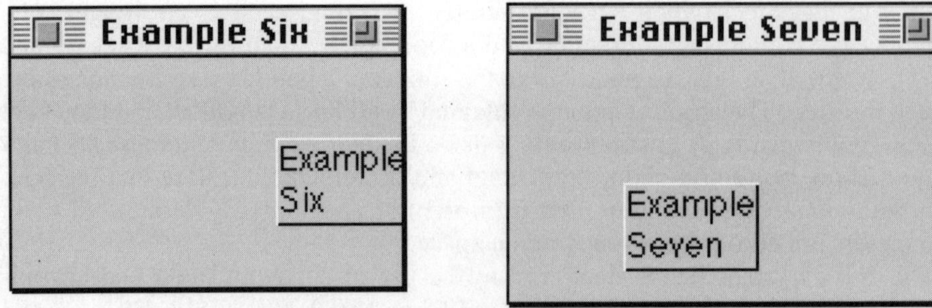

Figures 30.8 and 30.9 Using a **Layout** to specify the location of a component.

Exercise 30.13

Rewrite the examples above using a BorderedWrapper.

Exercise 30.14

Experiment with different layouts by modifying the examples above.

30.9 Summary of VisualPart class hierarchy

As an example of a framework structure, Figure 30.10 shows the structure of the components of an Inspector. From this and the above description, we can identify three characteristics:

- An instance of (some subclass of) DependentPart is usually the leaf in the framework structure. For example, the instance of TextCollectorView in Figure 30.10.
- An instance of Wrapper (or one of its subclasses) is an interior node of the framework – it contains a single component. As an example, see the many instances of BorderedWrapper in Figure 30.10.
- An instance of CompositePart (or one of its subclasses) is an interior node of the framework – it contains an arbitrary number of wrappers, each of which contains a single component. For example, in Figure 30.10, the instance of BorderDecorator (a subclass of CompositePart).

Exercise 30.15

Try inspecting the internal structure of a VisualWorks window on the screen. The easiest way to do this is to interrupt the image (with <control-c>) with the cursor over

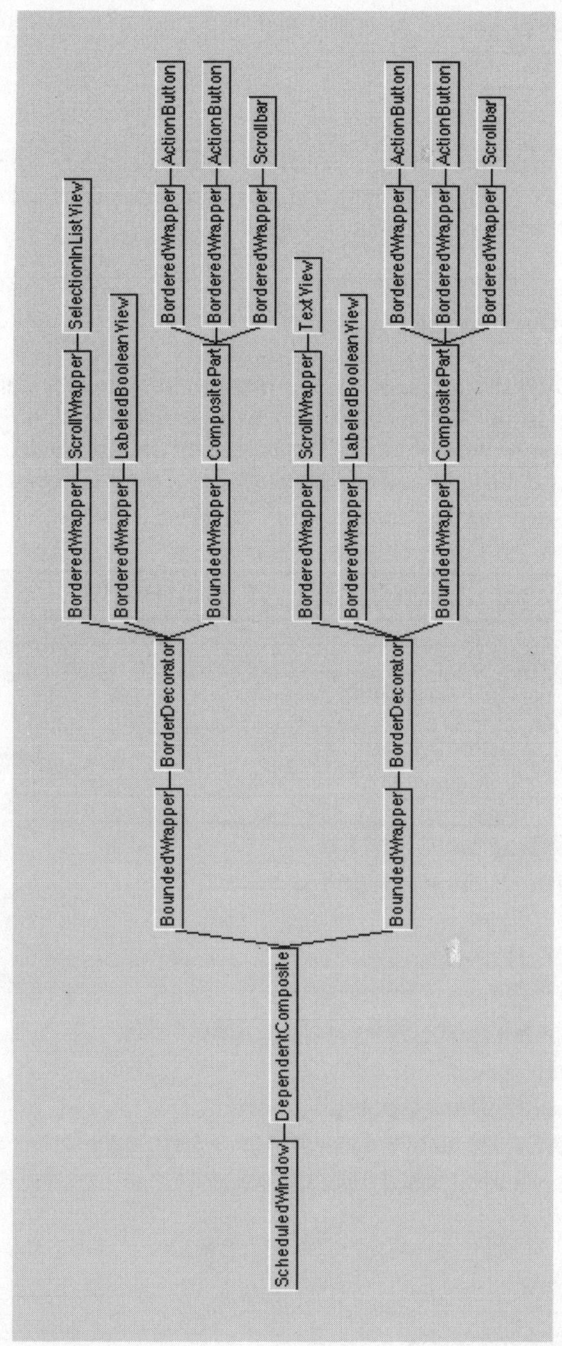

Figure 30.10 The internal arrangement of an Inspector.

a VisualWorks window. Use the Debugger and Inspectors to explore the window structure.

Exercise 30.16

Browse the three class hierarchies rooted at DependentPart, Wrapper and CompositePart. Try to understand how and why new behavior is added in each subclass. You may find the class comments helpful.

30.10 The displayOn: message

All views respond to the message named displayOn:. This message causes some aspect of a model to be displayed. It usually contains a sequence of expressions which send messages to the instance of GraphicsContext provided as the argument. For example, Figure 30.11 shows the displayOn: method for class ListView.

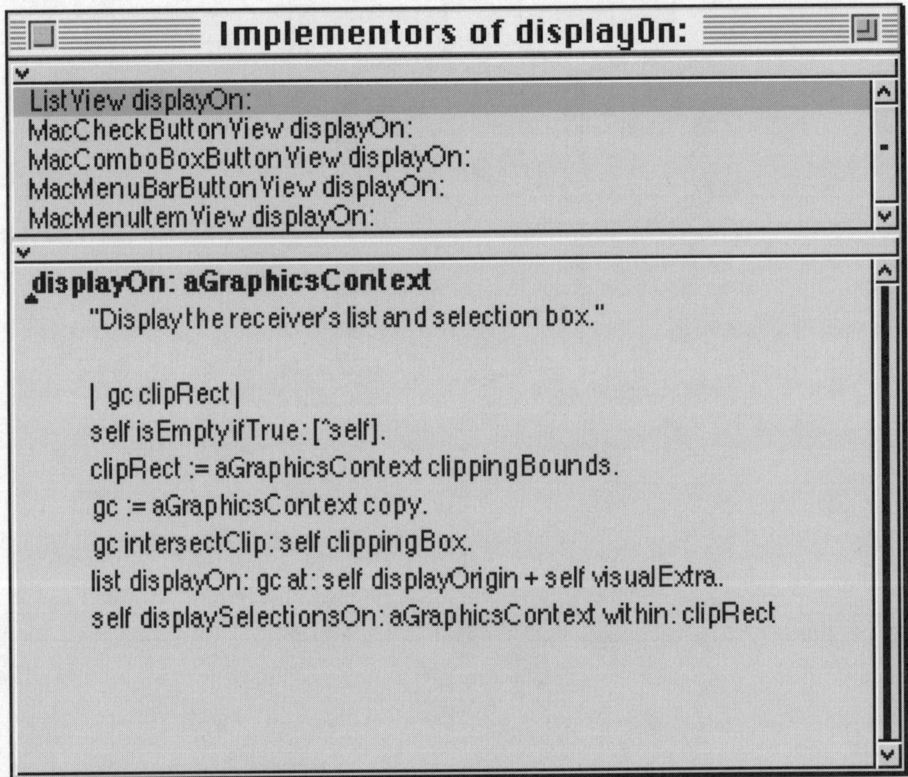

Figure 30.11 An example **DisplayOn:** method.

30.11 Invalidation

When a view realizes that its display contents are no longer correct (perhaps due to an update: message from the model), it should send itself either invalidate or invalidateRectangle: with a Rectangle argument to indicate the invalid area. This message will travel up the parts framework to the object at the top (usually a ScheduledWindow) which will accumulate all the Rectangles and then send a message to its component to redraw itself (by sending a displayOn: message with an appropriately clipped GraphicsContext).

The accumulation of invalid areas is integrated into the damage repair mechanism. When the window is told (by the platform's window manager) that an area is damaged (for example, when first opened or later obscured by another window), it uses the same mechanism to redisplay the damaged areas. This technique helps avoid unnecessary repainting of windows and associated flicker.

The delay between the top component being told about an invalidation and it actually sending a displayOn: message to its component can be substantial (especially when there is significant computation). It can be told to repair damage immediately by using the invalidateRectangle:repairNow: message with true as the second argument. Alternatively, a view can ask for all outstanding damage in its framework structure to be repaired immediately by sending itself the message repairDamage.

Exercise 30.17

Browse the methods described above.

30.12 Example: ClockView

In the example below we provide a worked example of a fully functioning view to represent a clock. This example will re-use some of the code first described in Chapter 25.

The class ClockView is a subclass of VisualPart. It contains two instance variables – clockProcess and running – which will be used to represent the timing process of the clock and to indicate if the clock is running (respectively).

```
VisualPart subclass: #ClockView
  instanceVariableNames: 'clockProcess running'
  classVariableNames: ''
  poolDictionaries: ''
  category: 'View examples'
```

We require two methods to start and stop the timing process (in protocol control):

```
start
   "start the clock"

   running
      ifFalse:
            [clockProcess resume.
            running := true]
stop
   "stop the clock"

   running
      ifTrue:
            [clockProcess suspend.
            running := false]
```

We also require two methods, initialize and release, to instantiate and terminate the timing process (in protocol initialize-release).

```
initialize
   "initiate the clock process
   This message is received when the instance is created"

   | delay |
   super initialize.
   running := false.
   delay := Delay forSeconds: 1.
   clockProcess :=[
      [self invalidate.
   "Causes the window view to re-display"
         delay wait] repeat] newProcess.
   self start
release
   "terminate the process
   This message is received when the window is closed"

   self stop.
   clockProcess terminate.
   super release
```

Now we add the displayOn: method, which displays the current time on the GraphicsContext argument (in protocol displaying).

```
displayOn: aGraphicsContext
   "display the time"
```

Figure 30.12 A VisualWorks Clock.

```
Time now printString asComposedText displayOn: aGraphicsContext
```

Finally, we have to add a method called preferredBounds, which will return a Rectangle specifying the preferred size of the ClockView (in protocol bounds accessing).

```
preferredBounds
    "answer my preferred bounds (actually the bounds of the text I'm going to
    display)"

    ^Time now printString asComposedText preferredBounds
```

To test the ClockView, we place an instance of it in a ScheduledWindow (Figure 30.12):

```
| window |
window := ScheduledWindow new.
window label: 'Clock'.
window component: ClockView new.
window open
```

Exercise 30.18

Experiment with the example above.

Exercise 30.19

Using a CompositePart, create a window containing many instances of ClockView.

Exercise 30.20

(Hard.) Consider modifying ClockView so that it displays a clock face in either a conventional analog style or a digital style.

30.13 Summary

The 'view' component of the MVC mechanism is represented by classes VisualPart and ScheduledWindow – class ScheduledWindow provides the outer container view with connections to the platform window manager; and the abstract class VisualPart provides behavior for the components of a window. One of the most important methods that these classes provide is displayOn:, taking an instance of GraphicsContext as its argument. This method has multiple implementations specific to each 'view' class.

The final element of the MVC triad is the controller. In the next chapter we describe the classes that represent this element.

31 Controllers

The mechanism of controllers is considered in this chapter. The basic control loop in class Controller is described, including the way in which control is passed from one controller to another, and from one window to another. Additionally, we describe mouse and keyboard interaction, and give examples to modify the cursor shape.

This chapter also considers the additional support provided by major subclasses of Controller: StandardSystemController, ControllerWithMenu and NoController. The interaction between StandardSystemController and ScheduledWindow is also described.

31.1 Introduction

A *controller* is the final element of an MVC structure. In Chapter 29 we said that a controller provides the user with the means to interact with its view and/or model. Fundamentally, therefore, a controller is concerned with user *input* whereas a view is concerned with (screen) *output*. Views and controllers are configured to work together in pairs (a controller *must* have a view), in such a way that the controller is invisible to the user – it makes a view *appear* to respond to mouse and keyboard activity.

The responses that we expect a controller to provide, in response to user input, include the following:

- Produce a menu containing operations that may be performed on the model or the view
- Inform the model or view about the selections (e.g. from a list) made using the mouse
- Capture and interpret keyboard presses

- Control the location and appearance of the cursor, or
- Any combination of the above.

Each instance of ScheduledWindow and each component view (an instance of View, CompositeView, or their subclasses) has a controller. Therefore, in a structure of visual parts, the user may interact with many controllers. For example, in an Inspector, if you select an item from the left-hand pane with the mouse, the window's controller and the list view's controller are involved in interpreting the mouse activity. In particular, the window's controller would respond to the <window> button being pressed, and the view's controller would respond to activity of the <select> and <operate> buttons. This 'flow of control' between controllers is managed by the controllers themselves. The means by which a controller determines whether it wants control or decides to hand control to some other controller is fairly complex, but follows a well-defined pattern.

31.2 Class Controller

It should come as no surprise to discover that controllers are represented by instances of class Controller (or one of its subclasses). In order to coordinate its view and model, class Controller has two instance variables, view and model, which are usually initialized by view: and model: messages sent by the controller's view. Class Controller also contains an additional instance variable, named sensor, which is an instance of InputSensor (or one of its subclasses) and which provides low-level support for the mouse and keyboard input devices. (Class InputSensor is described later in this chapter.)

Class Controller provides a default 'control sequence' for responding to user input. The methods in class Controller that provide this behavior are overridden by its subclasses to produce specialized behavior. Therefore, although not strictly an abstract superclass, instances of class Controller are rarely useful.

31.3 Flow of control

Earlier we mentioned that a controller is responsible for coordinating the flow of control between it and other controllers, and the sequence of control within itself. It's important here to make the distinction between the flow of control *between* windows and the flow of control *within* a window. Although the mechanisms for both are generally similar, the fact that the windows are also managed by the platform window manager introduces some small inconsistencies.

Since only one window can have control at one time, there needs to be another object whose role is to determine which window should be given control. This role is filled by an instance of class ControlManager. There is only one active instance of ControlManager in the VisualWorks image, represented by the global variable ScheduledControllers. Its instance variable (confusingly called scheduled-Controllers) is a collection containing the controller of each ScheduledWindow (hence the 'Scheduled' in ScheduledWindow). As each instance of Scheduled-Window is opened (by sending it the message open), its controller is added to the collection of controllers maintained by ScheduledControllers.

ScheduledControllers determines which window controller wants control by sending each of them in turn the message isControlWanted. The first controller to respond true to this message is sent the message startUp. (Both of these messages will be described later.)

It is the responsibility of the window's controller to determine which of the window's subcomponents desires control. It does this by sending the message subViewWantingControl to the window. The window then asks its component which subcomponent wants control by sending it the message objectWanting-Control.

When a component receives the message objectWantingControl it asks its controller (if it has one) if it wants control by sending it the message isControl-Wanted. If the component is a composite, it may forward the objectWanting-Control message to each of its subcomponents, and so on. The first component to respond true to the message objectWantingControl is then sent the message startUp by the window's controller. The component redirects the message to its controller, giving it control, beginning what is known as the 'control sequence'. When the controller first gets control, it sends itself the message controlInitialize, then controlLoop, then controlTerminate.

Within the controlLoop method, a controller first checks to see if it still has control by sending itself the message isControlActive. If the corresponding method returns true, the controller sends the message controlActivity to itself, then repeats the isControlActive test. If the isControlActive message returns false, the control-Loop sequence finishes. Subsequently, control is regained by the object that sent the startUp message.

The controlActivity method may contain code to deal with various input events, such as key presses, and mouse activity. The default implementation of control-Activity (in class Controller) simply passes control to the next level (a controller of a component of this controller's view) by sending itself the message controlToNext-Level. The controlToNextLevel method determines whether there is a component with a controller wanting control (using subViewWantingControl). The control-Activity method should be redefined in subclasses when the controller wants to perform some action. Let's go over some of the other messages that we mentioned above:

isControlWanted – The controller determines whether it wants control. This is often accomplished by sending itself the message viewHasCursor.
isControlActive – Similarly, the controller determines whether it is active.

controlInitialize – Occasionally redefined in subclasses to perform suitable initialization of the controller when it gains control, for example changing the cursor shape. The default implementation (in class Controller) simply returns self.
controlTerminate – Occasionally redefined in subclasses to shut down this controller cleanly when it gives up control. The default implementation returns self.

Exercise 31.1

Browse class ControlManager and inspect the global variable ScheduledControllers.

31.4 Specialized controllers

The methods corresponding to the messages controlActivity, isControlActive, and isControlWanted are the ones that are re-implemented by subclasses of class Controller to produce specialized behavior. (Occasionally, controlInitialize and controlTerminate are also re-implemented – as shown later in an example.)

When building an MVC application it may be necessary to implement your own class of controller. However, it's often possible to use an existing Controller subclass directly, or use it as a superclass for your own controller class. To assist you in your decision, in this section we present a summary of the major subclasses of Controller.

Class StandardSystemController

A subclass of Controller, class StandardSystemController, is unusual because it is designed to work only with instances of ScheduledWindow (or one of its subclasses). It is StandardSystemController that provides the standard <window> menu and its corresponding operations (close, move). It is also important to note that the collection of controllers maintained by ScheduledControllers are instances of StandardSystemController (or occasionally a subclass).

In addition to providing methods corresponding to the <window> menu options, class StandardSystemController also re-implements the controlActivity method. In brief, this method starts a Menu (Chapter 28) if the <window> button is pressed, otherwise it sends the controlActivity message to its superclass. The Menu is retained by a class variable named ScheduledBlueButtonMenu.

Exercise 31.2

Why does StandardSystemController use a class variable to represent the menu, rather than an instance variable?

Exercise 31.3

Where is the class variable ScheduledBlueButtonMenu initialized?

Exercise 31.4

Browse class StandardSystemController, paying particular attention to the other methods that it re-implements.

Class NoController

Another subclass of Controller is class NoController. As its name suggests, an instance of NoController refuses to accept control, thus preventing its view or model from being edited or manipulated. This behaviour is especially useful for a message view which only displays status information.

Exercise 31.5

How do instances of class NoController refuse to accept control? *Hint*: browse the class, especially the methods isControlActive, isControlWanted, and startUp.

Class ControllerWithMenu

ControllerWithMenu is another subclass of Controller. It provides a mechanism to start a menu when the <operate> mouse button is pressed. It acts as an abstract superclass for application-specific controllers (although instances of it may be used via sophisticated programming) that require a menu of options.

The menu is referenced via the controller's instance variable menuHolder (usually an instance of ValueHolder (Chapter 29), or PluggableAdaptor (Chapter 33)) whose *value* is a Menu. The method that initializes menuHolder is called initializeMenu, and is therefore ripe for re-implementing in a subclass that requires a specialized menu.

ControllerWithMenu re-implements several of Controller's methods. The most interesting of these is controlActivity (see Figure 31.1). As you can see, if the <select> or <operate> mouse buttons are pressed, the messages redButtonActivity or yellowButtonActivity are sent to the receiver, respectively. (In Chapter 4 we mentioned that Smalltalk refers to the mouse buttons in terms of their color, so it's necessary to remember the mappings: red (<select>), yellow (<operate>) and blue (<window>).) The yellowButtonActivity method starts the Menu referenced by menuHolder and sends the message selector corresponding to the user's menu selection to the receiver.

Exercise 31.6

Browse class ControllerWithMenu. What other Controller methods does the class re-implement?

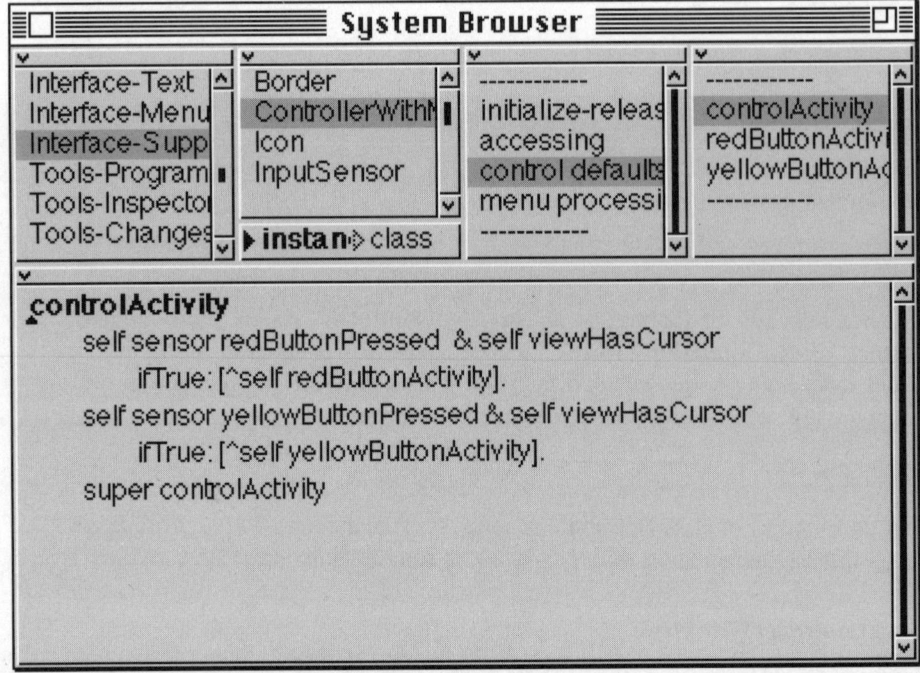

Figure 31.1 The **controlActivity** method in class **ControllerWithMenu**.

Exercise 31.7

Browse the subclasses of ControllerWithMenu. How many of them re-implement the initializeMenu method? Do all of them use a class variable to reference the Menu?

31.5 Class InputSensor

We mentioned earlier that class Controller has an instance variable named sensor that is expected to reference an instance of InputSensor or one of its subclasses. In fact, all the controllers in the VisualWorks image reference an instance of TranslatingSensor, except those controllers that are instances of StandardSystem-Controller. Each StandardSystemController shares an instance of WindowSensor with its window. Both are subclasses of InputSensor, with TranslatingSensor providing a little extra functionality to translate coordinates according to the coordinates of the controller's view.

Class InputSensor therefore provides a number of methods to determine which mouse button is pressed, the current position of the cursor, and the characters entered at the keyboard. The messages are described below:

cursorPoint – returns a Point indicating the cursor's position in local coordinates, i.e. in the coordinates of the controller's view.
globalCursorPoint – returns the location of the cursor in screen coordinates.
waitButton – the cursor position the next time any button is pressed.
waitClickButton – the cursor position the next time any button is pressed *and* released.
waitNoButton – the cursor position the next time any button is released.

For example, evaluate the following expression, using **print it** to see the result.

```
ScheduledControllers activeController sensor waitClickButton
```

It's also possible to determine which mouse button is pressed. Each of the following return a Boolean:

```
redButtonPressed
yellowButtonPressed
blueButtonPressed
noButtonPressed
anyButtonPressed
```

Similarly, we can test if a key has been pressed on the keyboard by sending a sensor the message keyboardPressed.

Exercise 31.8

Browse class InputSensor and its subclasses.

Exercise 31.9

(Hard.) Write some code in a Workspace which will continuously print the location of the cursor in the Transcript until the <select> mouse button is pressed.

31.6 Class Cursor

It's important to distinguish between a sensor and a cursor. In the section above we described how a sensor may be interrogated for its cursor position. Class Cursor represents the physical *display* of a cursor shape. There are many messages contained in the class protocol constants which, when received by class Cursor,

Table 31.1

wait
execute
normal
read
write
hand
crossHair
origin
corner

produce instances of the class. Some of the messages, and their corresponding cursor shapes, are in Table 31.1.

To display a cursor shape at the cursor position, send an instance the message show. Alternatively, send it the message showWhile: with a block argument. For example:

```
Cursor hand showWhile: [(Delay forSeconds: 5) wait]
```

Exercise 31.10

Browse class Cursor and display some instances.

31.7 Example: ClockController

Here we will give a small example of building a controller class, to be used with the ClockView class described in Chapter 30. Initially, we will produce one that uses the <select> and <operate> mouse buttons to start and stop the clock, respectively. Later, we provide some exercises to modify its behavior.

First, let's define our new Controller subclass:

```
Controller subclass: #ClockController
    instanceVariableNames: ''
    classVariableNames: ''
    poolDictionaries: ''
    category: 'View-Examples'
```

We mentioned above that the Controller class hierarchy provided a means of specialization – the difficulty is knowing which method to override. In this case we override the default controlActivity method, since our controller has to interpret mouse activity. The method is usually contained in the control defaults protocol:

```
controlActivity
    "determine which mouse button has been pressed (if any) and send the
    appropriate message to my view"
    self sensor redButtonPressed ifTrue:[^view start].
    self sensor yellowButtonPressed ifTrue: [^view stop].
    ^super controlActivity
```

And that's it! We have defined the class and added the necessary method. Now to try it out, we must first redefine ClockView so that it is a subclass of View (and therefore inherits the ability to use a controller):

```
View subclass: #ClockView
    instanceVariableNames: 'clockProcess running'
    classVariableNames: ''
    poolDictionaries: ''
    category: 'View examples'
```

Finally, we have to connect the controller to the view:

```
| window view |
window := ScheduledWindow new.
window label: 'Controlled Clock'.
view := ClockView new.
view controller: ClockController new.
window component: view.
window open
```

Exercise 31.11

Type in and evaluate the code above.

Exercise 31.12

Add one method that causes the clock to start when the cursor enters the view. *Hint*: browse the method controlInitialize.

Exercise 31.13

Similarly, add one method that stops the clock when the cursor leaves the view.

Exercise 31.14

Modify the two methods you added above so that the cursor changes to an 'hourglass' shape when it is within the view.

31.8 Summary

Class Controller provides the default behavior corresponding to the last element in the MVC triad. It manages the flow of control between windows and between the components of a window. Subclasses of class Controller provide specialized behavior to support (for example) window control and menu control. Each controller has a *sensor* which provides a connection to the mouse and keyboard. In the next chapter we describe how to build a VisualWorks application that brings together a model, a view and a controller, to provide an example of the use of the MVC mechanism.

32 An interactive application – dice

This chapter presents a step-by-step introduction to constructing MVC applications using a very simple example: a dice. The abstract model is constructed first (a number between 1 and 6 which can be changed randomly), followed by a view which can represent the value on the screen as a number. A controller is added next, which is progressively refined to add further functions. Finally, a view that represents the number as 'spots' with the conventional layout is given, and refined to improve its performance.

32.1 Introduction

We have considered the properties of models, views and controllers separately in previous chapters. Here, we implement a complete package, consider its drawbacks, and refine it in the light of our observations. Again, it is recommended that the reader work through this example using a running VisualWorks image.

32.2 Separating the model and its view

What we want to achieve here is an application modeling the properties of a dice. (Strictly speaking, the correct singular form is *die*. However, following modern usage, the word *dice* will be used for both singular and plural forms.) Physically, a dice is a cubical block with spots representing the numbers from one to six on its faces. However, the *function* of a dice is to generate a random number. This could be done in a number of different ways: a hexagonal disk made into a spinning top, for example, or an electronic noise generator circuit.

We will use this insight to separate the abstract functionality (the *model*) from the visible representation (the *view*) in our implementation. The model is very simple, merely requiring some way of maintaining a current value that can be changed randomly. The view is much more complex; it has to display the model's state in an acceptable fashion. For example, it is the view's function to determine the size and position of the displayed spots (see later).

The role of the controller can also be determined by considering the real-world situation. We interact with ('roll' or 'throw') a dice in a manner which communicates only the desire to see another randomly selected number. Thus, our controller should respond to input events (clicking the mouse buttons, for example) by informing the model to change its state randomly. As we shall see, all the usual functions expected of VisualWorks windows (such as moving or collapsing) will be provided using existing classes.

One of the problems with using the Model–View–Controller mechanism in VisualWorks is deciding where to start! As the environment encourages incremental application development, it can be difficult to know which class to create first. As a general guide, however, the best place to start is by constructing the model, or at least enough of the model to provide some useful operations. Frequently, the model can be tested independently before any view or controller is implemented, using Inspectors or by printing messages in the Transcript.

When the model is working correctly, part of the view structure should be implemented. Initially it should be coupled with an instance of NoController, so that no application-specific control is provided. Again, the view–model combination can be tested without a controller. The controller should then be added, with the appropriate mouse and keyboard actions.

Once the first attempt at an application is completed, it should be refined to include all desired functionality in the model, improve the quality and performance of the view, and add further options to the controller. As new functions can be added readily, the package can be modified to reflect changes in requirements or feedback from users.

32.3 Developing the model Dice

For a package using one or more new classes, we should always create a new class category. This keeps associated classes together in the System Browser, and makes it easier to refer to a single application. You can create a new category (call it 'Games–Dice') using the System Browser and the <operate> button menu in the top-left pane.

The model is a new class, Dice, which acts as a holder for an integer between 1 and 6. It has no special features inherited from other classes in the image, other than making use of a dependency mechanism. For this reason we make Dice a subclass of Model, since we wish to inherit Model's refined dependency mechanism. Using the template in the System Browser, you can create a new class Dice with superclass Model in category Games-Dice (Figure 32.1). This also declares a single instance variable value.

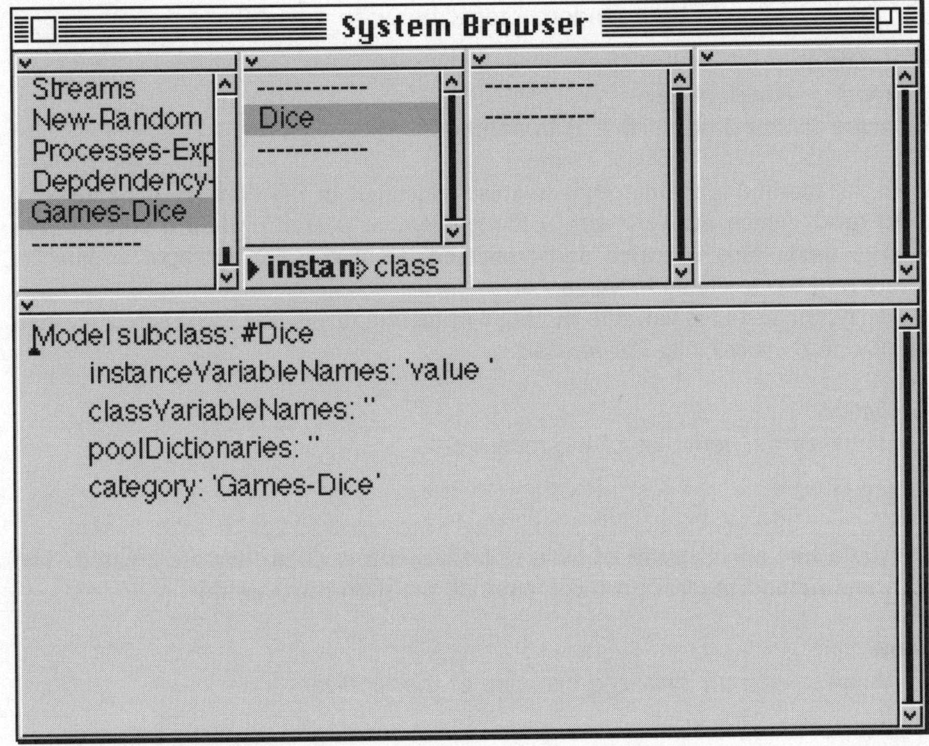

Figure 32.1 Creating a model – class **Dice**.

Clearly, we require a method which permits other objects to enquire about the value. The method value simply answers with the instance variable, and is the sole method in this class's accessing instance protocol.

```
value
   "Answer with the current value held by the receiver"

   ^value
```

Since we definitely do not want other objects to be able to modify the state of the Dice arbitrarily, we encapsulate our state by refraining from implementing any protocol to set the variable value. Instead, we want instances of Dice to be able to respond to a message roll (in instance protocol modifying), which sets value to a randomly selected integer between 1 and 6.

```
roll
    "Set my value to be a random integer between 1 and 6"

    | rand |
    rand := Random new.
    value := (rand next * 6 + 1) truncated
```

When this method is evaluated, it creates an instance of Random (see Chapter 18), called rand, which answers with a Float between 0 and 1 when it receives the message next. This is scaled and truncated, so that a SmallInteger within the correct range is assigned to value.

Clearly, the instance variable will need to be initialized. We can create a method initialize in protocol initialize-release.

```
initialize
    "Initialize the variables of the receiver"

    value := 1
```

We would like all instances of Dice to be initialized when they are created. The following method in class protocol instance creation provides this.

```
new
    "Answer with an initialized instance of the receiver"

    ^super new initialize
```

This completes the first version of our model dice. We can test our model by creating and inspecting an instance of Dice, using the expression:

```
Dice new inspect
```

Selecting the value item displays the number referenced by the instance variable. Typing, selecting and evaluating the expression:

```
self roll
```

in the right-hand pane of the Inspector (see Figure 32.2) will modify the instance variable. (There is always the possibility that the new random value will be 1!) Verify this yourself by deselecting and reselecting the value instance variable in the Inspector.

Exercise 32.1

The roll method unnecessarily creates a new instance of Random each time the Dice is 'rolled'. Re-implement the method to use the same instance during the lifetime of a

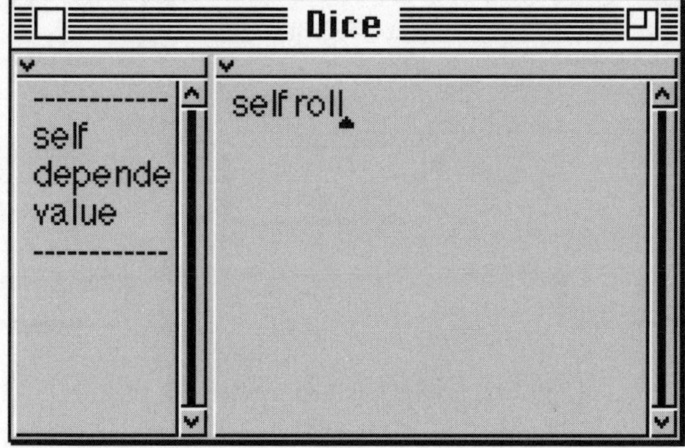

Figure 32.2 Inspecting an instance of **Dice**.

dice. (*Hint*: another instance variable is required.) Alternatively, use the same instance of Random for all Dice. (*Hint*: consider using a class variable.)

Exercise 32.2

The instance initialization method always sets the Dice model to the same value on creation. Modify the initialization method to ensure that a Dice has a random value after creation. (*Hint*: you already have a method to set the state randomly.)

Exercise 32.3

When testing the view, it may be useful to have a dice that behaves more predictably, simply incrementing value when rolled and wrapping round from 6 to 1. Implement a subclass of Dice (called TestDice) which has this property.

Exercise 32.4

Selecting self in an Inspector on a Dice displays 'a Dice'; this uses the default implementation of printOn: defined in class Object. Add a method to Dice that overrides this method so that a Dice is printed with both its class name and its current value.

32.4 A simple view for Dice

Here, we will construct the minimum useful view for use with Dice, called DiceView. To simplify the view structure, we will start by displaying a digit corresponding to the value held by the model.

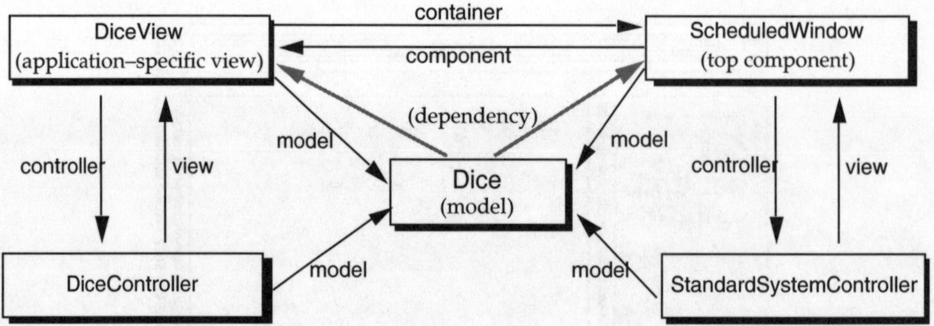

Figure 32.3 Views and controllers for **Dice**.

We will wish to make the view for Dice scheduled, so that it behaves like all other views in the image. Consequently, we will insert our DiceView as a component of a window which is an instance of ScheduledWindow. This also means that we can use the <window> button menu provided by StandardSystemController easily.

In Chapter 29 we considered how the view and controller interact with each other and with the model. An instance of View (or its subclasses) has instance variables referring to the model and the controller; similarly, an instance of Controller (or subclasses) has instance variables referring to the model and view. The communication between the model and the view uses the *dependency* mechanism (see Chapter 27). The relationship between our model, views and controllers is illustrated in Figure 32.3 (compare this relationship with that described in Figure 29.2).

Class DiceView will be a subclass of View, so that we can inherit all functionality to access models and controllers (see Chapter 30). Again, you can create this new class (with no instance variables) using the System Browser.

The basic function of a view is to display some aspect of its model appropriately. To do this, we add a method to DiceView to override the displayOn: method in the displaying protocol of class VisualPart (above View in the class hierarchy) which does nothing (remember that the displayOn: method is the means by which a VisualPart may display some aspect of its model). For simplicity, we will display the value from the model as a single digit at the top-left of the view. In the method below, we transform the value to a graphic object, in this case an instance of Text, by first creating a String:

```
displayOn: aGraphicsContext
    "Display the model's value as a digit."

    model value printString asText displayOn: aGraphicsContext at: 10 @ 10
```

(The displaying of Text was covered in Chapter 20.)

We will be using the dependency mechanism (Chapter 27) to provide the communication from the model to its view. We achieve this by inheriting the update: method in class DependentPart (the superclass of View), which invalidates the view. However, we shall need to modify the roll method in our Dice class to ensure it notifies its dependents that it has changed. We do this via the changed message. Our original roll method will become:

```
roll
    "Set my value to be a random integer between 1 and 6"

    | rand |
    rand := Random new.
    value := (rand next * 6 + 1) truncated.
    self changed
```

Finally, we need some class protocol to create a suitable view for a Dice. More precisely, we want to create a window which is an instance of ScheduledWindow together with an associated StandardSystemController so that the window can be *scheduled*. That is, the window's controller should be able to be included in the list of controllers managed by the global instance of class ControlManager called ScheduledControllers. This means it will behave like all other VisualWorks windows on the screen (see Chapter 30). For example, the normal <window> button menu functions, such as resizing and collapsing, are provided.

Here, we provide a method, conventionally called openOn:, which creates and schedules an instance of DiceView as the component of a ScheduledWindow. By convention, this method appears in the class protocol instance creation of class DiceView. The model for both the view and the window is expected to be the same instance of class Dice.

```
openOn: aDice
    "Create an instance of the receiver in a ScheduledWindow"
    "DiceView openOn: Dice new"

    | window diceView wrapper |
    window := ScheduledWindow
                    model: aDice
                    label: 'Dice'
                    minimumSize: 60 @ 60.
    diceView := self model: aDice.
    wrapper := BorderedWrapper on: diceView.
    Wrapper insideColor: ColorValue white.
    wrapper borderWidth: 2.
    diceView controller: NoController new.
    window component: wrapper.
    window open
```

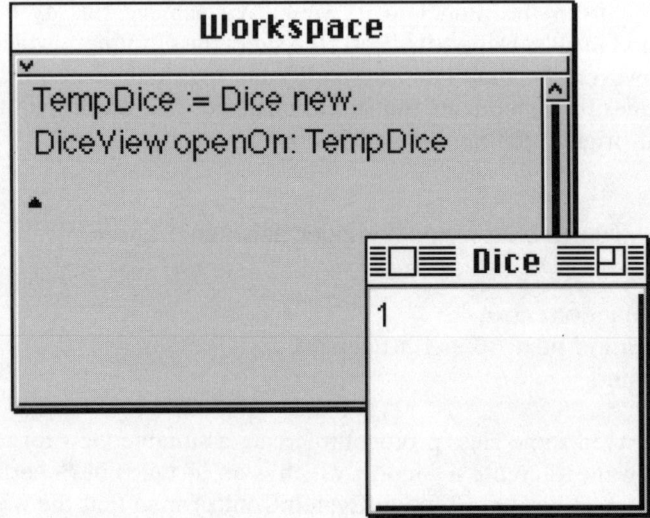

Figure 32.4 Viewing the **Dice**.

This method explicitly sets the border width and inside color for the wrapper. The default color (black) is used for the border. An explicit minimum size is set for the window, so that the window is at least big enough to display a character but the default maximum size is accepted. The open message to the window causes it to become scheduled.

You should note that the controller initially associated with DiceView is an instance of NoController, but will be replaced by a DiceController later. An instance of the default controller class (StandardSystemController) for the window is provided automatically.

We are now in a position to test the view–model combination, even though we have not yet constructed a controller. Evaluating the expressions:

```
TempDice := Dice new.
DiceView openOn: TempDice.
```

causes an instance of Dice to be assigned to the variable TempDice and then a DiceView is created on this Dice (see Figure 32.4). TempDice should be declared as a global variable. You may be prompted for a position and size for the window in the usual way. Note that the usual <window> button menu options, including **collapse** and **close**, should work.

Once the Dice has been opened, the expression:

```
TempDice roll
```

causes the Dice to change; this should be reflected in the window opened previously. We can also demonstrate the ability to have several views on the same model by opening a second DiceView on the same Dice, by evaluating the expression:

```
DiceView openOn: TempDice.
```

Sending the roll message to the model should cause its dependent views to be updated.

Exercise 32.5

Modify the displayOn: method so that the digit is displayed in the center of the view. (*Hint*: remember that a view responds to a bounds message with a Rectangle describing its bounding box.)

Exercise 32.6

The simple displayOn: method above does not put the digit in the exact center of the view. This is because the display reference point of the Text created is in its top-left corner, which is aligned with the center of the view's bounds. Rewrite the displayOn: method to place the displayed digit in the exact center of the view. (*Hint*: the expression someString asComposedText answers with an instance of ComposedText which may be asked for its bounds.)

Exercise 32.7

Try increasing the size of the digit displayed by the DiceView (*Hint*: Consider specifying a style to be used by the ComposedText.)

Exercise 32.8

Create a new version of the displayOn: method in which the color displayed inside the wrapper is different. (*Hint*: you will need an expression like wrapper insideColor: ColorValue lightGray.)

Exercise 32.9

Create a new version of the openOn: method so that a fixed-size window is used. (*Hint*: browse the methods in the accessing protocol of class ScheduledWindow.)

Exercise 32.10

The 'roll' action is not very realistic at present, as it only changes value once. Modify the roll method in class Dice so that the dice goes through several intermediate values with a delay between each. What happens on the view?

Exercise 32.11

For the intermediate values of the dice to be displayed, an additional update: method must be written in class DiceView. This method will override the one inherited from class DependentPart. Chapter 30 described the invalidation messages available to force an *immediate* damage repair. Implement the necessary update: method so that the Dice's intermediate values are displayed.

32.5 The DiceController

Now that we have demonstrated the Dice and its views working correctly, we want to create a suitable controller. In this case, we will create a class DiceController that is a subclass of Controller. Edit and accept the template in the System Browser to define the new Controller subclass.

```
Controller subclass: #DiceController
  instanceVariableNames: ''
  classVariableNames: ''
  poolDictionaries: ''
  category: 'Games-Dice'
```

Note that no new instance or class variables are required in this case.

Here, we want to be able to roll the dice by clicking the <select> button over the DiceView. To do this, we merely need to add a method to DiceController to override the controlActivity method defined in class Controller.

```
controlActivity
  "If my <select> button is pressed, roll the model, then
  wait for the button to be released"

  self sensor redButtonPressed
    ifTrue: [ model roll.
          self sensor waitNoButton].
  ^super controlActivity
```

This method checks to see if the <select> mouse button is pressed by sending redButtonPressed to the sensor. If so, the roll message is sent to the model; then we wait until the <select> button is released. In either case, the controlActivity method defined in class Controller is evaluated.

You should note that, for this controller, we do not need to perform any special action when control is passed to the DiceController or when it gives up control. Thus, we do not need to override the controlInitialize or controlTerminate messages. Similarly, we are using the default isControlActive method, which simply tests if the cursor is over the view's displayed area and that the <window> button is not pressed.

Finally, we have to install an instance of DiceController when a DiceView is opened on a Dice. To do this, we modify the openOn: method in the class protocol of DiceView:

```
openOn: aDice
    "Create an instance of the receiver in a ScheduledWindow"
    "DiceView openOn: Dice new"

    | window diceView wrapper |
    window := ScheduledWindow
                model: aDice
                label: 'Dice'
                minimumSize: 60 @ 60.
    diceView := self model: aDice.
    wrapper := BorderedWrapper on: diceView.
    wrapper insideColor: ColorValue white.
    wrapper borderWidth: 2.
    diceView controller: DiceController new.
    window component: wrapper.
    window open
```

Exercise 32.12

Now that we have a controller, we do not need a global variable in order to be able to send messages to roll the dice. Implement an open method in DiceView class protocol instance creation, which creates a new instance of Dice for each view–controller combination. (*Hint*: use the existing openOn: method.)

Exercise 32.13

Modify the controlActivity method so the dice is 'rolled' for as long as the mouse button is held down. (*Hint*: you have to remove only one expression to achieve this.)

Exercise 32.14

In some cases it is convenient to be able to send a message to an object to 'open a view' on that object, in the way in which, for example, the message inspect is interpreted by Object. Implement an open message in instance protocol viewing of Dice to open a scheduled window on an instance of Dice.

Exercise 32.15

Open an Inspector on the dice application and look at the instance variables.Possibly the easiest way to do this is to interrupt the DiceController when it is active (use

<control-c> when the DiceView is selected), open a Debugger and inspect the controller's view instance variable.

32.6 Refining the view

Clearly, the present approach used by DiceView for displaying the value of a Dice as a digit is not particularly attractive. We would really like to display the values as 'spots' in their conventional positions.

The following re-implementation of the displayOn: method creates a small EllipticalArc (called spot) contained within a FillingWrapper, with a diameter which is one-fifth of the minimum horizontal and vertical extents of the view's bounds. (Class EllipticalArc is described in Chapter 15.) The spot is then displayed in the desired positions, depending on the value of the model.

```
displayOn: aGraphicsContext
    | box cent spotWidth spotHeight spot offset |
    box := self bounds.
    cent := box center.
    spotWidth := box width // 5.
    spotHeight := box height // 5.
    spot := (EllipticalArc boundingBox:
                        (0@0 extent: spotWidth @ spotHeight)) asFiller.
    offset := cent - (spotWidth // 2 @ (spotHeight // 2)).
    (#(1 3 5 ) includes: model value)
      ifTrue: [spot displayOn: aGraphicsContext at: offset].
    (#(2 3 4 5 6) includes: model value)
      ifTrue:
        [spot displayOn: aGraphicsContext
              at: offset - (cent - box topLeft // 2).
        spot displayOn: aGraphicsContext
              at: offset + (cent - box topLeft // 2)].
    (#(4 5 6) includes: model value)
      ifTrue:
        [spot displayOn: aGraphicsContext
              at: offset - (cent - box topRight // 2).
        spot displayOn: aGraphicsContext
              at: offset + (cent - box topRight // 2)].
    6 = model value
      ifTrue:
        [spot displayOn: aGraphicsContext
              at: offset - (cent - box leftCenter // 2).
        spot displayOn: aGraphicsContext
              at: offset + (cent - box leftCenter // 2)]
```

You should note how the spot size and positions are related to the view's bounds. Effective use is made of several messages understood by class Rectangle. Also, you should observe how literal arrays and the includes: message are used to perform the case analysis; this technique is useful in a variety of circumstances. Finally, you can see how the temporary variables box and cent are used to reduce the amount of recomputation of values.

However, experimenting with the new version of DiceView reveals that there is a pause between clicking the mouse button and the appearance of the spots. This is because we are creating a new 'spot' EllipticalArc every time the view is displayed, and this operation takes some time.

We can substantially improve the performance by judicious use of caching in the view. We do not need to recompute the spot every time, but only when the *bounds* changes; i.e. when the view is resized by the user. The simplest way to do this is to add three instance variables to DiceView. One (called spot) retains the EllipticalArc used to display the spot, and the other two (spotWidth and spotHeight) retain the width and height of the spot respectively. These variables only need to be modified when the bounds of the view is changed. When the view subsequently redisplays the spot, the displayOn: method uses the cached variables. You should note that we are effectively increasing the lifetime of the variables involved, and we should expect this to reduce the amount of recomputation required.

First, we should re-define class DiceView, adding the instance variables described above, as follows:

```
View subclass: #DiceView
  instanceVariableNames: 'spotWidth spotHeight spot'
  classVariableNames: ''
  poolDictionaries: ''
  category: 'Games-Dice'
```

Now, create a protocol bounds accessing. Here we add the method bounds:, which is sent to a window's components when it is opened or resized.

```
bounds: newBounds
  "Re-compute my instance variables when my bounds changes"

  spotWidth := newBounds width // 5.
  spotHeight := newBounds height // 5.
  spot := (EllipticalArc boundingBox: (0 @ 0 extent: spotWidth @
  spotHeight)) asFiller.
  ^super bounds: newBounds
```

The bounds: method creates a suitably sized EllipticalArc (within a FillingWrapper) and stores this in the instance variable spot. It also updates spotWidth and spotHeight, before forwarding the message to its superclass.

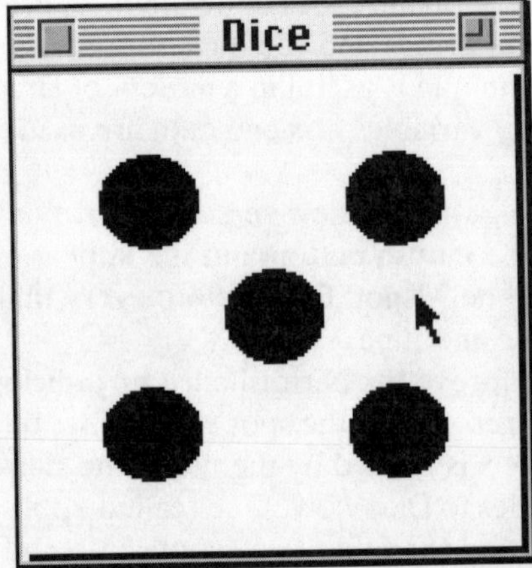

Figure 32.5 The final display of the **Dice**.

Finally, we modify the displayOn: method to display the EllipticalArc in appropriate places depending on the model's value. The result of the modifications is shown in Figure 32.5.

```
displayOn: aGraphicsContext
   | box cent offset |
   box := self bounds.
   cent := box center.
   offset := cent - (spotWidth // 2 @ (spotHeight // 2)).
   #(1 3 5) includes: model value)
     ifTrue: [spot displayOn: aGraphicsContext at: offset].
   (#(2 3 4 5 6) includes: model value)
     ifTrue:
       [spot displayOn: aGraphicsContext
             at: offset - (cent - box topLeft // 2).
       spot displayOn: aGraphicsContext
             at: offset + (cent - box topLeft // 2)].
   (#(4 5 6) includes: model value)
     ifTrue:
       [spot displayOn: aGraphicsContext
             at: offset - (cent - box topRight // 2).
       spot displayOn: aGraphicsContext
             at: offset + (cent - box topRight // 2)].
   6 = model value
     ifTrue:
       [spot displayOn: aGraphicsContext
```

```
        at: offset - (cent - box leftCenter // 2).
    spot displayOn: aGraphicsContext
        at: offset + (cent - box leftCenter // 2)]
```

Exercise 32.16

Use the deterministic dice class TestDice developed in Exercise 32.3 to test that the new displayOn: method works as expected.

Exercise 32.17

We are, of course, not limited to the restrictions of the real world in our implementation of dice. Modify the displayOn: method in DiceView so that it can display patterns of up to nine spots. Implement a subclass of Dice which generates random values between one and nine, and use it to test the improved displayOn: method.

Exercise 32.18

In Exercise 32.17, we allow the *same* view to represent several (slightly) different models. Modify the openOn: method in class DiceView to provide the window with a different label, depending on the class of the model. (*Hint*: the expression anObject class name answers with a Symbol representing the class of anObject.)

Exercise 32.19

Experiment with different colors for the dice spots. (This is more interesting if you have a color monitor!)

Exercise 32.20

A more ambitious task is to implement a view that can display a Dice in a quite different manner. For example, you might like to display the dice as a six-sided disk, or using a three-dimensional representation of a cube.

32.7 Additional control features

As a final refinement, we will add a menu to our DiceController. To be consistent with the operation of other views in the image, we will provide an application-specific menu which is attached to the <operate> mouse button, and retain the present function of the <select> button.

In order to use menus effectively, we will have to redefine DiceController to be a subclass of ControllerWithMenu (see Chapter 31). We will also require one class variable (DiceMenu) to hold an instance of Menu (see Chapter 28) which is common to all instances of DiceController. No instance variables are required. You should define the new version of DiceController as illustrated below.

```
ControllerWithMenu subclass: #DiceController
   instanceVariableNames: ''
   classVariableNames: 'DiceMenu'
   poolDictionaries: ''
   category: 'Games-Dice'
```

Make sure that you remove all the old methods in class DiceController.

For our initial version, we will have only one item on the <operate> button menu, which simply rolls the dice. We will need some class initialization protocol to set up the Menu.

```
initialize
   "Initialize the class variable"

   "DiceController initialize"

   DiceMenu := Menu labels: 'roll' values: #(rollDice)
```

Note the inclusion of the expression DiceController initialize in the comments. Remember to evaluate this expression after you have accepted the method in order to initialize the class variable. This expression should be re-evaluated whenever the class initialization method is redefined.

The implementation of the method controlActivity in ControllerWithMenu sends one of several messages to self, depending on which mouse button is pressed. For example, if the <select> button is pressed, the message redButtonActivity is sent. We want to override the default implementation of redButtonActivity in order to send the roll message to the model. We do this as follows:

```
redButtonActivity
   model roll.
   self sensor waitNoButton
```

The default implementation of yellowButtonActivity in class ControllerWithMenu is to start up the menu contained by its instance variable menuHolder (see Chapter 31). This variable is assigned by the method initializeMenu, which should be added to our instance protocol, as below:

```
initializeMenu
   self menuHolder: (ValueHolder with: DiceMenu)
```

The message corresponding to the item selected from the menu is sent to the designated message receiver; by default, the receiver is the controller which started the menu. In this case, there is only one message (rollDice) which can be sent, as defined in the class initialization method above, so we must add an instance method corresponding to that message:

Figure 32.6 Using the new **DiceController**.

```
rollDice
  model roll
```

The method rollDice corresponds to the **roll** option on the Menu and sends the message roll to the model.

This completes the new version of the DiceController. Evaluating the expression:

```
DiceView open
```

should create a DiceView with an instance of the new DiceController attached (see Figure 32.6). You should verify that the <select> and <operate> button functions are as expected, and that the normal <window> button functions are still available.

We might also like to include keyboard input to our dice application. We can override the controlActivity method in ControllerWithMenu to check for keyboard input before passing control to its superclass.

```
controlActivity
  self sensor keyboardPressed
      ifTrue:
          | char |
          [char := self sensor keyboardEvent keyCharacter asLowercase.
          char = $r
              ifTrue: [model roll]
              ifFalse: [view flash]].
  ^super controlActivity
```

If a key is depressed on the keyboard, the character code is read from the sensor (via the message keyboardEvent) and converted to lower-case. If the character is

$r, a message roll is sent to the model, otherwise the message flash is sent to the view.

Exercise 32.21

Add a **spawn** option to the DiceController <operate> button menu, which creates and schedules a new DiceView on the same model. You might also like to add a keyboard command (use the character <s>) to spawn a new view.

Exercise 32.22

If the controller instance variable is not initialized when an instance of View (or a subclass) is created, then a controller of a default class is created when required. The method defaultControllerClass implemented in class View answers with class Controller. Modify the implementation of DiceView to use this default controller mechanism. (*Hint*: you should remove the controller creation expression in the openOn: method.)

Exercise 32.23

(Hard.) Try putting several instances of Dice and their corresponding DiceViews into a single window. (*Hint:* browse class CompositePart.)

Exercise 32.24

Consider implementing better (or just different) ways of viewing a Dice.

32.8 Summary

This chapter stresses the importance of incremental development of MVC applications, constructing first the 'model', then the 'view' and finally the 'controller'. Note that the model Dice contains no reference to a user interface. By using the dependency mechanism, we ensure that when the model changes (e.g. the value of the Dice), the view is informed.

The view of the Dice is represented by class DiceView, which we implemented as a subclass of View. By inheriting the behavior of View, it was only necessary to implement a displayOn: method to display the value of the Dice. Similarly, by inheriting the behavior provided by Controller, we only had to implement a controlActivity method to provide user interaction. The second version of DiceController inherited from ControllerWithMenu, so that we could easily provide a menu. We continue our description of MVC in the next chapter, where we examine how to create dialog boxes programmatically, extending those already described in Chapter 28.

33 Building a dialog box

To round off our description of the Model–View–Controller structure, we will briefly examine some view–controller components which support *push-button* actions. We have already seen some of these in operation – Chapter 28 gave examples of how to use existing Prompters and Confirmers. In this chapter we will look at how to build some of your own.

VisualWorks provides several classes that assist in the construction of dialogs. These are useful for a variety of user interactions (some of which you have used) including prompters, field-based entry, buttons, sliders, etc. (Chapter 34 discusses the use of 'canvasses' which facilitates the creation of dialogs using a window-building metaphor.)

33.1 Class DialogView

The DialogView class is a subclass of CompositeView (Chapter 30). It provides methods for constructing composite dialogs that contain a variety of visual components, some of which we have already mentioned. We shall see more kinds of components shortly.

The default controller of a DialogView is an instance of DialogCompositeController. This decides which of the components require control and enhances the usual control sequence to provide the user with the ability to 'tab' between text fields. Components can be added to an instance of DialogView from top to bottom using a variety of messages:

```
addColumn: aCollection fromX: leftFraction toX: rightFraction collect: aBlock
addRow: aCollection fromX: leftFraction toX: rightFraction collect: aBlock
addTextFieldOn: aModel initially: aString
addTextLabel: aString
addWrapper: aWrapper atX: aFraction
addVerticalSpace: anInteger
```

We'll look at examples of several of these messages later.

Exercise 33.1

Browse some of the class messages of DialogView (e.g. choose:labels:values: default:).

33.2 Dialog components

Each active component view in a DialogView (i.e. one with which the user may interact) must have a model. The model can be any object, but is typically either an instance of ValueHolder (see Chapter 29) or a PluggableAdaptor (see later).

Having populated an instance of DialogView, it may be sent the message open. This creates and schedules a ScheduledWindow containing the DialogView. The controller of a ScheduledWindow containing a DialogView is an instance of DialogController. Class DialogController is a subclass of StandardSystem-Controller, and disables the <window> button menu. It also retains control until the user has responded to the dialog.

Instead of building a specialized component view it's often possible to use an instance of an existing view class, providing suitable parameters. In the following sections we briefly describe three of the most commonly used views: Labeled-BooleanView, FractionalWidgetView, and ComposedTextView:.

Class LabeledBooleanView

A LabeledBooleanView allows the state of a boolean variable to be toggled, and may also be used as a 'trigger' (see later). An instance sends its model the message value to discover its current state, and value: to change that state. Instances of ValueHolder are useful here!

Instances of LabeledBooleanView can take on many visual representations. Sending one of the following messages in Table 33.1 causes its visual appearance to be modified accordingly. Additionally, the programmer may specify an Image or a ComposedText to be displayed, passing it as the argument to a beVisual: message. To specify two different visual objects, one for 'off' and one for 'on', use the following message:

Table 33.1

Message	Off	On
beCheckBox	☐	☒
beRadioButton	○	⦿
beSwitch	▷	▶
beToggle	□	■
beTrigger	(no image)	

```
beVisual: offImage ifTrue: onImage
```

To set the label of the view, use the label: message.

The view's controller (an instance of WidgetController) only responds to the <select> button. It should be initialized to behave suitably using one of the following messages:

beButton – set model to true only *while* the <select> button is pressed. For example, a scroller.
beSwitch – set model to true *as soon as* the <select> button is pressed. For example, using a widget to start up a pull-down menu.
beToggle – toggle the model's state when the <select> button is *clicked*. For example, a check box.
beTriggerOnUp – set model to true when the <select> button is *released*. For example, the class-instance switch on the System Browser.

The following expressions first create and populate an instance of DialogView, and then schedule it on the screen (Figure 33.1):

```
| dialog model typeButton quitButton |
model := ValueHolder newBoolean.
dialog := DialogView model: model.
dialog addTextLabel: 'Car Specification'.
dialog addVerticalSpace: 10.
typeButton := LabeledBooleanView model: ValueHolder newBoolean.
typeButton label: 'Estate'; beRadioButton.
typeButton controller beToggle.
dialog addWrapper: (BoundedWrapper on: typeButton) atX: 0.
dialog addTextFieldOn: ValueHolder newString initially: 'model'.
quitButton := LabeledBooleanView model: model.
quitButton label: 'Quit'; beTrigger.
quitButton controller beTriggerOnUp.
dialog addVerticalSpace: 10.
dialog addWrapper: (BorderedWrapper on: quitButton) atX: 0.5.
dialog open
```

Note that in the example above, the final message is to an instance of DialogView, not a ScheduledWindow. This causes the dialog to be modal.

Exercise 33.2

Modify the appearance and behavior of the button in the example above.

Class FractionalWidgetView

The class FractionalWidgetView provides 'sliders'. The model of an instance of this class must respond to the message value with a number between 0 and 1 (or a Point

Figure 33.1 An example of a **DialogView**.

with coordinates between 0 and 1). Similarly, the model must understand value: – the argument is a number between 0 and 1 (or a Point). ValueHolders are useful here too.

A slider may be one-dimensional – vertical or horizontal – or two-dimensional; the following messages are used to initialize its orientation:

```
beHorizontal
beVertical
beTwoDimensional
```

Exercise 33.3

Extend Exercise 33.2 to include an instance of FractionalWidgetView.

Class ComposedTextView

Class ComposedTextView is an (indirect) subclass of View (Chapter 30). Its instances expect a model to respond to value and value: (i.e. an instance of some subclass of ValueModel). Additionally, the model should respond with an instance of String or Text. We give an example of using a ComposedTextView later in this chapter.

33.3 Class PluggableAdaptor

When a dialog does not stand alone but is integrated into a larger model, a ValueHolder will not be sufficient within a LabeledBooleanView, as the binary state will be part of the model. A class called PluggableAdaptor (a subclass of Value-Model – Chapter 29) provides a level of indirection between instances of Labeled-BooleanView and the model. The view and its controller send the standard

Table 33.2

getBlock: firstBlock putBlock: secondBlock updateBlock: thirdBlock	Explicitly specify the contents of each block
selectValue: aValue	This initializes the receiver to act like a boolean that is true when the model's value is equal to aValue.
getSelector: getSymbol putSelector: putSymbol	Substitute getSymbol and putSymbol for value and value: respectively
collectionIndex: anIndex	Access the given element of the model, which should be some kind of collection that responds to at:, etc.
performAction: aSymbol	Send the selector aSymbol to the model when the PluggableAdaptor receives the message value:.

messages value and value: to the PluggableAdaptor, which it converts into arbitrary actions defined by three blocks (instance variables of the Pluggable-Adaptor): getBlock, putBlock and updateBlock. An overview of the mechanism is:

- getBlock is evaluated to *get* the value. The getBlock is evaluated with one argument, the model.
- putBlock is evaluated to *set* the value. The putBlock is evaluated with two arguments, the model and the new value. (The putBlock may also be used to indicate a *trigger* message to be sent to the model.)
- updateBlock is evaluated to handle an update from the model; if it returns true, the dependents of the PluggableAdaptor (i.e. its view) are notified. The updateBlock is evaluated with three arguments, the model, the update aspect, and the update parameter.

In addition to an explicit message to specify the contents of the blocks, there are four convenience messages provided to initialize instances of PluggableAdaptor (see Table 33.2).For example, the code below provides an alternative user interface to an instance of Dice, introduced in the previous chapter (Figure 33.2). Note how a PluggableAdaptor is used as the model for an instance of ComposedTextView.

```
| comp model adaptor trigger button textView window |
window := ScheduledWindow new.
window label: 'Dice'.
model := Dice new.
comp := CompositePart new.
adaptor := (PluggableAdaptor on: model).
adaptor getBlock: [:m | m value printString]
           putBlock:[:m :v | ]
           updateBlock: [:m :v :p | true].
```

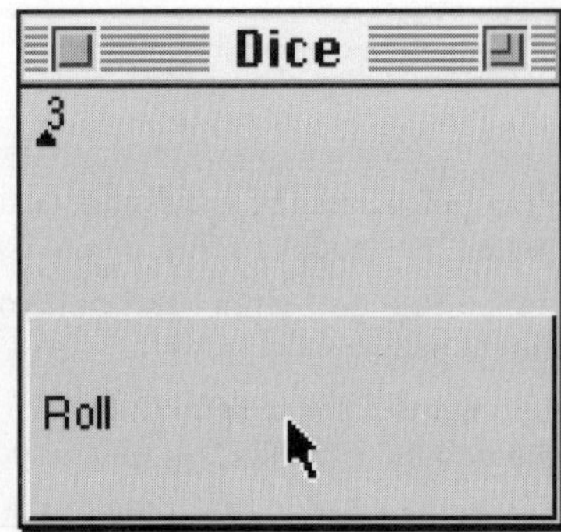

Figure 33.2 An alternative interface to a **Dice**.

```
textView := ComposedTextView model: adaptor.
textView controller: NoController new.
comp add: textView in: (0 @ 0 extent: 1 @ 0.5).
trigger := PluggableAdaptor on: model.
trigger performAction: #roll.
button := LabeledBooleanView model: trigger.
button label: 'Roll'; beTrigger.
button controller beTriggerOnUp.
comp add: button borderedIn: (0 @ 0.5 corner: 1 @ 1).
window component: comp.
window open
```

Exercise 33.4

Experiment with modifications to the example above.

Exercise 33.5

Browse and try the example in class WidgetController.

33.4 Summary

As you have seen in this chapter and Chapters 30 and 32, programmatically creating a window or a Dialog box can be a time-consuming affair. In the next chapter we explore the use of Canvasses, which provide a means of creating a window by using the mouse to position widgets on a window.

34 Using a Canvas*

We have seen how to build interactive applications using MVC and the dependency mechanism. In this chapter we introduce a simplifying layer that sits on top of MVC that takes care of many of the details of window development such as the layout of widgets and their properties. The same application may be deployed on several different window systems by emulating the appropriate look-and-feel.

We will not attempt to give detailed coverage in this chapter, for that we refer you to the VisualWorks' manuals from ParcPlace. However, we will attempt to provide a brief review of the functionality provided by the Canvas mechanism, an explanation of where it fits into the development process and a discussion of its benefits and limitations.

34.1 Overview

VisualWorks provides window painting functionality. The 'design' for a window is created by 'painting' on a 'Canvas', and is called a 'window specification'. A window specification is represented as a class method of some application-specific class (usually a user-defined subclass of ApplicationModel – see later), and is usually named #windowSpec. The contents of the specification are used by a *builder* object (an instance of UIBuilder) at run time to create a window. The window is associated with an instance of the class which contains the specification method.

There are a number of tools provided to help with the painting, defining and testing of Canvasses. These will be covered in more detail later in the chapter.

In brief, the iterative process for developing or modifying a Canvas is as follows:

* This chapter was written in collaboration with Laura Hill.

- Open a new or existing Canvas.
- Drag widget icons from the 'Palette' to an appropriate place on the Canvas.
- Enter properties for each widget. These properties include color, layout and font, etc. as well as an *aspect* selector that is sent to an instance of the application-specific class to return the model for the widget. Properties are entered using a 'Properties Tool' which is divided into pages (see later).
- Install the Canvas – this creates a window specification method in a class determined by the programmer. If the class has not yet been defined, a class definition dialog will appear.
- Use the 'Definer' Tool to create instance variables and instance methods in the class, corresponding to the models and methods expected to be found. (Optional.)
- Write supporting code (for example, the message selector sent by an Action Button).
- Test the interface.

You may have noticed that this sequence contradicts the 'recipe' we presented in Chapter 32. In a later section we provide a modified recipe for use with Canvasses.

34.2 Summary of parts

The Canvas mechanism introduces many extensions to those that we have described thus far in this book. In the following sections we discuss these in more detail.

Class ApplicationModel

In Chapter 29 we discussed the difference between an application model and a domain model. Using a Canvas, the definition of the application model is largely unchanged, except that perhaps it includes more functionality than might be the case in a traditional MVC application. For simple applications it may not be necessary to have complex models for many of the views. Quite often, an instance of ValueHolder will suffice. In that case, the idea of a domain model can sometimes get lost.

The abstract class ApplicationModel is the class intended to be the superclass of almost all application models (just as Model is intended to be the superclass for all domain models). It defines behavior to open, close and coordinate windows. To open a window defined in a subclass of ApplicationModel, send the message openInterface: *aWindowSpecName* to the class. If the name of the window specification is #windowSpec, the message may be shortened to open. The method corresponding to this message is implemented in class ApplicationModel; it creates an instance of the application model class and assigns it an instance of UIBuilder. It is this latter object that then interprets the window specification,

Table 34.1

VisualWorks description	Abstract superclass	Comment
Application	ApplicationModel	Basic application model behavior
Dialog	SimpleDialog	Model dialog application model
Data Form	LensDataManager	Application model for database windows, holding query specifications as well as window specifications.
Database Application	LensMainApplication	Database application root class, holding main window specification, data model specification and database connection.

causing MVC structures to be instantiated, i.e. views to be created, models to be connected to those views and controllers to be attached. These views are inserted into a new instance of ApplicationWindow that is then opened on the screen. The model for the window is the instance of the class that was sent the open message.

In addition to class ApplicationModel described above, VisualWorks provides three more abstract superclasses which are used to represent different kinds of application. All four are described in Table 34.1.

The application model class that contains your window specification will be a subclass of one of the abstract superclasses described in the table, and become the application model for the application. All windows opened from the application will emulate the default look-and-feel specified in the Settings Tool unless specifically overridden.

Exercise 34.1

Browse class ApplicationModel.

Widgets

VisualWorks comes with a set of ready-made widgets that can be placed directly on a Canvas using a drag-and-drop interaction. The widgets are contained in a Palette (Figure 34.1), usually positioned adjacent to the Canvas. The following widgets are included (described left to right, top to bottom):

- Action Button – A button that triggers some action when clicked.
- Check Box – A button that represents a boolean state of its model.
- Radio Button – A button, usually one of a group, which displays as 'on' when its *select* property is equal to the value held by its model.
- Label – A textual or graphical label.

Figure 34.1 The Palette.

- Input Field – A field in which data may be entered and displayed in one of many formats, including: string, symbol, text, number, password, date, time, boolean. May be read-only.
- Text Editor – Resembles a Workspace, has the same properties as an Input Field.
- Menu Button – A button that displays a menu and puts the user's selection into the button's model. May also be used to select actions to be performed.
- List – A list of objects (may be single or multiple selection).
- Combo Box – A combination of a Menu Button and an Input Field. Used to restrict user input.
- Divider – A horizontal or vertical line.
- Box – A box drawn around a particular region of the window. May have a label.
- Region – A rectangular or elliptical visual region. May have color properties.
- Slider – A widget to provide selection from a numeric range.
- Table – A tabular representation of information. May be a two-dimensional list or a collection of objects displayed in rows.

- Data Set – A list of similar objects, for example the rows of a database. Information is presented in a tabular form similar to a Table. Provides more extensive control over columns than a Table.
- Notebook – Similar to that seen in the Help Browser.
- Subcanvas – Another Canvas, used within the current Canvas.
- View Holder – A place holder for a widget not available from the Palette. The *view* property is a selector that, when sent to the application model, returns an instance of some subclass of VisualPart.

The Charts package, available from ParcPlace, adds a 'chart' icon to the palette. Additionally, third-party vendors are beginning to provide new widgets fully integrated with the Palette.

Models

Most of the widgets mentioned above are designed to have a model that responds to ValueModel protocol (often instances of ValueHolder) so that the interface between widget and model is clear, concise and consistent across the entire VisualWorks framework. The model for a particular widget is determined by sending the selector specified in the widget's *aspect* property to the instance of the defining class associated with the UIBuilder. Widgets that do not require a model have no *aspect* property.

Dividers, Boxes and VisualRegions need no model – they are merely decorative. Action Buttons and Labels reference an instance of the defining class as their model. Check Boxes, Radio Buttons, Input Fields, Text Editors, Menu Buttons, Combo Boxes and Sliders expect an instance of ValueHolder (or an instance of a class that behaves like ValueHolder) as their model.

A List widget, a DataSet widget, and a Notebook widget each expect an instance of SelectionInList as its model. SelectionInList is a subclass of Model that has two instance variables: listHolder and selectionIndexHolder. Both of these are ValueHolders, one containing the list itself and one the selected numeric index into the list (in a MultiSelectionInList the selectionIndexHolder contains a Set of indices).

A Table widget requires the most complex model of all, an instance of TableInterface. Instances of TableInterface contain much information on the presentation of the table (e.g. the width, format and label for each column). In addition, TableInterface has an instance variable – selectionInTable – that references an instance of SelectionInTable. (This class provides similar behavior to SelectionInList.) The class has two instance variables: tableHolder and selectionIndexHolder that contain respectively a table (either an instance of TwoDList or TableAdaptor) and a selectionIndex (an instance of Point).

A Subcanvas does not have a model *per se* – it is merely a collection of other widgets according to the layout and definition of some other Canvas. Each of those widgets will have a model according to the above guidelines.

A View Holder must define its own model (if necessary) according to the needs of the particular instance of VisualPart returned.

Exercise 34.2

Browse classes SelectionInList, TableInterface and SelectionInTable.

Dependencies

As described in Chapter 29, a model uses a dependency mechanism to notify its views that it has changed. Views and controllers have direct access to each other and to their model, but the model has no direct knowledge of its views. Using a Canvas does not alter this paradigm. Part of a UIBuilder's task when transforming a Canvas specification into a window is to set up the dependencies. It does a good job! You don't need to do anything. That is part of the beauty of requiring all models to be polymorphic with ValueModel; VisualWorks knows just what to expect.

Because the underlying models all have ValueModel behavior, there are some additional ValueModel methods that help a programmer to create further dependencies. For example,

onChangeSend: *aSelector* to: *anObject*

This method creates an instance of DependencyTransformer that watches for update: messages coming from the receiver, and sends *aSelector* to *anObject* when one is received. This saves the developer from having to implement an update: method in the class of *anObject*. It further limits the update traffic because *anObject* will only receive update messages from those instances of ValueModel in which it has registered an interest.

34.3 Tools

VisualWorks comes with a variety of graphical tools to help you build your application. The Launcher (Figure 34.2) offers access to some of the tools by way of

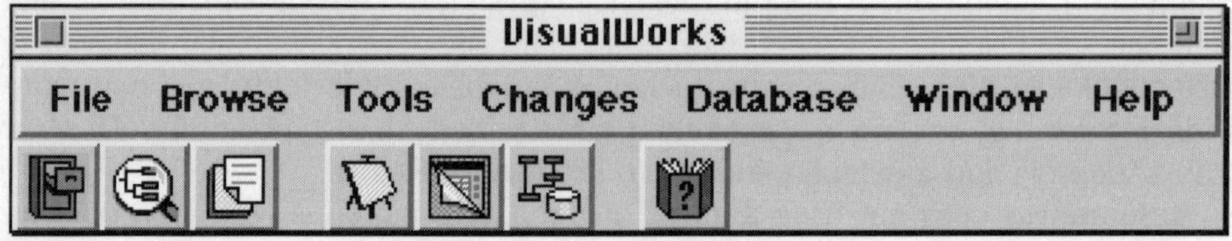

Figure 34.2 The Launcher.

Figure 34.3 The **Tools** menu of the Launcher.

Table 34.2

Canvas	Opens a new Canvas, usually accompanied by a Palette and a Canvas Tool window.
Resource Finder	A window that lists all the classes in the image for which Resources have been defined. A Resource may be a Canvas, a Menu or an Image. From the Resource Finder you can start the application, edit a Resource, browse a class or remove a Resource.

two icons (Table 34.2), the remainder are available from the **Tools** menu (Figure 34.3). The other tools are described later in this chapter.

When a Canvas is opened for editing, it is accompanied by a Palette (see earlier) and a Canvas Tool window (Figure 34.4). The Canvas Tool provides access, via its menu bar, to operations also available from the <operate> menu of the Canvas

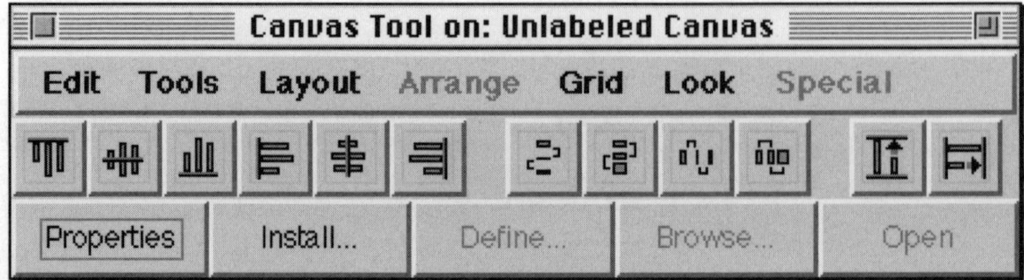

Figure 34.4 The Canvas Tool.

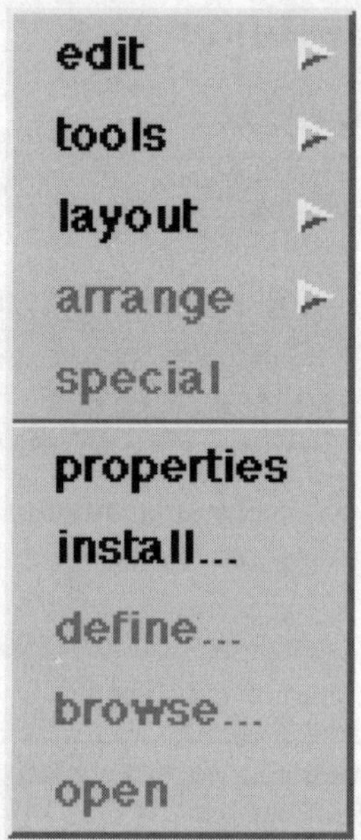

Figure 34.5 The <operate> menu from a Canvas.

(Figure 34.5). The first six icons of the Canvas Tool are used for the horizontal and vertical alignment of widgets. The next four icons are used for vertical and horizontal distribution, and the last two are used for vertical and horizontal size equalization. The bottom row of buttons are used in the stages of the Canvas specification process described earlier. Each button becomes enabled as its stage in the process is reached. For example, the **Define** button is disabled until the Canvas is installed.

The **Grid** submenu offers control of the mechanism used to position widgets (Figure 34.6) and the **Look** submenu offers a choice of look-and-feel preferences (Figure 34.7). However, the selection made here only applies to the current Canvas (to allow the developer to see how the Canvas would look on other platforms). When a window is opened, its look-and-feel will be derived from the preferences specified in the Settings Tool (Chapter 5).

The Definer is one additional tool that may be launched from the Canvas Tool, or the <operate> menu of a Canvas. The Definer writes class and method definitions in the class on which the Canvas is installed according to the properties specified for each widget. Usually this involves adding an instance variable to the class definition for each widget's *aspect* and accessing methods in the 'aspect' protocol for each instance variable. The Definer contains an **Add Initialization** option, which (if checked) causes the accessing methods to return defaults if the variable is uninitialized. (If the instance variable is nil, the method creates a new instance of the expected model for that widget (e.g. ValueHolder with: nil, SelectionInList new) and returns that after assigning it to the instance variable.)

34.4 Building an application

Let's revisit the MVC 'recipe' from Chapter 29. Using a Canvas may simplify some steps:

1. Build your *domain model*. This step is still necessary for most applications. However, if your domain model is very simple – for example, a counter that simply holds a number and increments – you may not need to define separate classes. In this case, you may derive the variables for the application model class directly from the Canvas. This does not mean, however, that you should start building an application by going directly to Canvas painting. It is important to design your domain model, even if you later simplify into ValueHolder models in the application model rather than separate classes.
2. Build your *application model*. First, design your application model – make sure you understand what responsibilities it has.

Here we depart from the recipe in Chapter 29:

3. Design your Canvas. Use the iterative process described earlier to paint the Canvas, select properties and define models. If you need specialized views (i.e. views that are not included in the Palette) use the View Holder widget to set a place in the Canvas for them. Then you need to build a view, build a controller for that view if necessary and hook this view up to the View Holder widget by way of its property selector.
4. As long as you have subclassed your application model class from Application-Model you are done. The window may be opened by sending the message open

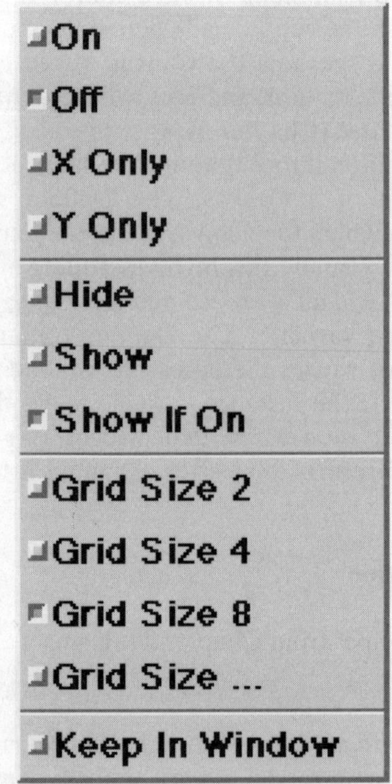

Figure 34.6 The Grid Control menu.

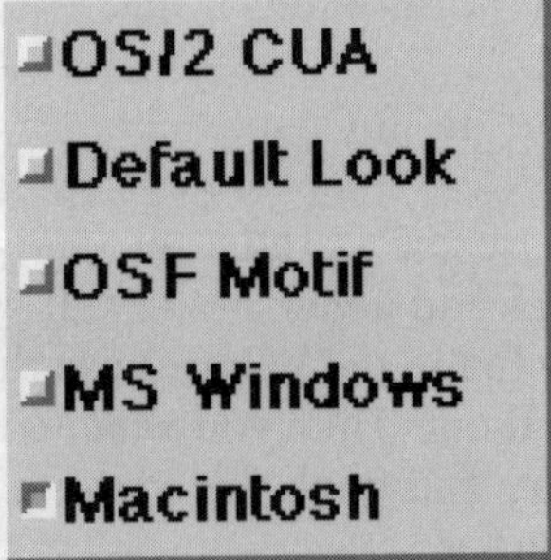

Figure 34.7 The menu to control look-and-feel.

to your class, or openInterface: aSpecName if the name of your specification is not #windowSpec.

5. Iterate until cooked.

34.5 Example: a different dice

Let's look at the dice example from Chapter 32. If we were to create the Dice application using a Canvas, much of the code would remain the same because we would have to create a specialized view (to display the dots), with specialized controller behavior (to roll the Dice). However, until the point when we decided to use a special controller, we could have used a Canvas to design the window, run the Definer and our application would be complete.

However, as an example, let us produce a slightly different Dice example – one in which we display the value of the Dice in an Input Field and use an Action Button or a menu option to roll the Dice. First, open a new Canvas, and set the 'Basics' properties of the window according to Figure 34.8. Install the Canvas on a new class, called VWDice, and define it as an 'Application', as a subclass of ApplicationModel. Use the default specification name #windowSpec. Now browse the class and add two instance variables: value and rand.

In Figure 34.8, we have defined a menu, named #diceMenu, as the menu for the window. Open a Menu Editor to define a menu as in Figure 34.9, build it and test it, then install it in class VWDice as #diceMenu. (Note that 'Roll' and 'rollDice' are separated by a <tab>.)

Now add a Label, Input Field and Action Button to the Canvas, similar to Figure 34.10. (Note that the appearance of your Canvas may differ from Figure 34.10, according to the platform on which you are working.) For each of the widgets, set their properties according to Figures 34.11 to 34.15.

Install the Canvas again, to save the changes you have made, and then add the following two methods to class VWDice:

```
initialize
    "Initialize the instance variables of the receiver."
    super initialize.
    value := ValueHolder with: 1.
    rand := Random new.
rollDice
    "Roll the dice."
    value value: (rand next * 6 + 1) truncated.
```

Note that for this example we are assuming that our domain model (value) is simple enough to be represented by an instance of ValueHolder.

Finally, select the Input Field widget on the Canvas and define a model for it, as shown in Figure 34.16.

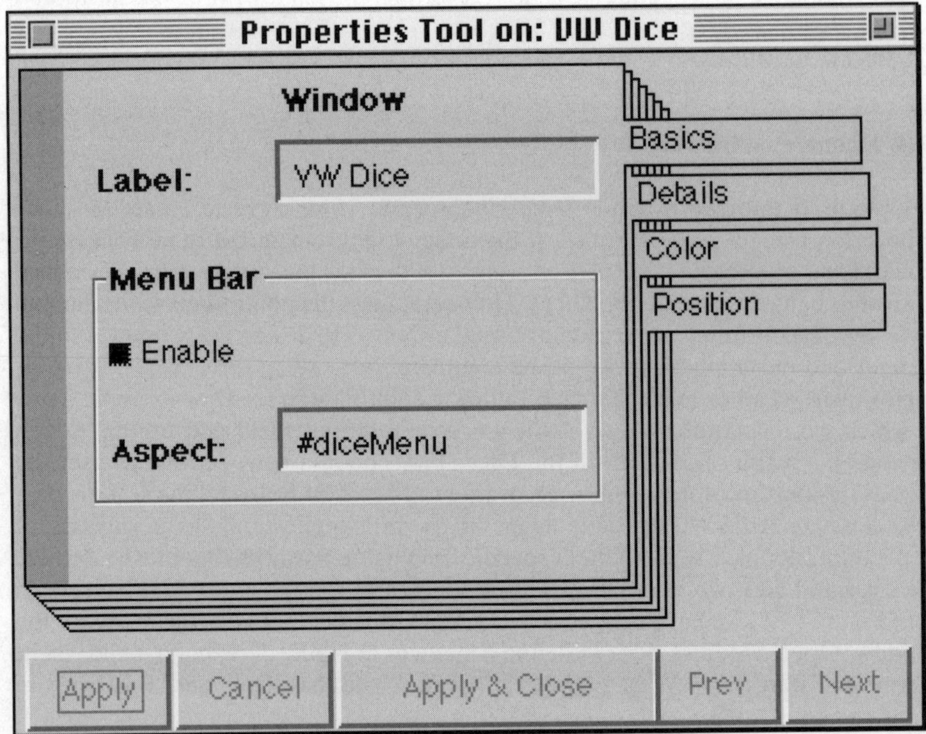

Figure 34.8 The properties of the window.

If you now start the application (from the Canvas, the Canvas Tool, or the Resource Finder), you should find that it works as intended, appearing similar to Figure 34.17.

Exercise 34.3

Modify the look-and-feel selection to discover how your application would appear on other platforms.

Exercise 34.4

Experiment with changing the properties such as font, color and position on the widgets in the example above, as well as the alignment options available in the Canvas Tool.

Exercise 34.5

(Hard.) Modify the example above to incorporate class DiceView from Chapter 32.

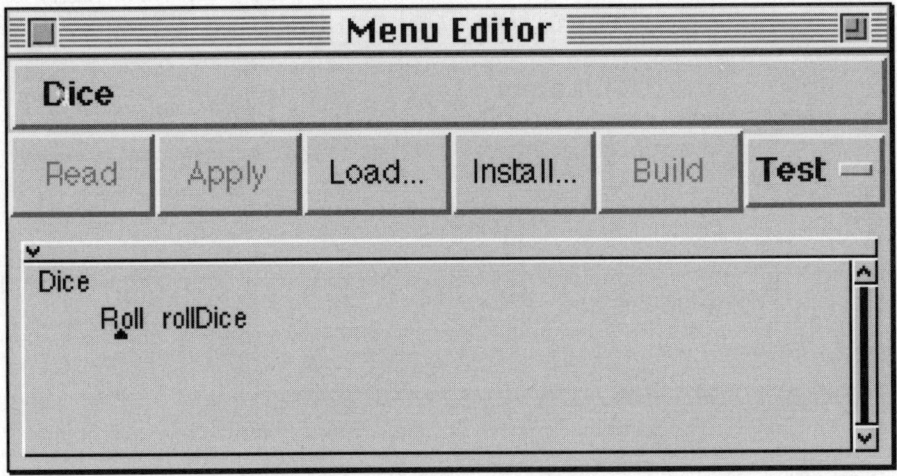

Figure 34.9 The definition for the window's menu.

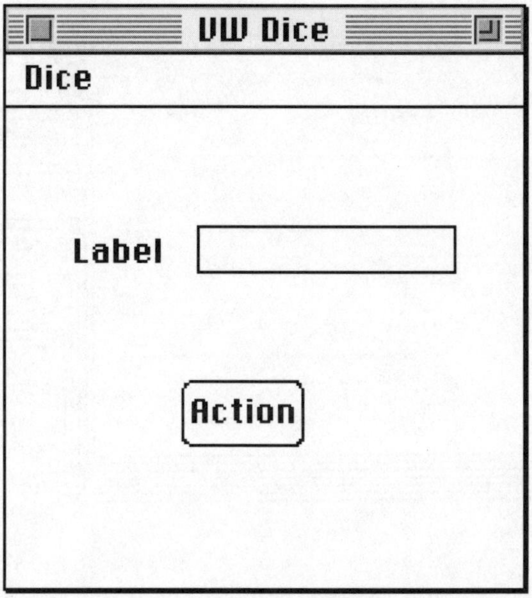

Figure 34.10 The Canvas for the dice.

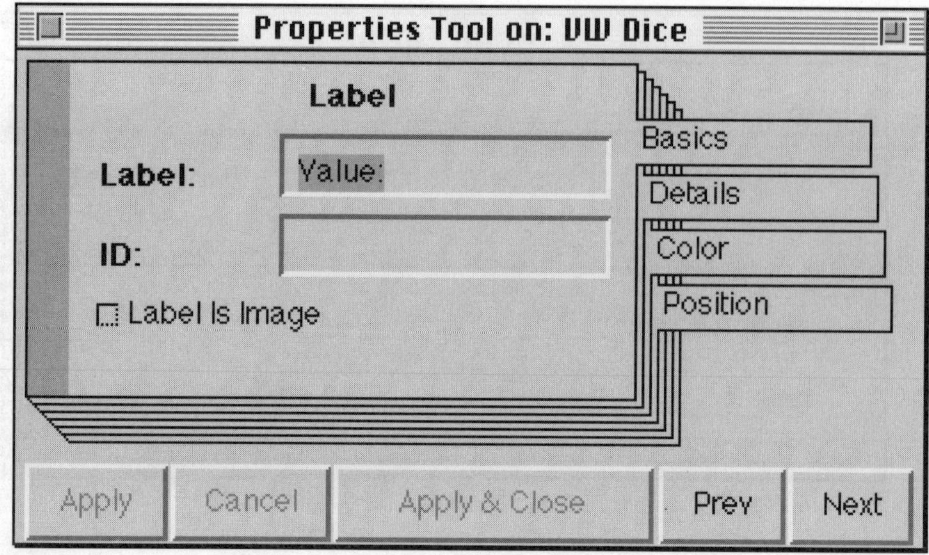

Figure 34.11 The properties for the Label widget.

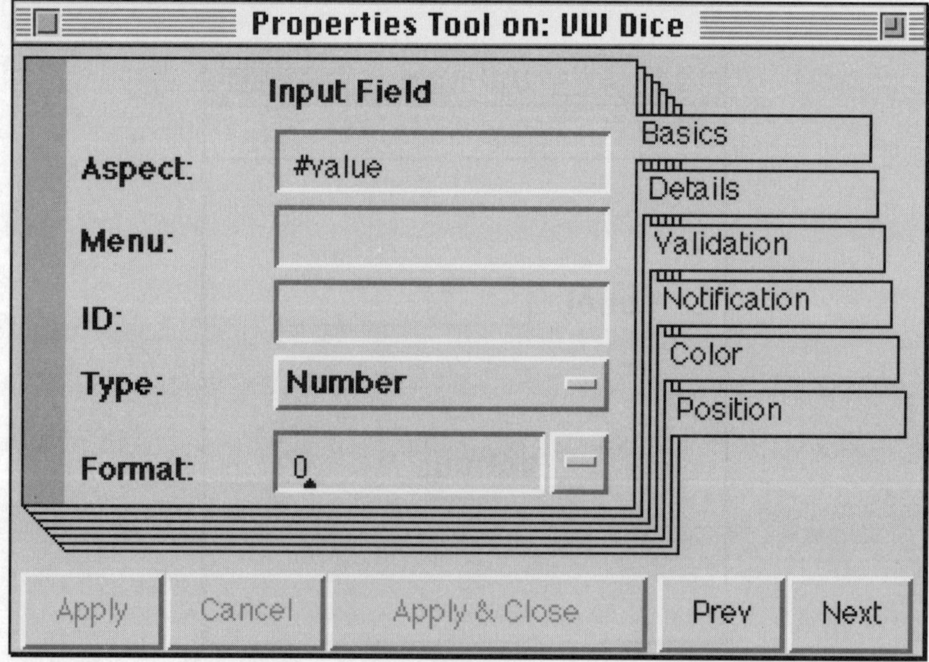

Figure 34.12 The 'Basics' properties for the Input Field.

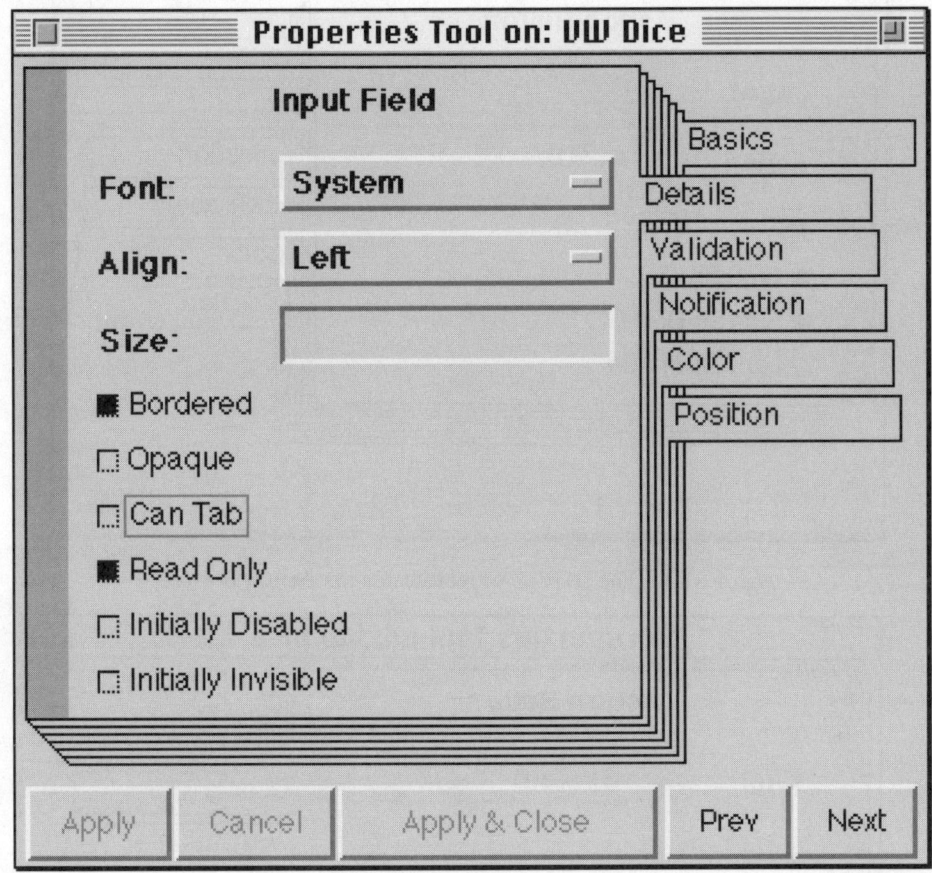

Figure 34.13 The 'Details' properties for the Input Field.

34.6 Benefits of using a Canvas

Why learn MVC? It's hard! Using a Canvas is a great time saver. It gives immediate feedback during user interface design and greatly simplifies the process of arranging the components. However, underneath the simplicity of predefined views and controllers and models that all behave the same way, lies the full power and complexity of MVC. Your knowledge of MVC will allow you to debug errors, to develop new views when they are not found on the Palette, and to extend VisualWorks to satisfy your requirements more fully.

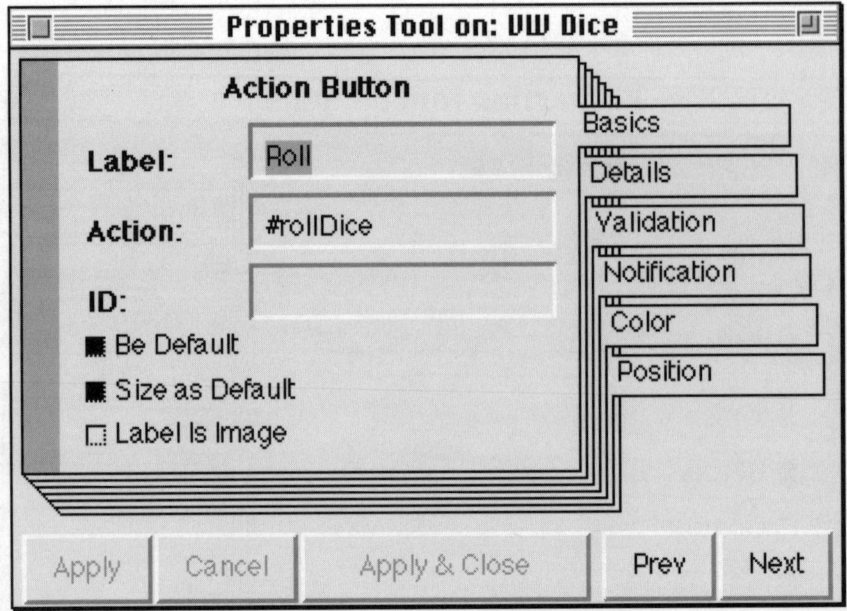

Figure 34.14 The 'Basics' properties for the Action Button.

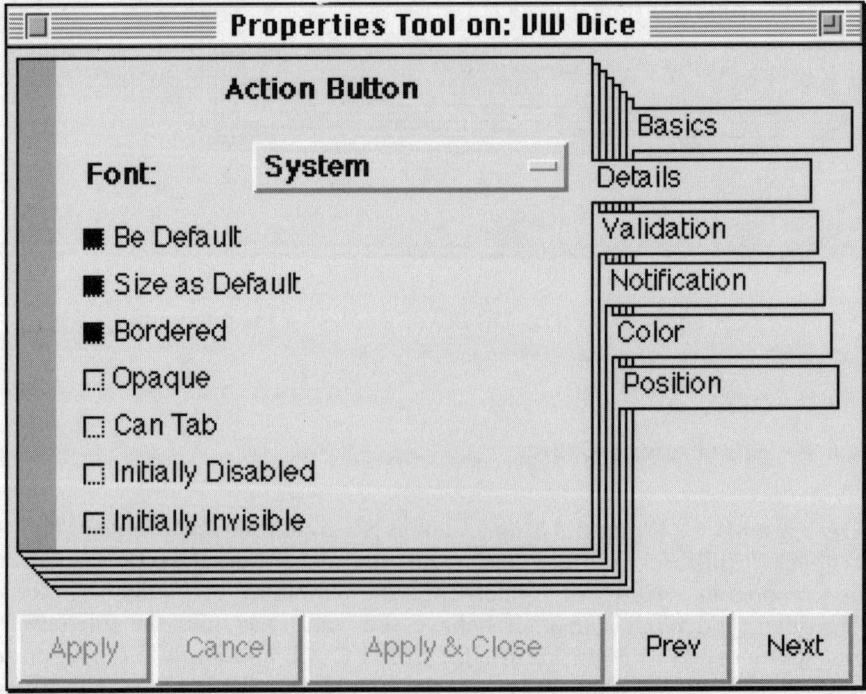

Figure 34.15 The 'Details' properties for the Action Button.

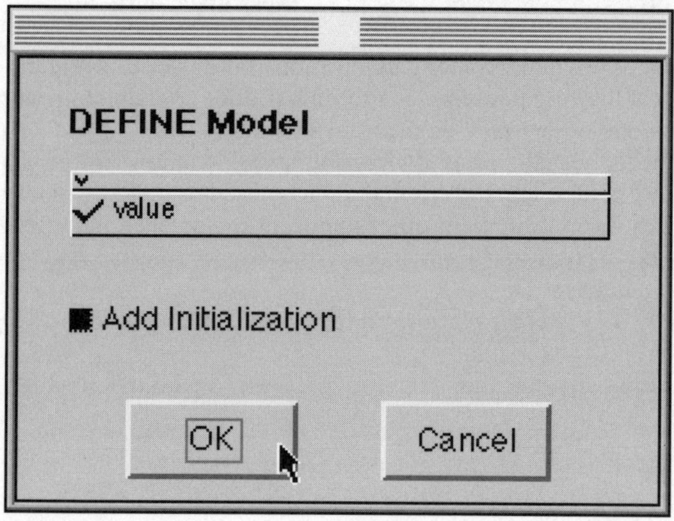

Figure 34.16 Defining a model for the Input Field.

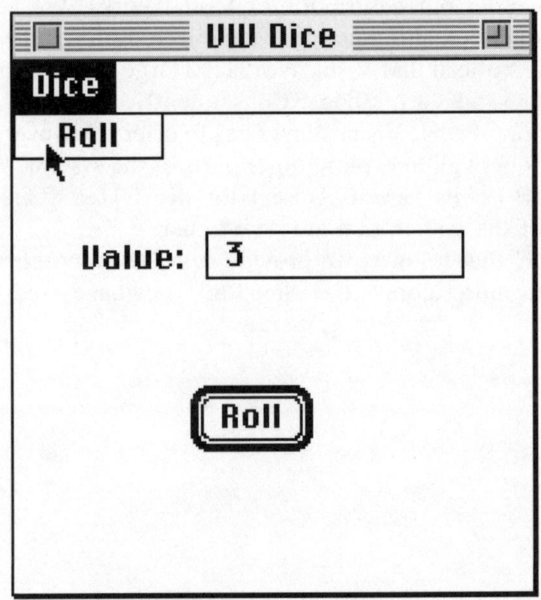

Figure 34.17 The complete Dice application.

In summary, the benefits of using the Canvas mechanism are:

1. It masks MVC making many applications far easier to program.
2. It is not a limiting paradigm – although it does contain many consistent views and models, others may be incorporated easily.
3. It supports visual reuse by consolidating window information in small, accessible components which may then be used as building blocks in other user interfaces, used directly in other applications, or even inherited.
4. It provides a good start for novices, especially for interfaces to applications that browse databases.
5. It greatly assists cross-platform development, being able to 'adopt' look-and-feel.

However, don't assume that you can get away without knowing the Smalltalk language!

Exercise 34.6

In Chapter 33 we introduced an example to use instances of DialogView and LabeledBooleanView; try to rewrite that example using a Canvas.

34.7 Summary

This chapter concludes our description of VisualWorks. We hope that you have enjoyed reading the book and found it a valuable addition to the ParcPlace manual set. You may have noticed that VisualWorks is a large system, containing hundreds of classes and thousands of methods. Consequently, we have been able to cover only a small fraction of what VisualWorks has to offer. However, we hope that you now feel confident enough to explore other parts of the system. We have both been using Smalltalk-80 (in its various guises) for nearly ten years, and yet we still encounter parts of the system that are new to us!

In the Appendix that follows, we provide some extra pointers for those of you wishing to learn more about the Smalltalk language and the VisualWorks environment.

Appendix: references and pointers

No, this isn't a chapter about the problems of dereferencing, or how to manage pointers to objects – after all this is Smalltalk, not C++! Here we briefly outline some references to other useful material, user groups, and other sources of information. In addition, we provide some pointers to available Smalltalk source code. Lastly, we give solutions to the most common 'bugs' encountered by newcomers to VisualWorks.

A.1 References

There are four magazines that cover Smalltalk and other object-oriented issues, all published by SIGS publications in the USA: *Hotline on Object-Oriented Technology, Object Magazine*, *The Journal of Object Oriented Programming* and *The Smalltalk Report*. These frequently contain articles on Smalltalk, ranging from low-level implementation problems to higher-level issues such as programming style. (Roxanna Rochat's technical report *In Search of Good Smalltalk Programming Style* (Tektronix Technical Report CR8619) provides sound advice for those embarking on Smalltalk development.)

For those with an interest in wider object-oriented programming issues we recommend Brad Cox's excellent book *Object-Oriented Programming: An Evolutionary Approach*. David Taylor's book, *Object-Oriented Technology: A Manager's Guide*, provides an alternative perspective on the use of object-oriented techniques.

One topic that we deliberately decided not to address in this book was that of object-oriented analysis and design, for which there are numerous books available. Some of the most popular are given below:

Booch, G., *Object-Oriented Analysis and Design with Applications*, Second Edition, Benjamin/Cummings, 1991.

Coad, P. and Yourdon, E., *Object-Oriented Analysis*, Second Edition, Yourdon Press, 1991.

Jacobson, I., Christerson, M., Jonsson, P., and Overgaard, G., *Object-Oriented Software Engineering*, Addison-Wesley, 1992.

Rumbaugh, J., Blaha, M., Prelermani, W., Eddy, F., and Lorensen, W., *Object-Oriented Modeling and Design*, Prentice Hall, 1991.

Wirfs-Brock, R., Wilkerson, B., and Wiener, L., *Designing Object-Oriented Software*, Prentice Hall, 1990.

As well as paper-based media, there are several electronic sources of information. The most widespread of these is *UseNet*, the bulletin board system used by huge numbers of people to communicate about computing matters and many others besides. (Available via the Internet.)

UseNet consists of thousands of 'news groups', each of which has a name indicating its contents. The news groups are arranged in a hierarchical structure, so that the name of each news group indicates its place within that structure. For example, there is a group for computer languages called 'comp.lang' and one specific to Smalltalk called 'comp.lang.smalltalk'. Additionally, there is a general news group for all things relating to object technology called 'comp.object'.

There is also a Smalltalk frequently asked questions ('FAQ') document, distributed by Craig Latta (latta@xcf.berkeley.edu.) that contains a list of frequently asked questions (and their answers) about the Smalltalk programming language and environment. It is posted to the UseNet news group 'comp.lang.smalltalk' and is available via anonymous FTP from xcf.berkeley.edu as file misc/smalltalk/FAQ/SmalltalkFAQ. It can also be obtained by sending electronic mail to Smalltalk-request@xcf.berkeley.edu with the subject line 'request for FAQ'.

For those of you wanting a more interactive means of communication, there are several special interest groups you can join. Because of the British bias of the authors, the one with which we are most familiar is the Object-Oriented Programming and Systems special interest group of the British Computer Society (BCS-OOPS). (Membership is not restricted to British residents.) It produces a regular newsletter and holds frequent seminars, including an annual 'Object Technology' three-day event. (Those readers on the other side of the Atlantic may be interested in the annual ACM SIGPLAN Conference on Object-Oriented Systems, Languages and Applications – OOPSLA.)

A.2 Pointers

The last five years has seen a huge increase in the number of Smalltalk-related products and services. We don't have the space to describe all of them here, so we will concentrate on some of the more popular. For further information, consult *The*

Smalltalk Resource Guide, which contains a directory of Smalltalk products and services. It is published and distributed by Creative Digital Solutions, 293 Corbett Avenue, San Francisco, USA. Alternatively, the annual *International OOP Directory* (published by SIGS) contains a wider selection of contacts and reference material.

Before we outline a few of the commercial products, it's worth describing some of the vast amount of material that's available in the public domain, as a result of either research projects or the altruism of a few individuals. First, the research projects. (Much of this information was drawn from the Smalltalk FAQ described above.)

CoolDraw

CoolDraw is a constraint-based object-oriented drawing framework (originally called 'ThingLab'). It is similar to other MacDraw-like packages with one major exception: everything in CoolDraw is done with constraints. The system is written in Smalltalk-80 release 4.1. CoolDraw is available via anonymous FTP from ursamajor.uvic.ca in ftp/ursa/constraints/CoolDraw.

The Grapher

You have already seen the result of using the 'Grapher': it was used to produce the figure of the VisualPart class hierarchy in Chapter 30. The current version of the Grapher was written by Mario Wolczko, and is based loosely on the one written for version 2 of Smalltalk by Steve Messick and Chris Jacobson of Tektronix. It is available from the Manchester 'Goodies' Library (see below).

SmallDraw

SmallDraw is a very simple structured graphics editor that was originally written to run under Smalltalk-80 release 4.0, by Dan Benson of Siemens Corporate Research, Inc. (dbenson@scr.siemens.com). SmallDraw is available via anonymous FTP from st.cs.uiuc.edu as /pub/st80-vw/SmallDraw.VW.

Smallmusic

Based at Berkeley, a work group has been formed to discuss and develop an object-oriented software system for music, using Smalltalk-80. The electronic mail address for the group is smallmusic@xcf.Berkeley.EDU. The abstract and outline to their working paper is available via anonymous FTP from ccrma-ftp.stanford.edu as pub/st80/OOMR6.t.

In the descriptions above, we indicated the anonymous FTP sites where access to source code was available. Two sites act as large Smalltalk archives containing many interesting and varied sources:

The Manchester Smalltalk 'Goodies' Library

Host: mushroom.cs.man.ac.uk (Manchester University, Dept of Computer Science). This archive contains much Smalltalk source code ('goodies'), all of which can be 'filed-in', mostly for Smalltalk-80 (ParcPlace releases 2.1 to 4.1, and VisualWorks), and some for Smalltalk/V. (A few items cannot be copied outside the Manchester University Dept of Computer Science – these are unreadable by ftp users. If you try to access an item and permission is denied, you may assume that it is one of these items.)

The directory hierarchy is (roughly) organized by origin of goodie. Thus, the top-level directories include: 'lancaster' (source from Lancaster University), 'manchester' (local source, subdivided by Smalltalk version), 'misc' (miscellaneous sources), 'parc' (sources from ParcPlace), 'uiuc' (a mirror of the Smalltalk archive on st.cs.uiuc.edu – see below), 'usenet' (sources from comp.lang.smalltalk).

Should you have any problem accessing the archive, or queries of any sort, please send electronic mail to the manager, at lib-manager@cs.man.ac.uk.

The UIUC archive

Host: st.cs.uiuc.edu (University of Illinois at Urbana-Champaign, Dept of Computer Science). UIUC keeps local files and a 'mirror' of the files at Manchester.

In the following sections we describe several of the commercial software products with which we have experience. Contact names and addresses can be found in *The Smalltalk Resource Guide* mentioned earlier.

ENVY/Developer

ENVY/*Developer* (ENVY is a registered trademark of Object Technology International Inc.) is a multi-user environment designed for Smalltalk development. The product's configuration management and version control system provides the controls necessary for large-scale Smalltalk development. ENVY/*Developer* also includes a framework to promote corporate re-use of object-oriented components and enable multi-platform development. It additionally includes a high-speed object storage and retrieval utility.

HP Distributed Smalltalk

HP Distributed Smalltalk is an implementation of the CORBA (the Object Management Group (OMG) consortium's specification of a Common Object Request Broker Architecture) 1.1 standard for distributed object systems. It is supported on the HP 9000 series 700 and 800 systems running HP-UX, IBM RS/6000 running AIX and Sun Sparcstations running SunOS and Solaris.

HP Distributed Smalltalk is a tool set that enables rapid development of multi-user enterprise-wide Smalltalk solutions. It extends VisualWorks 2.0 to make an object-oriented development environment for creating and running CORBA-compliant distributed applications.

ObjectExplorer

The Object Explorer for VisualWorks is a visual object inspection and documentation tool. (You may have noticed that we have used it to produce some of the figures in this book to explore the relationships between objects.) It is being used in some of the largest (and smallest) Smalltalk projects to reduce training time, improve development productivity, and document finished code.

ReportWriter

ReportWriter is a query and reporting application that is fully integrated with VisualWorks. ReportWriter supports queries and reports using the domain model contained in Smalltalk as well as database schema-oriented reports. It supports fonts, control breaks, full event-driven formatting, device-independent output, and a callable run-time reporting engine. Any data which is accessible from Smalltalk can be included in reports including SQL, OODB, image, and file-based information.

Runtime Packager

From Advanced Boolean Concepts, this product automates the process of creating VisualWorks images for deployment to endusers. It provides the necessary facilities to locate referenced versus unreferenced classes and methods and to remove the unreferenced items from the run-time image. In addition, it can strip and save a ready-to-run image without additional run-time support code. Runtime Packager can also significantly reduce run-time image size, permitting applications to run on smaller end-user machines with greater responsiveness.

A.3 Troubleshooting

During the many years we have been using Smalltalk, we have noticed that newcomers to the environment often make similar mistakes or encounter similar problems. In the following sections we describe some of these and provide example solutions.

Closed Launcher?

If you inadvertently close the Launcher, you'll soon discover that you no longer have access to the usual means of opening new windows, saving your image, etc. As long as you have a window open in which you can evaluate code – such as a Workspace, Transcript, etc. – you can open a new Launcher by evaluating the expression

```
VisualLauncher open
```

Missing sources?

If you move the location of your VisualWorks image you may find that when browsing sources you see t1, t2, etc., instead of the more familiar variable names. In addition, you may find that methods no longer have comments.

Remember that the source of all code in the image is kept in two files: the sources file (containing the code of the basic classes – called visual.sou) and the changes file (with all the changes and additions you have made – initially called visual.cha). When you are browsing code, the System Browser asks the default instance of SourceFileManager (there's only ever one) to find the sources and changes files. If the SourceFileManager refers to non-existent files, then the Browser decompiles the bytecodes, resulting in t1, t2, etc.

To solve the problem, open the Settings Tool and find the page that specifies the location of files (Figure A.1). (The Settings Tool is described in Chapter 5.) Amend the locations appropriately, and accept the changes.

Growing image?

If you find that your image 'grows' whenever you save it (i.e. the size of the image file increases), this may be the result of two possible causes:

1. You have decided to store objects in the image, rather than using an external database or filing system – no problem.
2. You are inadvertently storing objects in the image, because for some reason they are not being destroyed by the garbage collector – this *is* a problem.

The usual reason for an object not being destroyed by the garbage collector is because the object is 'rooted' – i.e. it is referenced by, or has a reference to, one or more objects that are global variables. For example, a window is not garbage-collected until its controller is removed from the collection of scheduledControllers managed by the global instance of ControlManager. Typically, there are three possible solutions.

Release methods

We noted in Chapter 27 that the dependency relationships (e.g. used by an MVC application) may need to be taken apart explicitly. This usually requires a release method containing expressions to set variables to nil, terminated by the expression super release.

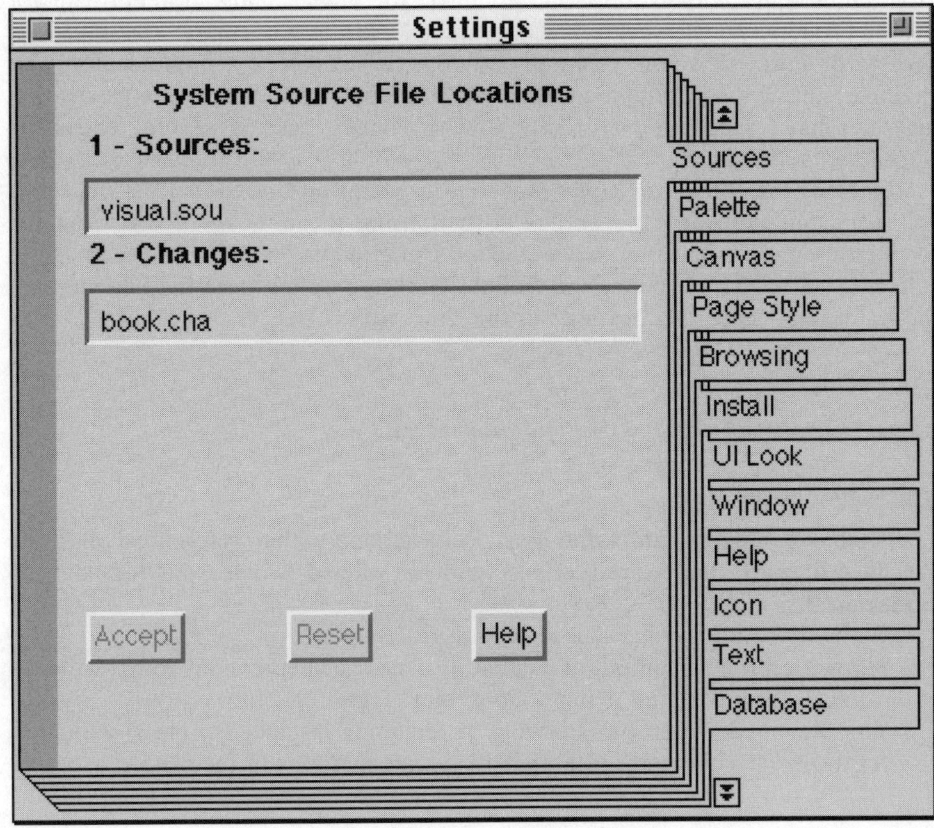

Figure A.1 Setting the location of the source files.

Exercise A.1

Browse all implementors of release.

DependentsFields

If you remember (from Chapter 27), DependentsFields is a class variable (an IdentityDictionary) of class Object. It is used as part of the dependency mechanism for those classes that are not a subclass of Model. Although DependentsFields is not a global variable, because it is a class variable of class Object, it may be accessed as if it were. Therefore you should be able to inspect DependentsFields by evaluating the expression DependentsFields inspect in a Workspace.

If your release methods have been correctly implemented, you should find that DependentsFields is empty (after closing all the windows connected with your VisualWorks application). (This is not strictly true – for example, certain advanced programming techniques rely on an entry for classes ObjectMemory and/or SystemDictionary.) However, if DependentsFields is not empty, this does not necessarily imply that your release methods are not correctly implemented. For example, during the development stages of your application the release mechanism may not have functioned correctly (due to bugs), causing several entries in DependentsFields.

Removing the entries is simple. Open an Inspector on DependentsFields, select an item from the left pane and remove it using the remove option from the <operate> menu. Once you have emptied DependentsFields, force the image to collect its garbage by selecting the **Collect Garbage** option from the **File** menu of the Launcher – note the messages in the Transcript.

Exercise A.2

Inspect DependentsFields and take any action necessary.

Undeclared variables

The global variable Undeclared is a PoolDictionary that references all those variables that are 'undeclared'. Each item has one of two reasons for being in Undeclared:

1. When accepting a method, or evaluating a message expression, you identified a variable as 'undeclared' from a Confirmer (Figure A.2); or
2. You redefined a class by removing or renaming instance (or class) variables, yet those variables were referenced by some methods of the class.

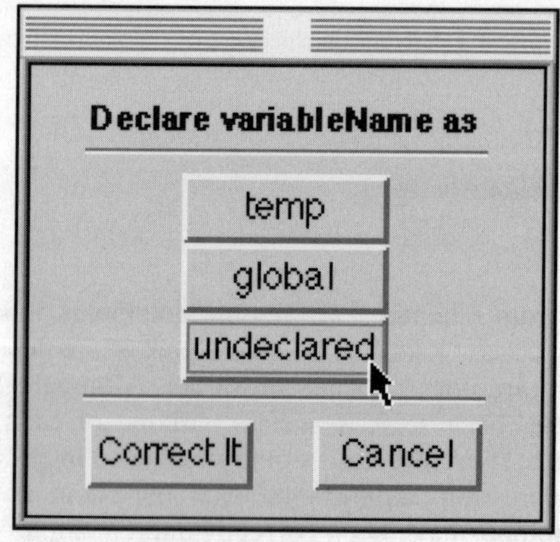

Figure A.2 Identifying an 'undeclared' variable.

Whatever the reason, the variables should be removed from the PoolDictionary. However, it's always wise to check first if there are any references to the variables (as in case (2) above). To find references to undeclared variables open an Inspector on Undeclared, and for each variable in turn, select the **references** option from the <operate> menu. If there are references for a variable, you will be provided with a Browser containing the methods in which the variable is referenced. It's usually fairly straightforward to fix this: either remove the methods (if they are no longer required) or declare the variable. After tidying up the references to each undeclared variable (or if it has no references), remove it from the Dictionary using the **remove** option from the <operate> menu.

It's worth inspecting Undeclared occasionally, as undeclared variables can often be the source of subtle bugs (an undeclared variable behaves as if it is a global variable).

Exercise A.3

Inspect Undeclared and take any action necessary.

A.4 Summary

Object-oriented technology seems to be the current 'flavor of the month' – portrayed by the computing press as the next 'silver bullet'. All aspects of software development are now considering the use of object-oriented techniques: analysis and design, software engineering, user-interface design, database design, to name but a few. From its beginnings as a language to 'support children of all ages in the world of information' (Ingalls, D., 'The Smalltalk-76 Programming System Design and Implementation', *Proceedings of the Fifth Annual ACM Symposium on Principles of Programming Languages*, ACM, p.9), Smalltalk has consistently been one of the leaders of the object-oriented movement.

For those of you new to Smalltalk, or object-oriented technology in general, the references at the beginning of this Appendix provide a good starting-point for your journey of discovery.

Index